'Throughout his book, Asbridge resists the temptation to provide a simple, seamless narrative. Instead, he builds up his account of critical moments by leading the reader through the various (sometimes contradictory) layers of contemporary evidence . . . If this approach provides the text with a vivid directness, so too does the author's (for once, literally) foot-slogging research. Asbridge has walked large tracts of the crusader's route through Syria and Palestine, and his sensitivity to topographical detail – and its tactical importance to the campaign – gives his account the tightly focused immediacy of travelogue'

John Adamson, *Sunday Telegraph*

'[A] substantial book, [in which] there is plenty to discover . . . Asbridge [tells] of astonishing heroism, together with rapidly escalating sadism and atrocity . . . His pace is tremendous, and he has a remarkable feel for place. It certainly helps that, like so many Crusaders nine centuries ago, Asbridge has himself walked 350 miles from Antioch towards Jerusalem: his book is all the better for it'

Diarmaid MacCulloch, *Guardian*

'Nuanced and sophisticated . . . The first, very considerable, merit of [this] book . . . is that Thomas Asbridge, while fully aware of the modern perspectives, presents the story to us from the point of view, principally, of the Crusaders themselves . . . Thoroughly documented and academically respectable, [it is an] admirable example of narrative history written with the general reader in mind. Nobody can read [*The First Crusade*] without acquiring a better understanding of the Middle Ages and the medieval mind; nor, I would think, without developing an admiration for the courage, tenacity, and even the idealism of the Crusaders. To that extent, [it] may be called revisionist history'

Allan Massie, *Literary Review*

'Salutary reading . . . the first book on the subject to get us close to the way the crusaders thought and felt, when they mistook massacre for charity and bloodshed for penance'

Felipe Fernández Armesto, *The Times*

'Asbridge's outstanding new history eyes with understanding and unsqueamishness the mixed motives of the Crusaders . . . The savagery of the triumphant Christian warriors seemed to shock and delight contemporary commentators in equal measure. It is this duality of passion, religious and murderous, that Asbridge analyses with such skill . . . Asbridge's tactful and sympathetic approach to the fragmentary and partial nature of the primary sources, his ability to sustain a gripping narrative, to develop the personalities of the principals, to inspire both admiration and regret for the achievements of these medieval adventurers, all combine to make this one of the most distinguished books yet launched on the current wave of enthusiasm for history'

Graham Anderson, *Oxford Times*

'Although well-researched, the book wears its scholarship lightly and reads like a work of fiction, complete with vivid characters such as Stephen of Blois and Godfrey of Bouillon. This will, no doubt, become required reading on many a university's history course, but it is also a fascinating and lively account that will readily appeal to the ordinary reader'

Stephen Stewart, *Glasgow Herald*

'Thomas Asbridge's account of this First Crusade has vividly brought the event to life . . . everyone should read this book'

Medieval History

'[Asbridge's] prose is straightforward yet gripping . . . his scholarship thorough and careful; here is an author whose passionate engagement transcends the divide between the academic and general reader . . . he is that rare breed of historian whose painstaking research does not compromise his readability'

Jason Taliadoros, *The Age*

THE
FIRST
CRUSADE

THE
FIRST
CRUSADE

A New History

THOMAS ASBRIDGE

FREE PRESS

First published in Great Britain by The Free Press in 2004
An imprint of Simon & Schuster UK Ltd
A Viacom company
This edition published, 2005

1 3 5 7 9 10 8 6 4 2

Simon & Schuster UK Ltd
Africa House
64–78 Kingsway
London WC2B 6AH

Simon & Schuster Australia
Sydney

www.simonsays.co.uk

A CIP catalogue for this book is available from the British Library.

ISBN: 0-7432-2084-6

Typeset by M Rules
Printed and bound in Great Britain by
Cox & Wyman Ltd, Reading, Berks

PICTURE CREDITS
pp. 1, 8, 15, 21: British Library
pp. 7, 11, 22: Susan B. Edgington
pp. 3, 4, 12, 14: Bibliothèque Nationale de France
pp. 5, 9, 30: Agence Photographique de la Réunion des Musées Nationaux
pp. 6, 13: The Walters Art Museum, Baltimore
pp. 2, 10: The Art Archive
pp. 16, 17, 18, 19, 23, 24, 25, 26, 27, 29: Thomas Asbridge
p. 20: AKG-images
p. 28: Hulton Getty

FOR CHRISTINE AND ELLA

CONTENTS

PREFACE

The First Crusade stands as one of the most remarkable episodes in European history. It saw tens of thousands of people embark on an extraordinary 3,000-kilometre journey to the Holy Land, their aim to recapture Jerusalem from Islam in the name of the Christian God. Facing bone-crunching exhaustion, deadly disease, wretched starvation and bloodthirsty battle, these crusaders demonstrated a capacity for intense religious devotion as well as appalling brutality. Against all odds and at dreadful cost in terms of human suffering, they prevailed. The events of the crusade were so dramatic, its impact so colossal as to inspire countless generations, across nine centuries, to grapple with its history. All have struggled to comprehend such a powerful and disturbing event. Most have assumed that Europe was driven to crusade by some form of pre-existing genetic hatred for Islam, and that a desperate clash between these two civilisations was all but inevitable. In the modern era, analysis of the First Crusade has been drawn in other directions. In its various incarnations over the last 150 years, the expedition has been all but stripped of its devotional context to become little more than a grand but greedy raid, presented as the first glorious flowering of western colonialism and exposed as conclusive evidence of medieval Europe's spectacular barbarity.

In recent decades the intense efforts of historians in Europe, the Near East and North America have honed and reshaped our understanding of the crusade's origins, progress and impact. But, to date, no scholar has drawn together these strands of research to present a new analytical narrative of the expedition, accessible to a wide audience. This book will not attempt to present the definitive history of the First Crusade; such a feat would be all but impossible. Drawing upon cutting-edge scholarship, original research and an intimate knowledge of the Levant, it will shed new light upon the expedition's inception, explaining what motivated such a multitude of Europeans to join the crusade; it will retell the story of its participants' incredible journey, asking how a venture devoid of centralised leadership and seemingly prosecuted with little or no forward planning avoided immediate annihilation; and it will assess the true nature of relations between Christendom and Islam at the time of the crusade and demonstrate how they were transformed by the attack on the Holy Land.

I began writing this book three years ago, but it is really the product of a far more enduring passion for crusading history. I was first introduced to the wondrous tale of the First Crusade by the inspirational teaching of Richard Mole. Even then, at the age of sixteen, I was captivated and soon decided that I wanted to devote my life to the study of the crusades. Now, nearly two decades later, I count myself very lucky to have found my way into academic life and a career as a medieval historian.

Along the way I have been helped by many friends and mentors, but I would here like to express my particular thanks to those who, in one way or another, have shaped my approach to this book. Peter Edbury, Professor of Medieval History at the University of Cardiff, and Jonathan Riley-Smith, now Dixie-Professor of Ecclesiastical History at Emmanuel College, Cambridge, guided me through university life as an undergraduate and postgraduate, teaching me the principles of historical research and the value of critical analysis. It is my sincere hope that they will not judge this, my first attempt to bring the medieval world alive for a wider audience, too harshly.

Thanks are also due to a number of other crusade scholars, most notably to Professor Malcolm Barber and Dr Susan Edgington for reading drafts of this book and proffering valuable advice, and to Dr Jonathan Phillips for his continued friendship and encouragement. I am indebted to many of my colleagues in the Department of History at Queen Mary, University of London, not least for the provision of research leave in which to complete this book. Without the advice of Professor Peter Hennessy I might never even have begun, and the fact that my sanity survived the actual process of writing relatively intact owes much to the treasured friendship of Dr James Ellison and Kathryn Mallen.

My work also benefited enormously from the patient faith of Andrew Gordon, my editor at Simon & Schuster. The finished text of the book owes much to his warm encouragement and astute editorial judgement.

I would also like to thank the staff of the Institute of Historical Research, London, where much of this book was written, and the Department of History at the University of Reading for providing a generous travel grant to enable me to walk 350 miles along the route of the First Crusade from Antioch to Jerusalem in the summer of 1999. My experiences during that journey, alongside my other varied travels in the Levant, provided invaluable background for the book.

I have been lucky enough, through all my academic career, to benefit from the unerring support of my family. This book has been no exception, but I must express a special vote of thanks to my parents for demonstrating immense forbearance during the rather tortured last months of writing as I sought to complete the text and adjust to the wonderful but exhausting duties of fatherhood.

I wish to give my deepest, most heartfelt thanks to my wife, Christine. Through long months and years of writing and research she has stood by my side, offering unflinching support, acting as a sounding board for my ideas and providing the most constructive criticism of this work. Above all, she brought the miracle that is our daughter Ella into the world and held all our lives together as I finished this book.

Just before this book was completed, my agent, Giles Gordon, died after a sudden accident. Without Giles' sage guidance I would never have had the opportunity to bring my vision of the First Crusade to a mainstream audience. I will always regret that he was not able to read this book in its final form, but I hope he would have approved. I will miss him very much.

THOMAS ASBRIDGE
London, November 2003

LIST OF MAPS

CAST OF CHARACTERS

Popes

Gregory VII (1073–85) Hardline champion of the Papal Reform Movement

Urban II (1088–99) Launched the First Crusade at Clermont in 1095

Crusaders

Adhémar of Le Puy Bishop of Le Puy in southern France and papal legate on the crusade

Raymond of Toulouse Count of Toulouse and lord of St Gilles; secular leader of the southern French crusaders

Bohemond of Taranto Son of Robert Guiscard and leader of the southern Italian Norman crusaders

Godfrey of Bouillon Duke of Lower Lotharingia and leader of a contingent of crusaders from Lotharingia and Germany

Robert of Normandy Son of William the Conqueror and duke of Normandy; leading figure among the northern French crusaders

Robert of Flanders Count of Flanders and leading figure among the northern French crusaders

Stephen of Blois Count of Blois and leading figure among the northern French crusaders

Hugh of Vermandois	Count of Vermandois in northern France and brother to King Philip I of France
Tancred of Hauteville	Bohemond of Taranto's young and adventurous nephew
Baldwin of Boulogne	Count of Boulogne; Godfrey of Bouillon's ambitious brother
Peter the Hermit	Charismatic preacher and nominal leader of the People's Crusade
Peter Bartholomew	Provençal visionary who 'discovered' the Holy Lance

Byzantines and Armenians

Alexius I Comnenus	Emperor of Byzantium (1081–1118); founder of the great Comneni dynasty
Manuel Boutoumites	Greek general who oversaw the crusader siege of Nicaea
Taticius	Greek guide who accompanied the crusaders to Antioch
Thoros	Armenian ruler of the city of Edessa; adoptive father of Baldwin of Boulogne
Firuz	Armenian resident of Antioch who betrayed the city

Muslims

Kilij Arslan	Seljuq Turkish sultan of the Rüm in Asia Minor
Yaghi Siyan	Governor of the city of Antioch
Duqaq of Damascus	Seljuq ruler of the Syrian city of Damascus; led first Muslim relief force on Antioch
Ridwan of Aleppo	Seljuq ruler of the Syrian city of Aleppo; led second Muslim relief force on Antioch
Kerbogha	Ruler of Mosul and renowned general; leader of a massive Muslim army to relieve Antioch
Al-Afdal	Ruler of Fatimid Cairo

THE
FIRST
CRUSADE

I

HOLY WAR PROCLAIMED

A race absolutely alien to God has invaded the land of Christians, has reduced the people with sword, rapine and flame. These men have destroyed the altars polluted by their foul practices. They have circumcised the Christians, either spreading the blood from the circumcisions on the altars or pouring it into the baptismal fonts. And they cut open the navels of those whom they choose to torment with loathsome death, tear out their most vital organs and tie them to a stake, drag them around and flog them, before killing them as they lie prone on the ground with all their entrails out. What shall I say of the appalling violation of women, of which it is more evil to speak than to keep silent?

On whom, therefore, does the task lie of avenging this, of redeeming this situation, if not on you, upon whom above all nations God has bestowed outstanding glory in arms, magnitude of heart, litheness of body and strength to humble anyone who resists you.[1]

This horrific imagery and forceful exhortation launched the First Crusade. On the last Tuesday of November, in the year 1095, Pope Urban II delivered an electrifying speech to a crowd outside the

southern French city of Clermont. Christians living in the East, he
alleged, were enduring dreadful oppression and abuse at the hands of
their 'savage' Muslim masters, and the epicentre of Christian
tradition, the Holy City of Jerusalem, likewise lay in the grasp of
Islam. In the face of these intolerable 'injuries', Pope Urban called
upon Catholic Europe to take up arms and prosecute a vengeful
campaign of reconquest, a holy war that would cleanse its participants
of sin. When he proclaimed that those fighting as 'soldiers of Christ'
would be purified by the fire of battle, his words set Christendom
alight.

In the weeks and months that followed, the pope's impassioned
appeal swept across Europe, prompting some 100,000 men and
women, from knight to pauper, to take up the call – the largest
mobilisation of manpower since the fall of the Roman Empire. One
such was the great Norman warrior Bohemond of Taranto. Immersed
in the bitter siege of the rebellious southern Italian city of Amalfi,
Bohemond apparently underwent a dramatic conversion when news
of the gathering crusade arrived. Calling for his most lavishly wrought
cloak to be brought forth, he had this treasured garment cut to pieces
in front of an astonished assembly. Fashioning the cloth into crosses,
he then proudly displayed this badge upon his sleeve as a visible sign
of his commitment to the cause and distributed the remainder among
the enthralled audience. Together they abandoned the siege to fight
a new war, leaving the air afire with their battle cry: 'God's will! God's
will!'[2]

This titanic expedition, known to history as the First Crusade,
marked a watershed in relations between Islam and the West. This
was not the first war between Christians and Muslims, but it was the
conflict that set these two world religions on a course towards deep-
seated animosity and enduring enmity. Between 1000 and 1300 CE
Catholic Europe and Islam went from being occasional combatants
to avowed and entrenched opponents, and the chilling reverberations
of this seismic shift still echo in the world today.

The First Crusade stands at the heart of this transformation because it effected change on two intertwined levels: 'reality' and 'myth-history'. In 'reality', the actual progress of the crusade brought Islam and the West into fierce physical conflict, but need not necessarily have prompted an irrevocable divide. Even before the expedition was over, however, its events began passing into 'myth-history', as contemporaries sought to record and explain its remarkable progress, asking why it had happened, who had participated and why, and how the expedition had affected the world. Indeed, from its genesis, the history of the crusade was blurred by distortion. The image of Muslims as brutal oppressors conjured by Pope Urban was pure propaganda – if anything, Islam had proved over the preceding centuries to be more tolerant of other religions than Catholic Christendom. Likewise, the fevered spontaneity of Bohemond's decision to take the cross, dutifully recorded by one of his followers, was almost certainly a façade masking calculated ambition.[3]

THE WORLD OF POPE URBAN II

The man who unleashed the First Crusade was born to the noble de Lagery family in the northern French town of Châtillon-sur-Marne around the year 1035. Baptised Odo, he is known in the annals of history by another name, for upon ascending the throne of St Peter in Rome in his fifties he followed papal tradition, breaking with his past to become Pope Urban II. But, in spite of this transformation, Urban remained a man of his time, his upbringing and earlier career leaving an unquestionable imprint upon his papacy and serving to shape the momentous call to arms that shook Europe at the end of the eleventh century.[4]

European society

Urban's target audience in 1095 was the aristocracy of France, the very group into which he had been born, a violent warrior class, fighting for survival amid bloodthirsty lawlessness. One thousand years earlier, the region we would think of today as France had been overrun and absorbed by the relentless expansion of the Roman world. For centuries the province enjoyed relative peace and prosperity within the protective fold of this empire, but from the later fourth century CE onwards Rome's dominion began to falter, as the force of its law, culture and society receded. The Roman Empire did not implode in one sudden, spectacular moment – rather, it decayed incrementally, and, with the gradual evaporation of its power, the way opened for 'barbarian' peoples to supplant, mimic and finally extinguish Rome's authority. Between the fifth and seventh centuries, groups like the Visigoths, Avars and Lombards redrew the map of Europe, leaving a bewildering patchwork of diverse, warring realms where unity had once prevailed. In north-eastern Gaul one such group, the Franks, came to prominence around 500 CE, carving out a kingdom with which historians now associate their name – Francia, or France – Urban's homeland.[5]

By 800 CE a descendant of the Franks, Charlemagne, had amassed such a collection of dependencies – encompassing regions that would today make up much of France, Italy, Germany and the Low Countries – that he could claim to have restored the glory of the Roman Empire in the West. France and Europe as a whole enjoyed a return to some semblance of centralised authority under Charlemagne and his successors, the Carolingians.[6] But by the year 1000 this had dissolved under the weight of bitter succession disputes and harrowing Viking invasions. Without the controlling hand of centralised rule, disorder spread and effective power devolved into the hands of acquisitive warlords. At the time of Pope Urban II's birth in the eleventh century, only the barest remnant of a Frankish realm survived, and any glimmer of unified French identity endured only in the imagination. The titular kings of France struggled even to control a small territory centred around Paris, while the Frankish realm fractured into numerous dukedoms and counties whose power eclipsed that of the royal house. 'France' was even divided linguistically, with two distinct languages – Languedor and Langue-doc – prevailing in the north and south respectively. The people eventually attracted to Urban's crusading ideal in 1095 were certainly not all from France, but contemporaries who wrote about this expedition, especially those looking in from outside western Europe, tended to categorise all its participants under the single term 'Franks'. Although somewhat misleading, it has therefore become common practice to describe the First Crusaders as the Franks.[7]

Urban II grew up within the Champagne region of north-eastern France, in an intensely localised environment. Here, as in the rest of Europe, even nobles could expect to live their entire lives without travelling more than a hundred kilometres from home. The warrior aristocracy held sway, a class, dominated by the knightly profession, bound by a complex network of lordship, vassalage and obligation – what in the past has been called the 'feudal system' – at the heart of which lay an exchange of military service in return for tenure of a territory or 'fief'. Champagne, and France in general, may not, as historians once thought, have been in a state of utter, chaotic savagery, but Urban was still born into an extraordinarily violent society, dominated by bloody feud and vendetta. Even the more peaceable nobles engaged in rapine and plunder as a matter of course, and vicious internecine struggles for power and land were a fact of daily life.[8]

Medieval Christianity

For all the violence and mayhem of Urban's childhood world, he was, from his earliest days, surrounded by and immersed in the Christian religion. The medieval society in which he lived was obsessively dedicated to this faith, almost every feature of daily existence being conditioned by its doctrines. Europe's devotion to Christianity can be traced back to the fourth century CE, when the Roman emperor Constantine the Great embraced Christian dogma, injecting this small-scale eastern Mediterranean sect into the lifeblood of Rome. Pumped through the arteries of the empire, Christianity eventually became the state religion, displacing paganism. In a strange quirk of history, the earthly power that had overseen the execution of Christ now catapulted his teachings on to the world stage. Even as Rome's might crumbled, this creed continued to spread to almost every corner of Europe, and by the eleventh century the region could accurately be described as western Christendom. Following what would today be thought of as Roman Catholicism, its people can most precisely be termed the 'Latins' to distinguish them from adherents of the various other branches of Christianity.[9]

In Urban's day, this faith dominated and dictated everyday life to an extent that can seem almost inconceivable to a modern observer attuned to the attitudes and preconceptions of an increasingly secularised contemporary society. Urban lived in an authentically spiritual age, one in which there was no need to question the existence of God because his absolute power was plain for all to see, made manifest on earth in the form of 'miracles' – the sudden curing of a 'blind' man after prayer, the 'divine punishment' of a murderer struck by lightning. Events that would today be interpreted as natural phenomena, or put down to the vagaries of chance, served to confirm the efficacy of the Christian message to a medieval audience. In eleventh-century Europe, the full pantheon of human experience – birth, love, anger and death – was governed by Christian dogma, and the cornerstone of this system of belief was fear. Medieval minds were plagued by one overwhelming anxiety: the danger of sin. In death, it was believed, every human soul would be judged. Purity would bring everlasting paradise, but an eternity of gruesome torment awaited those polluted by sin. This universal obsession, shared by king and peasant alike, shaped all custom, morality and law.* Urban's early life,

---

*In an age before printing, when illiteracy was the norm across all levels of society, the threats posed by sin and damnation were pressed home through dreadful, arresting imagery. Religious art was the mass media of the central Middle Ages, and the frescoes and stone sculptures that decorated churches provided graphic representations of the danger of impurity. Any visitor to the Cathedral of St

like that of his contemporaries, was essentially a struggle to avoid sin and attain heavenly salvation.[10]

The problem was that sin and temptation were everywhere. Natural human impulses – hunger, lust, pride – all carried inherent dangers, and the Bible failed to offer medieval mankind a clear-cut definition of an 'ideal' Christian lifestyle. In Late Antiquity some Christians had gone to extremes to avoid worldly contamination: the celebrated fifth-century hermit St Simeon spent forty-seven years in lonely isolation atop a pillar in northern Syria, striving for purity. By Urban's day, a more attainable path to perfection had become popular in western Europe. Monasticism, in which Christians dedicated their lives to prayer and the service of God within an enclosed environment, embracing the principles of poverty, chastity and obedience, was accepted as the pinnacle of spiritual existence. It was this path to 'perfection' that Urban eventually chose to follow. As a young man, he was sent to study at the cathedral school in Rheims and soon joined the Church, attaining the position of archdeacon, an indication that Urban had probably been a younger son and was therefore not bound to a knightly future.[11]

Remaining in Rheims until his mid-thirties, Urban then made a dramatic decision. We might imagine that, as a member of the Church, he was already cradled in the bosom of Christian purity, but in reality the eleventh-century clergy were a notoriously dissolute bunch. Priests and bishops often reaped rich profits from land, some

---

Lazare in Autun, Burgundy, to the south of Urban's homeland, could not fail to get the message, for the arch above the main entrance contained a stunning sculpted tableau of the Last Judgement. Carved in the first decades of the twelfth century by the master craftsman Giselbert, the weighing of souls – the moment at which a human's worth would be measured – is depicted with agonising clarity, as a grinning devil strives to tip the scales in his favour and then drag condemned souls into hell. Elsewhere, giant demonic hands reach out to strangle a sinner, with the utter horror of the moment etched on to the victim's face. Confronted with these ghastly images, and the equally compelling representation of the blessed lifted into eternal paradise by graceful angels, it is little wonder that medieval Christians were fixated upon the battle against sin.

ATLANTIC

OCEAN

Boulogne
FLANDERS Amiens
Caen Rouen Rheims
NORMANDY Paris
Chartres Troyes
Tours Blois Dijon
Poitiers Cluny
FRANCE Lyons
Clermont
Bordeaux Valence
Toulouse LANGUEDOC PROVENCE
Montpellier

Cologne
GERMAN
Bouillon Mainz Prague
Trier Worms Regens
LORRAINE Toul
CHAMPAGNE ALSACE
EMPIRE
Basel A L P S
Milan
LOMBARDY Venice
Piacenza
Genoa Bologna
Pisa

LEON AND CASTILE
PORTUGAL
ARAGON
Barcelona
Toledo

CORSICA
Rome
Ostia
Sales
SARDINIA

M e d i t e
e
r

SIC
MALTA

Western Europe in 1095
(Land over 1000 metres/3281 feet is shaded)

0   100   200   300 miles
0   100 200 300 400 500 km

might marry, hold two or three ecclesiastical offices at once and perhaps even fight in wars. Around 1068 Urban turned aside from this worldly 'secular' arm of the Church to become a monk, although his decision was probably inspired by a mixture of personal ambition and piety. He was professed into perhaps the most influential and respected monastery of the day, the Burgundian house of Cluny, an institution just reaching the apogee of its power. Cluny epitomised two interlocking concepts: liberty and purity. In an age when even monasteries commonly fell prey to worldly contamination, as lords, princes and bishops sought to meddle in their affairs, Cluny had one massive advantage. From the moment of its birth, in the early tenth century, it had been placed under the direct protection of the pope in Rome. Immune from local interference, Cluny was effectively its own master, free to appoint its own abbots, govern as it saw fit and pursue monastic perfection in true isolation. Under the guidance of its energetic and long-lived abbot, Hugh (1049–1109), the monastery itself grew to accommodate three times as many monks, and a vast new abbey church was built that would become the largest enclosed space in western Europe. At the same time, the tendrils of Cluniac power continued to spread across Latin Christendom, as existing monasteries in France, Germany, Spain, England and northern Italy reformed to adopt Cluniac principles. By the end of the eleventh century, more than 11,000 monks in some 2,000 religious communities had joined the Cluniac movement. Even within this vast, supranational edifice, Urban's piety and administrative skill did not long go unnoticed. He rose to become grand prior of Cluny, second in command to the abbot, and helped to cement the monastery's reputation as a bastion of uncompromising spiritual purity.[12]

But Urban's career was not to end within the confines of a monastery. As a papal protectorate, Cluny had long enjoyed an intimate, mutually beneficial alliance with Rome. It is no surprise then that Urban's position within the monastery brought him to the notice of the pope. Around 1080, he was recruited to become cardinal-bishop of Ostia, one of the most powerful ecclesiastical offices in Italy. Urban had now entered the inner sanctum of spiritual authority, but he could not have arrived at a more tumultuous moment, for the papacy was in the midst of a ferocious dispute.

The medieval papacy

To understand the arena now confronting Urban, one must first appreciate the differences between the theoretical and actual status of the medieval papacy. In Christian tradition there were five great centres of ecclesiastical power on earth, five patriarchates, of which Rome was just one. But late-eleventh-century popes claimed pre-eminence among all these on the basis that Christ's chief apostle St Peter had been the first bishop of Rome. Scripture indicated that St Peter had been empowered by Christ to manifest God's will, becoming, in essence, the most potent spiritual figure on earth. The papacy maintained that an unbroken chain of descent ran from St Peter across the centuries, connecting all popes and thus making them successors to this authority. Indeed, it went one step further, arguing that this unique 'apostolic power' was not handed down from pope to pope and thus subject to dilution, but was instead directly conferred, fresh and unsullied, upon each new incumbent of the office. As far as Rome was concerned, this meant that papal authority was unassailable and infallible. Medieval popes thus regarded themselves as the world's foremost spiritual power and believed they were entitled to exert absolute control over the Latin Church of Europe.[13]

When Urban joined the Roman camp, however, the reality of papal authority was but a pale, almost pathetic, reflection of these lofty aspirations. Far from being recognised as the leader of the Christian faith on earth, the pope struggled to manage the spiritual affairs of central Italy, let alone all western Christendom. The theoretical underpinnings of papal power had for centuries lain dormant and untapped, as the office of pope remained mired in localised interests and abuse, and any attempts to break free of these confines faltered in the face of massive obstacles.

The same centrifugal forces that had fragmented political power in the wake of the Roman Empire's decline worked simultaneously to disorder and dislocate ecclesiastical authority. By the year 1000, bishops in England, France, Germany, Spain and even northern Italy had little or no expectation of, nor reliance upon, guidance from the pope, sitting in impotent isolation upon the throne of St Peter in Rome. Accustomed to the practice and rewards of independent government, these prelates were unresponsive, even resistant, to any shift towards centralisation and conformity.

At the same time, any hope of wielding absolute ecclesiastical power in Europe was unrealistic, because the dividing line between the spiritual realm of the Church and the temporal world of kings, lords and knights was at best blurred, at worst non-existent. In the medieval age, these two spheres were so intertwined as to be practically inseparable. Kings, believing themselves to be empowered by divine mandate, felt a responsibility to care for and, if necessary, govern the Church. Meanwhile, virtually all bishops wielded a measure of political authority, being major landholders in possession of their own wealth and military forces. To curb the political independence of these powerful figures, many kings sought to control the selection, appointment and investiture of churchmen based within their realm, even though in theory this was a papal prerogative. At the end of the first millennium of Christian history, the Latin Church was in disarray and the limited efforts to control it were being offered not by the papacy, but by secular rulers.

It was not until the mid-eleventh century that the first significant steps towards redressing this imbalance were taken. Amid a general atmosphere of heightened devotional awareness, inspired in part by the example of monasteries like Cluny, western Christians began to look at their Church and perceive sickness. A clergy rife with abuse and 'governed' by a powerless pope offered little prospect of guiding society towards salvation. Arguing that the Latin Church would have to clean up its act, starting in Rome itself and working outwards, a 'Reform Movement' emerged, advocating a twin agenda of papal empowerment and clerical purification. This campaign enjoyed some early success, establishing a rigorous new process for electing popes and launching public attacks on vices such as clerical marriage and the buying and selling of ecclesiastical office.[14]

The champion and chief architect of the cause was Pope Gregory VII (1073–85), the very man who recognised Urban's talents and brought him to Italy. A profoundly ambitious, wilful and intransigent figure, Gregory fought harder than any pope before him to realise the potential of his office, struggling to unify and cleanse Latin Christendom under the banner of Rome. With audacious single-mindedness, he identified what he believed to be the root cause of the Church's problems – the polluting influence of the laity – and then set about attacking it with near-rabid tenacity, in what has been termed the 'Investiture Controversy'. Gregory was not interested in tempered diplomacy or negotiated reform – he went straight for the jugular of the mightiest secular force in Europe, hoping to cow the rest of Christendom into submission by example.

In 1075 Gregory banned the German king Henry IV, a man who could trace the lineage of his office to Charlemagne and beyond, from interfering in the affairs of the Church. When Henry resisted, Gregory mobilised the ultimate weapon in his arsenal. As yet possessing no military might with which to coerce, he chose instead to strike Henry with spiritual censure. In February 1076, he excommunicated the most powerful Latin Christian alive and instructed the king's subjects to renounce him. So dramatic was this act that legend later declared it to have caused the ancient papal throne of St Peter to crack in two. Ejecting Henry from the Church, denying his status as a Christian, was an immense gamble; should Gregory's edict be ignored, his bluff would be called and his authority shattered, but were this condemnation to be heeded, then the Roman pontiff, who just decades earlier had seemed a marginal nonentity on the European stage, would be confirmed as the arbiter of ultimate justice.

In the final analysis, Gregory's strategy did not succeed, his papacy ending with the glorious ambition of papal empowerment unrealised. Henry's excommunication did initially prompt the king to adopt a more penitent stance, but the pope soon overplayed his hand, enraging his enemies and alienating supporters with his radical and unbending vision of spiritual reform and his intensely personal, autocratic notion of papal authority. Along the way, Gregory experimented with the concept of a papal army, a move that prompted indignation in some quarters but broke crucial ground on the road towards the concept of crusading.

It was into a world of unrealised papal aspirations and seething diplomatic discord that Urban was propelled by his appointment as prelate of Ostia *c.* 1080. In spite of Gregory VII's hard-line fanaticism and failing fortunes, Urban remained among his staunchest allies, backing up his publicly avowed support for the beleaguered pontiff with sterling service as papal legate to Germany between 1084 and 1085. He had, nonetheless, to witness Gregory's ultimate decline, as Henry IV had his own candidate, Clement III, declared pope and finally moved in to occupy Rome itself. On 25 May 1085, Pope Gregory VII died in ignominious exile in southern Italy. In the chaos that followed his death no obvious candidate immediately emerged to champion the Gregorian cause or challenge the authority of the German anti-pope. The first, short-lived choice of a successor was not consecrated until May 1087, and, after his death in September of that same year, it took a further six months of infighting before Urban II could step forward to assume the office of pope.[15]

Given the extraordinary impact he was to have upon European history, the most striking feature of Urban's early pontificate was the position of extreme weakness and vulnerability from which he began. In 1088, the Latin West seemed ready to turn its back upon the Gregorian party. Urban had to contend with Clement III, the rival German claimant to the papal throne, and recovered possession of the Lateran Palace in Rome in 1094 only through bribery, and even then his hold over the city was precarious. But he did gradually restore papal authority. A far more skilful diplomat than his predecessor, in his dealings with the secular and ecclesiastical powers of Europe Urban chose to encourage gradual change through cautious suggestion rather than affect brazen dominance. He also adopted a more flexible approach to reform and its implementation, stressing inclusion rather than retribution when dealing with transgressors. This temperance won back a good deal of support for the papal cause. Urban capitalised upon the network of contacts established during his days at Cluny and worked to rejuvenate the web of aristocratic clients, known as 'the faithful of St Peter', that had grown up under Gregory VII. Rejecting despotism in favour of consultative government, Urban was the first pope to institute a functioning *curia Romana* or papal court, in which he worked alongside ecclesiastical advisers instead of presenting himself as the sole, perfected mouthpiece of St Peter.

By 1095, Urban's restrained touch had begun to pay off, bringing the doctrine of reform to regions that Gregory's closed fist had failed to penetrate. The papacy was at last beginning to recover some of its international prestige. Rome's power was still far from universal, however, when in March Pope Urban convened a major ecclesiastical council at the southern Italian city of Piacenza. It was during this meeting that a fateful embassy arrived bearing envoys from Constantinople (modern-day Istanbul), capital of the mighty Greek Christian Empire of Byzantium. Beset by aggressive Islamic neighbours, these Byzantines appealed for military aid from their Christian brethren in the West. The pope's initial reaction was to urge 'many to promise, by taking an oath, to aid the emperor most faithfully as far as they were able against the pagans', but this seems to have provoked little or no reaction. The idea of promoting a more vigorous response was, however, beginning to take shape in Urban's mind. Before the year was out, and with the backbone of papal authority barely rebuilt, he would issue a call to arms that would drive a multitude of Latins swarming to the gates of Constantinople and beyond.[16]

THE CRUSADING IDEAL

In the autumn of 1095, with the power of Rome taking its first tentative steps towards recovery, Pope Urban II made a grand preaching tour of France. It was during this visit to his old homeland that Urban launched the First Crusade. He called upon the warriors of the Latin West to avenge a range of ghastly 'crimes' committed against Christendom by the followers of Islam, urging them to bring aid to their eastern brethren and to reconquer the most sacred site on earth, the city of Jerusalem. This speech, the moment of genesis for the concept of a crusade, bound the Christian religion to a military cause. To understand how the pope achieved this fusion of faith and violence and why Europe ultimately responded to his appeal with enthusiasm, we must begin by asking what prompted Urban to preach the crusade when he did.

The threat to Latin Christendom?

The first point to acknowledge is that the call to arms made at Clermont was not directly inspired by any recent calamity or atrocity in the East. Urban's sermon may have been stimulated, at least in part, by the Byzantine appeal for military aid received some eight months earlier at the council of Piacenza, but this request was not itself tied to any recent Greek defeat, resulting instead from decades of mounting Muslim aggression in Asia Minor (modern-day Turkey). And although the Holy City of Jerusalem, the expedition's ultimate goal, was indeed in Muslim hands, it had been so for more than 400 years – hardly a fresh wound. At the start of the eleventh century, the Church of the Holy Sepulchre, thought to enclose the site of Christ's crucifixion and resurrection, had been partially demolished by the volatile Islamic leader known to history as the Mad Caliph Hakim. His subsequent persecution of the local Christian population lasted for more than a decade, ending only when he declared himself a living god and turned on his own Muslim subjects. Tensions also seem to have been running high in 1027, when Muslims reportedly threw stones into the compound of the Holy Sepulchre. More recently, Latin Christians attempting to make devotional pilgrimages to the Levant, of whom there continued to be many, may have reported some difficulties in visiting the Holy Places, but the volume and severity of such complaints was far from overwhelming.[17]

The reality was that, when Pope Urban proclaimed the First Crusade at Clermont, Islam and Christendom had coexisted for centuries in relative equanimity. There may at times have been little love lost between Christian and Muslim neighbours, but there was, in truth, little to distinguish this enmity from the endemic political and military struggles of the age. When, in the seventh century, Muhammad first revealed the teachings of Allah and Islam exploded out of the Arabian peninsula, the eastern Roman Empire of Byzantium faced a seemingly unstoppable tide of expansion. Arab forces swept through Palestine, Syria and Asia Minor, finally breaking upon the walls of the Greek capital, Constantinople. As the years passed, Islam and Byzantium developed a tense, sometimes quarrelsome respect for one another, but their relationship was no more fraught with conflict than that between the Greeks and their Slavic or Latin neighbours to the west.[18]

At the other end of the Mediterranean, Islamic forces had overwhelmed the Iberian peninsula in 711 CE. So dynamic was their advance that only the might of Charlemagne's grandfather, Charles the Hammer, could turn them back from the borders of France and the heartlands of Latin Christendom. Partially detached from the rest of Europe by the physical barrier of the Pyrenean mountains, these Muslims settled in Spain and Portugal, leaving the indigenous Christians only a thin sliver of territory in the north. Muslim power held fast for generations, allowing culture, learning and trade to flourish, and Islamic Iberia blossomed into one of the greatest centres of civilisation in the known world. When decay and political fracture finally set in during the eleventh century, the surviving Christian realms of the north were quick to capitalise. In the decades leading up to the First Crusade, the nature of Iberian Latin–Muslim contact did alter: animosities hardened; the Christians went into the ascendant; and the frontier dividing these two faiths gradually began to inch southwards. But even in this period the scavenging Latins were far more interested in draining the Muslim south of its fabled wealth than they were in prosecuting any sort of concerted religious warfare. When blood was shed in battle, it was usually the result of Christian in-fighting, fractious squabbling over the spoils.[19]

At the end of the eleventh century, Christendom was in one sense encircled by Islam, with Muslim forces ranged against it to the east along Byzantium's Asian frontier and to the south in the Iberian peninsula. But Europe was a long way from being engaged in an urgent, titanic struggle for survival. No coherent, pan-Mediterranean onslaught threatened, because, although the Moors of Iberia and the Turks of Asia Minor shared a religious heritage, they were never united in one purpose. Where Christians and Muslims did face each other across the centuries, their relationship had been unremarkable, characterised, like that between any potential rivals, by periods of conflict and others of coexistence. There is little or no evidence to suggest that either side harboured any innate, empowering religious or racial hatred of the other.[20]

Most significantly, throughout this period indigenous Christians actually living under Islamic law, be it in Iberia or the Holy Land, were generally treated with remarkable clemency. The Muslim faith acknowledged and respected Judaism and Christianity, creeds with which it enjoyed a common devotional tradition and a mutual reliance upon authoritative scripture. Christian subjects may not have been able to share power with their Muslim masters, but they were given freedom to worship. All around the Mediterranean basin, Christian faith and society survived and even thrived under the watchful but tolerant eye of Islam. Eastern Christendom may have been subject to Islamic rule, but it was not on the brink of annihilation, nor prey to any form of systematic abuse.

It is true that, ten years before the council of Clermont, Iberia entered a period of heightened religious intolerance. In 1086, a fanatical Islamic sect invaded Iberia from north Africa, supplanting surviving, indigenous Muslim power in the peninsula. This new regime set about resisting and then repelling the acquisitive Christian north, scoring a number of notable military victories that re-established the balance of power in Islam's favour. This did cause a reaction in the Latin West. In 1087 the king of France urged his subjects to offer military support to their Iberian brethren, and a number of French potentates duly led companies across the Pyrenees, among them a number of knights who later joined the First Crusade. Then in 1089 Pope Urban II took a limited interest in Iberian affairs. He focused his attention upon the ancient Roman port of Tarragona in north-eastern Spain, a city which had for generations lain in ruins, adrift amid the unclaimed wasteland between Christian and Muslim territory. Urban sponsored the rebuilding of Tarragona as a papal protectorate, but, although he created a new archbishopric there and construction was apparently begun, it is not clear whether the port was actually reoccupied. Iberia did serve as something of a testing ground for crusading ideology, because Urban offered a remission of sin to those engaged in the restoration of Tarragona, but his involvement on the peninsula was still extremely limited and there was no direct link between the needs of this theatre of conflict and his eventual decision to launch a campaign to the Levant.[21]

Pope Urban's motives in 1095

The problems addressed by the First Crusade – Muslim occupation of Jerusalem and the potential threat of Islamic aggression in the East – had loomed for decades, even centuries, provoking little or no reaction in Rome. Urban II's decision to take up this cause at Clermont was, therefore, primarily proactive rather than reactive, and the crusade was designed, first and foremost, to meet the needs of the papacy. Launched as it was just as Urban began to stabilise his power-base in central Italy, the campaign must be seen as an attempt to consolidate papal empowerment and expand Rome's sphere of influence. It was no accident that Urban chose to unleash the concept of crusading in

France, a region in which his roots gave him connections and local knowledge, and over which the papacy had long wished to strengthen its hold. Indeed, the crusade was just one of the weapons used in pursuit of this agenda, Urban's entire grand tour of France in 1095–6 being a transparent attempt to manifest papal authority.

But for Urban the real beauty of the crusade was that it also had the potential to fulfil a range of other papal ambitions. Since the start of his pontificate, Urban had sought to re-establish friendly contact with the Greek Church of Byzantium, whose relationship with Rome had soured after the two Churches were, in 1054, forced into schism by a heated disagreement over liturgical practice. Orchestrating a positive response to the Byzantine appeal for military aid promised to cement a new period of détente with Constantinople. At the same time, it offered the prospect of expanding Latin influence over the Levantine Church in Asia Minor, Syria and Palestine, a significant step along the road towards papal pre-eminence in all Christendom.

The First Crusade also held more altruistic benefits. It is likely that Urban earnestly desired to help his Byzantine brethren and those eastern Christians living under Islamic rule. Although probably aware that the latter were not suffering desperate abuse, he still sought to liberate all Christendom, thus ending any threat of oppression. And while the Muslim rulers of the Holy Land might have been willing to grant pilgrims access to the sacred sites of Jerusalem, in Urban's mind it was still infinitely preferable for that revered city to be under Christian control. At the same time, he came to realise that the very means by which these goals might be achieved could also serve to purify the Latin West. Having grown up among the Frankish aristocracy, the pope was only too aware of the spiritual dilemma facing this knightly class. Bombarded by a stream of warnings about the dreadful danger of sin, but forced to resort to soul-contaminating violence in order to fulfil their duty and defend their rights in this lawless age, most nobles were trapped in a circle of guilt, obligation and necessity. As Roman pontiff, the father of the Latin Church, Urban was personally responsible for the soul of every single Christian living in the West. It was incumbent upon him to lift as many of his flock as possible towards salvation. The campaign launched at Clermont was therefore, in one sense, designed to answer the prayers of a polluted class in Urban's care, because it offered the nobility a new path to redemption. The message in 1095 was that knights would now be able to prosecute violence in the name of God, participating in a holy war.[22]

The long road to holy war

Turning bloodshed into a sacred act required the pope to reconcile Christian teaching with the ruthlessness of medieval warfare. With the preaching of the First Crusade the Latin Church went far beyond simply condoning violence; it energetically encouraged military conflict and promoted carnage as an expression of pious devotion. This sanctification of warfare, in which two seemingly immiscible elements – violence and Christianity – were fused, now stands as the defining characteristic of the First Crusade, the feature which has catapulted this expedition into the popular imagination and aroused generations of scholarly attention. The very concept of Christian holy war, of which the crusade was the dominant species, can elicit a sense of dismay and censure in modern observers, who view it as a distortion of Christ's teaching, an abomination that directly contradicts his promotion of pacifism. Many are driven to ask how the medieval papacy could have developed such an extraordinary concept.[23]

In fact, the First Crusade was not utterly abnormal, but an extreme product of concerns common to all ages of human society: the need to contain mankind's innate appetite for violence; and the desire to distinguish between 'good' and 'evil' warfare. Across millennia of recorded history and in every corner of the planet, civilisations have struggled to control and harness human aggression, most often by categorising certain types of bloodshed as acceptable and outlawing or vilifying the remainder. Even modern societies posit a moral distinction between 'private' murder and killing performed in the midst of sanctioned 'public' warfare. Ruling elites also tend to promote their own wars as justifiable and those of their enemies as morally corrupt. The medieval theory of crusading similarly sought to redirect the energies of Europe's feuding warlords, channelling their bloodlust out beyond the borders of the Latin West for the 'good' of all Christendom. In the long term, however, this approach to the management of violence had a bleak and lasting impact upon the relationship with Islam.

This still begs the question of how Christianity, seemingly a pacifistic religion, was so readily militarised. Pope Urban II did not conjure the idea of a crusade from thin air, nor did he consider the concept of holy war to be revolutionary or even novel. In his mind, centuries of Christian, and even pre-Christian, tradition legitimised the principles espoused at Clermont. It was inevitable that his ideas would be influenced by precedent because eleventh-century Latin society was profoundly retrospective. Being Christian to the core, it accepted two immutable truths: scripture, the cornerstone of the faith, was utterly unassailable, the unquestionable word of God; and at the moment of its foundation by St Peter, the Roman Church had been a precise expression of divine will, the Lord's design for mankind made manifest on earth. These two ancient rocks of perfection left a heavy imprint upon the medieval mind. Fixated by this vision of a golden age in which the apostles supposedly created an ideal Christian order, and governed by an immoveable, authoritative text, the medieval world was obsessed with the past.

But Urban and his contemporaries viewed their Christian history through a cracked and clouded lens. The glorious 'perfection' of a bygone era to which they aspired too often owed more to fiction than to fact. The sheer malleability of history – stretched and distorted by the imprecisions of memory and twisted through wilful manipulation and forgery – meant that the 'past' that informed and enabled Urban's sanctification of violence was actually a shifting, tangled web of reality and imagination. Although the pope earnestly believed that the campaign he preached in 1095 conformed to Christ's teaching, a deep chasm separated the ideals promoted by scripture and those that sustained the concept of crusading.

Weathered by a thousand years of human history, Christian attitudes to violence had undergone an incremental but drastic transformation.

Christianity does, at first glance, appear to be an unquestionably pacifistic faith. The Gospels of the New Testament record numerous occasions when Jesus seemed to reject or prohibit violence: his Sermon on the Mount recommended a policy of peaceful resistance in the face of aggression, turning the other cheek in response to a blow; he instructed his followers to offer love to their enemies; and, at the moment of his betrayal by Judas in the Garden of Gethsemane, when St Peter sought to defend Christ from his captors, Jesus ordered the apostle to sheath his sword, cautioning that he who lived by violence would die by violence. At the same time, the Old Testament appears to offer incontrovertible guidance on the question of violence when Moses reveals the divine law 'thou shall not kill' in the Ten Commandments.

Urban's vision of his religion was, however, coloured by the work of Christian theologians who, in the course of the first millennium CE, decided that scripture might not actually offer such a decisive or universal condemnation of violence and warfare. In part, these theorists were initially sent scurrying to reconsider Christian doctrine by the living reality with which they were confronted. It was always going to prove difficult to maintain an unwavering policy of pacifism in the face of mankind's inherent bellicosity, but, with the conversion of the Roman Empire, it became virtually impossible to sustain the absolute rejection of violence. From the fourth century onwards, Christianity underwent a gradual but deep-seated transformation as it fused with a Roman 'state' for which warfare was an essential feature of existence. Attempting to balance the proscriptions of faith with the needs of empire, some of the earliest Christian scholars, known as the founding fathers or patristic writers, sought to refine man's understanding of the message contained in the Bible. They did not have to look far to realise that, on the question of violence, scripture was riddled with apparent contradictions.

In spite of its stated ban on bloodshed, Mosaic Law actually endorsed military defence in the face of aggression. Elsewhere, the Old Testament went even further. Being an ongoing history of the Hebrews' long struggle for survival, it describes a series of holy wars, conflicts sanctioned and supported by divine licence, in which God was held to be the author of victory. To patristic theologians, these examples appeared to indicate that, under the right circumstances, even vengeful or aggressive warfare might be permissible. Even the New Testament, if judged from a certain perspective, could appear to be ambivalent in its approach to physical conflict. Jesus had after all said that he came to bring not peace but a sword, and at one point had used a whip of cords to drive moneylenders out of the temple.

The most influential patristic writer to grapple with these problems was the north African bishop St Augustine of Hippo (354–430 CE), perhaps the most eminent theologian in all Christian history and author of a long series of works exploring human existence and religious devotion. St Augustine's work on Christian violence laid the foundation upon which Pope Urban II eventually erected the crusading ideal. St Augustine argued that a war could be both legal and justified if fought under strictly controlled conditions. His complex theories were later simplified and consolidated to produce three prerequisites of a Just War: it must be proclaimed by a 'legitimate authority', like a king, prince or bishop; it ought to have a 'just cause', such as the recovery of lost property or defence against enemy attack; and it should be fought with 'right intention', that is without cruelty or excessive bloodshed. These three Augustinian principles were the basic building-blocks of the crusading ideal. But, although Augustine's work shaped the format and nature of Pope Urban II's crusade sermon at Clermont, it did not actually provide the western Church with a working doctrine of holy war. St Augustine broke Latin Christian theology from the shackles of pacifism, and his ideas gradually filtered down into European society, helping to salve general anxieties about the relationship between faith and military service. But there were distinct limitations to his theory as it was applied to the medieval West. It was seen to demonstrate that certain forms of necessary, public warfare might be 'justified' – that is, acceptable and lawful in the eyes of God.[24]

A significant conceptual divide separates this from 'sanctified' violence. This latter form of warfare was not deemed simply to be tolerable to God, a potentially sinful act to which he was prepared to turn a blind eye because its evil would lead to a greater good. Instead, a holy war was one that God actively supported, even demanded, which could be of spiritual benefit to its participants. Pope Urban's crusading ideal was an extension of this second class of sanctified warfare, but it was not until the eleventh century that the Latin Church really developed a working theory of holy war.

Between the age of St Augustine and the council of Clermont, western Christendom gradually became acculturated to the concept of sanctified violence. This was an incremental, organic process, marked by sporadic episodes of theological experimentation, not a driven programme of linear development. Before the year 1000, the papacy occasionally dabbled in the rhetoric of holy war when facing significant threats. In the ninth century, two successive popes sought to rally military support by promising rather vaguely defined spiritual benefits – a 'heavenly reward' or 'eternal life' – to those who fought and died in defence of Rome. But this type of appeal seems to have garnered only a limited response and soon fell into disuse. At the same time, Latin society underwent a fitful awakening to the idea that 'just wars' might encompass elements of sacred obligation or reward. The prominent role of Carolingian bishops in sponsoring, even directing, brutal campaigns to conquer and convert the pagans of eastern Europe helped stimulate the idea that warfare might have a pious goal. The Christianisation of Germanic 'barbarian' traditions also encouraged reverence for the martial qualities of the warrior class and the adoption of the ritual blessing of the weapons of war by the clergy. It was a relatively small step to imagine that esteemed Christian knights, bearing sanctified arms and armour, might be capable of performing some sort of devotional service to God. Even so, at the turn of the millennium, any receptivity to the potential sanctification of violence was still balanced by an ingrained, almost instinctive suspicion that, amid the endemic disorder afflicting society, much of the 'public' warfare proclaimed as 'just' by feuding lords was, in fact, illicit and thus sinful.

It was not until the second half of the eleventh century that Latin Christendom truly began to edge towards the acceptance of sanctified violence and thus became receptive to the idea of crusading. The first step was the accelerated incidence of papally sponsored warfare. With elements of the Reform Movement urging Rome to pursue an energetic policy of empowerment, successive popes began taking a more active interest in the protection of their Italian territories and the extension of their international influence. It soon became apparent that, if Rome wished to stand on the world stage, it would, on occasion, need some form of material military power with which to enforce its spiritual will. It was nothing new for the papacy to seek martial support from its secular allies; the difference was the degree of its direct, even personal, involvement in warfare. In 1053, Pope Leo IX (1049–54) actually participated in a battle against the aggressive Norman adventurers who had recently invaded southern Italy, offering his supporters absolution from sin as reward for their military service. A decade later, one of Leo's successors, Alexander II (1061–73) lent papal support to Christians fighting against Islam in Iberia, suggesting that this type of warfare might, of itself, be penitential.[25]

Pope Gregory VII and sanctified violence

During the pontificate of Gregory VII the doctrine and application of sacred violence underwent a radical transformation. Gregory's ambitious and uncompromising vision of papal authority prompted him to pursue the sponsorship and sanctification of warfare at an unprecedented pace. His work created the platform upon which Urban stood in 1095. Possessed by an intensely personal notion of his office and believing more wholeheartedly than any pope before him that he was the literal, living embodiment of St Peter, Gregory was utterly convinced that he could wield full apostolic authority on earth. In his mind, there seems to have been no question but that the pope should have total, unchecked control over the spiritual wellbeing of mankind. He was, equally, in no doubt that this power took precedence over that exercised by kings and princes. To realise this audacious ideal, Gregory took a massive step towards the militarisation of the Latin Church. He decided that what Rome really needed was not the martial backing of potentially unreliable secular allies, but a fully fledged papal army owing its allegiance, first and foremost, to St Peter.

In pursuit of this goal, Gregory made a series of sweeping pronouncements that slowly percolated throughout western society, threatening to reshape the Latin world order. He set about reinterpreting Christian tradition in order to establish a precedent for his combative policies. Centuries earlier, patristic theologians had described the internal, spiritual battle waged against sin by devoted Christians as the 'warfare of Christ'. In time, it became popular in learned circles to conceive of monks as the 'soldiers of Christ', ascetics armed with prayer and ritual, engaged in a metaphorical war with temptation. Gregory appropriated this idea and twisted it to suit his purpose. He proclaimed that all lay society had one overriding obligation: to defend the Latin Church as 'soldiers of Christ' through actual, physical warfare.

The laity had, in recent decades, been encouraged to reimagine their spiritual relationship with God and the Latin Church in terms that mirrored the structure of temporal society. With God conceived of as 'lord' and 'ruler' of the 'kingdom' of heaven, Christians were conditioned to believe that they owed him loyalty and service as they would a mortal king. To turn this diffuse theory into reality, Gregory harnessed and adapted a popular fixture of Christianity. Latin Europe was accustomed to the notion that saints – Christians who had lived meritorious lives or been martyred, and thus, in death, attained a special place in heaven – deserved reverence. Throughout the West, men and women championed patron saints, offering them dutiful veneration in return for protection and support. Gregory sought to transform this localised patchwork of allegiance by harnessing the universal appeal of St Peter. Rome had, for some time, described its supporters as *fideles beati Petri*, the 'faithful' of St Peter. But Gregory chose to focus on a different aspect of the word *fideles*, emphasising its implication of service and vassalage to suggest that all Latin Christians were, in fact, 'vassals of St Peter' and so by implication vassals of the pope.

By fusing the vision of Christendom as God's 'kingdom', the practice of venerating saints and the feudal connotations of the term *fideles*, Gregory concocted an elaborate justification for his claim that all lay society owed him a debt of military service. In truth, much of Europe would not have fully understood this intricate web of distorted precedent and warped tradition, and certainly, in the divisive atmosphere of the Investiture Controversy, not all Latins answered Gregory's call to obedience. But he did manage to recruit a powerful network of *fideles* willing to do the bidding of Rome, many of whom would later support Urban's crusade.

The most devoted and influential of these *fideles* was Countess Matilda of Tuscany, the great matriarch of northern Italy. Ruling one of the grandest princedoms in Europe, Matilda commanded respect in all corners of western Christendom. The not inconsiderable military resources of this 'daughter of St Peter', as she liked to be known, lent real force to the papal cause. As a wealthy patron Matilda also attracted some of the finest minds in Europe to her lavish court. Men like Anselm of Lucca, a master of canon law (the history of Church law and papal judgements) and the arch propagandist Bonizo of Sutri set out to shore up the theological underpinnings of Reform policy and cement the doctrine of Christian warfare. Throughout the 1080s, their work served to consolidate Gregorian theories in some areas and to fuel the pursuit of papal authority in others. This 'think tank' amassed an array of textual authorities with which to defend Matilda's reputation and rebut any criticism of the papacy's militarisation. Anselm scoured the annals of ecclesiastical law in search of precedents for the sanctification of violence, while Bonizo wrote a series of popularised, polemical histories of the Church, designed to demonstrate that God actually had a long record of endorsing holy war. One of their colleagues, John of Mantua, even managed to reinterpret a key pacifistic passage in scripture. John noted that, although Christ had ordered St Peter to sheathe his sword in the Garden of Gethsemane, he had not told him to cast it aside. On this basis, John maintained that Jesus had, in fact, wanted his chief apostle to keep the weapon by his side for use at a later date. John's allegorical argument was that, while God did not intend the pope to wield the 'sword' in person, he did expect him to direct a material 'weapon' – the armed laity – in defence of Christendom. The work carried out at Matilda's court played a vital role in the genesis of the crusading ideal, serving to assemble and shape centuries of Christian thought on the question of violence into a coherent theory of sanctified violence, a resource upon which Urban would later draw.

Working alongside these Matildine scholars, Gregory VII made the leap from concept to practice, taking significant steps towards the creation of a papal army and marking a distinct turning point on the road leading to Urban II's speech at Clermont. Early in his pontificate, Gregory laid plans for a grand military enterprise that can be regarded as the prototype for a crusade. In 1074 he tried to launch a holy war in the eastern Mediterranean that would, had it come to fruition, have borne a striking resemblance to the campaign initiated by Urban II in 1095. Gregory sought to recruit lay military support in France and Germany for an expedition to bring aid to the Greek Christians of Byzantium, who were, he claimed, 'daily being butchered like cattle' by the Muslims of Asia Minor. He proposed to lead this bold defence of Christendom in person, declaring that the venture might take him all the way to the Holy Sepulchre of Jerusalem, and expressed the hope that success might bring about the reunification of the eastern and western Churches under the authority of Rome. Although Gregory declared in a letter of December 1074 that he had already amassed an army 50,000 strong –

a claim that was sheer fantasy – his grandiose project soon fizzled out, tarnished by its intimate association with Gregory's own personal authority and then extinguished by the scouring wind of the Investiture Controversy.

Gregory's planned expedition did, nonetheless, begin to crystallise the ideal of holy war. His predecessor had already implied that violence in the service of God might be meritorious; Gregory's 1074 scheme explained why. The spiritual benefits of participating in his campaign still seem to have been somewhat vague, described simply as a 'heavenly reward', but the reason why such a prize might be on offer was made much clearer. Gregory argued that his projected war would be fought in defence of the Christian faith and that the very act of bringing aid to Byzantium was an expression of love for one's Christian brethren and thus charitable. This formula of charitable defence made it much easier for contemporaries to believe that fighting in a holy war might truly earn them merit in the eyes of God. Events later in Gregory's pontificate also helped to clarify the penitential nature of sanctified violence. In the midst of the Investiture Controversy he urged Matilda of Tuscany to fight Henry IV 'for the remission of her sins' and instructed her 'to impose on [her] soldiers the danger of the coming battle for the remission of all their sins'. The scholar Anselm of Lucca later interpreted this to mean that participation in this war had the same purificational value as other forms of penance precisely because it promised, just like a pilgrimage, to be both difficult and perilous.

For all this, Gregory VII cannot be regarded as the sole architect of the crusading ideal. He certainly never successfully launched a campaign on the scale of the First Crusade, nor was he particularly concerned to direct the energy of sanctified violence against Islam. But he did break crucial ground on the road to the idea of crusading. Gregory's radical, unrelenting drive towards militarisation prompted considerable criticism in ecclesiastical circles, as he was accused of dabbling in practices 'new and unheard of throughout the centuries'. His vision was so extreme that, when Urban II offered a more measured ideal, he appeared almost conservative in comparison and attracted little censure.[26]

Gregory's achievements and those of his predecessors also meant that, by the start of Urban's pontificate in 1088, the concept of holy war had been formulated. The Latin West had been acculturated to the idea that certain classes of violence might be justified, and was slowly waking up to the notion that warfare directed by the papacy might have a penitential character and thus be capable, in some sense, of cleansing the soul of sin. Within a year of his assumption of the papal throne, Urban had begun to experiment with this new weapon: participants in the reconstruction of Tarragona were offered a remission of sin, but on this occasion the pope achieved a subtle shift of theological emphasis by equating this merit to that of a pilgrimage to Jerusalem. In the years that followed, as the Gregorian papacy slowly enjoyed a renaissance of authority, Urban pondered the full potential of sanctified violence. It was only at the council of Clermont, in the wake of the appeal at Piacenza, that the full range of his ambition became evident.

THE SERMON AT CLERMONT

The First Crusade was proclaimed in November 1095 during Urban II's momentous visit to France. His was the first journey made by any pope outside Italy for almost half a century. With the ongoing Investiture Controversy and the recent diminution of papal authority, the journey north of the Alps was designed to affirm Urban's legitimacy and assert Rome's presence in his old homeland. Even with the papal reputation besmirched by years of chaotic conflict, Urban's grand tour of the region cannot have failed to impress. It had been decades since most of the towns and villages through which his lavish entourage passed had witnessed a visit from a bishop or prince, let alone that of a pope accompanied by a host of senior clergymen. For many, this was the spectacle of a lifetime.

To rally the Latin Church to his cause, Urban called the clergy to a grand ecclesiastical council. Held in late November at Clermont, in the Auvergne region of south-eastern France, this meeting was attended by some twelve archbishops, eighty bishops and ninety abbots – not a massive assembly by medieval standards, but the largest of Urban's pontificate to date. For more than a week, the council considered an array of ecclesiastical business, as Urban sought to disseminate his plans for the continued reform of the Church. Then, on 27 November, with the council drawing to a close, the pope announced that he would deliver a special sermon to an open-air assembly held in a field outside Clermont. Urban probably arranged for this public spectacle in the hope that his preaching would draw a large crowd, and later tradition maintained that the meeting had to be moved outside because of the sheer weight of numbers that gathered to hear him speak, but in reality perhaps only 300 or 400 people braved the chill November air. These select few were to bear witness to a captivating sermon.[27]

Pope Urban's message

Unless new evidence comes to light, we will never know exactly what Pope Urban II said in his momentous sermon. Even though this speech initiated a campaign that would change the face of European history, no precise record of Urban's words survives. In the years that followed, a number of men, including three eyewitnesses, did record versions of his address, but all of them wrote after the end of the First Crusade. Their accounts must, therefore, be read with a healthy dose of suspicion in mind, given that their versions of the events at Clermont were composed with the benefit of hindsight. They knew only too well what powerful emotions Urban's words would stir in western Christendom, the tide of humanity that would respond to his call and the dreadful progress of the crusade that followed. Only by carefully cross-referencing these versions of Urban's sermon with the pope's own letters, composed around the time of the council of Clermont, can we approach some understanding of his message and intentions.

We know that Urban urged western Christendom to pursue two interlocking goals: the liberation of the eastern Churches, most notably by bringing military support to the beleaguered Byzantine Empire; and the reconquest of the Holy Land, in particular the city of Jerusalem. From the start, he conceived of the campaign as a war of defence and repossession. The crusade was not launched as an evangelical enterprise to bring about the conversion of Muslims, forced or voluntary, but to protect and recover Christian territory. This was to be a war of religion, but one that focused upon physical power, not ephemeral theology. Rather than emphasise complex questions of dogma and creed, Urban promoted a war that his audience could understand, stressing the theme of Christian brotherhood and highlighting the fact that all Latin knights had a duty to defend Christ's patrimony by participating in an impassioned battle to recover the Holy Land.[28]

His appeal seems to have been loosely structured around the three Augustinian principles of Just War – legitimate authority, just cause and right intention – bolstered by remodelled Gregorian ideals. He took 'just cause' as the key theme for his proposed campaign, launching into a polemical oration, peppered with inflammatory images of Muslim atrocities.

We want you to know what grievous cause leads us to your territory, what need of yours and all the faithful brings us here. A grave report has come from the lands of Jerusalem and from the city of Constantinople that a people from the kingdom of the Persians, a foreign race, a race absolutely alien to God . . . has invaded the land of those Christians [and] has reduced the people with sword, rapine and fire.[29]

A central feature of Urban's doctrine was the denigration and dehumanisation of Islam. He set out from the start to launch a holy war against what he called 'the savagery of the Saracens', a 'barbarian' people capable of incomprehensible levels of cruelty and brutality.

Their supposed crimes were enacted upon two groups. Eastern Christians, in particular the Byzantines, had been 'overrun right up to the Mediterranean Sea'. Urban described how the Muslims, 'occupying more and more of the land on the borders of [Byzantium], were slaughtering and capturing many, destroying churches and laying waste to the kingdom of God. So, if you leave them alone much longer they will further grind under their heels the faithful of God.'[30] The pope also maintained that Christian pilgrims to the Holy Land were being subjected to horrific abuse and exploitation. While the wealthy were regularly beaten and stripped of their fortunes by illegal taxes, the poor endured even more terrible treatment:

> Non-existent money is extracted from them by intolerable tortures, the hard skin on their heels being cut open and peeled back to investigate whether perhaps they have inserted something under it. The cruelty of these impious men goes even to the length that, thinking the wretches have eaten gold or silver, they either put scammony in their drink and force them to vomit or void their vitals, or – and this is unspeakable – they stretch asunder the coverings of all the intestines after ripping open their stomachs with a blade and reveal with horrible mutilation whatever nature keeps secret.[31]

These accusations had little or no basis in fact, but they did serve Urban's purpose. By expounding upon the alleged crimes of Islam, he sought to ignite an explosion of vengeful passion among his Latin audience, while his attempts to degrade Muslims as 'sub-human' opened the floodgates of extreme, brutal reciprocity. This, the pope argued, was to be no shameful war of equals, between God's children, but a 'just' and 'holy' struggle in which an 'alien' people could be punished without remorse and with utter ruthlessness. Urban was activating one of the most potent impulses in human society: the definition of the 'other'. Across countless generations of human history, tribes, cities, nations and peoples have sought to delineate their own identities through comparison to their neighbours or enemies. By conditioning Latin Europe to view Islam as a species apart, the pope stood to gain not only by facilitating his proposed campaign, but also by propelling the West towards unification.

Urban did, however, have one major problem at Clermont. No recent, overwhelming calamity or crime stood out to act as the igniting spark of his holy conflagration. To ensure that his sermon prompted a fevered response, the pope worked hard to lend his appeal some sense of burning urgency. A heated theological schism had for decades divided Rome and Constantinople, but Urban nonetheless emphasised the shared Christian heritage that united East and West, suggesting that Latin Christendom had a fraternal obligation to act. According to one account, Urban urged his audience 'to run as quickly as you can to the aid of your brothers living on the eastern shore'; in another he is reported as encouraging them to think of eastern Christians as 'your blood brothers, your comrades-in-arms, those born of the same womb as you, for you are sons of the same Christ and the same Church'. He also capitalised upon the immediate devotional resonance of Jerusalem, describing the Holy City as 'the navel of the world', the birthplace of all Christian faith and scene of Jesus' life, death and resurrection. Urban hoped that the image of a captive Jerusalem would be so distressing as to prompt an immediate reaction, and he is recorded exhorting his listeners to 'be especially moved by the [fate of the] Holy Sepulchre of Our Lord and Saviour, which is in the hands of unclean races'.* The pope may have also played on the theme, previously used by Gregory VII, of the 'kingdom of God', representing the Holy Land as Christ's 'realm' or 'patrimony' and reminding Latin Christians of their obligation to defend their lord's territory.[32]

---

*It was also a popularly held belief that the 'Last Days' prophesied in the Bible – when all mankind would be judged and the 'saved' would enter eternal paradise – could only come to pass once the city of Jerusalem was once again in Christian hands. The First Crusade was thus viewed by some as a crucial step towards the realisation of Christian destiny.

The pope promoted the crusade as a distinct form of warfare, set apart from the grubby contamination of the inter-Christian struggles afflicting the West. According to one account, he proclaimed:

> Let those who in the past have been accustomed to spread private war so vilely among the faithful advance against the infidels . . . Let those who were formerly brigands now become soldiers of Christ; those who once waged war against their brothers and blood-relatives fight lawfully against barbarians; those who until now have been mercenaries for a few coins achieve eternal rewards.[33]

This approach was an offshoot of the Augustinian principle of 'right intention', requiring a Just War to be fought with restraint and control. Urban suggested that 'normal' violence was both illegal and corrupting, that only a war fought under regulated conditions could be considered licit or sanctified. But he proclaimed that in this campaign the regulating factor would be not the degree of brutality, but rather the 'alien' status of its target. Earlier in the eleventh century, the papacy had encouraged lay society to adhere to the Peace and Truce of God movements, codes of practice which sought to limit the places and times at which violence might be inflicted. The underlying assumption of these conventions was that not all violence was equal in the eyes of God. For the Peace and Truce, the distinction lay in degrees of sinfulness: violence carried out on a holy day or against a cleric was worse than an attack upon a layman during the week. Pope Urban twisted and extended this idea, declaring that the crusade would be a distinct class of warfare, prosecuted under a particular set of controlled conditions. In this instance, however, the 'controlling' feature that established a 'right intention' had nothing to do with degrees of violence or the tempered prosecution of warfare. Instead, it was entirely dependent upon the 'alien' nature of the enemy to be confronted. The expedition would be 'just' because it was directed against 'inhuman' Muslims, not because it was executed with moderation. This may, to some extent, help to explain why the First Crusaders proved capable of such extreme brutality.[34]

A *new form of holy war*

Perhaps the most significant feature of Pope Urban's sermon at Clermont was the formula of sanctified violence he associated with the proposed campaign. His predecessors, like Gregory VII, had experimented with the concept of holy war, seeking to promote the idea that military service in the name of God might bring participants a spiritual reward. But, more often than not, their calls to arms had attracted only a limited response. In one sense, Urban followed their lead: he promised that Latins who fought to protect their eastern brethren and recapture Jerusalem would enjoy a remission of sin, that is a cleansing of the soul. But he took a crucial further step, refining the ideological framework of sanctified violence to produce a new model of sacred warfare that, for the first time, truly resonated with the needs and expectations of medieval Europe. It was this new recipe for salvation that produced such an electric reaction among his audience.

Urban performed a relatively simple feat. He repackaged the concept of sanctified violence in a devotional format that was more comprehensible and palatable to lay society. Earlier popes may have argued that holy war could purify the soul, but Latin arms-bearers seem to have harboured nagging doubts about the efficacy of this notion. Urban sold the idea in terms that were familiar, convincing and attractive.

Western Christians were programmed to think of themselves as being critically contaminated by sin and conditioned to pursue a desperate struggle for purification through the outlets of confession and penance. Among the most recognised and fashionable of penitential activities in the eleventh century was the practice of pilgrimage. These devotional journeys to sites of religious significance were specifically designed to be gruelling, potentially dangerous affairs and thus capable of purging the soul. Urban's sermon at Clermont interwove the theme of holy war with that of pilgrimage to produce a distinct, new class of sanctified violence: a crusade. In this sacred expedition, the purificational properties of fighting for Christ were married to the penitential rigours of the pilgrim's journey, creating ideal conditions for the cleansing of sin. In this First Crusade, Urban's target audience, the Frankish knights of western Europe, would be able simultaneously to pursue two of their favourite pastimes – warfare and pilgrimage – in a devotional activity that seemed to them a natural extension of current Christian practice. This crusade promised to engender an unquestionably purgative atmosphere within which the intense burden of transgression and guilt might be relieved. The allure of this armed pilgrimage was all the more intense because its ultimate target was the premier devotional destination in Christian cosmology, the most revered physical space on earth: the Holy City of Jerusalem.

Jerusalem has a singular devotional resonance for three of the world's great religions, being the third city of Islam and the centre of the Christian and Judaic faiths. By the end of the eleventh century, it was popular in the Latin West to conceive of the city and its surroundings as a physical relic of Christ's life. Pope Urban was fully conscious of the almost irresistible appeal of the Holy City, and he took pains to underline its significance during his sermon. According to one account, he proclaimed that since 'we derive the whole of our Christian teaching from the fountain of Jerusalem' and because 'the [Holy] Land itself and the city in which Christ lived and suffered are known to be holy on the evidence of scripture', all Christian knights should feel impelled to answer his call to arms:

You, dearest brothers, must take the greatest pains to try to ensure that the holiness of that city and the glory of his Sepulchre will be cleansed . . . You, Christian soldiers, may justly defend the freedom of the fatherland by the exercise of arms. [And] if you believe that you ought to take great pains to make a pilgrimage to the graves of the apostles [in Rome] or to the shrines of any other saints, what expense of spirit can you refuse in order to rescue, and make a pilgrimage to, the Cross, the Blood, the Sepulchre?[35]

The spiritual rewards offered by Urban for making this armed pilgrimage to Jerusalem were immensely attractive, but not theologically audacious. Later, unsanctioned preachers did extend and simplify Urban's message, but the pope himself never suggested that joining the crusade would 'magically' guarantee all participants a place in heaven. To a modern observer, the very idea of fighting to purify one's soul might seem absurd and irrational, but Urban's vision of the crusade indulgence was firmly grounded in medieval reality. He conceived of the purificational properties of the crusade in terms that mirrored current devotional practice, incorporating existing language and ritual to produce a system that, in eleventh-century terms, offered a clear and rational pathway towards salvation.

Having modelled the crusade as an armed pilgrimage, Urban expressed the spiritual benefits of the campaign in penitential terms. Before 1095, under typical circumstances, a Latin knight concerned for the purity of his soul and fearful of the fires of hell would confess his sins to a cleric, receive an appropriate penance (such as fasting or a pilgrimage) and, upon completion of this 'punishment', be absolved. The expedition preached at Clermont represented a new form of 'super' penance: a venture so arduous, so utterly terrifying, as to be capable of cancelling out any sin. Participants would still have to confess their transgressions to a member of the clergy, but the crusade would replace any necessary penance. Answering Urban's call to arms, therefore, offered the arms-bearers of Europe a powerful new penitential option, but one that was cloaked in the apparatus of accepted custom. For the first time, fighting in the name of God and the pope brought with it a spiritual reward that was at once readily conceivable and deeply compelling: a real chance to walk through the fires of battle and emerge unsullied by sin.[36]

2

AFIRE WITH CRUSADING FEVER

At first glance, it might appear that Pope Urban's sermon at Clermont had an almost miraculous impact, that his words fell like fiery sparks upon bone-dry tinder, instantaneously igniting the imagination and enthusiasm of Latin Christendom to produce an extraordinary, unprecedented, perhaps even inexplicable, response.

In the twelve months following the council of Clermont, somewhere between 60,000 and 100,000 men, women and children, drawn from across the face of western Europe, answered the pope's rallying cry. This was, of course, not a full mobilisation of all Latin manpower. To be sure, more people stayed at home than took the cross. But it was, nonetheless, a gathering of human force and resources on a scale unparalleled in this age. Contemporary observers from within Europe and without gazed in wonder, sure in the knowledge that they were witnessing an event unique in living memory. Struggling to find an explanation for this phenomenon, they looked to the hand of God, or even the Devil. In the last century, historians have been driven to devote more analytical energy to rationalising this explosion of crusading fever than to almost any other feature of the expedition. They have grappled with a series of complex but crucial questions. What emotions and impulses inspired such a mass of Latin humanity to set out on crusade? How and why did the call to aid the eastern Churches and free Jerusalem spread across Europe with such power and rapidity? Did Pope Urban II actually appreciate the sheer elemental dynamism of the message he unleashed at Clermont?[1]

The answers to all these queries are, at best, circumspect and approximate. Just as we can do nothing more than estimate the number of thousands who responded to the crusading ideal, so too, with the surviving evidence, we can gain only a limited insight into their motivation and intent. In any case, it would be a gross oversimplification to suggest that such a host of individuals might be driven by a single set of beliefs and desires. Likewise, the precise details of the mechanisms of crusade dissemination and recruitment, and the full range of Urban's expectations, must remain in the shadowy half-light between theory and demonstrable reality. This is not to suggest that these lines of enquiry are without value – just the opposite. Even the partial traces of evidence and explanation are profoundly revelatory. Observing the impact of the crusading ideal is akin to tracing the spread of a virulent disease within a living organism. The dispersal and effect of an illness may disclose a great deal about the nature of the afflicted host. Similarly, even limited success in charting the response to Urban's preaching can furnish significant insights into the nature of eleventh-century society. It can, perhaps, even offer a brief glimpse into the essence of the medieval mentality. Exploring the motives and intentions of the First Crusaders as they took the cross may also help to explain their reactions to the appalling trials and remarkable triumphs of the next four years.

POPE URBAN'S EXPECTATIONS AND INTENTIONS

In the past, historians have suggested that when Urban II preached the First Crusade at Clermont he actually expected only a few hundred knights to answer his call – that, in effect, the pope was caught entirely off guard by the tidal wave of enthusiasm that swept across Europe and, as a consequence, rapidly lost control of the shape and format of the expedition. In fact, a significant corpus of evidence suggests that he harboured fairly grand ambitions for this project and had a real sense of its potential scale and scope. Certainly in the months following the council of Piacenza (1–7 March 1095), where Urban first received the Byzantine appeal for aid, and perhaps even earlier, he developed the idea of a penitential armed pilgrimage to Jerusalem that might simultaneously bring military reinforcement to eastern Christendom and expand the sphere of papal influence. This is not to suggest that the crusade was the only thing on the pope's mind, but it was a significant feature of his evolving reform agenda. At the same time, Urban began making preparations to ensure that his proposed expedition would meet with a positive response, tapping into the surviving network of *fideles beati Petri* established under Pope Gregory VII, including Matilda of Tuscany. It is striking how many of the prominent nobles who took the cross after Clermont were themselves *fideles*, or were connected to this group through marriage or family. Between his arrival in France in July 1095 and the start of the council of Clermont on 18 November, Urban visited a series of prominent monasteries, including his former house of Cluny. He also met and primed the two men whom he hoped would champion the crusading cause.[2]

Priming the core

The first of these was Adhémar of Le Puy, a figure who would become the spiritual shepherd of the First Crusade. Born into a noble family, possibly that of the counts of Valentinois, Adhémar was appointed bishop of Le Puy, in the Auvergne region of south-eastern France, at some point between 1080 and 1087. He had also probably completed a pilgrimage to Jerusalem before 1087. As a prominent Provençal bishop, Adhémar soon became an ally and associate of the region's most powerful secular ruler, Raymond of Toulouse. The bishop, evidently a firm supporter of the Gregorian papacy, was chosen by Urban II to play a pivotal role in the forthcoming expedition. In August 1095, soon after his arrival in France, the pope journeyed to Le Puy, where he must have met Adhémar. Here, and perhaps on other occasions over the coming months, the two discussed Urban's crusading project, agreeing a plan to orchestrate its reception and prosecution. Unfortunately, no record of these conversations survives, but we can be virtually certain that they took place because the events that followed were clearly stage-managed. Adhémar of Le Puy duly attended the council of Clermont and listened intently to Urban's crusading sermon on 27 November. Then, as soon as the pope fell silent, Adhémar stepped forward to take the cross, becoming the first ever crusader. According to one eyewitness, after Urban had preached the campaign to the East:

The eyes of some were filled with tears, some were frightened and others argued about this matter. But among all at the council – and we all saw him – the bishop of Le Puy, a man of great repute and the highest nobility, went up to the lord pope with a smiling face and on bended knee begged and beseeched his permission and blessing to make the journey.[3]

Bishop Adhémar had effectively been planted in the audience to ensure that the pope's words met with a warm reaction. On the following day, it was announced that Adhémar would be the official papal representative, or legate, on the coming crusade. Urban himself later wrote that:

We appointed in our place as leader of this journey and labour our dearest son Adhémar, bishop of Le Puy. It follows that anyone who decides to go on this journey should obey his orders as though they were our own and should be entirely subject to his power to 'loose and bind' in any decisions that appear to concern this business.[4]

The pope had chosen Adhémar to lead the expedition to

Jerusalem, endowing him with absolute spiritual authority over the crusaders. In this position, the bishop of Le Puy proved to be a skilled and patient conciliator, a valuable voice for reason and a staunch advocate of Urban's policy of détente with the Greek Church of Byzantium. But, although the pope may have envisaged the crusade as a pious armed pilgrimage, he must have known that to succeed the expedition would still require practical military direction and inspirational generalship. Adhémar possessed some talent as a strategist, he may even have had a degree of skill as a military leader, but, with Church law technically forbidding him from actually fighting in battle, the bishop could never truly fulfil the role of overall commander-in-chief of the crusade.[5]

Before the council of Clermont, the pope also approached a second figure, one with the potential to provide this type of leadership – Raymond of Toulouse. Born the second son of Count Pons of Toulouse c. 1042, Raymond initially acceded to the relatively small Provençal lordship of St Gilles, with the county passing to his elder brother. But a combination of good fortune, canny diplomacy and resolute determination eventually enabled Raymond to supplant his sibling, assume lordship of the county of Toulouse and cultivate an impressive network of power and influence. By 1095 he was the dominant secular lord in south-eastern France. Raymond had not always been an ally of the Gregorian papacy, indeed Pope Gregory VII actually excommunicated him on two occasions, but by the 1080s a repentant Raymond had come back into the fold and soon developed into an ardent supporter of the Reform Movement and an avowed *fidelis beati Petri*. He confirmed his friendship with Pope Urban II in 1090 by renouncing all rights to the Church of St Gilles, a prerogative that his family had previously usurped. Being one of the most powerful princes in all Latin Christendom and a steadfast ally of the papacy, Raymond was, in many ways, the natural choice as secular leader of Urban's projected crusade.

Later traditions and legends actually suggest that he was almost predestined to fill this position, being accustomed to the prosecution of campaigns against Islam and familiar with the journey to Jerusalem. In the twelfth century, it was believed that Raymond had fought against the Moors of Iberia in the 1080s, losing an eye in combat, but this story cannot be verified. An obscure Syrian contemporary recorded an even more improbable tale of Raymond's exploits. The count had, he maintained, completed a pilgrimage to Jerusalem before 1095, but upon reaching the Holy City had had his eye pulled out of his head as punishment for refusing to pay an exorbitant Muslim tax on Latin pilgrims. Apparently, Raymond then returned to the West, carrying his eyeball in his pocket as testament to his suffering. The count may have lost an eye in the course of his life – both stories revolve around an explanation of this striking feature of his appearance – but there is no reliable evidence to suggest that he had any experience of travel to the Levant predating the First Crusade.

Nonetheless, as with Adhémar, we can be almost certain that, in the months before the council of Clermont, Urban met with Raymond of Toulouse to discuss the shape and execution of the proposed expedition. Raymond did not himself attend the sermon at Clermont, but the very next day ambassadors arrived to pledge his resolute support for the campaign; the lightning rapidity of this reaction indicates forward planning. But if the count, like Adhémar, had been brought in to lend his seal of approval to the crusading enterprise, then it seems strange that Raymond chose not to attend the council itself. His absence may, perhaps, have been caused by disagreement over the leadership of the expedition. Raymond certainly coveted the post of commander-in-chief. He was well qualified to perform this role, not least because he could draw upon an immense reservoir of wealth with which to fund the endeavour, and his extant friendship with Adhémar of Le Puy made him the obvious candidate for a secular lord to work alongside the papal legate. In fact, his decision to pledge his support on 28 November, the very day upon which Adhémar was appointed, suggests that they had intended to enrol in the crusade as joint leaders in a package deal.

Unfortunately for Raymond, the pope stubbornly refused, either at Clermont or in the months that followed, to confirm the count's status publicly. Urban may have prevaricated because he expected the Byzantine emperor to assume command of the expedition once it reached Constantinople. But, whether or not there was an open dispute, almost eight months passed before Raymond made a public declaration of his commitment actually to join the crusade.

Even without official papal endorsement, Raymond of Toulouse was, to begin with at least, the most powerful First Crusader. Being in his mid-sixties and thus at quite an advanced age by medieval standards, he was undoubtedly the elder statesman of the expedition, but the passing years seem to have weakened his physical constitution, leaving him more prone to bouts of illness and infirmity. Yet, even if his body did sometimes show signs of frailty, his mind remained resolute. Proud, self-possessed and obdurate, Raymond devoted the resources of his capacious treasury and the full force of his political acumen and accumulated military expertise to the crusading cause. He was undoubtedly driven by a determination to fulfil his vow and recover Jerusalem, but as the expedition progressed it became increasingly obvious that he was struggling to reconcile this pious goal with his own ambition for power. Before the end, Raymond would reveal that he was obsessed with the mantle of overall command and was keenly aware that the Latin conquest of the Levant might also fuel his own territorial ambitions.[6]

Spreading the word

As well as priming two of the main players in the crusade before Clermont, Urban also took great care to publicise the call to crusade. Already by December 1095, Urban was able to claim in a letter to the people of Flanders that his sermon at Clermont was 'widely known', and he followed up this initial address with an extended preaching tour that crisscrossed much of France. This was designed to broadcast the crusading appeal while promoting Urban's reform agenda and stimulating the recognition of papal authority. Between December

1095 and September 1096 the pope visited Limoges, Le Mans, Bordeaux, Toulouse and Montpellier, among other towns and cities, and presided over major councils at Tours in March 1096 and Nîmes in July 1096, before finally returning to Italy. During this grand tour, he consecrated numerous churches and altars and lent his support to a massive ecclesiastical building programme, all of which served to engender an aura of Roman primacy. For a man probably now in his sixties, Urban demonstrated immense energy and resilience through these long months, but his efforts paid off. Seizing every possible opportunity to preach the expedition to Jerusalem, the pope drew enormous crowds, and a wave of crusading enthusiasm took hold. One eyewitness recalled the impact of his presence at Limoges:

> We saw [the pope] with our own eyes and we were in the crowds of the faithful at his consecrations ... In a good sermon he encouraged the people standing there to take the road to Jerusalem. Thanks be to you, O Christ; for you watered the swelling corn which grew from the seed sown by him, not only in our region, but also throughout the world.

The compelling impact of his words, the theatre of these mass rallies and the air of authority surrounding the papal office combined to produce a super-charged atmosphere in which many found it impossible to resist the crusading message. The full impact of Urban's preaching is revealed by the fact that a high proportion of the First Crusaders now known to us through historical record came from regions in and around the path of his campaigning trail.[7]

Crusade recruitment was a central theme of Urban's extensive tour of France, and he made assiduous efforts to sponsor and cultivate the expedition launched at Clermont, all of which points to the fact that he did, to some extent, plan or anticipate the response to his initial preaching. The pope would, it seems, never have been content to allow the crusade message to languish in obscurity, nor would he have been happy for it to produce only 200 to 300 recruits. Urban knew that he was unlocking a powerful and compelling ideal in November 1095. But, even so, he was still surprised by the mercurial speed and astounding magnitude of the reaction.

The rapid spread of crusading fever can, in part, be explained by the fact that it was not just Urban himself who promoted the expedition after Clermont. He encouraged all bishops present at the councils of Clermont and Nîmes to preach the crusade in their own dioceses. His preaching tour also stimulated a number of public assemblies at which the crusade was proclaimed in his absence, prompting frenzied masses to take the cross. At Rouen, the enthusiasm generated by one of these gatherings got so out of hand that it prompted a full-scale riot. At the same time, unofficial preachers also began to broadcast versions of Urban's appeal across Europe. Before long, the pope realised that he was in danger of losing control of the entire enterprise. Chief among his concerns was the knowledge that the crusade was spontaneously attracting thousands of recruits from a diverse cross-section of society – ecclesiastics, peasants, women and children, the old and infirm – and Urban had never intended or expected these non-combatants to become participants. In the autumn of 1096 he felt it necessary to warn the Latins of northern Italy and Iberia that 'we do not allow clerics or monks to [take the cross] unless they have permission from their bishops and abbots'. He went on to remind these bishops that they 'should also be careful not to allow their parishioners to go without the advice and foreknowledge of the clergy'. By this point, recruitment had obviously outstripped papal expectations and was threatening to tear Latin society apart at the seams. Zealous young men were abruptly deciding to desert house and home to join the crusade, prompting Urban to recommend in addition that they should not be allowed to 'rashly set out on such a long journey without the agreement of their wives'. At this point, Urban effectively passed the buck. Having lost full, centralised control of the crusade, he began to demand, rather unrealistically, that local bishops intervene to re-establish order. Many of these possessed neither the ability nor the will to exert such authority, but an even more fundamental problem was that as a sub-species of pilgrimage, the crusade was a penitential act, and thus both voluntary and open to all Christians. The very feature that had made Urban's message so palatable – its packaging within an existing framework of devotional practice – meant that the principle of unrestricted participation was imported into, and imposed upon, the precepts of crusading, making it all but impossible to control recruitment.

The pope also became concerned that the irresistible allure of the crusade was drawing valuable manpower away from Iberia. He wrote to the Christian nobility of northern Spain, advising them that 'if any of you has made up his mind to go to [the East], it is here instead [in Iberia] that he should try to fulfil his vow, because it is no virtue to rescue Christians from the Saracens in one place, only to expose them to the tyranny and oppression of the Saracens in another'.[8]

Even though Urban had anticipated a warm response to his proposed armed pilgrimage, he was still caught off guard by the full passion of Latin Europe's enthusiasm. By the end of 1096, he had to face up to the stark reality that the crusader 'army' would be an entirely different creature from that which he had hoped for. The pope had set out to attract recruits from a specific demographic sector: the knightly aristocracy. This was the class within which Urban himself had been raised, whose strengths, aspirations and fears he knew only too well, and although he did not specifically target the Champagne region of his youth, he did demonstrate a more general affinity with his homeland by directing the full force of his initial preaching towards the nobility of France before later broadening his appeal to include the arms-bearers of western Germany, the Low Countries and Italy.

THE FIRST CRUSADERS

Urban judged that these knights, termed in Latin *milites*, possessed of martial prowess, financial resources and an active sense of devotional obligation, offered the best hope of transforming his crusading ideal into a living reality. Above all else, he knew that for the expedition to succeed it would need to be powered by a ferocious fighting force, and knights, the elite warriors of eleventh-century Europe, were the obvious choice. Urban himself explained in a letter that 'we were stimulating the minds of knights to go on this expedition, since they might be able to restrain the savagery of the Muslims by their arms and restore the Christians to their former freedom'.[9]

Knights in the eleventh century

Skilled as they were, knights were not part of a full-time standing army. They were soldiers, but they also had other roles, as lords or vassals, landholders and farmers. In any one year they might expect to be engaged in warfare for no more than a few months, and even then not necessarily by fighting in a familiar, established network, group or formation. We should not envisage the knights of the First Crusade as grand, chivalric warriors, riding into battle astride giant warhorses, clad in splendid Gothic plate armour and wielding massive lances. It would be more than a century before advancements in technology and custom combined to bring the concept and practice of medieval knighthood into full flower. But, for all this, the knights of the eleventh century were the best fighters available to Pope Urban.

In 1095, the knightly class was still at an embryonic stage of development. The rising costs associated with functioning as a knight, primarily related to equipment and training, made it increasingly difficult for men of less affluent backgrounds to operate as *milites*, although, as yet, the class was not the exclusive preserve of the aristocracy. Virtually all male members of the lay nobility were expected to carry out the duties of a knight, and most wealthier lords retained the service of a number of *milites* as vassals, under contract to protect and farm their lands in return for military service. This enabled poorer individuals to attain the status of a *miles*, acquiring the tools of the trade through employment.

By the time Urban preached the crusade at Clermont, the key

characteristics of knighthood – a distinct range of equipment and a consequent style of warfare – were coalescing across Latin Christendom. What really marked out a knight was his ability to fight as a mounted warrior. In the eleventh century, warhorses were, by modern standards, quite small, perhaps on average twelve hands in height, what would today be classified as little more than a pony. Nonetheless, they were prohibitively expensive to purchase and even more costly to maintain, requiring feed, horseshoes and quite probably the constant care of what would later be called a squire. Buying a warhorse was the equivalent of today taking out a mortgage on a house, with all the pain of the initial outlay, followed by a lifetime of upkeep payments. This was made all the worse by the fact that most knights also had to keep at least one other, lighter mount upon which to travel.

But these precious warhorses seem to have given warriors a distinct edge in combat, offering the advantages of speed, mobility and force. The exact nature of mounted warfare at the time of the First Crusade is unclear. Military practice was struggling to incorporate and exploit technological advancements, but the pace of change was often slow. As late as 1066, Anglo-Saxon warriors rode to the Battle of Hastings, but then promptly got off their horses to fight on foot because they were not used to mounted combat. The adoption of the stirrup, giving the rider greater stability, allowed knights to employ increasingly heavy spears or lances, couched under the arm. In time, this led to the development of the most famous feature of knightly warfare: the heavy cavalry charge, in which tightly packed groups of knights rode into enemy formations at speed, delivering the dreadful 'shock' impact of their lances and ripping their opponents to shreds. To be effective, this type of manoeuvre required considerable expertise, demanding trust and social cohesion, and in 1095 its use was still being refined. The First Crusaders deployed massed cavalry charges, and the expedition's finest generals experimented with the tactical possibilities of this 'weapon', but we should not imagine that the knights who marched off to Jerusalem were used to fighting in tight, disciplined formations, nor that they could be controlled in battle with chesspiece-like precision. On the whole, fighting on the crusade was a bloody, ragged affair, characterised by chaotic close-quarter combat. Under these conditions, it was the Latin knights' ruthless brutality that made them such a potent force.

The knights targeted in Pope Urban's preaching were typically also equipped with an array of arms and armour. Most would have worn a conical steel helmet, perhaps over a mail hood or coif, and a thigh-length mail shirt over a padded jerkin. These would not have been capable of resisting a solid cut or thrust, but did offer protection from glancing blows. In one hand, knights generally would have carried a more formidable defence: a large, usually kite-shaped, wooden shield, sometimes bound with iron. In the other, they would have held one of a selection of mêlée weapons. Chief among these were the lance or spear, which could be couched or thrown over arm, and the sword, usually of the one-handed variety, measuring around eighty centimetres in length, a heavy, but finely balanced, blunt-tipped bludgeoning tool. Mastering these weapons of war required long hours of dedicated training (time that was often available only to the wealthy), an abundance of physical energy and a steely nerve. It was not uncommon for nobles to spend the majority of their youth honing their martial skills – one prominent crusader, Godfrey of Bouillon, was already noted as an accomplished warrior at the age of sixteen – but rigorous military instruction carried its own inherent dangers, and knights were frequently injured, maimed or even killed in training.

Late-eleventh-century knights were almost always accompanied by at least four or five support crew, men who could act as servants, tending to their master's mount, weaponry and general welfare. Pope Urban knew that each knight he attracted to the crusading cause would bring additional manpower with him, men who could, when necessary, add to the ranks of the second major type of medieval warrior: the infantryman. From a historical standpoint, this group, known simply in Latin as *pedites* (literally, those on foot), represents a far more amorphous, indefinable mass. The composition of the infantry component of a typical Latin army was extremely fluid, being made up of an unpredictable combination of knights' followers, peasants and even, as became common on the crusade, knights who had lost their mounts. We know far less about their standard equipment, although we can guess that they employed a similar assortment of hand weapons – spears and swords, as well as daggers, clubs and axes. Perhaps the greatest challenge faced by any medieval general was to achieve a successful amalgamated strategy, employing knights and infantry in concert. During a campaign both groups might be expected to move at an equal pace; after all, even knights would have spent most of their time walking alongside their mounts. But it was in combat that the real problems of co-ordination arose, because soldiers on foot were simply incapable of traversing the battlefield at the same speed as horsemen. The danger, evidenced by the events of the crusade, was that exploiting the rapid manoeuvrability of a cavalry force might isolate and expose the infantry.

One additional form of weaponry available to both knights and infantry was the bow. Archers, generally operating longbows of about two metres in length and capable of delivering arrows to a distance of 300 metres, were a common feature of most infantry forces. Being cheap to make, relatively easy to maintain and useful as a hunting tool, these simple bows were a mainstay of the poorer elements within an army, but at the same time they represented an extremely valuable military resource. If deployed with care, a group of archers could unleash wave upon wave of arrows, each capable of piercing almost any type of body armour, wreaking havoc among enemy forces. Bowmen were the particular scourge of the otherwise well-protected knight, and contemporary writers occasionally describe, in awe, how proud horsemen were annihilated by a rain of missiles, their bodies so peppered with arrows as to be likened to hedgehogs. By 1095, some warriors were also using a simple form of crossbow. Expensive, cumbersome and terribly slow to reload, this weapon could, nonetheless, propel a heavy quarrel with such force that at close distance it might penetrate seven centimetres into solid wood. The potential impact of a crossbow bolt upon an armoured knight was so devastating that the papacy sought, in the twelfth century, to ban their use in an early form of arms treaty. But this weapon is known to have seen some action during the First Crusade, most notably in the hands of Godfrey of Bouillon.

In spite of the fact that Pope Urban lavished praise upon the knights of France, celebrating their martial virtues, the reality was that the type of warfare generally practised by the warriors of Europe did not actually mirror the varied demands of his proposed expedition to Jerusalem. Late-eleventh-century Latin knights and their followers were accustomed to short-term campaigns and small-scale skirmishing. Most were ill prepared for the strategic and logistical exigencies of long-range marches across foreign soil. Many would never have participated in a grand setpiece battle, because these massive, unpredictable engagements were usually avoided at all costs. But there was one form of military engagement with which European armies were familiar and in which they could boast considerable expertise that might be applicable to the coming crusade: siege warfare.

By 1095, castles and fortifications were a military mainstay of Latin Christendom's socio-political landscape. In a land subject to violence and disorder, the physical protection offered by strongholds enabled the ruling classes to maintain strategic, economic and administrative control of their territory. Castles, serving as nails to hold together the fabric of medieval society, were almost ubiquitous, while virtually every town or city was, to one degree or another, fortified by the likes of walls or a citadel. In the prevalent atmosphere of acquisitive internecine conflict, it was common for forts, castles and towns to face regular attack. Indeed, with kings and princes seeking to control their subjects, and local lords struggling to carve out and retain their own semi-independent territories, the ebb and flow of politico-military conflict was expressed in almost seasonal recourse to siege and counter-siege. As technology improved and the use of stone became more prevalent than that of wood, and walls and towers became higher, thicker and stronger, so the bickering potentates of western Europe sought to develop ever more ingenious and effective ways to overcome them.

When the First Crusade was preached, most Latin knights were intimately acquainted with the techniques and technology of siege warfare. Among the weaponry that they were accustomed to employ was a range of large-scale projectile weapons. These stone-throwing devices, usually powered by either torsion or counterweights, could vary considerably in size and power. The smallest might only be able to catapult a five-kilogram rock some seventy-five metres, while massive engines might be capable of sending large boulders or even, under more gruesome circumstances, whole human bodies the same distance. All of these machines were, however, difficult to construct and relatively immobile once erected. Harking back to ancient Roman terminology, eleventh-century writers used a variety of words, such as *petraria*, *mangana* and *mangonella*, to refer to these weapons, but, as yet, no uniform vocabulary of warfare was in place, and it can thus be very difficult to know what type of machine was being described.[10]

The leading crusaders

Pope Urban II set out to attract the fighting manpower of Europe, dominated by the mounted knight and skilled in vicious skirmishing and siege warfare, to his crusading cause. To tap into this pool of military manpower and expertise, he directed his preaching, first and foremost, at the lay aristocracy. Urban knew that, with the nobility on board, retinues of knights and infantry would follow, for even though the crusade required a voluntary commitment the intricate web of familial ties and feudal obligation bound social groups in a common cause. In effect, the pope set off a domino effect, whereby for every noble who took the cross a chain reaction was initiated, with that principal vow standing at the epicentre of an expanding wave of recruitment.

If he was really to capitalise upon the pyramidal hierarchy that held sway in medieval Europe, Urban needed to attract recruits from the highest echelon of western society. But it is a striking fact that not a single Latin monarch participated in the First Crusade. In the past, historians have suggested that this 'failure' was actually part of the pope's master plan; that he deliberately sought to discourage the involvement of kings in the hope of more readily maintaining papal control over the expedition. In reality, Urban did go some way towards courting the enthusiasm of the European monarchy. Given the recent history of conflict and hostility between the Gregorian papacy and the king of Germany, Urban must have known that Henry IV would reject the crusading ideal. In England, William the Conqueror's son and heir William Rufus was embroiled in a struggle to subdue his realm and could ill afford a protracted absence on crusade, but he did lend the expedition considerable financial support. It was the king of France, Philip I, who came closest to joining the enterprise.

Far weaker than either his English or German counterpart, Philip had enough trouble controlling the region around his capital city of Paris, let alone trying to manifest his will throughout the territory we would think of today as France. His participation in the crusade might, nonetheless, have proved fortuitous, given his ideological status and fiscal resources. Philip certainly showed some enthusiasm for the proposed campaign, presiding over a council to discuss its prosecution on 11 February 1096, attended by his brother, Hugh of Vermandois, and a selection of his nobles. That same night saw a spectacular but disturbing lunar eclipse, during which the moon turned blood red, a phenomenon which seemed a portent of the king's future. The problem was that, officially at least, Philip was in bad odour with the pope. Four years earlier, the king had fallen in love with Bertrada of Montfort, wife to the powerful Frankish magnate Fulk IV, count of Anjou. In a scandal of international proportions, Philip abandoned his own wife, entering into a bigamous marriage to Bertrada. When he sought to extract an official recognition of this illicit union from the bishops of France, Rome decided it could no longer turn a blind eye and promptly excommunicated the king. This shameful predicament rumbled on up to the council of Clermont and beyond. Negotiations towards a resolution proceeded throughout Urban's grand preaching tour of France; indeed in July 1096 he was assured that a repentant Philip was now willing to renounce Bertrada. But in the end the king's amorous heart got the better of him and, as an excommunicate, being in no position to take the cross, the opportunity to crusade passed him by.[11]

The First Crusade may not have attracted the participation of kings, but the cream of western Christendom's nobility was drawn to the venture, members of the high aristocracy of France, western Germany, the Low Countries and Italy, from the class directly below that of royalty. Often bearing the title of count or duke, these men could challenge or, in some cases, even eclipse the power of kings. Certainly they wielded a significant degree of independent authority and thus, as a group, can most readily be termed 'princes'. Raymond of St Gilles, count of Toulouse, who had expressed his intention to join the crusade so soon after the sermon at Clermont, was among the mightiest of their number. His age and financial resources placed him in a strong position to challenge for the position of overall military commander of the crusade.

But Raymond was not the only prince to take the cross. In the summer of 1096 the southern Italian Norman, Bohemond of Taranto, committed himself to the expedition in a theatrical public ceremony. In the course of the eleventh century, Norman adventurers had, through dogged resolve and martial skill, forced their way on to the southern Italian peninsula, carving out independent territories that eventually coalesced to form a Norman kingdom of Sicily. Bohemond was fathered by one of the chief architects of this process, Robert 'Guiscard', that is Robert 'the Wily'. Some forty years of age when he took the cross, Bohemond was a striking figure. One Byzantine eyewitness described him in rather fanciful language:

Bohemond's appearance was, to put it briefly, unlike that of any other man seen in those days in the Roman world, whether Greek or barbarian. The sight of him inspired admiration, the mention of his name terror . . . His stature was such that he towered almost a full cubit over the tallest men. He was slender of waist and flanks, with broad shoulders and chest, strong in the arms . . . The skin all over his body was very white, except for his face which was both white and red. His hair was lightish-brown and not as long as that of other barbarians (that is it did not hang on his shoulders) . . . His eyes were light-blue and gave some hint of the man's spirit and dignity . . . There was a certain charm about him [but also] a hard, savage quality in his whole aspect, due, I suppose, to his great stature and his eyes; even his laugh sounded like a threat to others.[12]

His arresting physical attributes were married to a formidable personality, driven by unquenched ambition and empowered by martial genius. Bohemond joined the crusade already a gifted and experienced military commander, one near-contemporary describing him as 'second to none in prowess and in knowledge of the art of war'.[13] Bohemond learned his trade in the brutal struggle to secure Norman control of southern Italy. In this, his chief opponents were the Byzantines, the most persistent challengers for possession of the region. To counter their meddling, Bohemond's father in 1081 launched an audacious, pre-emptive expedition against the empire's holdings along the eastern shores of the Adriatic, designed to establish a new Norman lordship in the Balkans. In the four years that followed, Bohemond, acting initially as lieutenant to his father, and then for long periods as overall commander-in-chief, fought a protracted, but ultimately unsuccessful, campaign against the Greeks.

The trials of this dogged conflict furnished him with an invaluable military education. He garnered some knowledge of leadership from the stern example set by his father – on the eve of the first major battle against the Byzantines, Robert reportedly burned his fleet, closing the door to escape in order to harden the resolve of his wavering troops. Participating in the seven-month investment of Durazzo, the chief Greek outpost on the Adriatic, exposed Bohemond to the realities of siege warfare. Having surrounded the city from June 1081 to February 1082, enduring a bitter winter, the Normans appeared to be making little progress. It was not until Robert Guiscard orchestrated a betrayal from within that Durazzo actually capitulated – a lesson on the merits of bribery and deceit that would influence Bohemond's conduct on crusade. Then, between the spring of 1082 and the winter of 1083, he personally led a daring expeditionary raid across the Balkan wilds, securing notable victories in two pitched battles against the Byzantine emperor Alexius. The prolonged trans-Adriatic campaign also taught Bohemond the value of naval support and supply.

In the end, the Normans overstretched their resources and the Greeks were able to reoccupy the Balkans. But, for Bohemond, this practical experience of war, encompassing generalship, battle tactics, campaign strategy and military logistics, served as an outstanding preparation for the rigours of the First Crusade, not least because it brought him into contact with Muslim mercenaries employed in the Byzantine army and gave him an excellent working knowledge of the Balkans. There was, of course, a price to pay for this schooling. The 1081–5 campaign caused an almost irreparable fracture in Norman–Byzantine relations. Bohemond was left nursing frustrated territorial ambitions in the eastern Adriatic, while the Emperor Alexius developed a deep-seated distrust of the Norman princeling.

Already petering out, the Balkan expedition came to a decisive end with the death of Robert Guiscard in July 1085. This proved to be a severe blow to Bohemond's prospects. Although he was Robert's eldest son, his father had, soon after his birth, divorced his mother on grounds of consanguinity and remarried an Italian princess with whom he sired a second son. Named Roger – he was later given the appellation 'Borsa', meaning 'Moneybags', because he reputedly loved nothing more than to count coins – Robert, in honour of his new wife, designated him rather than Bohemond heir to southern

Italy. Upon his father's death, Roger Borsa moved quickly to claim his inheritance, cutting a costly deal with his uncle, the count of Sicily, in return for confirmation of his status as Robert Guiscard's sole successor. With Roger in control of almost all of southern Italy, Bohemond suddenly found himself virtually penniless.

For the next decade, Bohemond fought an extended, sniping war to scrabble back control of some territory in the regions of Apulia and Calabria. One of his earliest successes was the occupation of Taranto, the town with which historians traditionally associate his name, though the real jewel of his hard-won lordship was the major port of Bari. By 1095, Bohemond had managed to establish a significant foothold in the extreme south of the Italian peninsula, but the full range of his ambitions was still largely held in check by the machinations of his brother and uncle. His restless energy and martial expertise seemed to make him an ideal candidate for crusade recruitment.

Bohemond was acquainted with the expedition's architect, Pope Urban II. The southern Italian Normans had been intermittent allies of the Reform papacy throughout the second half of the eleventh century and, at the start of his pontificate, Urban cultivated their support. Given that his sister was a *fidelis beati Petri*, familial connections may have brought Bohemond into the Reform circle. He certainly met Urban on at least three occasions, first at the council of Melfi in September 1089, and twice in 1092–3, when the pope actually visited Taranto.[14] And it is quite possible that he attended the council of Piacenza in March 1095, at which the initial appeal from the Greeks was announced.

The problem was that Bohemond's past history of bitter conflict with the empire did not sit well alongside Urban's espoused policy of détente with Byzantium. The Norman may have been well suited to meet challenges of a long-distance campaign to the Holy Land, but it must have been obvious to all that he might find it difficult to sustain a co-operative alliance with his old enemy Alexius. When Bohemond did eventually take the cross, many suspected that he was actually planning a renewed offensive against the Greeks, and one contemporary even circulated the fantastical suggestion that the entire crusade was a plot, cooked up by Urban 'on the advice of Bohemond', who hoped that the expedition would facilitate his plan for a new Balkan campaign.[15]

In reality, Bohemond's recruitment was a mixed blessing. His gift for generalship promised to give the crusader host a much-needed edge in battle, but his presence threatened to undermine the critical Latin–Byzantine coalition. Bohemond did, however, bring one further asset to the cause. His decision to take the cross prompted an experienced, if not especially numerous, band of southern Italian Normans to join up, and among their number was a young man who would become a renowned champion of the crusading cause – Bohemond's own nephew, Tancred of Hauteville. Barely twenty years of age, possessed of limited military experience, but apparently able to converse in Arabic, Tancred quickly assumed the position of second-in-command of the loose contingent that followed Bohemond into the East. Tall, blond and powerfully built, Tancred was profoundly ambitious and untiringly energetic.[16]

It is a striking testament to the power of the crusading message unleashed by Urban II that it also stirred the hearts of men who, before 1095, had been avowed enemies of the Reform papacy. One such, Duke Godfrey of Bouillon, from the region of Lotharingia, stood entirely outside the network of papal supporters who formed the backbone of crusade recruitment. He had no history of collaboration with the Reform party, nor any known connections to the *fideles beati Petri*. In fact, he was openly hostile to the First Crusade's grand patron, Matilda of Tuscany. A staunch ally to Henry IV of Germany, Godfrey had actually participated in the siege of Rome. In spite of all this, he took the cross.

Godfrey was said to have been 'tall of stature, not extremely so, but still taller than the average man. He was strong beyond compare, with solidly built limbs and stalwart chest. His features were pleasing, his beard and hair of medium blond.'[17] He was born around 1060, the second son of the count of Boulogne, and could trace his lineage back to Charlemagne, a connection much romanticised by later commentators on the crusade. With the county passing to his elder brother, Godfrey faced limited prospects, but gained the title of duke of Lower Lotharingia when designated heir to his childless uncle and namesake, Godfrey the Hunchback, the estranged husband of Matilda of Tuscany.

In reality, the volatile region of Lower Lotharingia proved almost impossible to govern, his ducal title rather hollow, but he did control one significant stronghold – the castle of Bouillon, in the Ardennes, some seventy kilometres north of Verdun. Godfrey had some experience of warfare, but none of command, and no particular reputation for personal piety, being a known despoiler of Church land. It has been suggested that, in joining the expedition to Jerusalem, he was merely following the fashionable practice of his more esteemed northern French neighbours.

For all this, Godfrey demonstrated unbending dedication to the crusading ideal. The later tradition that he swore never to return from the crusade was probably false, but he did prove to be among the least self-serving of the Latin princes, and the most committed to completing the pilgrimage to the Holy Land.[18] Godfrey was joined at the last minute by his brother, Baldwin of Boulogne, a figure who, like Tancred, would emerge from relative obscurity in the course of the crusade, demonstrating a bullish tenacity in battle and an almost insatiable appetite for advancement. Baldwin was apparently darker haired but paler skinned than his brother and was said to have a piercing gaze.[19]

These five princes – Raymond of Toulouse, Bohemond of Taranto, Godfrey of Bouillon, Tancred of Hauteville and Baldwin of Boulogne – shaped the course of the First Crusade. It was they who stood at the heart of this astonishing expedition, whose skill, ambition and devotion drove the enterprise, and by turns threatened to rip it apart, and they whose lives were utterly transformed by the crusading experience.

The other princes

Other Latin princes answered the pope's call to arms as well. Among these, the pre-eminent figure in terms of lineage was Hugh of Vermandois, brother of King Philip I of France, to whom historians have sometimes appended the rather misleading appellation 'Magnus' (the Great). Hugh was certainly proud of the royal blood flowing through his veins, but the actual physical resources at his command were quite limited. The small county of Vermandois seems to have furnished him with a relatively meagre fortune, and he managed to attract only a small contingent of followers to join him on crusade.

Robert Curthose, duke of Normandy, was also well connected, being the eldest son of William the Conqueror and brother to William Rufus, king of England. Although apparently possessed of an easygoing geniality, he later gained a reputation for indolence and a fondness for the finer comforts of life, but this probably owed more to his ineffective governance of Normandy than to any innate flaw of character. As duke, Robert faced almost constant harassment from his acquisitive brother, who pursued the reunification of his father's cross-Channel realm with dogged determination. In the years leading up to 1095, with the region beset by 'terrible disorder', Robert found it increasingly difficult to maintain control. One twelfth-century observer actually maintained that the duke took the cross only to escape the pressures of rule, but this seems unlikely given that Robert appears all along to have planned to return to Europe upon completion of the journey to Jerusalem.

Robert of Normandy began the crusade in the company of two other princes, Stephen, count of Blois, his brother-in-law, and Robert II, count of Flanders, his cousin. Together, this tight-knit kinship group led a large northern French contingent of First Crusaders. Stephen was reputed to have been one of the richest lords in France, but little is known of his career before 1095, save that he was married to one of the most formidable women of the age, Adela, daughter of William the Conqueror. Robert of Flanders may have been inspired to take the cross by the example of his sadistic father and namesake who, less than a decade earlier, had completed a pilgrimage to Jerusalem as penance for his brutal and exploitative rule. Along the way, he had established a relationship with the Greek emperor Alexius, to whom he later sent 500 knights to aid in the defence of Byzantium.[20]

Almost all of these princes had experience of battle, but only Robert of Normandy and Bohemond had commanded large armies, and Bohemond alone had any familiarity with the Muslim world of the eastern Mediterranean. With Raymond of Toulouse's ambition to be recognised as commander-in-chief of the expedition still unfulfilled by the end of 1096, the First Crusade began without any obvious or accepted secular leader. Contrary to all the precepts of military convention, its armies would have to function without a single authoritative voice of command.

The challenge of controlling thousands of crusaders was going to be immense, all the more so because they were not drawn from a uniform or united source. Each prince who committed to the expedition brought with him a small party of his closest intimates, including members of his household – perhaps a seneschal, marshal or constable – his servants, a chaplain and even his huntsman. Major princes, like Godfrey of Bouillon, Bohemond of Taranto and Robert of Normandy, also attracted much looser, more fluid bands of followers, based on the bonds of lordship and family and perpetuated by common ethnic or linguistic roots. Stephen of Blois' party, for example, drew in many knights from his homeland region of Chartrain, some of whom were his vassals, but others simply informal supporters who were often powerful lords in their own right. The concept of national identity had little force in the eleventh century, but like-minded crusaders tended to club together. Four relatively distinct contingents evolved: the northern French under the two Roberts and Stephen; an array of Lotharingians and Germans travelling with Godfrey of Bouillon; the southern French and Provençals under the direction of Raymond of Toulouse; and

Bohemond's company of southern Italian Normans. Evident tension, even open antipathy, persisted between the northern and southern French; they did, after all, have a history of enmity and spoke different languages, Languedor and Languedoc.

The First Crusade was thus a cellular, organic entity. It would be unrealistic, in 1096 at least, to speak of a single crusading army, because the Latin forces were actually made up of a disparate, even divided, array of contingents, between which there was considerable potential for conflict, and within which there were frequent opportunities for mobility through transferral of allegiance. Not surprisingly, contemporaries found it nearly impossible to estimate the size of such a diffuse force with any accuracy. Many resorted to wildly improbable figures of 500,000 or more. By our best estimate some 7,000 knights took the cross and were accompanied by perhaps 35,000 armed infantry. A horde of anywhere between 20,000 to 60,000 non-combatants attached itself to this militarised core. The not inconsiderable task confronting the crusader princes was to enforce some semblance of unity and direction upon this shifting mass. Their one advantage was that this somewhat haphazard host shared a powerful, unifying goal.[21]

TAKING THE CROSS

Most First Crusaders joined the expedition to Jerusalem at emotionally charged gatherings, where, having been whipped up into a frenzy by a rousing sermon on the virtues of the crusading ideal, they made a public commitment to the cause. This involved two ritual elements: the giving of a solemn vow to see the pilgrimage to the East through to the end by visiting the Holy Sepulchre of Jerusalem; and the adoption of a physical representation of the cross – a symbol which was just then becoming a popular totem of Christian devotion – to be carried on their person until the return journey to the West had been completed. By these two steps, the Church sought to capture and solidify the explosive force of the crusading message, using the binding, legal force of the vow and the instantly recognisable, visual symbol of the cross to ensure that the initial spontaneous enthusiasm actually resulted in participation. One contemporary later described Urban at Clermont declaring that:

> Everyone who has decided to make this holy pilgrimage and has made a promise to God and has vowed that he will pour himself out to him as a living, holy and pleasing sacrifice must bear the sign of the Lord's cross on his front or breast. Anyone who after fulfilling his vow wishes to return must put the sign on his back between his shoulder blades.[22]

The crusaders certainly seem to have felt that these rites set them apart from the rest of society, their insignia proclaiming to all that they bore the status and obligations of armed pilgrims, and the burden of duty conferred by them later proved to have the power both to compel and inspire. But, for all their binding force, these rituals seem, at least in 1095–6, to have been relatively informal. There was probably no exact or established formula of words for the vow taken, nor does there seem to have been a universally recognised method for acquiring or wearing the cross. Most crosses seem to have been provided by the clergy, but Bohemond furnished his followers with theirs by cutting up his own cloak, while Godfrey of Bouillon's chaplain, Abbot Baldwin, dispensed with a cloth badge entirely, having his cross branded into the flesh of his forehead, a practice which was apparently quite widespread. Like so many features of crusade recruitment and practice, the rituals associated with taking the cross developed organically.[23]

Initial motives

It was once fashionable to suggest that the First Crusaders were primarily inspired to take the cross by greed, that the crusade was a grand adventure, offering the aspirant knights of Europe an opportunity to amass untold fortunes of treasure and territory. It is true that, even at Clermont, Pope Urban II appears to have been aware that his audience might be attracted to the crusading cause by avaricious impulses. The decree describing the expedition that was recorded in the canons of the council stated: 'Whoever for devotion alone, not to gain honour or money, goes to Jerusalem to liberate the Church of God can substitute this journey for all penance.'[24]

It has also been suggested that the appetite for materialistic gain was amplified by the wretched standard of living enjoyed by most Latins at the end of the eleventh century. A severe drought had afflicted much of France in the years before 1096, leading to a series of poor harvests and the resultant spread of famine. Then, while the crusade was actually being preached, the region was hit by outbreaks of ergotism, a rather grim disease caused by eating bread made from mouldy rye. The theory is that, faced by these horrors, the Latin West responded with rapturous enthusiasm to the image of the Levant as 'a land flowing with milk and honey'. The evidence provided by one contemporary observer certainly supports this idea, because he wrote that 'it was easy to persuade the western Franks to leave their farms. For Gaul had been afflicted for some years, sometimes by civil war, sometimes by famine, sometimes by an excessive death rate. Finally a plague ... had terrified the people to the point at which they despaired of life.' Another contemporary conceded that it was difficult to be sure that all crusaders were driven by pure motives:

> Different people give different reasons for this journey. Some say that in all pilgrims the desire has been aroused by God and the Lord Jesus Christ. Others maintain that the French lords and most of the people have begun this journey for frivolous reasons and that it was because of this that setbacks befell so many pilgrims ... and for that reason they cannot succeed.[25]

Of all the theories assigning acquisitive motives to the First Crusaders, the most enduring and influential has been the idea that the expedition was almost exclusively populated by land-hungry younger sons, deprived of inheritable territory at home in the West by the law of primogeniture, and thus desperately eager to establish new lordships in the East. This image is, however, profoundly misleading.[26]

Some crusaders might fit this paradigm, at least to a degree – Bohemond of Taranto, for example, was certainly alive to the possibility that the journey to Jerusalem might furnish opportunities for the conquest of territory – but they were very much in a minority. For every crusader like Bohemond, there were countless more who, like Stephen of Blois and Robert of Flanders, already enjoyed secure possession of adequate, even expansive lordships. Some crusaders did, of course, at least entertain the possibility that they might end up settling in the Holy Land. In spite of his own immense Provençal power-base, Raymond of Toulouse seems to have had his eye on Levantine relocation and travelled east in the company of his third wife, Elvira.[27]

The reality was that most crusaders were inspired by a complex combination of motives; many must have harboured hopes that in the course of this devotional pilgrimage they might reap some personal gain. But perhaps the most significant insight into the medieval mentality offered by the First Crusade is the unequivocal demonstration that authentic Christian devotion and a heartfelt desire for material wealth were not mutually exclusive impulses in the eleventh century. We now know that greed cannot have been the dominant motive among the First Crusaders, not least because, as recent research has shown, for most participants the expedition promised to be utterly terrifying and cripplingly expensive.

The prospect of such a massive journey into the unknown – Jerusalem was more than 3,000 kilometres away and most crusaders would never before have travelled more than 100 kilometres from home – left many almost paralysed with fear. The acute anxiety expressed by Stephen of Blois when making a donation to a local abbey just prior to his departure for the East was reflective of the emotions felt by many crusaders: '[May God] pardon me for whatever I have done wrong and lead me on the journey out of my homeland and bring me back healthy and safe, and watch over my wife Adela and our children.' Many who answered Urban's call to arms fully expected to die in the venture, and they tried to brace themselves to enter the scouring fire of holy war. Most also had to face virtual penury just to afford the exorbitant cost of crusading. Recent estimates suggest that, in order for the average knight to meet the costs of the coming campaign in terms of equipment, supplies, horse and servants, he would have had to raise five times his annual income. Many families endured major financial sacrifices to enable their kin to afford to crusade. Most tellingly of all, we know with the benefit of hindsight that only a handful of crusaders actually stayed in the Levant after the expedition, and among the returning majority none came home laden down with riches.[28]

If pure greed did not propel the crusaders, should we then assume that, above all, Christian piety inspired tens of thousands to risk their lives and livelihoods? This vexed question, fraught with difficulty and blighted by unsubstantiated impression, has occupied generations of historians, but some real progress has been made in recent years. Nevertheless, the severe limitations of the available evidence mean that we are still able to attempt only an approximate reconstruction of the motives and intentions of one particular class of crusader: the lay aristocracy. Alone in all medieval society, this upper echelon – the knightly elite – left a discernible imprint on the fabric of history during the process of taking the cross and preparing for the campaign, offering us fleeting, but instructive, insights into their state of mind. Of other social groups, in particular the poor, tens of thousands of whom are known to have joined the crusade, no authentic, first-hand trace survives. They appear in the written record, if at all, as shadowy imaginings, their ideas, aspirations and beliefs recreated by the pens of contemporary aristocratic observers. So on this most taxing question of motivation we must make do with what we can and consider the nobility.

Even here we should acknowledge that our evidence has been at least partially filtered. Our primary resources are the legal documents, or charters, drawn up by aristocratic crusaders to settle their affairs prior to departure for the Levant. It is rather ironic that, in this sphere of evidence, administrative efficiency is actually the enemy of historical exactitude. Charters drawn up, for example, under the rigorous standards of twelfth-century English governance tend to be precise, well-ordered documents and thus intensely formulaic and often quite boring. Luckily for us, those originating amid the relative disorder of late-eleventh-century French record keeping, just when the First Crusade was launched, tend to be far more invigorating. Roving, even rambling affairs, they frequently digress from the minutiae of financial exchange and legal rights to record a bewildering array of incidental information, including personal histories and human emotions, current affairs and infamous scandals, the strange and miraculous – all appear in a captivating kaleidoscopic slice of medieval experience. Crucially, they appear to offer a direct window into the minds of aristocratic crusaders. But even with this treasure trove of material, we must exercise some caution, because most nobles were actually illiterate and, since the majority of extant charters relate to transactions with monasteries, almost all surviving documents of this type were, in fact, physically written by monks. We cannot, therefore, discount the possibility that the revelatory lens of charter evidence has been subtly coloured by clerical hands, tainted by monks' intensely Christian outlook and fanatical obsession with spiritual devotion.[29]

The mindset of the lay aristocracy

Even bearing this caveat in mind, the evidence for the aristocratic response to the crusading message strongly suggests that spiritual concerns dominated the minds of the Latin nobility as they took the cross. To understand why this was so, we must first reconstruct the devotional landscape in which they lived. On this plane of medieval society, laymen were intimately connected to the monastic profession. With the Church and regional clergy still in relative disarray, eleventh-century nobles were reluctant to turn to their parish priests or even local bishops for spiritual guidance. Instead, they looked for succour from monastic institutions like Cluny, champions of devotional purity on the cutting edge of Christian ideology. When Pope Urban II launched the First Crusade, all across the Latin West his target audience, the knightly aristocracy, was engaged in a symbiotic union with monasteries. Every knight who joined the expedition to Jerusalem probably enjoyed some form of monastic association, be it through patronage and the donation of wealth or through the presence of a familial member who had entered a religious house. Monastic institutions shaped the nobility's conception of the Christian cosmos: knights were effectively conditioned to view, interpret and interact with the spiritual world around them through terms of reference and rituals defined by monks.[30]

The most powerful feature of this programming was an acute awareness of the danger of sin and an associated terror at the prospect of damnation. All medieval society was preoccupied with the pursuit of purity, but the knightly aristocracy, forced by the nature of its profession into daily contact with contaminants such as violence and personal wealth, seems to have been particularly prone to harbour an obsession with spiritual infection and the afterlife. The constant inner struggle it faced was evoked by the early-twelfth-century biographer and confidant of Tancred of Hauteville:

Frequently [Tancred] burned with anxiety because the warfare he engaged in as a knight seemed contrary to the Lord's commands. The Lord, in fact, ordered him to offer the cheek that had been struck together with his other cheek to the striker; but secular knighthood did not spare the blood of relatives. The Lord urged him to give his tunic and his cloak as well to the man who would take them away; the needs of war impelled him to take from a man already despoiled of both whatever remained to him. And so, if ever that wise man could give himself up to repose, these contradictions deprived him of courage.[31]

Tancred and knights like him across Europe were trapped – their secular obligations made sin inevitable, but monks cautioned them that their transgressions would, in the afterlife, trigger the most gruesome torments. On closer examination, we might, in fact, expect Tancred and his contemporaries to have been rather confused about the exact consequences of their sins because, around 1095, they were not actually being offered a particularly clear or concise vision of what would happen to their souls after death. Nascent Christian theology bombarded them with a complex jumble of images and ideals, a bewildering mosaic of ritual, custom and belief that, to a modern observer, can appear convoluted and even contradictory, but from which three dominant, interwoven strands emerge.

First, the Church maintained that the Day of the Last Judgement was fast approaching – it had of course been 'approaching' since the earliest Christian era – when good would finally be separated from evil through the 'weighing' of every human soul. Alongside this single apocalyptic event, Latins were also inculcated with a second strand of belief: that they would personally face some form of judgement immediately upon death and that any taint of sin would earn them punishment. Third was an overwhelming belief in the efficacy of alms-giving.

One of the main salvific remedies proffered by the Church to counter the threat of judgement and damnation was the giving of alms, which might be loosely defined as the donation of financial resources to religious communities, often in the form of title to land or rights to its revenue. These transient, material possessions could not, the Church argued, be taken into the afterlife, but might be used to ease the path towards the true Christian 'inheritance', the kingdom of heaven. Like pilgrimage, alms-giving might be undertaken as an appointed penance or be a voluntary propitiary down-payment. In quantifying the purificational impact of such endowments, the

Church was careful to avoid any direct assertion that Christians might crudely buy their way to salvation, preferring instead to suggest that donors might, in God's eyes, become enshrouded in an aura of merit. Nevertheless, most laymen imagined a direct link between donation and salvation. The benefaction of monastic communities like that of Cluny was deemed particularly efficacious, because its monks, engaged day and night in almost constant prayer, transformed every Cluniac monastery into an overflowing super-generator of redemptive energy. Alms-giving to such an institution allowed one to tap into this powerhouse of salvation, because every lay donor name was included in the monastery's prayers. Most religious houses were associated with a particular saint or saints, and lay donation was also believed to earn the favour of these Holy Dead, ensuring an easier passage through the rigours of temporal existence.

An illustrative example is that of the southern French noble Gaston IV of Béarn. A *fidelis beati Petri* who had campaigned against the Moors of Iberia in 1087, he took the cross in 1096 and joined Raymond of Toulouse's crusading contingent. Earlier, in 1091, Gaston decided to donate some property to the Cluniac house of St Foi, Morlaas in Gascony. At the same time he confirmed the gifts made by his father years earlier. The charter recording this transaction states that Gaston acted for the benefit of his own soul and those of his wife and children, and in the hope that 'God may help us in this world in all our needs, and in the future grant us eternal life'.

In some ways, the rather fragmentary devotional framework which encapsulated the concepts of apocalyptic threat, immediate judgement and propitiary alms-giving might seem to beg more questions than it answered. What, for example, was supposed to happen to a soul between death and the advent of the Last Judgement? Was it possible to attain immediately the delights of heaven or to be eternally condemned to the torments of hell, or were all souls awaiting the Apocalypse in some form of limbo? Could alms-giving or pilgrimage actually cleanse the soul of sin or did it simply cancel out the earthly or heavenly punishment due for transgression?

In later centuries Latin theologians tackled these concerns with varying degrees of success, but for the knights who encountered the crusading message in 1095 the prevailing matrix of belief remained only partially realised or reconciled. For all this, it lost nothing of its power to compel or control. Eleventh-century society seems simply to have filled in the gaps left by this emergent construct, giving rise to devotional customs that actually served to intensify the binding force of the Latin faith. Uncertainty about the afterlife stimulated a popular belief in an embryonic version of purgatory, a shadowy 'middle place' between heaven and hell. It was assumed that, unless one was so utterly dissolute as to earn immediate damnation, this halfway house would be the first destination of all laymen upon death – so powerful and enveloping was the contamination of sin, it was deemed inevitable that every normal human would need to endure at least a period of purification in the hereafter. What is worse, with the souls of the dead mired in an indeterminate purgatorial sentence, Latin nobles not only had their own souls to worry about – they had to answer for the fate of their dead relatives as well. Knights like Tancred, shouldering this heavy burden of responsibility, sought to salve their anxious conscience.

By the end of the eleventh century, social convention and devotional custom dictated that, alongside other penitential acts like pilgrimage, the lay aristocracy should, for the betterment of their own souls and their ancestors' spiritual wellbeing, maintain networks of monastic patronage and donation. The developing theory of purgatory also lent permanent force to any act of endowment. Monasteries frequently appended what amounted to insurance policies to the contracts made with lay donors. Known technically as malediction clauses, these threatened dire spiritual consequences and pronounced elaborate curses upon any noble who chose to renounce his own property transactions or interfere in those of his ancestors. Had Gaston of Béarn chosen, in 1091, to reclaim rather than confirm his father's grants to St Foi, he would have anticipated not only a personal punishment, but the infliction on his ancestor of unspeakable torments in limbo.[32]

The knightly aristocracy targeted by Pope Urban II's crusading appeal in 1095 was thus locked into an enduring and overpowering system of monastic patronage. These men were not simply savage brutes, bent on vendetta and violence, they were also, in medieval terms, devout Christians engaged in a constant but seemingly hopeless battle against transgression. Through the intimate devotional interface enjoyed with religious communities they were conditioned to view monastic life as the quintessence of spiritual perfection, but, bound to the duties of knighthood, that cloistered road to salvation was closed to them. The vow required of participants in the crusade seemed to mirror that made by postulant monks, suggesting that the expedition to Jerusalem had now opened up a new path to the kingdom of heaven. Indeed, one contemporary was prompted to observe:

> God has instituted in our time holy wars, so that the order of knights and the crowd running in their wake . . . might find a new way of gaining salvation. And so they are not forced to abandon secular affairs completely by choosing the monastic life or any religious profession, as used to be the custom, but can attain some measure of God's grace while pursuing their own careers, with liberty and in the dress to which they are accustomed.[33]

The thrilling allure of this new opportunity, coupled with the reassuringly traditional penitential context of Urban's proposed armed pilgrimage, rendered the crusade almost irresistible. Tancred's reaction, like that of thousands of his fellow knights, was apparently electric:

> After the judgement of Pope Urban granted remission of all their sins to all Christians going out to fight the gentiles [non-Christians], then at last, as if previously asleep, [Tancred's] vigour was aroused, his powers grew, his eyes opened, his courage was born. For before . . . his mind was divided, uncertain whether to follow in the footsteps of the Gospel or the world.[34]

His biographer employs heavily romanticised imagery, almost encouraging us to imagine Tancred reborn as a superhero at the moment he took the cross, but the central message of the text – that spiritual devotion was the driving force behind crusade recruitment – is echoed by a wealth of charter evidence detailing aristocratic preparations for the expedition to Jerusalem.

Preparing the soul and body

Having taken the cross in emotional and often spontaneous rituals, most First Crusaders received the traditional symbols of the pilgrim – the staff and purse – at a secondary ceremony, held days, weeks or even months after the initial public commitment to the cause.* For the lay aristocracy, this presentation often took place within the confines of their local monastery and coincided with the finalisation of a whole swathe of spiritual and functional preparations, the details of which are now enshrined in charter records. This evidence reveals that most prospective crusader knights shared three concerns: fear of the coming campaign; a desire to depart on this sacred expedition with a clear conscience and in a penitent frame of mind; and a practical need to raise large sums of money with which to fund their exploits. Many turned to the established custom of devotional donation to resolve all three problems in one. The year 1096 saw a huge burst of activity, as hundreds of nobles sought to put their affairs in order, settling outstanding disputes with religious communities and disposing of an array of property in return for hard cash or equipment.

The Church stood to gain a great deal from this wave of penitent desperation, and most found it to be an extremely profitable year. But, in the months following the council of Clermont, so many knights looked to sell or mortgage property for money that the market eventually suffered from a glut of land and a shortage of hard coinage

---

*The First Crusaders' status as pilgrims also afforded them a range of benefits traditionally associated with that penitential activity, including the protection of their property and land by the Church in their absence.

to pay for it. Religious houses swept up estates for a fraction of their actual value, but still struggled to free up sufficient financial resources to meet the demand for transactions. At one point, the bishop of Liège was apparently forced to strip the jewels from every reliquary in his cathedral and all those in nearby churches to raise 1,300 silver marks and three gold marks, the mortgage price of Duke Godfrey's castle at Bouillon. No ecclesiastic could afford to mortgage Robert of Normandy's entire duchy, so he turned to his brother, William Rufus, who duly raised 10,000 silver marks in return for rights to Normandy and all its revenues for five years.

Raymond of Toulouse was one crusader who made careful preparations for the expedition to Jerusalem. To secure the favourable intercession of the Virgin Mary he made a large donation to the cathedral of Le Puy, in return for which a candle was burned in front of her statue for the remainder of his natural life. Raymond explained that he had made this gift 'for the redemption of my crimes and those of my parents and for the honour and love of St Gilles, whom I have frequently offended by many kinds of injuries'. He also took care to clear the decks with the abbey of St Gilles, resolving a longstanding dispute over territory in their favour.

Godfrey of Bouillon likewise sought to settle his affairs. He sold or mortgaged every scrap of disposable property he could muster to the bishops of Verdun and Liège, raising valuable cash for himself and his brother Baldwin of Boulogne, and ending bitter quarrels with both pontiffs. One document noted that the brothers had been 'seized by the hope of an eternal inheritance and by love, prepared to go to fight for God in Jerusalem and sold and relinquished all their possessions'. They certainly continued to enjoy familial support while on crusade, for in 1098 their mother, Countess Ida of Boulogne, endowed a local monastery 'for the safety of her sons, Godfrey and Baldwin, who have gone to Jerusalem'. Godfrey did, however, leave a door open for his return to the West, maintaining an option to redeem the mortgage on the castle of Bouillon and taking care to ask his overlord, Henry IV of Germany, for permission to leave for Jerusalem.

When juxtaposed with this rich mosaic of evidence for pious motivation, the once-fashionable myth that the crusaders were self-serving, disinherited, land-hungry younger sons must be discarded. Crusading was indeed an activity that could bring spiritual and material rewards, but it was in the first instance both intimidating and extremely costly. Devotion inspired Europe to crusade, and on the road to Jerusalem the First Crusaders proved time and again that their most powerful weapon was a shared sense of purpose and an indestructible spiritual resolution.[35]

PETER THE HERMIT AND THE 'PEOPLE'S CRUSADE'

> While the leaders, who needed to spend large sums of money for the great retinues, were preparing like careful administrators, the common people, poor in resources but copious in number, attached themselves to a certain Peter the Hermit, and they obeyed him as though he were the leader, as long as the matter remained within our own borders.[36]

Thus did one contemporary describe the impact of the enigmatic demagogue Peter the Hermit, the most famous 'popular' preacher of the campaign to Jerusalem and figurehead of what has become known as the 'People's Crusade'. In line with the tenor of this extract, historians long thought that two distinct movements emerged in response to the crusading ideal: an official expedition, dominated by the lay aristocracy and inspired by the preaching of Urban and his clergy; and a swarming horde of ignorant peasants, goaded by the fiery sermons of largely unsanctioned charismatic preachers into a frenzied, uncontrollable mob.

In reality, there was no clear-cut division between the forces, ideas and individuals that drove lordly knights and bedraggled paupers to embark on the crusade. Approved as well as unauthorised preachers spread the crusading message across Europe, their orations stirring both rich and poor to action, while Pope Urban's grand tour of France roused a broad cross-section of society. Nor was there necessarily a massive difference between the rituals engaged in by noble and by impoverished crusaders at the moment of taking the cross.[37]

The problem is that, when dealing with what might be termed the popular preaching of the crusade and the response it engendered, we are forced to adopt the vocabulary of the ambiguous and indefinite. We know that the majority of crusaders came from the middle and lower classes, but, of these tens of thousands of men, women and children, virtually no direct evidence survives. As in so many ages of humanity, the voice of the masses remains unheard, its story untold. We know, too, that Pope Urban empowered a number of freelance preachers to disseminate his call to arms throughout the Latin West, but of their identities or the message they propagated only the barest hints remain.[38]

Only Peter the Hermit, whose dynamic preaching was most likely not endorsed by the papacy, has found a place in the annals of history. Indeed, for centuries he was actually regarded as the man who originally conjured up the idea of crusading. Peter was unquestionably an exceptional individual, possessed of a singular talent for oration. Describing his career, one near-contemporary wrote:

A certain priest, Peter by name, once a hermit, who was born in the city of Amiens which is in the west of the kingdom of the Franks, was the first to urge steadfastness in this Journey [to Jerusalem] with all the inspiration he could. In Berry, a region of the aforesaid kingdom, he became a preacher of the utmost persuasiveness and oratory.[39]

At first glance he must have looked like a vagabond, such was his penchant for extreme austerity and his disregard for physical cleanliness. One man who met Peter sought to describe his curious nature, recalling that:

outdoors he wore a woollen tunic, which revealed his ankles, and above it a hood; he wore a cloak to cover his upper body, and a bit of his arms, but his feet were bare. He drank wine and ate fish, but scarcely ever ate bread. This man, partly because of his reputation, partly because of his preaching, [assembled] a very large army.[40]

Another near-contemporary noted that 'he was small in stature and his outward form was contemptible, but greater valour ruled in his slight frame. For he was sharp witted, his glance was bright and captivating, and he spoke with ease and eloquence.'[41] Today, Peter's evident asceticism, repellent appearance and unusual eating habits might lead him to be shunned by society. To an eleventh-century audience, his peculiar habits simply indicated an unearthly piety, imitating the life of Christ's apostles, and served to amplify the magnetic impact of his sermons. As a youth he may have undergone some form of scholastic education, he undoubtedly spent some years as a recluse, but by 1095 he had already developed a burgeoning reputation as an itinerant preacher, advocating devotional poverty and a return to simple Christian virtues. One eyewitness recalled:

> We saw him wander through cities and towns, spreading his teaching, surrounded by so many people, given so many gifts, and acclaimed for such great piety, that I don't ever remember anyone equally honoured . . . whatever he did or said seemed like something almost divine. Even the hairs of his mule were torn out as though they were relics . . . a novelty loved by the common people.[42]

Even before the crusade was conceived, Peter's astounding gift for public speaking enabled him to incite a passionate, even hysterical response in his listeners. In this he was not unique: medieval society seems to have been particularly prone to demagogic influence, and within a few decades charismatic heretics were enthralling western audiences, the followers of one being so mesmerised that they ended up drinking his bathwater as a holy elixir.[43]

Until the mid-nineteenth century, historians believed that Peter had played a central role in the genesis of the First Crusade. This tradition, now widely discounted, depended on a story circulated in the West in the first decades of the twelfth century. This maintained that Peter had, even before the council of Clermont, made a pilgrimage to the Holy Land. Upon visiting Jerusalem, he supposedly witnessed first-hand the ritual abuse of indigenous Christians under Islamic rule, and in an audience with the city's senior churchman, the patriarch, heard tales of unbearable suffering. Distraught, the hermit sought solace in the Church of the Holy Sepulchre, where, so the story goes, 'since he was exhausted by prayers and vigils, he was overtaken by sleep. And the majesty of the Lord Jesus was shown to him in a vision.' In this moment of revelation, Peter was promised that he would receive from the patriarch 'letters of our mission with the seal of the Holy Cross, and you will hasten as quickly as possible your journey to the land of your people, you will disclose the malicious acts and injustices inflicted on our people and holy place, and stir the hearts of the faithful to the cleansing of the holy places in Jerusalem'. Having fulfilled this prophecy, the hermit returned to Europe, gained an audience with the pope and persuaded Urban that he should launch a crusading appeal.[44]

There may be some credence to the idea that Peter bore a letter allegedly lending divine sanction to the expedition to the Holy Land, because another chronicle described the hermit 'carrying round a letter which he claimed to have fallen from heaven, stating that all Christendom from all parts of the world must migrate in arms to Jerusalem [and] drive out the pagans'.[45] But there is no evidence to suggest that Peter did visit the Levant prior to November 1095, nor is it possible to confirm that he ever met or was sanctioned by Pope Urban.

The hermit was, nonetheless, already preaching the crusade with zealous enthusiasm by the end of 1095. In the months that followed, his ministry spread from Berry through northern France and into Germany, and wherever he spoke the fires of crusading fervour ignited. Peter had already proved that he could work wonders with the message of ascetic piety, but once he began to exhort the merits of a devotional pilgrimage to recapture Jerusalem the effect was almost miraculous. Unfortunately no record of his sermons survives, so we cannot know whether he distorted Pope Urban's vision of the crusade, nor can we reconstruct the spiritual benefits he promised to participants. But the impact of his preaching is clear. One near-contemporary noted that his words attracted the clergy, the lay aristocracy and 'all the common people, as many sinful as pious men, adulterers, murderers, thieves, perjurers, robbers . . . every sort of people of the Christian faith, indeed even the female sex'. A Greek observer who lived through the crusade recalled that, 'as if he had sounded a divine voice in the hearts of all, Peter the Hermit inspired the Franks from everywhere to gather together with their weapons, horses and other military equipment'.[46]

Within six months of Clermont, Peter had moved thousands to take the cross. Many were desperately poor peasants, but there were also nobles among his followers, including the French knight Walter Sansavoir. While the pope and his clergy extolled the virtues of the crusade, urging judicious preparation and broadcasting 15 August 1096 as the expedition's official departure date, Peter the Hermit, alongside other charismatics (similar to him but unrecorded), roused the faithful to more urgent and ecstatic action. A breakaway group under Walter Sansavoir set off on 21 May, and in the weeks and months that followed more than 15,000 men, women and children left their homes for the East. It was this largely uncontrollable, ramshackle horde that would act as the vanguard of Pope Urban's grand expedition, a first wave of crusaders that did not conform to his orderly plans and threatened to derail the entire campaign even before it had properly begun.

THE JOURNEY TO BYZANTIUM

As the fire of crusading enthusiasm spread across Europe in 1096, tens of thousands of Latin Christians prepared to leave their homes and take up the long road to Jerusalem. The first crusaders began setting off from France and Germany in late spring, small bands of peasants and a few knights, often inspired by popular preachers like Peter the Hermit, that gradually coalesced into a number of larger, loosely formed contingents. This initial wave of 'pilgrims' has come to be known as the People's Crusade.

Few among them could have truly understood the sheer, daunting scale of the journey on which they had embarked. Driven by a surge of spontaneous enthusiasm, most set out with little forethought or preparation. Jerusalem, their goal, lay thousands of kilometres away, across harsh terrain, much of it held by enemy forces. Lacking the financial resources even to consider taking ship over the Mediterranean, they had but one option – to walk the entire way. It was an extraordinarily foolhardy undertaking that would see many of them dead or destitute before they had even left the West.

There was one obvious route to follow in the initial stages, the ancient pilgrim road to Asia Minor that ran along the River Danube into the recently converted kingdom of Hungary. But while still in their homelands many of these 'poor' crusaders became embroiled in one of the blackest, most bloodthirsty episodes in all medieval history. Revealing the full power of the crusading message to inspire horrific violence and incite profound racial hatred, these 'soldiers of Christ' turned their weapons against an 'enemy' near at hand – the Jews of Europe. This flood of anti-Semitism spread like a contagion from the crusaders to the local Christians of central and eastern Europe. Together they conspired to perpetrate a series of murderous attacks upon the Jews, a people who had for generations lived in peace among them, in what has been called 'the first holocaust'.[1]

The pogroms began as early as December 1095 with anti-Semitic riots in Rouen, and by early 1096 anxious French Jews were warning their German brethren to be wary of these new crusaders. Just a few months later, between May and July 1096, the Rhineland Jews fell victim to sadistic persecution as a tide of anti-Jewish sentiment swept eastwards through Germany and beyond. Beginning in Speyer, incidents soon followed at Trier, Metz, Regensburg and Cologne, among other cities, with perhaps the most infamous and disturbing attacks taking place at Worms and Mainz. Historians long believed that these atrocities were the work of uncontrolled peasant mobs, a vile distortion of the crusading ideal at the hands of the undisciplined, illiterate masses.[2]

The unsettling reality is that, although peasants did make up a large proportion of the People's expedition, most contingents in this first wave of the crusade were actually led, and quite efficiently controlled, by knights, many of them powerful Latin aristocrats. Indeed, a Jewish eyewitness recorded that his people had been abused by 'both princes and common folk [who] placed an evil sign upon their garments, a cross, and helmets on their heads'.[3] One of the largest groups gathered at Mainz in late May: Germans led by the powerful noble Emicho, count of Leiningen; Swabians under Count Hartmann of Dillingen; and a well-equipped and well-organised army of crusaders from France, England, Flanders and Lotharingia, including the notable lords Drogo of Nesle and William the

Carpenter. Certainly no rabble, this contingent, thousands strong, was a potent military force. Even princes from the main, second wave of the crusade may have been guilty of anti-Semitic tendencies, as Godfrey of Bouillon is reported to have extorted 500 silver pieces from the Jews of Mainz and Cologne in return for promises of protection that he failed to fulfil.[4]

The pogroms of 1096 were not simply random, rogue incidents, nor were they necessarily misrepresentative of the ideals that drove many First Crusaders. But why did an expedition preached as a war of reconquest against Islam result in the murder of Jews? Even Latin contemporaries were unsure, one noting:

> I know not whether by a judgement of the Lord, or by some error of mind, they rose in a spirit of cruelty against the Jewish people scattered throughout these cities and slaughtered them without mercy . . . asserting it to be the beginning of their expedition to Jerusalem and their duty against the enemies of the Christian faith.[5]

Two forces seem to have been at work, stimulated by the crusading message that Urban had shaped. Characterising Muslims, the expedition's projected enemies, as a sub-human species, the pope harnessed society's inclination to define itself in contrast to an alien 'other'. But tapping into this innate well-pool of discrimination and prejudice was akin to opening Pandora's Box. A potentially uncontrollable torrent of racial and religious intolerance was unleashed.

The First Crusade was also styled, perhaps most forcefully by popular preaching, as a war of retribution to avenge the injuries supposedly meted out against Christendom by Islam. This message, itself a ghastly distortion of reality, was ripe for further manipulation. The dreadful power of these twin impulses was underscored by a Jewish near-contemporary. Recreating a discussion of ideology among a group of crusaders, he imagined them proclaiming:

Behold we journey a long way to seek the idolatrous shrine and take vengeance upon the Muslims. But here are the Jews dwelling among us, whose ancestors killed [Jesus Christ] and crucified him groundlessly. Let us take vengeance upon them. Let us wipe them out as a nation. Israel's name will be mentioned no more. Or else let them be like us and acknowledge [Christ].[6]

Cloaked in an aura of divine sanction, these Latins gave free rein to long-simmering animosity, subjecting the followers of Judaism to a ruthless programme of violence, extortion and forced conversion. Wherever they went, the crusaders' blind hatred, greed and bloodlust infected local Christian townspeople, turning them against their Jewish neighbours. In all this, the German Church maintained a disapproving but largely ineffectual stance. Its bishops knew full well that Rome did not advocate the victimisation of Jews and that canon law explicitly prohibited forced conversion. Some, like the bishop of Speyer, duly worked to protect imperilled Jewish citizens, offering them shelter and support. Yet others looked on unmoved or, worse still, collaborated in the attacks.[7]

Of all the crusaders implicated in this inexcusable episode, none eclipsed the notoriety of Emicho of Leiningen, the self-styled champion of this holocaust. Decades later one Jewish observer recalled how:

Count Emicho, the persecutor of all Jews, may his bones be ground up between iron millstones . . . became head of the bands and concocted the story that an emissary of [Christ had] given him a sign in the flesh indicating that, when he would reach Byzantium, [Christ would] crown him with a royal diadem.[8]

His crimes and those of his followers were recorded with distressing clarity by both Jewish and Christian contemporaries. Today their words afford us a tangible and disquieting sense of the shock, fear and horror associated with these incidents. Most powerful is the Hebrew chronicle written soon after 1096 by an anonymous Jew based in Mainz, many of the details of which are confirmed by the early-twelfth-century Rhineland Christian historian Albert of Aachen.[9]

Having been largely thwarted at Speyer by the efforts of its bishop, Emicho's band descended upon the city of Worms on 18 May 1096. According to the Mainz Chronicle, they soon hit upon a devious scheme to incite the local populace to carnage:

> They took a 'trampled corpse' of theirs, which had been buried thirty days previously, and carried it through the city, saying, 'Behold what the Jews have done to our comrade. They took a gentile and boiled him in water. They then poured the water into our wells in order to kill us.'[10]

By the time violence erupted in the streets, many Jews, forewarned by the events in Speyer, had already sought the protection of the bishop of Worms. They looked on from the sanctuary of his palace, as those of their brethren that had chosen to remain at home were 'killed like oxen and dragged through the market places and streets like sheep to the slaughter'. Only those who accepted forced conversion to the Christian faith were spared. Their own safety was, however, short lived. Emicho's mob laid siege to the bishop's domicile, and once they broke in the purge continued. Some Latins seem to have been killing their 'enemy' on sight, but most sought first to compel them to accept Christianity using the most brutal tactics. The Mainz Chronicle described the suffering of Isaac of Worms:

> They put a rope around his neck and dragged him throughout the entire city, through the mud of the streets, up to the place of their idolatry. His soul was still bound up in his body. They said to him: 'You may still be saved. Do you wish to convert?' He signalled with his finger – for he was unable to utter a word with his mouth, for he had been strangled – saying: 'Cut off my head!' and they severed his neck.

It is at Worms that we first hear reports of entire Jewish families committing suicide in order to avoid the Latins' swords or the noose of Christianity. By 20 May the Jews of Worms had been all but eradicated.[11]

Then on 25 May Emicho trained his dreadful gaze upon the city of Mainz. Here the Jewish population again tried to take refuge with the local archbishop. Albert of Aachen wrote that he finally agreed to offer them shelter after payment of an 'incredible amount of money', but then did little to resist Emicho's band once it had forced its way into the city:

> Breaking the bolts and doors, they killed the Jews, about 700 in number, who in vain resisted the force and attack of so many thousands. They killed the women, also, and with their swords pierced tender children of whatever age and sex . . . Horrible to say, mothers cut the throats of nursing children with knives and stabbed others, preferring them to perish thus by their own hands.[12]

Less than a month after the first contingents set out, this first wave of the crusade had crushed the Rhineland Jews with merciless efficiency and barbaric glee. Even to this day, dirges honouring the victims of these massacres are recited in synagogues around the globe. Emicho's band, and numerous other groups of crusaders like them, had given an early indication of what dark horrors this holy war might bring.

For Emicho at least, the crusade was nearly over. In August his powerful army, laden down with booty, reached the borders of Hungary upon the banks of the Danube. Refused entry because of their reputation for rapacious brutality, they laid siege to the border fortress of Wieselberg for three weeks, demonstrating considerable military aptitude, but all to no avail. The king of Hungary eventually routed them in battle and their band fragmented. Emicho fled back to Germany, while some of his key followers, like Drogo of Nesle, Thomas of Marle and William the Carpenter, found their way to Italy, where they later hooked up with the second wave of crusader forces.

Other sections of the People's Crusade traversed eastern Europe with less difficulty. Walter Sansavoir enjoyed a relatively easy and uneventful passage. Peter the Hermit, at the head of a large band of French and Germans, may have been involved in the anti-Semitic pogrom at Cologne, but managed to reach the Balkans by midsummer. Numerous other bands, of which no detailed records survive, also made the journey. Collectively, however, this first wave of the crusade had gained a well-earned reputation for violence and volatility.[13]

THE MAIN ARMIES OF THE FIRST CRUSADE

The armies of the great princes mobilised between August and December 1096. More than 40,000 knights and footsoldiers, accompanied by a mass of non-combatants, set out for the Holy Land. This mass migration created an unprecedented upheaval in Latin society. In less than half a year, a whole swathe of European aristocracy vanished, many never to return. Countless lordships and households were stripped of men and left in the care of wives, family, monasteries or the Church. Across western Christendom, crusaders swallowed their fears and left their old lives behind them. For many, leave-taking was an emotional experience. One northern French crusader recalled how 'husband told wife the time he expected to return, assuring her that if by God's grace he survived he would come back home to her', but nevertheless she mourned the loss of her spouse 'who she was losing in this life as if he were already dead'.[14]

Although this second wave of crusaders was somewhat better prepared and organised than the first, there still remains a question mark over the degree of logistical planning entered into by the princes, primarily because our sources reveal little on the subject. Most would have had some idea of what route they might take to the East. Bohemond, for one, had a good knowledge of the Balkans, while Robert of Flanders' father had completed a pilgrimage to Jerusalem only a few years earlier, and Robert must have heard tales of the journey. Pope Urban's advice to the princes seems to have been to set out after the mid-summer harvests had brought in supplies and head for Constantinople, where they could expect guidance and assistance from the Byzantine emperor Alexius I Comnenus. Many crusaders may even have expected the emperor to assume overall leadership of the expedition at this point. A collective decision certainly appears to have been made to muster the disparate crusader armies at the great capital of Byzantium, an obvious choice given that the city was a natural stopping-off point on the overland route to the Levant, and that one of the crusade's central goals was to bring aid to the Greeks.

Many crusading nobles also made careful financial preparations for the expedition, liquidating property rights to free up portable wealth and accrue equipment and mounts. Archaeological and textual evidence indicates that the Latins brought a wide array of European coinage with which to trade during the journey east, seven separate currencies being noted in Raymond of Toulouse's contingent alone.

Some thought may have been given to the need for naval support. Urban certainly sought to involve two of the great maritime powers of the age, sending envoys to the semi-autonomous Italian port of Genoa in July 1096 and later contacting its rival Pisa, but no precise evidence of these negotiations or their outcome survives. The vast majority of the second wave of crusaders chose not to make a direct sea crossing to the Holy Land, opting instead for predominantly land-based routes to Constantinople. Nonetheless, English, German and Genoese fleets did find their way into the eastern Mediterranean in the course of the crusade, although their exact relationship to the expedition is unclear.[15]

That seems to have been the extent of the Latin princes' planning. They forsook complex logistical networks and the burden of long chains of supply. Rather than attempt to carry or bring in the vast quantity of food and equipment needed en route, they chose instead to survive through subsistence: in friendly territory, relying upon markets and what little they could forage from nature; in enemy

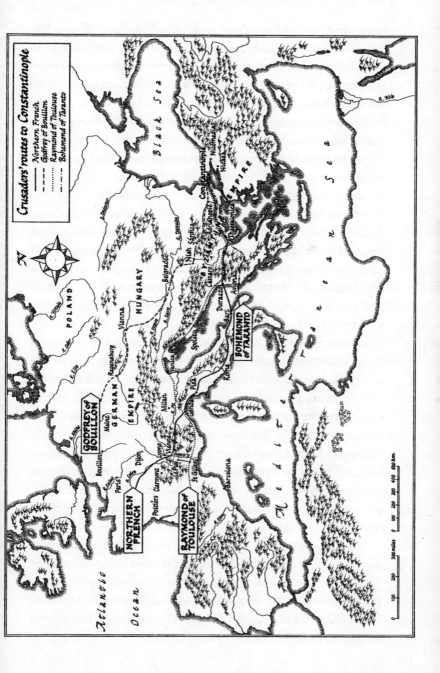

Crusaders' routes to Constantinople
— Northern French
– – Godfrey of Bouillon
· · · Raymond of Toulouse
–·– Bohemond of Taranto

lands, turning to wholesale scavenging and rampant pillage. This process of living off the land, often hand to mouth, helps to explain why the crusaders developed an increasingly voracious appetite for plunder as the expedition progressed. It also accounts for the campaign's early shape and form.

One key consequence of the Latin approach to supply was that it made practical sense for the various contingents of the First Crusade to travel separately. If the pope had ever imagined that its forces would muster at a single location in the West, this idea soon fell by the wayside once the full scale of recruitment became clear. Gathered together, a host numbering in excess of 60,000 people might strip a region of resources in a day; broken down into smaller armies, there was a far better chance of survival. This consideration, alongside the natural tendency to congregate in ethnic and linguistic clusters and the lingering air of suspicion between old opponents like the northern and southern French, prompted the crusaders to march out of Europe in four fairly distinct groups.

It also followed that these armies, which were anyway setting out from distinct regions of the West, would have the best chance of success if they followed different routes to Constantinople. Travelling, as they would be, through allied Christian lands, they would hopefully have no need for massed military manpower and little to gain from following in each other's footsteps down a broken but denuded path.

Thus it was that, from the late summer of 1096, the Latin princes led their forces to Byzantium along three major trans-European arteries, ancient pilgrim routes to the East that traced the crumbling remains of once great Roman roads. Hugh of Vermandois was the first to depart in late August, leading a relatively small band of followers over the Alps, down through Italy to the southern port of Bari, from whence he took ship across the Adriatic. Hugh may have been at the vanguard of the crusading host, but he arrived on the borders of Byzantium under the most inauspicious circumstances. His vessel foundered on the Dalmatian coast and, shipwrecked, he had to suffer the humiliation of being rescued by the Greeks.[16]

The main force of northern French crusaders, consisting of the combined armies of Robert of Normandy, Stephen of Blois and Robert of Flanders, set off along the same route to southern Italy in the early autumn, meeting up with Pope Urban along the way at Lucca in late October. By the time they reached the southern end of the peninsula they were informed that it was too late in the season to make a safe crossing of the Adriatic, but for some unknown reason Robert of Flanders refused to wait. He detached his army from the larger host and set sail into winter seas. His passage to Dalmatia and beyond must have been extremely uncomfortable, but no record of it survives. Robert of Normandy and Stephen, meanwhile, elected to sit out the winter. Their wealth enabled them to await spring in considerable comfort, but some of their followers were less fortunate. Fulcher of Chartres, a priest who began the crusade in Stephen's army and later wrote one of the major Latin histories of the expedition, remarked of this period that 'many of the common people who were left [to look after themselves] and who feared privation in the future sold their weapons and again took up their pilgrims' staves and returned home as cowards'.

It was early April 1097 before the princes led those who remained on to ships at Brindisi. At first it appeared that all their waiting had been in vain, for one of the first vessels to set sail 'suddenly cracked through the middle for no apparent reason' and promptly sank. Four hundred crusaders drowned, although it was later rumoured that some of their bodies, discovered washed up on the shore, were found to bear the mark of the cross 'actually imprinted on the flesh . . . between the shoulders', a 'miracle' that was taken to indicate their martyrdom and God's unbroken approval. But at the time most onlookers were evidently horrified. Fulcher of Chartres noted that 'many faint-hearted who had not yet embarked returned to their homes, giving up the pilgrimage and saying that never again would they entrust themselves to the treacherous sea'. The majority remained, and four days later, with the winds finally favourable, made the voyage without further incident, landing near Durazzo.[17]

The massed ranks of the southern French contingent set out from Provence in late November 1096 under the direction of Raymond, count of Toulouse and Adhémar of Le Puy. Raymond's wealth and power had drawn in nobles from a wide orbit stretching across the county of Toulouse to include large sections of the duchy of Aquitaine. These included men possessed of considerable valour and skill at arms: Raymond, viscount of Turenne, whose father had just made a pilgrimage to Jerusalem in 1091; Gulpher, lord of Lastours, from the Limousin; and the adventurous knight Raymond Pilet. Having marched into northern Italy, this force had a number of options. By travelling south they could, like their northern brethren, take ship across the Adriatic, but this would necessitate a considerable delay until spring. They might also have headed east along the Via Gemina, the Roman highway to Belgrade, where they could link up with the great pilgrim route south to Constantinople. As it was, for reasons unknown, they took a more unusual route, striking south-east along the remnants of a Roman road down through the untamed terrain of the Dalmatian coast.

One member of this army, Raymond of Aguilers, a cleric who seems to have acted as one of Raymond of Toulouse's personal chaplains, wrote a history of the crusade from a Provençal perspective. He recalled this section of the journey with evident distaste, recording that they traversed 'a forsaken land, both inaccessible and mountainous, where for three weeks we saw neither wild beasts nor birds [but encountered] barbarous and ignorant natives'. By the time they reached Durazzo in early February 1097, everyone was thoroughly exhausted.[18]

Duke Godfrey of Bouillon became the figurehead for crusaders from Lotharingia and Germany. As well as his ambitious brother Baldwin of Boulogne, this contingent included, among others, the formidable German warrior Reinhard III, count of Toul. Departing in the late summer of 1096, this army followed the same pilgrim route taken by much of the People's Crusade, following the banks of the River Danube down into the heartlands of eastern Europe. But, upon reaching Hungary, Godfrey found, like Emicho of Leiningen before him, that the way ahead was barred. Choosing diplomacy over brute force, the duke dispatched one of his followers, Godfrey of Esch, who had taken the cross with his brother Henry, and was a former confidant of the king of Hungary, to negotiate passage. Although the king was initially reluctant after his experience of the People's Crusade, stiff terms were eventually agreed and Duke Godfrey's brother given as a temporary hostage to guarantee crusader discipline. The army eventually entered Hungary in September and enjoyed a peaceful passage to Belgrade.[19]

Living as they did on the fringes of the Byzantine Empire, the southern Italian Normans who congregated around Bohemond of Taranto had the shortest journey. Alongside Bohemond's nephew Tancred, this small but powerful contingent included the likes of Roger of Barneville, a ferocious Sicilian lord who also spoke Arabic. One member of this force, whose name has never been conclusively identified and may have been a cleric or knight, wrote a third eyewitness account of the First Crusade. According to this anonymous history, known as the *Gesta Francorum* (The Deeds of the Franks), the army crossed the Adriatic in October 1096 'at Bohemond's expense' to land south of Durazzo, a considerable outlay, but one that no doubt confirmed his status as leader.[20]

By these diverse routes, the second wave of crusaders arrived on the outer reaches of Byzantium, one Greek contemporary later remarking that 'like tributaries joining a river from all directions they streamed towards us in full force'.[21]

INTO THE EMPIRE

The First Crusaders reached the borders of the ancient Byzantine Empire in the summer of 1096, less than a year after Pope Urban's speech at Clermont. For the next twelve months they would pour through its lands like an unstoppable tide, sweeping across the

Balkans towards its opulent capital, Constantinople, and the Bosphorus Strait, a tiny strip of water separating Orient from Occident, to the very edge of the Islamic world.

The Byzantine world

Byzantium, the greatest Christian superpower of the medieval age, had an almost inconceivably long history, arching across centuries, back to a time even before the birth of Christ – the most enduring empire in human memory. It was, in fact, the sole surviving remnant of the classical Roman Empire. In 395 CE, when the horrific glory of Rome had already engulfed the known world for more than four centuries, its sprawling empire was judged unwieldy and its lands divided in two. After this date, the western half of the empire was ruled from Rome, while the East was governed from Constantinople. With Rome's dominion over Europe gradually dissolving from the fifth century onwards, only the eastern empire was left intact. It is this realm, which was to survive until 1453, that modern historians term the Byzantine Empire. In the eleventh century, though, its inhabitants thought of themselves, first and foremost, as Romans: the direct inheritors of Rome's power, wealth and culture. Their realm was, they believed, the very epicentre of civilisation, their emperor the most powerful man on earth.

In reality, Byzantium had for centuries been fighting an almost constant battle for survival, surrounded by enemies. When Muslim warriors began pouring out of Arabia in the seventh century, much of the eastern Roman Empire, including Syria and Palestine, was overrun. From this point forth, the Byzantines faced an unending struggle to hold on to Asia Minor against Islam. Indeed, Constantinople itself was besieged in 668 and again in 717. At the same time, ravening hordes of 'barbarians' surged out of the north and west – Bulgars, Petchenegs, Cumans – eating away at the empire's Balkan territory. At the start of the eleventh century Byzantium enjoyed something of a resurgence of wealth and power under the ferocious despot Basil II (976–1025), also known as Basil the Bulgar-Slayer. He earned this epithet through an act of unparalleled ruthlessness. Facing renewed Bulgar aggression in 1014, he outmanoeuvred and trapped their army, capturing 14,000 prisoners. The Bulgar Prince Samuel escaped, so Basil decided to send him a clear message about the dangers of threatening the empire. He chose to release rather than execute his prisoners, but had ninety-nine in every hundred blinded, leaving the hundredth man one eye with which to guide his mutilated companions back into Bulgar territory. The sight of this train of broken wretches crushed Samuel's spirit and he died of shock two days later.

Few of Basil's successors could match his cold-blooded yet visionary ambition, and the empire rapidly fell back into a state of chaotic decline after his death. In this unstable climate, the imperial throne became a seat of danger. Between the years 1025 and 1081 power changed hands thirteen times, as Constantinople burned with intrigue and successive emperors fell victim to violent *coups d'état*. In 1071 the Emperor Romanus Diogenes suffered the humiliation of defeat and capture at the hands of the Muslim Turks in the Battle of Manzikert, after which much of Asia Minor fell to Islam and the western frontier became destabilised. The once mighty edifice of Byzantium was on the brink of collapse, its treasury bankrupt, its armies ill deployed and its latest emperor aged and ineffectual.[22]

Alexius I Comnenus (1081–1118), a young general of aristocratic heritage, arrested this spiral of decline and, in the course of his long reign, initiated the process of rejuvenation. His daughter and biographer, Anna Comnena, offered this dramatised description of his appearance:

> Alexius was not a very tall man, but broad shouldered and yet well proportioned. When standing he did not seem particularly striking to onlookers, but when one saw the grim flash of his eyes as he sat on the imperial throne, he reminded one of a fiery whirlwind, so overwhelming was . . . his presence. His dark eyebrows were curved, and beneath them the gaze of his eyes was both terrible and kind.[23]

Alexius came to power in a bloodless coup, thanks to his proven military record and a network of noble support based on a carefully woven web of connections to the empire's most powerful families. An astute, measured politician and a wily diplomat, Alexius knew that to have any hope for a successful rule he would need to conjure two near miracles – survival in office and the rapid generation of vast amounts of cash. To preclude the almost unrelenting threat of assassination and rebellion, he conferred streams of empty titles on potential plotters, leaving them appeased and present, under his watchful eye, at the imperial court. Meanwhile, the treasury was restocked by wringing the empire dry through outrageously exorbitant taxation and, at a pinch, outright theft from the Church. Alexius used this wealth to recreate the aura of imperial munificence both within Byzantium and abroad, combining the raw purchasing power of money with the compelling image of unassailable majesty. Mixing bribery and intimidation, he shored up his political mandate at home, then gradually reasserted Greek supremacy on the international stage.

On the eastern frontier Alexius managed to halt the ongoing Muslim advance through a marriage of force and negotiation, but the Muslim Turks were still able to range freely across Asia Minor. In the northern reaches of Syria the valuable commercial centre of Antioch was lost, while closer to home the Turks maintained a tenacious foothold at the fortified city of Nicaea, just across the Bosphorus from Constantinople itself. The Greek capital held, but the Turks resisted Alexius' best attempts to dislodge them. Alexius judged that flushing out this enemy would require an injection of military ferocity from outside the borders of Byzantium, and the first and most obvious place to look was western Europe.[24]

The Latin West was, in many ways, the empire's most natural ally; the two worlds were, after all, both Christian. But the bond of this common faith was tempered by the fact that the Byzantines followed the Greek rather than Roman creed. Greeks and Latins had long disagreed on some facets of the Christian religion – the dating of Easter, the practice of prayer and ritual and the use of religious images – and the Greek Church, headed by the patriarch of Constantinople, also staunchly disputed the Roman pope's claim to universal primacy. These factors, alongside political and ethnic considerations, culminated in the eruption of an open rift between the two Churches in 1054, known as the Great Schism, the ecclesiastical equivalent of a breach in diplomatic relations. Channels were partially reopened within a few years, but the consequences of this fracture were still rumbling on in the background when Alexius came to power in 1081.

This spiritual friction was coupled with the *Realpolitik* of international relations. Just as the Christian lords of western Europe fought each other tooth and nail for power and wealth, so the religious fraternity failed to prevent Byzantium and the West from contesting political and economic domination of the Euro-Mediterranean world. The Greeks had long resented the fact that German kings habitually claimed the title of emperor, while more recently they had contested control of southern Italy and then the western Balkans with the Normans. The Greeks saw themselves as the cultured inheritors of Roman civilisation and regarded the Latins as little more than savage tribesmen, possessed of martial ferocity but otherwise to be scorned. In its dealings with the West, Byzantium thus generally adopted an arrogant, calculated stance, and certainly never regarded its neighbours as equals. But, as the eleventh century progressed and western Europeans began to make their presence felt on the world stage, this gap started to close. Byzantium might view the West with disdain, but the Latins increasingly looked back with a mixture of awed suspicion and budding assurance.

Alexius Comnenus had sought, since the start of his reign, to soothe tensions with western Christendom, encouraging compromise in the ecclesiastical sphere and reaffirming the empire's position as a major player in the arena of European politics. Like many emperors before him, he also maintained a significant western presence within the Byzantine military machine. For much of the eleventh century the core of the Greek army was actually manned by mercenaries, most notably in the elite Varangian Guard, dominated by Anglo-Saxon Englishmen and Scandinavian Vikings, whose duty it was to protect the emperor.[25]

Confronted in the mid-1090s with the problem of an intractable Islamic presence on the borders of the empire, Alexius weighed up the twin forces of Christian fellowship and simmering hostility, and decided to turn to the West for aid. To him this was not a sign of weakness or even parity, but an exercise in pragmatic manipulation. He had already forged an alliance with the major Latin noble Robert I, count of Flanders, father to the First Crusader. Contact was established when Robert passed through Constantinople on pilgrimage to Jerusalem c. 1091, and culminated in the dispatch of 500 western knights to aid Alexius' military efforts. The emperor was probably looking for a similar infusion of manageable Latin manpower when he sent envoys to the council of Piacenza in 1095. What he got was, of course, of an entirely different order of magnitude.[26]

The first wave: the fate of the People's Crusade

The conduct of the first wave of crusaders to reach his borders shocked and disturbed Alexius Comnenus. Even depleted as they were by death and desertion, the roving pilgrim bands of the People's Crusade seemed like a riotous flood of humanity that threatened to inundate the Byzantine Empire. So numerous were they that one Greek contemporary likened them to 'the sands of the sea shore and the stars of heaven'.[27] Of all the contingents that eventually reached Constantinople, only the progress of that led by Peter the Hermit is recorded in any detail. Once in Greek territory, Peter did his best to maintain discipline among his followers, but failed to prevent looters from ravaging the outskirts of Nish, one of the major towns on the route south, and suffered punitive attacks from its citizens as a result. The rest of the journey passed with relative ease, but, once he arrived at Constantinople on 1 August 1096, the problems of containment and restraint intensified. Now instead of a rambling gang of followers, Peter had to control the seething throng of crusaders that was gradually massing outside the Byzantine capital. Walter Sansavoir's contingent was already there, as was a large group of Italians; they were joined by a stream of French and German crusaders.

At first, Peter established cordial relations with Alexius. The emperor agreed to offer the Latins plentiful supplies and counselled them to await patiently the arrival of the main crusading armies before crossing the Bosphorus into hostile territory. But it was only a matter of days before rampant disorder set in. Even a Latin contemporary was forced to admit that 'those Christians behaved abominably, sacking and burning the palaces of the city, and stealing the lead from the roofs of churches and selling it to the Greeks, so that the emperor was angry and ordered them to cross the Bosphorus'.[28] Dismayed by this lawlessness and concerned for Byzantine security, Alexius saw little option but to deport these brigands to the exposed and alien shores of Bithynia in Asia Minor.[29]

Peter the Hermit's ineffectual leadership and the emperor's resolute response had now placed the People's Crusade in extreme peril. On around 7 August, the Franks were shipped across to the Gulf of Nicomedia and within a few days they had set up camp along its southern coastline at Civitot. Alexius continued to supply them with ample provisions, but they were, nonetheless, desperately isolated. Less than two days' march to the east stood the major Turkish stronghold of Nicaea, a powerful Muslim enemy, of whom these inexperienced and ill-prepared crusaders had little knowledge or comprehension. Rather than maintain a sensibly discreet profile, ravening Latin mobs soon began to trawl the surrounding countryside in search of plunder, allegedly subjecting the region to savage rapine: 'acting with horrible cruelty to the whole population, they cut in pieces some of their babies, impaled others on wooden spits and roasted them over a fire [while] the elderly were subjected to every kind of torture'.[30]

By September, expeditionary forces were ranging ever more boldly through the environs of Nicaea, stealing cattle and looting villages.

Then, towards the end of that month, a large group of Italian and German crusaders ravaged the nearby fort of Xerigordos. They were still revelling in pillage when a major force of Nicaean Turks suddenly arrived and surrounded them. Trapped inside the fort, the crusaders held out for eight days, but in the sapping late-summer heat they soon ran out of water. According to one near-contemporary, they were 'so terribly afflicted by thirst that they bled their horses and asses and drank the blood; others let down belts and clothes into a sewer and squeezed out the liquid into their mouths'.[31] With resistance fading, the Muslims broke in, slaughtering or enslaving the entire Latin force.

News of this defeat enraged the remaining crusaders camped at Civetot, and the more reckless began to advocate a direct counterattack on Nicaea itself. At that very moment, Peter the Hermit was in Constantinople bargaining with Alexius over provisions and thus unable to counsel caution. In the end, even Walter Sansavoir was convinced of the need for a pre-emptive strike and so, on 21 October 1097, the full fighting manpower of the People's Crusade marched out of Civetot, leaving 'only those without weapons and the sick . . . behind in camp'.[32] This was not, as historians once thought, a wretchedly feeble rabble. The army was led by reasonably skilful commanders like Walter Sansavoir and boasted a robust core of some 500 knights, alongside thousands of footsoldiers and peasants. This force was, however, undertaking a perilously risky operation against a largely untested enemy, endangering the entire first wave of the crusade for little or no reason.

Just a few hours after leaving the coast they ran into trouble. A formidable pack of Nicaean Turks had, it transpired, been planning their own attack that same day and the two forces met on the plains above Civetot. The Frankish knights put up strenuous resistance in the pitched battle that followed, but the awesome destructive power of the Turkish archers decimated the Latin ranks with wave upon wave of scything missiles. Walter Sansavoir fell, his body peppered by seven arrows, and around him the crusader army was all but annihilated. Years later, a Greek observer sorrowfully recalled that the number of Frankish dead was so great that their corpses formed a vast mound, adding, 'I will not say a mighty ridge or hill or peak, but a mountain . . . so huge was the mass of bones.'[33]

The Turks immediately followed up this bloody victory by falling upon the crusaders' camp at Civetot with merciless brutality. There they found 'the feeble and crippled, clerics, monks, aged women, boys at the breast, and put them all to the sword, regardless of age. They took away only the young girls and nuns, whose faces and figures seemed pleasing to their eyes, and beardless and beautiful young men.'[34]

The crusaders' first steps into Islamic territory had ended in utter catastrophe. Horrified by the news, Peter the Hermit convinced Alexius to send a rescue mission. A handful of survivors who had 'leapt into the sea [or hidden] in the woods or mountains' were picked up and brought back to Constantinople.[35]

The second wave: the princes' armies

The main armies of the First Crusade arrived in Byzantium between October 1096 and April 1097. Their crossing of the empire presented problems for Latins and Greeks alike. Many crusaders arrived expecting to be treated as valued Christian allies. One member of the southern French contingent recalled that 'we were confident that we were in our own land, because we believed that Alexius and his followers were our Christian brothers and confederates'. On the crucial question of food and supplies, the Latins assumed that these would either be provided free of charge or made available for purchase at reasonably priced markets. But, in the wake of the first wave's indiscipline, the Greeks, left anxious and belligerent, guarded their resources, offering only a limited stock of victuals at exorbitant rates. Disillusioned crusaders were forced to forage to make up the shortfall, but there was a fine line between foraging and raiding, and most princes struggled to keep their armies under control. Yet, even as tensions rose, ideological and pragmatic considerations encouraged Latin temperance. The princes knew that

Pope Urban wanted the crusade to reinforce Byzantium, and the majority were planning to offer service to the emperor, so the outbreak of open conflict was best avoided. Without imperial support, the expedition would also have little chance of crossing the Bosphorus. A northern French crusader observed that 'it was essential that all establish friendship with the emperor since without his aid and counsel we could not easily make the journey, nor could those who were to follow us by the same route'.[36]

Having experienced the chaotic passage of the People's Crusade, the Emperor Alexius, for his part, sought to manage this second wave with greater efficiency, shepherding the Franks through the heartlands of Byzantium as peaceably and rapidly as possible. He was undoubtedly shocked by the overwhelming and unwieldy scale of the crusade, and this has prompted many to believe that he viewed the expedition with inbred hostility from the start. Years later, his daughter Anna Comnena remarked that Alexius had 'heard a rumour that countless Frankish armies were approaching [and] dreaded their arrival, knowing as he did their uncontrollable passion, their erratic character and their irresolution, not to mention their greed'. Elsewhere she described the crusaders as 'all the barbarians of the West' and was particularly scathing in her descriptions of Bohemond as 'a habitual rogue' who was 'by nature a liar'. But these opinions were heavily coloured by hindsight, and, while there was distrust and friction, initially at least there was little open enmity between the Greeks and the crusaders. In 1096–7 Alexius wanted to contain, control and exploit the Franks, and so long as they toed the line he was prepared to offer them guidance and assistance.[37]

The main armies all reached Constantinople relatively intact. A rather bedraggled Hugh of Vermandois was the first to arrive in November 1096, trailed by Godfrey of Bouillon's contingent on 23 December. Raymond of Toulouse's and Bohemond's men followed in April 1097, and the bulk of the northern French forces did not appear until mid-May. All endured a degree of difficulty and danger in their journeys across the empire.

Alexius had sent high-ranking envoys at the head of substantial Byzantine forces to greet each army at the fringes of Greek territory. Officially they were there to act as guides and liaison officers, but in reality their primary remit was to shadow the crusader forces, policing Latin activity. This policy was a limited success: Godfrey's army traversed most of the northern pilgrim route without incident, passing Nish, Sofia and Philipopolis; Robert of Normandy and Stephen of Blois marched along the Via Egnatia, linking Durazzo to Constantinople, in the clement season of spring, moving with relative ease and rapidity. Full-scale warfare was avoided, as was widespread rape of the countryside.[38]

But there were flashes of hostility and open conflict. Raymond of Toulouse set out along the Via Egnatia in February and found the going far tougher. Although presented with letters of safe conduct by a member of the imperial Comneni family at Durazzo, the southern French struggled to find sufficient supplies and their wide-ranging foraging soon led to clashes with elements of the Byzantine army detailed to monitor their progress. Early in the journey, the papal legate Adhémar of Le Puy was attacked by Petchenegs, now loosely allied to the Greeks. Thrown from his mule and captured, the bishop was stripped of all his valuables and beaten over the head. He would probably have suffered an even worse fate but for the actions of one particularly acquisitive Petcheneg. Deciding that he wanted all Adhémar's treasure for himself, he set upon his fellow brigands, giving a group of crusaders time to come to the bishop's rescue. The trans-Balkan passage dragged on and by April the strain began to tell. When the people of Roussa offered a less than warm welcome, Latin discipline broke and the town was summarily stormed and sacked, an infringement that prompted retaliatory attacks from the Greeks. Raymond himself hurried on to Constantinople with just a handful of followers to restore relations with the emperor.[39]

Bohemond's contingent struck inland from the Adriatic coast at Avlona to join the Via Egnatia at Vodena, thus avoiding Greek scrutiny in the first part of the journey. Bohemond seems deliberately to have taken his time crossing the Balkans, perhaps waiting to see how the emperor dealt with other princes at Constantinople and formulating a strategy to turn events to his best advantage. Knowing that Alexius viewed the southern Italian Normans with profound unease because of the war of 1081–5, he apparently decided to give the emperor no grounds for early complaint, counselling his followers 'to be courteous and refrain from plundering that land, which belonged to Christians, and he said that no one was to take more than sufficed for his food'. This proved difficult to enforce, and the Byzantines and crusaders exchanged hostilities. In January 1097, livestock was stolen from the citizens of Castoria when they refused to sell supplies; while crossing the River Vardar on 18 February Bohemond's forces were attacked by imperial troops; and a few days later the crusaders sacked a small castle on the approach to Serres, apparently against Bohemond's wishes.

His conciliatory approach may simply have been a thin diplomatic veneer designed to mask his true intentions, because he was simultaneously probing the possibility of an anti-Greek alliance with other Latin princes. He tried to establish a line of communication with Godfrey of Bouillon, already camped outside Constantinople, proposing that they join forces and attack Alexius, but his envoys seem to have been intercepted. Intrigue was certainly in the air, because Godfrey was warned by his advisers to be wary of assassination attempts, even by such exotic methods as poisoned cloaks. With his schemes frustrated, Bohemond left the bulk of the army in the care of Tancred to pass Easter near Roussa and rode on to Constantinople to open negotiations with the emperor.[40]

The Graeco-Latin détente survived the piecemeal approach of the princes' armies towards the Byzantine capital, but an underlying current of mutual suspicion and ingrained antipathy was running dangerously close to the surface throughout the first half of 1097.

THE GREAT CITY OF CONSTANTINOPLE

The arduous journey from western Europe brought each contingent of the crusading host to the gates of Constantinople. There was no greater Christian city on earth. Its staggering size, exotic opulence and cosmopolitan populace astounded the Franks. One wrote:

> Oh what a noble and beautiful city is Constantinople! How many monasteries and palaces it contains, constructed with wonderful skill! It would take too long to describe all the wealth that is there of every kind, of gold, of silver, all types of clothes, holy relics . . . There are, I think, around twenty thousand eunuchs living there always.[41]

Poised as it was on an isthmus jutting out into the Bosphorus Strait – the thin body of water that connects the Mediterranean with the Black Sea and separates the European and Asian continents – the city was perfectly placed to exploit the pulsing trade route to the Orient. Known in antiquity as Byzantion (from which the word Byzantium is derived), it was renamed in honour of Constantine the Great when he chose it as the site of his new capital of the Roman Empire in 324 CE. The city was shaped into a rough triangle, two sides of which abutted the sea, and was enclosed within massive twin walls – to the landward side these presented an awesome, impenetrable barrier, seven kilometres long, up to five metres thick and twenty metres high. The huge size of this metropolis dwarfed the largest city in Latin Europe ten-fold; its teeming populace, perhaps 500,000 strong, could have inhabited an entire realm back in the West.

Alexius Comnenus was determined to protect this great city at all costs. So even though the crusaders had come to Byzantium as allies, the emperor forced them to camp outside Constantinople's walls. One Latin eyewitness recalled that 'we did not try to enter the city because it was not agreeable to [Alexius] for he feared that possibly we would plot some harm to him . . . [We could only] enter the city at the rate of five or six each hour. Thus while we were leaving, others were entering to pray in the churches.'[42] Those who were lucky enough to get in were greeted by sights of unparalleled grandeur. The colossal wealth of the Greeks was legendary, and the magnificence of their capital spoke of an empire possessed of immeasurable fortune and an ancient heritage.

The first stop of any crusader would have been the Basilica of St Sophia, the largest, most spectacular Christian church in the world. Built in the sixth century, its vast interior glistened, its walls, vaulted corridors and domes being covered with dramatic frescoes and mosaics whose craftsmanship far outstripped anything the Latins would have seen in western Europe. This giant structure was topped by an enormous dome more than fifty metres high and thirty metres wide. The basilica, like the city as a whole, was renowned for its collection of sacred relics. A visitor to Constantinople might see Christ's crown of thorns and pieces of the cross upon which he was crucified; the Virgin Mary's robe and locks of her hair; at least two heads of John the Baptist; and the bones of virtually all the apostles.

Elsewhere in the city, the Franks could marvel at countless wonders: the Forum of Constantine, dominated by a fifty-metre-high column, upon the summit of which stood a gigantic statue of the city's founder modelled as Apollo; the Hippodrome – an ancient stadium famed for its brutal chariot races, capable of seating a crowd of 100,000; and the Equestrian Statue of Justinian – a monumental marble column topped by a bronze of the emperor astride his horse, rendered three times life-size, holding his hand out to the east as a symbolic warning to the Persians.

The most esteemed visitors might gain access to the imperial residence itself, the Palace of the Blachernae, situated atop a hill in the north-west corner of Constantinople, overlooking the city and its surroundings. A crusader who saw it in the twelfth century wrote:

On its three sides the Palace offers to its inhabitants the triple pleasure of gazing alternately on the sea, the countryside, and the town. The exterior of the palace is of almost incomparable loveliness and its interior surpasses anything that I can say about it. It is decorated throughout with gold and various colours and the floor is paved with cleverly arranged marble.[43]

Confronted by this array of magnificence, most First Crusaders were utterly overawed. They had been born in the Latin West, where the distant echo of ancient Rome reverberated in the collective memory, the touchstone of a golden age in human history. Now, as they walked the streets of Constantinople, the glory and power of that empire seemed reborn, incarnate in living colour before their eyes. Few could have doubted that they had reached the mighty beating heart of western civilisation.

The oaths to Alexius

The Emperor Alexius looked to capitalise upon the splendour of his city. Having herded the crusade's second wave through the western reaches of the empire with some skill, he now had to deal with the Franks at the core of Byzantium. With the various contingents of the expedition projected to congregate at Constantinople, Alexius had an ideal opportunity to assert imperial authority over the venture, capitalising upon the imposing grandeur of the Byzantine court to dazzle the Latin princes into submissive accord. But the prospect of a potentially unruly Frankish horde gathering outside his walls filled the emperor with concern. He knew that, left to their own devices, the massed ranks of crusaders would become increasingly difficult to supply and their acquisitive eyes might even turn upon Constantinople itself. Indeed, soon after the first of the main armies under Godfrey of Bouillon had established camp on the outskirts of the city, tensions flared and there was open skirmishing between Baldwin of Boulogne and Byzantine troops.[44]

Alexius wisely chose to exploit the fragmented nature of the crusader host, dealing with each prince individually as he arrived at Constantinople and then avoiding a build-up of discontented Latins by shipping them across the Bosphorus as rapidly as possible. Once in Asia Minor they could be allowed to assemble without posing any direct threat to the Greeks. Anna Comnena recalled that the emperor 'used every means, physical and psychological, to hurry [the Franks] into crossing the straits', a clear instance of his prioritising Byzantine interests, because this policy exposed the second wave of crusaders to the same destructive fate suffered by the first.[45]

Before moving them on, however, Alexius was determined to establish a degree of control over the princes, harnessing the raw power of their armies to fulfil the needs of the empire and looking to capitalise upon any success they might enjoy.

Contrary perhaps to the crusaders' expectations, he had no plans personally to lead their expedition on to Jerusalem. The emperor's mind was instead focused upon two absolute and unwavering priorities: protecting the position of his fledgling Comneni dynasty and preserving the delicate balance of Byzantine security. Alexius was happy to assist the First Crusade, even keen for it to succeed, but he was never going to jeopardise Greek interests to further the Latin cause, and conducting a protracted campaign in the distant Holy Land would have exposed his rule to overthrow and the empire to invasion.

In lieu of direct participation, Alexius sought to bind the leading crusaders to him through bonds of service. Every Frankish prince or noble passing by Constantinople was called into the magnificent city for an audience with the emperor and required to offer him an oath of allegiance. After prolonged and fractious negotiation, Godfrey of Bouillon led the cream of Lotharingian aristocracy into the imperial palace around 20 January 1097 to find Alexius 'seated, as was his custom, looking powerful on the throne of his sovereignty, not getting up to offer kisses [of greeting] to the duke nor to anyone'. Maintaining this air of regal majesty, the emperor received their submission, thus apparently creating 'an unbreakable chain of complete trust and friendship' between them.[46]

The Latins' pledges had two components. The first was a solemn promise that 'whatever cities, countries or forts he might in future subdue, which had in the first place belonged to the Roman Empire, he would hand over to the officer appointed by the emperor'. This meant that any territory captured in Asia Minor and even beyond would have to be handed over to the Byzantines. The second part of the accord is much more difficult to pin down. It seems to have involved an oath of vassalage to Alexius, partly modelled on western forms of lordship, the precise details of which are impossible to recover. A bond of peace and mutual friendship was certainly implied; Alexius, as the senior partner, could direct the princes to do his bidding; they agreed not to harm the empire, but in return might expect imperial aid and counsel. It is extremely unlikely that, in connection with this last clause, Alexius ever formally affirmed his intention to join the crusaders on their march to Jerusalem. He was too agile a diplomat to commit himself in advance to such a risky venture. But the reciprocal obligations inherent in vassalic relations left the Franks expecting that he would reinforce their expedition at some point.[47]

Once Godfrey established the precedent of making this submission, most crusader princes followed suit without protest. With his thoughts of challenging the Greeks sidelined, Bohemond, for example, now sought to ingratiate himself with his former enemy. Arriving at Constantinople around 10 April, he was summoned to an audience and readily acquiesced to the oath. In return, he tried to convince Alexius to make him the *de facto* military commander of the crusade, but the emperor tactfully prevaricated.[48] Some, however, resisted Alexius' demands. As Raymond of Toulouse arrived in the city around 21 April, news reached him that the southern French forces trailing some days' journey behind had fallen prey to repeated attack. Suspecting foul play, he stoutly refused to proffer the same oath given by all the other princes, despite Alexius' best efforts to pressure him into submission. In the end, he agreed to a modified pact, vowing not to threaten the emperor's power or possessions. Modern historians have persistently maintained that Raymond's proud stance earned him Alexius' respect and friendship, uniting the two in an alliance that would endure through the course of the crusade. This is primarily based on the testimony of Anna Comnena, who, with the benefit of hindsight, wrote of Raymond in glowing terms, revealing nothing of the wrangling at Constantinople. In reality, there is nothing in Raymond's conduct to suggest that he and the emperor enjoyed an especially cordial relationship in 1097. Indeed, according to a member of Raymond's own army, he was actually plotting to attack the Greeks at this point. A number of lesser princes, including Tancred of Hauteville and Baldwin of Boulogne, are known to have initially avoided taking any oath, evading the emperor's net by immediately crossing the Bosphorus.[49]

Alexius had, nonetheless, asserted his dominance over the crusading elite and looked set to manipulate and exploit the expedition. With typical Byzantine largesse, he sweetened the act of capitulation by showering the Latin princes with lavish gifts. Godfrey acquired a mound of gold and silver from the imperial treasury, along with precious purple silks and valuable horses. He also received a hefty weekly stipend with which to purchase supplies for his army at local markets, although all of this soon poured back into Greek coffers. Bohemond was reportedly amazed and overjoyed when, after making his pledge, he was shown a room so packed with diverse riches 'that it was impossible for anyone to walk in it' and was told that the entire contents were his. Raymond of Toulouse alone gained little in the way of treasure because of his intransigence.[50]

The emperor also offered the Franks priceless intelligence about the challenges that lay ahead in Asia Minor. Bohemond is known to have consulted him about how to supply the Latin host during the initial penetration of this territory, and Alexius provided the princes with a clear explanation and analysis of the Muslim foe now confronting the First Crusade. Anna Comnena noted that the emperor 'warned [them] about the things likely to happen on their journey [and] gave them profitable advice. They were instructed in the methods normally used by the Turks in battle; told how they should draw up a battle-line, how to lay ambushes; advised not to pursue far when the enemy ran away in flight.' Later Alexius supplemented this tactical advice with an insight into his own pragmatic brand of politics, counselling the Franks to exploit the political and religious divisions that afflicted Islam.[51]

The world of Islam

The Muslim world with which Alexius sought to acquaint the crusaders had undergone a dramatic transformation in the four and a half centuries since Muhammad first proclaimed the faith in a distant corner of the Arabian peninsula. After the prophet's death in 632 CE, his successors prosecuted a series of wildly energetic military campaigns that saw the Islamic state sweep across the eastern Mediterranean, north Africa and Persia. The great cities of the East – Damascus, Baghdad and Cairo – all fell within a decade; Jerusalem, a city deeply revered as the site of Muhammad's ascent to heaven, was conquered in 638. By the start of the eighth century Islam had engulfed the Mediterranean world, to the east threatening Constantinople, in the west menacing southern France.

In spite of this extraordinary expansion, the Islamic state was, from early in its history, fundamentally and bitterly divided. Two sects claimed descent from Muhammad: to the north Sunni Islam was based at the Persian city of Baghdad, capital of what was known as the Abbasid caliphate; meanwhile, the southern Fatimid caliphate, centred on Cairo, adhered to the Shi'a form of Islam. By the start of the eleventh century, this grave breach had crippled the Muslim world, as the struggle between Sunnites and Shi'ites took precedence above all other affairs and the power of both Baghdad and Cairo stagnated.[52] In ethnic terms, Middle Eastern Islam had, up to this point, been dominated by Arabs and Persians, but from 1055 onwards an injection of new blood reinvigorated the Abbasid caliphate. Wild nomadic Turcoman tribesmen from the steppe-lands of Russia converted to Sunni Islam and overran Mesopotamia. When these Turks conquered Baghdad, their leader, an ambitious warlord named

Tughrul Beg, was proclaimed sultan (literally 'power') and his family, the Seljuqs, became the ruling dynasty of the Sunni north.

By the end of the eleventh century these Seljuq Turks held sway over Iran, Iraq, Syria and Palestine. The Egyptian Fatimids of Cairo had, for some years, been retreating in the face of this Seljuq aggression, and Alexius actually advised the crusaders to negotiate an anti-Turkish pact with them. A branch of the Seljuq family also seized control of much of Asia Minor after the Byzantines were crushed at Manzikert in 1071, and began styling themselves as the sultans of Rüm (the eastern Roman Empire).

It was these Seljuqs who would confront the First Crusade once it breached the frontier with Islam in 1097, and Alexius Comnenus did his best to prepare the Franks for their distinct brand of warfare. The traditional mainstay of their armies was the lightly armoured mounted warrior, astride a fleet-footed, agile pony, armed with a powerful composite bow that enabled him to loose streams of arrows from horseback. He might also be armed with a light lance, single-edged sword, axe or dagger. These troops relied upon speed of movement and rapid manoeuvrability to overcome their opponents. They classically employed two main tactics: encirclement, in which they would seek to surround an enemy on all sides in a fast-moving, swirling mass, while unleashing unending volleys of arrows; and feigned retreat, the technique of turning tail in battle in the hope of prompting your opponent to give chase, the indiscipline of which would break their formation and leave them vulnerable to sudden counterattack. This style of combat was still favoured by the Seljuqs of Asia Minor, but the Turks of Syria and Palestine had begun to adopt a wider array of Persian and Arab military practices, adjusting to the use of larger infantry forces and to the needs of siege warfare.[53]

The Muslims who met the crusaders in battle were skilled and ferocious warriors. They did not, however, see themselves as being engaged in a grand religious struggle with Christianity. The Muslim religion had, from its earliest days, embraced warfare. Muhammad himself prosecuted a series of brutal campaigns while subjugating

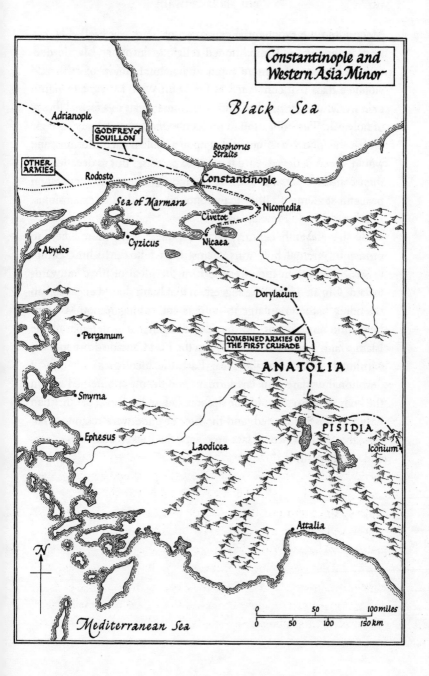

Constantinople and Western Asia Minor

Black Sea

Adrianople

GODFREY of BOUILLON

Bosphorus Straits

OTHER ARMIES

Rodosto

Constantinople

Sea of Marmara

Nicomedia

Civetot

Cyzicus

Nicaea

Abydos

Dorylaeum

Pergamum

COMBINED ARMIES OF THE FIRST CRUSADE

ANATOLIA

Smyrna

PISIDIA

Ephesus

Laodicea

Iconium

Attalia

N

0   50   100 miles
0   50   100   150 km

Mediterranean Sea

Mecca, and the exponential expansion of Islam was fuelled by raw Arab bellicosity and impassioned religious devotion. Islamic doctrine achieved a far more rapid and natural union of faith and violence than that concocted in the Latin West. By the late eighth century, Muslim jurists had enshrined these ideals in a formal theory of holy war. The obligation to prosecute *jihad*, the military struggle against the infidel, was incumbent upon all able-bodied Muslims, and would, it was believed, pave the way to paradise. But as decades and then centuries passsed, and the Islamic state began to focus upon peaceful settlement rather than conquest, the ideal of expansionist *jihad* gradually fell into abeyance.

By the eleventh century, Islamic powers were more likely to prosecute internal holy wars against their fellow Muslims, Sunni versus Shi'ite, than they were to turn the ideal of *jihad* outwards towards Christendom. The suggestion that Islam should engage in an unending battle to enlarge its borders and subjugate non-Muslims held little appeal; nor did the idea of unifying in defence of the Islamic faith and its territories. When the First Crusade drove into the Muslim heartlands of the Near East, the ideological impulse of devotional warfare thus lay dormant and deeply submerged within the body of Islam. It would be decades before the threat of Christian holy war was recognised, and the fires of *jihad* were reignited. For now, the crusaders would face an enemy that lacked their own energy and visionary unity.[54]

4

THE FIRST STORM OF WAR

In February 1097 the first wave of the main crusading army took a momentous step in the journey towards Jerusalem. Godfrey of Bouillon led his followers across the Bosphorus Strait and made camp on the northern shores of the Gulf of Nicomedia. The remaining Frankish contingents were to follow in the spring and early summer. Almost one and a half years after Pope Urban's speech at Clermont, with the long march to Constantinople behind them, the First Crusaders had reached the borders of the Muslim world.

In the event, Godfrey met little or no resistance when he crossed over to Asia Minor and, even isolated as he at first was from the rest of the crusade, his army remained largely unmolested. This was a real stroke of luck: in similar circumstances, the People's Crusade had been virtually annihilated. Had the major Muslim ruler in the region, Kilij Arslan, the Seljuq Turkish sultan of Rüm, chosen to pick off the individual contingents of the main crusading army as they landed, the entire Frankish expedition might well have collapsed.[1]

As it was, Kilij Arslan made a disastrous military blunder. Having defeated the People's Crusade with relative ease, he vastly under-estimated the strength of this second wave of crusaders and, rather than deal with them head on, he chose first to resolve a relatively minor territorial dispute far to the east. This would prove a costly error. In the interim, Godfrey and his fellow Latin princes were able to marshal their forces on the mainland of Asia Minor and turn their attention towards the jewel of Kilij Arslan's realm, his capital city, Nicaea.

THE SIEGE OF NICAEA

In early May 1097 about two-thirds of the crusading army set out for Nicaea. The forces led by Godfrey, Robert of Flanders, Hugh of Vermandois, and the southern Italian Normans, currently in the care of Tancred, first congregated at the town of Nicomedia. Here they were joined by Peter the Hermit, beleaguered leader of the People's Crusade, who had been eking out an existence around Constantinople and Bithynia since October 1096. Peter must have been glad to approach Nicaea from the north, rather than retrace his ill-fated steps from Civetot – a group of crusaders who took that route some weeks later were horrified and saddened to discover 'many severed heads and bones of the dead lying on the plains near [the] sea', the unholy graveyard of Peter's followers. Coming from Nicomedia, the main army chose to follow the ancient Roman road running south over the mountains to Nicaea. This route was direct, but heavily overgrown, so 3,000 men were sent ahead to clear the way with axes and swords, and then mark the route with crosses, establishing a well-defined line of communication back towards Constantinople. On 6 May Godfrey and his companions reached Nicaea, but even at this late stage, as the crusaders approached their first Muslim target, they were woefully unprepared for what one contemporary would later call 'the first storm of war'.[2]

Serving the emperor

The crusade was still operating as a rough conglomeration of Latin armies, with little or no central co-ordination, much less organisation.

Godfrey, Hugh, Tancred and Robert of Flanders seem to have moved on Nicaea without establishing a coherent plan of action, and their arrival was badly mistimed. When the city was reached on the 6th, their forces were left camped before it, isolated and inert, for eight dangerous days. It was not until the 14th, by which time Bohemond had arrived to solve the initial logistical problems surrounding the supply of food, that the crusaders moved in to lay siege to Nicaea. Even then they were fighting under strength, and it would be another two weeks before the full complement of the First Crusade's armies was brought to bear. This rather ramshackle, piecemeal deployment was extremely risky. Only Kilij Arslan's continued absence prevented an uncomfortable delay from becoming a potential disaster. The crusaders' lack of co-ordinated action and purposeful leadership was to some extent a symptom of their relationship with Byzantium.[3]

In besieging Nicaea, the crusaders were carrying out the emperor's will. They had come to Constantinople with half-formed ideas of aiding the eastern Churches and marching on Jerusalem, perhaps expecting the emperor himself to take personal command of the expedition. Alexius had other ideas. He certainly wanted to direct and make use of the crusading armies – after all they had come east, at least partially, in response to his call for military aid – and his primary goal was the recovery of Nicaea. The Seljuq capital was far too close to Constantinople for comfort, but the city had stubbornly resisted all of Alexius' attempts to recapture it. Indeed, one Greek source even suggested that 'the emperor, who had thoroughly investigated Nicaea, and on many occasions, judged that it could not possibly be captured'.[4] His plan was to throw his new weapon, the crusading horde, against the city, and then watch what happened from a safe distance. Alexius had absolutely no intention of leading the campaign in person, judging the 'barbarian' Franks to be too unpredictable and suspecting that this weapon might turn on its master. By avoiding direct involvement, Alexius was also able to maintain a thin façade of impartiality, leaving a door open for diplomacy and détente with Kilij Arslan should the siege fail. So it was that Alexius, ever the shrewd and calculating politician, established his camp at Pelekanum, to the west of Nicomedia.

It is true that the emperor put the interests of his empire above those of the crusade, even that he coldly exploited the Franks to further his own ambitions, and, on this basis, most modern historians have painted a picture of immediate tension and distrust when characterising the crusaders' relationship with Byzantium at Nicaea. This image has been shaped by eyewitness sources, who wrote with the benefit of hindsight, knowing how later events would poison relations. In reality, the siege of Nicaea was a largely collaborative venture, in which Latins and Greeks co-operated effectively, and the crusaders willingly fought for the Byzantine Empire. Even though Alexius refused to participate in person, it was of course in his interests to see the crusaders succeed at Nicaea. To this end, he nominated military advisers to support and oversee the Franks. Manuel Boutoumites, one of his most experienced lieutenants, accompanied Godfrey and the first group of crusaders to arrive at Nicaea. Indeed, Manuel was initially granted entry into the city to discuss a negotiated surrender, but, when this fell through, he lent his military expertise to the Latin siege preparations. A few weeks later, a second adviser, Taticius, arrived at the head of 2,000 Byzantine troops, to command the Nicaea campaign. Later he would become Alexius' chief representative among the crusaders. Taticius was an interesting choice; a member of the imperial household and experienced in battle, he was reportedly 'a valiant fighter, a man who kept his head under combat conditions', but he was, at the same time, a eunuch. He had an excellent knowledge of Nicaea's defences, having led the last Greek assault on the city more than a decade earlier. Taticius was a striking figure – born of half-Arab, half-Greek parentage, his nose had been cut off earlier in his military career and he wore a metal replica in its place.

Alexius also took steps to ensure that the crusaders had ready access to food and supplies. On his orders, the poorer Franks were given money and free provisions. Merchant ships were brought from across the Mediterranean to set up markets at the port of Civetot, where corn, meat, wine, barley and oil could be bought, while the traffic along the road back to Nicomedia must have been nearly constant. The Greeks were obviously committed to this complex web of logistical support, because, in spite of the immense size of the crusader army, we hear few reports of severe shortages or starvation. Later sieges would not always be so efficient.[5]

Even with Byzantine support, Nicaea's defences presented a formidable challenge. Today the ancient city has crumbled to become little more than a backwater village. Iznik, as it is now named in modern Turkish, is still surrounded by decrepit fortifications, but its quiet, unassuming pace of life gives little sense of its place in history. It is hard to imagine that this was once one of the great cities of Rome and Byzantium. In 325 CE the first Christian emperor of Rome, Constantine the Great, held a monumental Church council at Nicaea, attended by more than 300 bishops from across the known world, at which the Nicene Creed, which still serves to define the Christian faith, was adopted. When the First Crusade arrived in 1097 Nicaea remained an imposing stronghold. One Frankish eyewitness later recalled:

Nicaea [was] a city well protected by natural terrain and clever fortifications. Its natural defences consisted of a great lake lapping at its walls and a ditch, brimful of runoff water from nearby streams, blocking the entrance on three sides. Skilful men had enclosed Nicaea with such lofty walls that the city feared neither the attack of enemies nor the force of any machine.[6]

Located in a fertile basin, surrounded by hills, Nicaea lies on the eastern shore of the massive Askanian Lake, which stretches to more than forty kilometres in length. To the north, east and south a defensive wall, five kilometres long, enclosed the remaining three sides of the city, reaching to ten metres in height, punctuated by more than a hundred towers, and reinforced by a double ditch. Its capture would be no simple task, but the crusaders had one major advantage – sheer weight of numbers. When the siege began, in mid-May, the Franks were able to blockade only the city's northern and eastern gates, but by early June, with the majority of the crusader forces now assembled, it became possible to encircle Nicaea's land walls.[7]

In command of the masses

This was the first time that the main army of the First Crusade had come together. Franks, Greeks and Muslims alike were awestruck by the spectacle. One Byzantine contemporary described the crusaders as 'a countless multitude of locusts, so great as to resemble clouds and overcast the sun when it flew'. A Latin eyewitness recalled, 'Then the many armies there were united into one, which those who were skilled in reckoning estimate at 600,000 strong for war. Of these there were 100,000 fully armed men [and a mass of] unarmed, that is clerics, monks, women, and little children.'[8]

Medieval writers were notoriously poor judges of manpower, and these figures were probably a gross exaggeration, wild guesses designed to convey the enormous scale of the army. Even so, the First Crusade did represent the largest single mobilisation of European troops in centuries. At our best estimate, some 75,000 Latins gathered at Nicaea, of whom perhaps 7,500 were fully armed, mounted knights and a further 5,000 were infantry. This was, of course, a composite force, one mass made up of many smaller parts. All shared a common faith – Latin Christianity – but in other ways they were quite disparate, drawn from across western Europe, born into diverse political and cultural surroundings. Many had been enemies before the expedition began. They even faced a profound communication barrier: Fulcher of Chartres remarked, 'Who ever heard such a mixture of languages in one army, since there were French, Flemings, Frisians, Gauls, Allobroges, Lotharingians, Allemani, Bavarians, Normans, English, Scots, Aquitanians, Italians, Dacian, Apulians, Iberians, Bretons, Greeks and Armenians? If any Breton or Teuton wished to question me, I could neither understand nor answer.'[9]

To make matters worse, the crusade had no single leader. The pope's legate, or representative, Adhémar of Le Puy, could claim spiritual primacy, but overall strategic command could be contested by up to seven of the most powerful crusading lords, or princes. By the dictates of military logic, this would appear to have been a recipe for disaster. At Nicaea, the crusaders were, for the first time, forced to confront this problem. The Emperor Alexius might be the nominal leader of the campaign, but he had absented himself from the siege and, while his lieutenant Taticius was the official commander-in-chief, in practice he never wielded total power. From Nicaea onwards, the crusaders were forced to feel their way towards an organisational structure, through a process of experimentation and innovation. Within a few weeks they instituted a new decision-making structure – a council of princes – in which the highest echelon of crusade leaders, men such as Raymond of Toulouse and Bohemond of Taranto, met to discuss and agree policy. On the whole, this system was remarkably successful. One of its first pronouncements saw the creation of a common crusader fund through which all plunder could be channelled and redistributed.[10]

It was the council of princes that decided to adopt what might be termed a combined siege strategy to overcome Nicaea's defences. In this method two styles of siege warfare were deployed simultaneously. On the one hand, the Franks sought to blockade the city, cutting it off from the outside world and grinding it into submission through physical and psychological isolation, in a close-encirclement siege. At the same time, the crusaders actively pursued the more aggressive strategy of an assault siege. This involved building various machines of war – catapults, battering-rams, bombardment screens – which might allow them literally to bludgeon their way into the city through direct attack. On 14 May 1097 Bohemond and the southern Italian Normans made camp before Nicaea's northern gate, while Godfrey of Bouillon and Robert of Flanders were deployed to the east, and work began on a series of siege engines.[11]

The crusaders' arrival terrified the Turkish garrison of Nicaea. The city would probably have been manned by no more than a few thousand troops, each aware that Nicaea offered irresistibly ripe pickings to the massive Frankish horde. Kilij Arslan's capital stood not only as a bastion of the sultan's military and political pride, it was also home to his treasury. Under these circumstances, the garrison rightly judged that the crusaders would throw every resource into the siege. Against such odds, the Turks could not hope to prevail, and so in the second week of May they came close to agreeing terms with Manuel Boutoumites, the emperor's envoy. But, suddenly, they changed their minds and expelled him from the city.[12]

The first challenge

It was only on 15 May that the Franks found out why, when two Turkish spies were caught in the Frankish camp masquerading as Christians. One was killed during capture, but the other was immediately taken for interrogation. Threatened with torture and death, he quickly confessed everything. Kilij Arslan had returned from the east. Having finally realised how dangerous the crusaders might be, he had gathered a large army from across the sultanate of Rüm, and was even now camped in the steep hills to the south of the city, planning a counterattack the very next day. Contact had already been established with the Turks in Nicaea – hence their change of heart – and these two spies had been sent to observe the Frankish army and then carry final battle instructions to the garrison. Kilij Arslan's plan was to charge out of the southern hills at the third hour after dawn, enter Nicaea through the unblockaded south gate, regroup and then launch an immediate combined counterattack. Having told this story, the Turkish spy pleaded for his life, weeping, begging and even offering to convert to Christianity should he be spared, and eventually the princes took pity on him.[13]

The princes reacted quickly to these shocking revelations. They knew that Raymond of Toulouse and the Provençal army were already en route to Nicaea, and were, at that very moment, perhaps less than a day's march away to the north, along the road from Nicomedia. As dusk approached, messengers were dispatched urging haste, and the Frankish host kept nervous watch through the night. Finally, at dawn on 16 May, Raymond's men appeared out of the north. The crusaders' careful preparation of the old Roman road had paid off – news had reached the Provençals quickly and they had then been able to march along the clearly marked route through the night. In fact, Raymond of Toulouse arrived just in time. His army was still in process of setting up camp before Nicaea's southern gate when, just as the spy had predicted, Kilij Arslan's forces came pouring out of the hills.

He had come prepared for victory – his men carried ropes with which to bind the crusaders once they were taken captive – but, even without the Provençal reinforcements, Kilij Arslan would have been hard pressed to overcome the massive Latin army. With Nicaea's southern gate blocked, his troops were both outnumbered and isolated. He led an archetypal Seljuq Turkish army: thousands of lightly mounted, fast-moving archers, armed with powerful bone-and-horn composite bows. Faced with staunch resistance from the Provençals led by Raymond and Baldwin of Boulogne, hemmed in by the lake to the west and struck in the flank by Godfrey's and Bohemond's fierce cavalry charge from the east, the Turkish attack soon faltered. Realising that he was hopelessly outnumbered, Kilij Arslan fled the field south. It would be his only attempt to break the siege of Nicaea. In the days that followed, the renegade Turkish spy, whose predictions had proved to be accurate, went through a ritual of conversion and became a regular guest of the Frankish princes, to whom he was an intriguing curiosity. Soon his guards became relaxed in his company and in one careless moment took their eyes off him. Instantly seizing the opportunity, he 'flew across the city moat with a nimble-footed leap' and was soon pulled over the walls on a rope.[14]

In spite of this minor betrayal, the crusaders' first battle with a Muslim force had been a resounding success. Even Anna Comnena, not usually given to praising the Franks, described it as 'a glorious victory'. In truth, although the crusader defence had been well co-ordinated, Kilij Arslan escaped with most of his army intact. The real damage was done to his military prestige and the morale of Nicaea's garrison. In the aftermath of the fighting, 'the Christians cut off the heads of the dead and wounded and as a sign of victory they brought them back to their tents with them tied to the girths of their saddles'. Some were stuck on the ends of spears and paraded before the city walls, others were actually catapulted into the city 'in order to cause more terror among the Turkish garrison'. One Latin contemporary even suggested that a thousand Turkish heads had been sent to Alexius as a sign of victory.

Any medieval army knew the profound significance of morale amid the slow grind of siege warfare, and exchanges of horrific acts of brutality and barbarism were commonplace. For its part, the Turkish garrison soon retaliated, adopting a rather macabre tactic. The crusaders began to lead direct assaults upon the city and inevitably sustained some losses. One Latin eyewitness was disgusted by the Turks' treatment of these dead: 'Truly, you would have grieved and sighed with compassion, to see them let down iron hooks, which they lowered and raised by ropes, and seize the body of any of our men that they had slaughtered in some way near the wall. None of our men dared, nor could, take the body from them.' These corpses were robbed and then hung from the walls to rot, so as 'to offend the Christians by this inhuman conduct'.[15]

Closing in

With the first threat from Kilij Arslan repulsed, the crusaders sought to prosecute a direct assault. This would be a dangerous and exhausting process for defender and aggressor alike, and we hear that in the midst of the fighting, 'often, some of the Turks, often, some of the Franks, struck by arrows or by stones, died'. When early attempts to storm Nicaea's defences with ladders had failed, the crusaders concentrated their efforts almost exclusively upon creating a physical breach in the city's walls. This could be achieved through a variety of means. The safest, but technologically most advanced, was bombardment from a distance. The Franks built some stone-throwing machines, known as *petraria* or *mangonella*, which propelled missiles through the use of torsion or counterweights. Powerful machines could hurl massive rocks against their target, eventually causing walls to buckle and collapse, but at Nicaea the crusaders lacked the skills and craftsmen to build engines massive enough to damage the city's stout walls. Their bombardment was designed, instead, to harass the Turkish garrison and provide covering fire, under which they could employ a second technique.

If a besieging army could not topple walls from a safe distance, then the only alternative was to get in close and undermine the defences by hand. Just approaching the walls was, however, a lethal affair. The Turkish garrison had *ballistae* – giant crossbow-like devices used to hurl stones – and archers with which to defend their city: 'The *ballistae* of [Nicaea's] towers were so alternately faced that no one could move near them without peril, and if anyone wished to move forward, he could do no harm because he could easily be struck down from the top of a tower.' One crusader knight, Baldwin of Calderun, who had made many 'daring and rash' attempts to assault the city, 'breathed his last when his neck was broken by the blow of a hurled stone'. Another, Baldwin of Ganz, died during 'a careless rush at the city, his head pierced by an arrow'. If a crusader did, somehow, manage to reach the foot of the walls alive, he then faced an onslaught from above, as defenders atop the battlements gleefully rained rocks and a burning mixture of grease, oil and pitch down upon his head.[16]

The Franks experimented with a range of devices to combat these problems of direct assault, with varying degrees of success. Two prominent Latin lords, Henry of Esch, a member of Godfrey's contingent, and the German Count Hartmann of Dillingen, who had participated in the Jewish pogrom at Mainz, approached the challenge of this first crusader siege with enthusiasm. They pooled their resources and built what one contemporary called a *vulpus* or fox, to their own design and with their own money. This was apparently some form of bombardment screen, constructed of oak beams, under which infantry troops could advance on the walls, protected from Turkish missiles. Henry and Hartmann shrewdly decided to sit out the first test run of this contraption, and had to look on in horror as twenty of their men were crushed to death when 'the beams, the uprights and all the bindings came to pieces' and the *vulpus* collapsed at the foot of the walls.[17]

The Provençals adopted a more professional approach. Raymond of Toulouse employed a master craftsman to design and build a *testudo* or tortoise, a much sturdier, sloping-roofed bombardment screen. Under this protection, southern French crusaders were dispatched to undermine a tower on Nicaea's southern walls. One eyewitness described how, when they reached the fortification, 'sappers dug down to the foundations of the wall and inserted beams and pieces of wood, to which they set fire'. If carried out correctly, the siege technique they were attempting – that of sapping – could be extremely effective. The idea was to dig a tunnel beneath a section of wall, carefully buttressing the excavation with wooden supports as one went along. Once complete, the void was packed full of branches and kindling, set alight and left to collapse, thus bringing down the wall above it. Raymond's sappers managed to bring down a small section of one tower as night fell on around 1 June, but the Turkish garrison worked through the night to rebuild the defences so that by daybreak 'there was no chance of defeating them at that point'.[18]

In the end, the crusaders' best efforts at assault were thwarted by Nicaea's almost impregnable fortifications and the sheer energy and ferocity of the Turkish defence. Even Raymond of Aguilers, a chaplain in the Provençal army, was forced to admit that the Muslim garrison had made a 'courageous' effort. We hear, for example, of one unnamed Turkish soldier who went berserk and continued fighting, peppered with twenty crusader arrows. Even after 3 June 1097, when the Latin army was further strengthened by the arrival of the northern French, under Stephen, count of Blois, and Robert, count of Flanders, the city still refused to fall.[19]

By the second week of June, the crusaders realised that a new strategy was needed. Up to this point they had encircled Nicaea's three landward walls, but the fourth, westward face of the city, on the banks of the great Askanian Lake, lay open and unblockaded. The sheer size of this lake meant that its banks could not be effectively patrolled, and it became apparent that Turkish boats were bringing all manner of supplies into Nicaea without fear of attack. If this situation persisted and the city's walls held, Nicaea's garrison might realistically hope to hold out indefinitely. Around 10 June, the crusader princes met in council to discuss this problem, and within hours a messenger had been sent to the Emperor Alexius, carrying an audacious proposal. Control had to be taken of the Askanian Lake, but no navigable river offered ships access to its waters. The princes' solution sounded simple: if vessels could not be sailed to the lake, they would have to be carried. In practice, of course, the process of portaging large sailing boats almost thirty kilometres from the coast at Civetot to the shores of the Askanian Lake was no mean feat. Alexius agreed to supply the boats, under the command of Manuel Boutoumites and manned by a force of Turcopoles – well-armed Byzantine mercenaries of half-Greek, half-Turkish stock. Special oxen-drawn carts were constructed to bear this strange cargo through the hills of Bithynia. Late in the day of 17 June they reached the lake, but waited until the following dawn to set sail so that a combined lake- and land-based attack could be launched on Nicaea. The plan was to terrify the Turkish garrison into submission, driving home their isolation and the utter hopelessness of continued resistance. To this end, Alexius equipped the small Greek flotilla with more standards than were usual – so that the boats might appear more numerous than they really were – and a selection of trumpets and drums with which to create an intimidating racket. One Latin eyewitness described the scene:

At daybreak there were the boats, all in very good order, sailing across the lake towards the city. The Turks, seeing them, were surprised and did not know if it was their own fleet or that of the emperor, but when they realised it was the emperor's they were afraid almost to death, and began to wail and lament, while the Franks rejoiced and gave glory to God.[20]

The shock broke the Turkish garrison's will, and within hours they were suing for peace. After holding out for five weeks, Nicaea capitulated on 18 June. It was, however, the emperor's men, Manuel Boutoumites and Taticius, who actually took surrender of the city and raised the imperial standard. After all their efforts, the crusaders were left waiting outside the walls. Byzantine Turcopoles were set to guard the city's treasury and the crusaders were denied any chance of plunder. It was a precarious moment for Alexius' envoys: they may have had nominal authority over the campaign, but they were outnumbered both by the barely subdued Turkish garrison inside the city and by the acquisitive Frankish horde without. Had either side chosen to rebel, the Greeks would have been annihilated. As it was, the crusader princes kept their promise to return the city to the emperor, and the leading members of the Turkish garrison were quickly ferried out in small, manageable groups to Constantinople. There were some complaints among the Latin rank and file, worried that the captured Turks would soon be ransomed and thus free to fight the crusaders on another day, but even these were quickly silenced by the emperor's extravagant largesse. He knew only too well how to keep this 'mercenary' crusading army under control. One Frank recalled that, 'because he kept all [the money from Nicaea], the emperor gave some of his own gold and silver and mantles to our nobles; he also distributed some of his copper coins, which they call *tarantarons*, to the footsoldiers'.[21]

The fall of Nicaea was a product of the successful policy of close co-operation between the crusaders and Byzantium. The Franks would probably have enjoyed little success without Greek aid, while Alexius had needed the might of the Latin army to overcome Kilij

Arslan's capital.* One contemporary, reflecting upon the siege, wrote, 'Now that the storm of war had thus abated . . . the army of the living God spent the day in great rejoicing and exultation right there in the camp, because everything so far had gone well for them'. Their success had, however, been bought at a price. Many crusaders died in battle or from illness during the campaign. An eyewitness in Bohemond's army recalled that 'many of our men suffered martyrdom there and gave up their blessed souls to God with joy and gladness, and many poor starved to death for the Name of Christ. All these entered Heaven in triumph, wearing the robe of martyrdom.' Even at this early stage in the expedition to Jerusalem it seems that the crusaders believed that fighting and dying in the name of God cleansed them of sin and brought the gift of everlasting life.[22]

INTO ANATOLIA

Since passing through Constantinople, the leaders of the First Crusade had, in effect, been working for the emperor, fighting on the eastern border of Byzantium to recover Greek territory. With Alexius'

---

*There were other benefits from Nicaea's fall. Scores of Latin prisoners who had been held in the city were released. Among them was an unnamed nun who had followed Peter the Hermit to Asia Minor. She had been captured by a Turk and repeatedly raped by him and a number of other men. Upon her release, she recognised Henry of Esch among the crusader hosts and begged him to help her find some way to purify her soul. At last Bishop Adhémar himself prescribed a suitable penance: 'She was granted forgiveness for her unlawful liaison with the Turk, and her repentance was made less burdensome because she had endured this hideous defilement by wicked and villainous men under duress and unwillingly.' Thus it is clear that, in the eyes of the Church, by being raped she had committed a sin. But this was not the end of the story. According to one contemporary, the nun ran back to her Turkish captor on the very next day. The whole tale may well be a product of Albert of Aachen's imagination, and the nun's final change of heart, which he attributes to the innate and overwhelming lustfulness of females, seems particularly unlikely – how was it that her Nicaean 'lover' was not himself now a captive? – but it does serve as a vivid illustration of medieval preconceptions about women and sex.

primary objective achieved – the recapture of Nicaea – one question remained: what would the crusaders do now?

With this in mind, on 22 June the emperor called the Frankish princes to his camp at Pelekanum to discuss their plans. With the exception of Raymond of Toulouse and Stephen of Blois, who remained behind to protect the Latin camp, the cream of crusader aristocracy attended. By this point, most of the Frankish host shared one deep-held and compelling ambition – to march on Jerusalem and recover the Holy City for Christendom. Alexius probably had no idea what this 'barbarian' horde was capable of achieving. So far they had served his purposes well and, for the time being at least, there was no reason for him not to support their expedition. Once again, he seems to have offered the princes valuable advice on the political and strategic realities of the world they were planning to traverse. From this point on, we know that the crusaders discussed their next major goal on the road to Palestine – the vast, ancient city of Antioch, on the border between Asia Minor and Syria. They also followed Alexius' advice and dispatched envoys by ship to the Fatimid caliphate in Egypt, to discuss a possible treaty.[23]

There was no question in the emperor's mind that the crusaders would remain his servants. A member of Stephen of Blois' contingent pointed out that the Franks left Nicaea only 'once they had received permission from the emperor to depart'. Alexius also took the opportunity presented by the gathering at Pelekanum to reinforce his primacy. The oaths of allegiance given to him at Constantinople were restated, and any members of the crusader nobility who had managed to slip through the net, such as Tancred and Baldwin of Boulogne, were now pressed into pledging their obedience. Alexius' strategy was to assist the crusaders' cause and, as they marched across Asia Minor, follow in their wake mopping up any territory they conquered. To this end, he ordered Taticius, and the troops he had led to Nicaea, to accompany the Latin host. According to a Greek contemporary, Taticius' duty was 'to help and protect them on all occasions and also to take over from them any cities they captured, if indeed God granted them that favour'. Even at this stage, it is very unlikely that the emperor offered any firm commitment to lead Byzantine reinforcements himself in support of the crusade, although the Franks do seem to have been expecting to be joined by a large Greek army at some later date.[24]

Alexius' plan for controlled, constructive exploitation of the First Crusade had one major flaw. His power and influence over the expedition were almost absolute as it passed through Constantinople and besieged Nicaea, but, with every Frankish step into Anatolia (Central Asia Minor) and beyond, the crusade passed further out of the orbit of Byzantine authority. The spell of co-operation and subservience would continue to hold for months to come, but the level of collaboration experienced at Nicaea was never again repeated.

The Battle of Dorylaeum

The First Crusade left Nicaea in the last week of June 1097. By 29 June the entire army had assembled at a staging post one day's march to the south, at a bridge over the Göksu river. Its next major target was Antioch, hundreds of kilometres to the east, but to reach this the expedition would have to overcome two challenges. The first was the enormous size of the crusade. An army of roughly 70,000 people might take up to three days to march past a single point. Moving as one massed force would be incredibly unwieldy and place intense pressure on local resources, given that the Franks intended to continue their practice of foraging for food as they went. Logic dictated that the expedition should break into smaller contingents, travelling just as it had en route to Constantinople. But this approach had inherent dangers. The threat posed by the Seljuq Turks of Asia Minor may have been beaten back at Nicaea, but it had not been extinguished. The crusaders must have suspected that Kilij Arslan would, at some point, attempt a counterattack. By splintering into smaller armies the Latin host would lose its overwhelming numerical advantage.

Faced with a difficult choice, the princes elected to divide their forces in two, but maintain relatively close contact during the march. On 29 June, Bohemond's southern Italian Normans and Robert of Normandy's army crossed the Göksu, trailed at some distance by Godfrey of Bouillon, Robert of Flanders, Hugh of France and the southern French. They intended to rendezvous some four days' march to the south-east, at Dorylaeum, an abandoned Byzantine military camp.[25]

This was just the opportunity that Kilij Arslan had been waiting for. After his humiliating defeat at Nicaea on 16 May, he realised that every scrap of available manpower would be needed were he to have any hope of defeating the huge Frankish army. Putting aside past quarrels, he negotiated a pact with the Danishmendid Turks of northern and eastern Asia Minor and set off to intercept the crusaders. Even with this new larger army, he could ill afford to risk a full-scale battle against the massed Latin ranks. Instead, he hoped to pick off smaller portions of their army through ambush and guerrilla warfare. On the morning of 1 July 1097 he took his chance.

The first two days of Bohemond's and Robert of Normandy's march towards Dorylaeum had passed without incident. Scouts seem to have reported the presence of a Turkish force in the region as night fell on 30 June, but the princes must have judged this to be a small raiding party, because they took no steps to notify the second crusader force. This proved to be a fateful decision.[26]

A few hours after dawn on the following day, having just negotiated a small river crossing, the first crusader army reached an area of open ground at the junction of two valleys. Suddenly, a mass of Turkish horsemen appeared. Two Frankish eyewitnesses estimated their number at 360,000, but this is probably another wild exaggeration. Even so, the size of Kilij Arslan's force may have equalled or even exceeded that of this half of the crusading host. The Franks faced an appalling predicament: isolated and exposed, they were about to have their first, terrifying taste of Turkish horsemen in full flight.[27]

The crusaders were horrified. One member of Bohemond's army

recalled how the 'Turks began, all at once, to howl and gabble and shout, saying with loud voices in their own language some devilish word which I do not understand . . . screaming like demons'. Bearing down upon the stunned Latins was the very nightmare of which the Emperor Alexius had warned back in Constantinople – a rampaging pack of highly manoeuvrable mounted archers, itching to exploit the open ground, wheeling their nimble-footed horses in an encircling torrent, unleashing a deadly 'cloud of arrows'.

In a moment of extraordinary courage and composure, Bohemond and Robert kept their heads and stayed the pulse of panic rushing through their forces. They realised that, in the face of such an enemy, only steadfast unity offered any hope of survival – if the crusaders broke formation or sought to escape they would be mown down without mercy. As the Turks swarmed towards them, the princes sent an urgent appeal for reinforcement to the second crusader army and ordered a makeshift camp to be set up beside a nearby marsh. Into its centre were placed all the army's heavy gear, horses, women, children and other non-combatants, while the knights and infantry were deployed in a tight-knit defensive formation. One eyewitness remembered how 'after we had set ourselves in order the Turks came upon us from all sides, skirmishing, throwing darts and javelins and shooting arrows from an astonishing range'. In the race to establish a secure perimeter many of the Frankish peasants following the army were caught in the open and were soon butchered. Taking pity on them, one Frankish knight, Robert of Paris, broke ranks and rushed out to help them, but within seconds he was struck by an arrow and decapitated.

The princes' plan was to hold fast in close formation, stubbornly refusing to be drawn into open battle, while relying upon weight of numbers and superior armour to survive. They were playing a desperate waiting game, always hoping for the second army's arrival. Ranged against them was a seemingly endless, writhing multitude of Turks. One eyewitness believed that 'nearly all the mountains and hills and valleys, and all the flat country within and without the hills, were covered with this accursed folk'. To strengthen their resolve in the face of this swarm, the crusaders passed a morale-boosting phrase down the line: 'Stand fast together, trusting in Christ and the victory of the Holy Cross. Today may we all gain much booty.' At the same time, priests moved up and down the lines offering prayers of encouragement and receiving confessions, while women distributed water to stave off the day's heat.[28]

Inside the camp, many non-combatants were transfixed with fear. One clergyman in the crowd recounted how 'we were all huddled together like sheep in a fold, trembling and frightened, surrounded on all sides by enemies so that we could not turn in any direction'. At one point, some Turks actually broke through:

> The Turks burst into the camp in strength, striking with arrows from their horn bows, killing pilgrim foot-soldiers, girls, women, infants and old people, sparing no one on grounds of age. Stunned and terrified by the cruelty of this most hideous killing, girls who were delicate and very nobly born were hastening to get themselves dressed up, offering themselves to the Turks, so that at least, roused and appeased by love of their beauty, the Turks might learn to pity their prisoners.[29]

But still the crusader line held. Through five dreadful hours the Franks waited, held together by a potent mixture of faith, fear and fortitude, inspired by Bohemond's and Robert's immutable stance. This was an extraordinary feat of martial discipline, the product of inspired generalship. In the medieval age, successful military leaders could not simply depend upon strategic awareness or logistical skill. Unable to communicate detailed orders in the midst of fighting, a general was required to command by example, controlling his troops through sheer force of personality. In this context, Bohemond's and Robert's achievements in the battle near Dorylaeum were of the highest order.

At last, shortly after midday, the second crusader army arrived.

Godfrey, Hugh, Raymond of Toulouse and Adhémar of Le Puy raced to the battlefield, each leading a force of mounted knights. Adhémar sought to outflank the Turks, while the others joined forces with Bohemond and Robert to unleash a cavalry charge. There was no time to organise a well-ordered counterattack, but the Turks put up little resistance. They had harried the first Latin army through the day, enjoying little success. The prospect of facing the full force of a united crusader attack proved unpalatable. Having lost the chance to wipe out an isolated section of the Frankish host, Kilij Arslan realised he was beaten and fled the field. A member of Bohemond's army joyfully recalled their defeat: '[The Turks] fled very fast to their camp, but they were not allowed to stay there long, so they continued their flight and we pursued them, killing them, for a whole day, and we took much booty, gold, silver, horses, asses, camels, oxen, sheep and many other things.'[30]

The First Crusaders had had a close brush with disaster, but in the end they won a famous victory. One Syrian Muslim, writing in the mid-twelfth century, recalled that 'when news was received of this shameful calamity to the cause of Islam the anxiety of the people became acute and their fear and alarm increased'. Kilij Arslan's will, and that of the Seljuq Turks of Asia Minor, had been broken and from now on they largely avoided the Franks. The sultan himself fled eastwards, leaving a trail of destruction in his wake, having adopted a scorched-earth policy to deny the Latins access to crops and other supplies.

The battle near Dorylaeum was a bloody affair, leaving some 3,000 Muslims and 4,000 Christians dead, including William Marchisus, Tancred's brother. The crusaders spent three days camped by the battlefield, burying their dead and recovering their strength. Those that survived now had a bitter respect for Turkish warriors. One eyewitness remarked: 'What man, however experienced and learned, would dare to write of the skill and prowess and courage of the Turks . . . you could not find stronger or braver or more skilful soldiers.'[31]

Across the wasteland

After Dorylaeum the crusaders faced a different type of enemy. They now set out to cross the arid plains of Anatolia, where the ravages of Kilij Arslan's retreat and the blistering heat of mid-summer left 'a land which was deserted, waterless and uninhabitable'. One of Bohemond's followers wrote:

> We barely emerged or escaped alive [from this region], for we suffered greatly from hunger and thirst, and found nothing to eat except prickly plants which we gathered and rubbed between our hands. On such food we survived wretchedly enough, but we lost most of our horses, so that many of our knights had to go on as foot-soldiers, and for lack of horses we had to use oxen as mounts, and our great need compelled us to use goats, sheep and dogs as beasts of burden.[32]

Another contemporary recalled one day upon which the lack of water became so acute that:

> Overwhelmed by the anguish of thirst, as many as five hundred people died. In addition horses, donkeys, camels, mules, oxen and many animals suffered the same death from very painful thirst. Many men, growing weak from the exertion and the heat, gaping with open mouths and throats, were trying to catch the thinnest mist to cure their thirst. Now, while everyone was thus suffering with this plague, the river they had longed and searched for was discovered. As they hurried towards it each was keen because of excessive longing to arrive first amongst the great throng. They set no limit to their drinking, until very many who had been weakened, as many men as beasts of burden, died from drinking too much.[33]

It may seem remarkable that the deaths of animals were described in almost equal detail to those of men, but all the contemporary sources share this obsession with horses and pack animals. The crusading army relied upon the latter to transport equipment and supplies, while knights depended upon their mounts in battle. In the past, modern historians have emphasised the military advantage enjoyed by crusader knights because of their larger, stronger, European horses, but, in truth, most of these had died even before Syria was reached. Although a few of the richer princes were able to buy horses during the journey, much of the Frankish army was gradually transformed into an infantry-based force and, as the expedition progressed, the Latin cavalry became a less decisive weapon.[34]

IN SEARCH OF ALLIES

In early August the First Crusaders reached the region of Pisidia and, relieved to find 'a fertile country, full of good and delicious things to eat and all sorts of provisions', they stopped briefly to recover their strength. Some of the princes decided to engage in the preferred aristocratic pastime of the age, hunting. Unfortunately, in the midst of the chase, Godfrey of Bouillon was attacked by a savage bear and badly mauled. It was some time before he returned to full health.

The Franks advanced on Iconium, a well-fortified centre of Seljuq power, but by the time they arrived, in mid-August, the Turks had fled, and the crusade passed through the city without incident. By the end of the month, the expedition had reached Heraclea, where the Turkish garrison put up a brief, half-hearted defence before retreating. With the Seljuq overlords of Asia Minor on the run, the First Crusaders were now able to make contact with the region's indigenous population.[35]

Oriental Christians had been living in Asia Minor for centuries, ruled by the Greeks and, more recently, by the Muslim Turks. By the late summer of 1097, the crusade stood on the borders of a land inhabited by Armenians. Proud, fiercely independent Christians, they had no love of Seljuq domination, nor any burning desire to be reabsorbed by Byzantium. Some Armenian nobles had managed to hold on to their territories, surviving as client rulers to the Turks, feeding off the rising tide of discord as the edifice of Seljuq power in Baghdad crumbled. Others lived under direct Muslim rule, barely tolerating the presence of Turkish garrisons, eagerly awaiting an opportunity for freedom. The coming of the crusade wiped away the old order, offering Armenian and Latin alike the chance to benefit from co-operation and alliance.[36]

The Cilician expedition

At Heraclea the First Crusade faced a choice of routes onward through Armenian territory and into Syria. To the south and east the road led through the narrow defile of the Cilician Gates, across the fertile plains of Cilicia itself and then over the Belen Pass – a natural break in the Amanus mountains – to Antioch. This was the shortest, most direct path, but crossed two small passes that might easily be blocked by Muslim defenders. The alternative road led north through Cappadocia and then east, circling the formidable Anti-Taurus, a large craggy range of mountains. The main body of the crusading army chose to follow this longer route, while a small expedition, headed by two lesser-known princes – Baldwin of Boulogne, the brother of Godfrey of Bouillon, and Bohemond's nephew, Tancred – headed into Cilicia. This approach has long been misrepresented by modern historians, who argued that the northern route was adopted only because it traversed easier ground, and that Baldwin's and Tancred's sortie was simply a self-serving treasure hunt.

In fact, the Franks were following a more carefully conceived policy. The crusade was now but a short distance from the great city of Antioch. It would have to be taken if the expedition was to have any hope of reaching Palestine, and the princes must have known that this might require a long and exhausting siege. The strategy they pursued after Heraclea was shaped by the need to prepare for this Antiochene

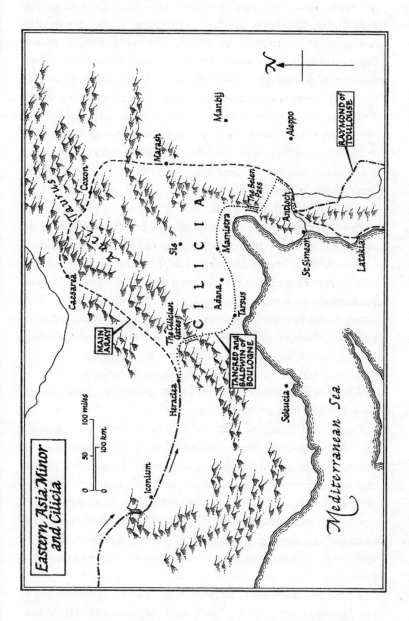

Eastern Asia Minor and Cilicia

Mediterranean Sea

MAIN ARMY

TANCRED and BALDWIN OF BOULOGNE

RAYMOND OF TOULOUSE

Taurus

Coxon

Marash

Manbij

Aleppo

Caesarea

Sis

Mamistra

The Belen Pass

Antioch

The Cilician Gates

Adana

Tarsus

St Simeon

Latakia

Heraclea

CILICIA

Seleucia

Iconium

0   50   100 miles

0   100 km.

campaign. By approaching Syria from two directions, in a pincer movement, the crusaders could establish contact with the Armenians of Cappadocia and Cilicia. The Franks might then aid their Christian brethren and establish an extremely useful network of alliances and foraging centres with which to supply the push into Syria. The princes were also expecting to be reinforced both by Byzantine troops and by later waves of crusaders, and the Cilician expedition would serve to secure the fastest road to Antioch.

Baldwin's and Tancred's expedition was not just an avaricious, independent adventure. Their strike south-east into Cilicia in mid-September 1097 was a deliberate and purposeful ploy, sponsored by the crusade leadership. Baldwin's and Tancred's selection as leaders of this venture depended in part upon their prominent familial connections, but their personal qualities must also have been a factor. Each man came from an eminent background and possessed ample military experience but, so far, the careers of both had been eclipsed by their more famous relatives: Godfrey and Bohemond. Baldwin and Tancred were profoundly ambitious men. Energetic, wily and skilful, they marched into Cilicia at the princes' bidding, all the while hoping that the expedition might catapult them to a new level of power and influence. The crusade's leaders may have intended this to be a closely co-operative mission, but the protagonists' acquisitive aspirations and fiery characters soon led to conflict.[37]

Baldwin of Boulogne set out with around 300–500 troops, including some prominent members of Godfrey's contingent, such as Reinhard of Toul and Baldwin of Le Bourcq. Tancred left with a smaller force, perhaps 100–200 strong and including his brother-in-law, Richard of Salerno. But, perhaps because he also travelled in the company of an Armenian guide, it was his group that found the fastest route through the unguarded Cilician Gates and beyond. Tancred was thus the first to arrive at Tarsus, a walled town to the south of the pass.[38]

Situated on the main route in and out of Cilicia and possessing a fine Mediterranean harbour, Tarsus was a natural centre of trade and commerce. Its ancient history already stretched back across 2,500 years when the crusaders arrived. Alexander the Great stopped here to swim in the River Cydnus, upon the banks of which Tarsus stood, during his all-conquering march into the Orient. In the first century BC, under the Romans, the town became the capital of Cilicia and its schools of philosophy achieved an international reputation. It was in Tarsus that Mark Antony first met Cleopatra, and later, one of its natives, St Paul the apostle, became a founding father of Christianity. But the inexorable passage of the ages undermined Tarsus' greatness. Over the centuries sedimentation gradually moved the Mediterranean coastline towards the south, and as town and port were separated trade faltered and Tarsus drifted into obscurity. Today, lying fifteen kilometres from the sea, the small town reveals little of its past. A stone archway – Cleopatra's Gate – still stands, commemorating her majestic arrival, but even this was built after the event as a tourist attraction in the second century CE. Local Turks have given it the less reverential nickname of 'The Bitch's Gate'.

In the eleventh century, however, Tarsus retained much of its classical glory and its pre-eminent status upon the Cilician plain was intact. Tancred approached this illustrious settlement on 21 September 1097. Its Turkish garrison raced out to do battle, but they were easily rattled and soon retreated back into Tarsus. The Franks quickly established a loose cordon around the town, and Tancred put on an elaborate show of preparing for the coming conflict, taunting the garrison, warning that his was but the vanguard of the crusading army, and that soon the great Bohemond would arrive. Tancred's crafty tactics of intimidation paid off. That night many of the Turks fled, and, in the morning, what remained of the garrison sought terms of surrender. Tancred's banner was soon raised on top of Tarsus' citadel, the mark of his right of possession, and, although his troops had not yet gained entry to the town, the first foray of his expedition seemed set to be a marked success.

Towards the end of that day, Baldwin of Boulogne arrived. At first both he and Tancred were relieved, each having taken the other to be a Turkish force, and they settled down to share a hearty feast beneath Tarsus' walls. By the following morning, however, a seed of envy had begun to grow in Baldwin's mind. Tancred may have been willing to offer his comrade a small portion of the treasures to be had from Tarsus, but he refused Baldwin's demand for an equal share. Both men had reasonable grounds for dispute: Tancred's force alone had orchestrated the town's surrender and his banner now flew, clear for all to see, marking, in accordance with western custom, his legal right to hold Tarsus unchallenged; for his part, Baldwin argued that they had begun the Cilician expedition as a co-operative venture and thus all spoils should be divided evenly.

Tancred had the stronger claim, but he was actually in quite a weak position. He was heavily outnumbered, as Baldwin had arrived with a force that was perhaps double the size of his own. Tancred had also failed to get a single crusader within Tarsus' walls. Sensing an opening, Baldwin arranged a secret parley with the Turks at which he put his case through an interpreter, skilfully weaving a web of persuasion around the garrison's hopes and fears. Tancred may, he argued, have the support of Bohemond, but he, Baldwin, was brother to Godfrey of Bouillon, the mightiest of all crusaders, who would surely trample Tarsus underfoot, obliterating all within its walls, should the town remain in Tancred's hands. The Turks' minds were soon turned: Tancred's banner was torn down, thrown into a nearby marsh and replaced by that of Baldwin.

When he saw Baldwin's banner flying above the town, Tancred realised that he had been outplayed. The insult to his pride was considerable, and a less calculating man might well have flown into a rage, but Tancred knew that any attempt to challenge Baldwin in combat would probably end in disaster. Within hours he had gathered together his troops and ridden off to the east.

Baldwin may have seen off his rival, but he had yet to assert full control over Tarsus. At first he was granted access to only two of the town's towers while the delicate negotiations surrounding the surrender were finalised. Baldwin was in no position to force the matter – his own army was too small to give him unquestionable military superiority, and the town's Armenian populace had not yet overcome their fear of the Turkish garrison.

Then, as day faded on 24 October, a force arrived at Tarsus. Some 300 southern Italian Normans, members of Bohemond's contingent, had been sent south from the main host to reinforce Tancred's group. Tired and hungry, they begged Baldwin to grant them shelter within the town, but for the moment he refused, fearing his position would be destabilised. This decision would have bloody consequences. In the dead of night, as Bohemond's men lay sleeping in the fields surrounding Tarsus, the bulk of the Turkish garrison managed to slip, unseen, out of the city. There they 'suddenly fell upon the Christian men who had surrendered their tired limbs to sleep . . . beheading some, slaughtering others, piercing others through with arrows, leaving [few] alive'. It must have been a swift but vicious assault, because no alarm was raised, and, with their grisly work done, the Turks raced off into the darkness.

With the coming of dawn, the atrocity was discovered and Tarsus thrown into chaos. Baldwin's enraged followers went on the rampage, butchering all remnants of the Turkish garrison. A wild rumour swept through the town that Baldwin was in some way implicated in the affair, and, fearing for his life, he locked himself in a tower and waited for the storm of vengeance to subside. He eventually convinced his men of his innocence and regained control of Tarsus, but the accusation of murder stained his reputation. Over the next week the town was combed for booty, although Armenian property was probably left untouched, and a sizeable Frankish garrison was installed. With Tarsus safeguarded, Baldwin and his remaining men set off east.[39]

Tancred had, meanwhile, found a new ally. Soon after leaving Tarsus he arrived at Adana. Today this bustling city dominates the entire Cilician region, but in 1098 it was just a small fortress town, inferior to Tarsus in both size and status. Adana had just succeeded in overthrowing its Turkish garrison in a brutal coup, and so Tancred found himself being warmly greeted by its new Armenian ruler, Oshin. This may have been something of a disappointment. Having played no part in Adana's liberation, Tancred was in no position to lay claim to the town. Unless he was prepared to take up arms against his Christian brethren, he and his men would once again be denied the rights of conquest and plunder. Oshin, himself a canny and ambitious noble, sensed that there might be a problem and quickly offered a solution. After becoming Tancred's client and ally, he would lead the Franks to another rich and prosperous town – Mamistra – which, Oshin promised, was weakly defended. This astute deflection of interest forestalled any conflict, and the friendship was sealed when Tancred's small army was reinforced with 200 Armenians.[40]

In the last days of September Tancred duly marched on Mamistra, a thriving commercial centre on the banks of the Pyramus river. Oshin's predictions proved accurate, and its Turkish garrison, terrified by the crusaders' burgeoning martial reputation, put up only cursory resistance. Tancred was eagerly welcomed by the Armenian population and accepted as Mamistra's new ruler. He was, at last, able to distribute a wealth of 'food, clothing, gold and silver' among his men as reward for their loyalty and patience. A few days later, Baldwin of Boulogne arrived in the region and established a camp on the opposite bank of the Pyramus. With the memory of Tarsus still fresh in everyone's mind, tensions were understandably high. Among Tancred's men, Richard of Salerno – one of the most prominent southern Italian Norman crusaders – stirred things up, arguing that revenge must be taken. Baldwin seems to have imagined that he could repeat his success at Tarsus, but on this occasion Tancred was in an entirely different position. With his Adanan allies, he could virtually match Baldwin for manpower, and, more importantly, he already had full control of Mamistra's fortifications. This time he would not back down.

With accusation and suspicion running rife, a confrontation was almost inevitable. When it came, it was short lived but brutal, and afterwards each side claimed the other had instigated the fighting. It may, in fact, have been little more than an impromptu brawl, but, all the same, a number of men were seriously injured, one or two were even slain, and captives were seized from both camps. Peace was restored the very next day and prisoners returned, but this was a dark and shocking episode: the knights of Christ had, for the first time, spilled one another's blood. Greed and ambition had brought discord to the crusade.

Following the mêlée at Mamistra, Tancred and Baldwin went their separate ways and would not meet again during the crusade. Baldwin was contacted by an Armenian noble named Bagrat, whom he had earlier befriended at Nicaea, and, lured east by the promise of fresh conquests, he left Cilicia behind him. Tancred garrisoned Mamistra with fifty knights and started out for the Belen Pass. He negotiated the crossing into Syria without difficulty, secured access to the port of Alexandretta and rendezvoused with the main crusading host as it marched on Antioch.[41]

In many ways, the Cilician expedition was a success: friendly relations were established with the Armenian population; the towns of Tarsus and Mamistra were garrisoned; and the direct route between Asia Minor and Antioch was secured. The venture also brought Baldwin and Tancred out of the shadows – from this point forth both would play prominent roles in the history of the crusading movement. The incursions into Cilicia may have served the overall interests of the expedition to Jerusalem, but they did, nonetheless, point towards a disturbing future, in which the pious vision of Jerusalem might be clouded, or even obscured, by personal rivalries and the temptations of wealth and power.

The journey of the main armies

While Tancred and Baldwin of Boulogne crossed Cilicia, the remainder of the crusading army forged a route north to Caesarea in Cappadocia and then south-east to reach Coxon in the first week of October. To this point the journey went well: Turkish garrisons fled as the host approached and no real resistance was encountered;

friendly relations were established with the local Armenian population, which provided plentiful supplies; and the Franks' role as servants of the Greek emperor was fulfilled, as Byzantine representatives were installed in command of two towns, Assan and Comana. At Coxon, Raymond of Toulouse, who had been ill for much of the journey from Iconium, recovered his strength. Around 7 October he dispatched a sizeable force, perhaps containing as many as 500 knights, south towards Antioch. This was in essence a scouting party, but Raymond may have been hoping to occupy Antioch before the rest of the crusade arrived, because he had heard a rumour that its garrison had deserted. When this proved to be false, the knight Peter of Roaix was sent with a small force, skirting around to the south of the city and into the Ruj valley, where, after brief fighting, he established a Provençal outpost.[42]

For the main army, the journey south from Coxon over a low-lying arm of the Anti-Taurus proved troublesome. A member of Bohemond's army described the experience:

> We set out and began to cross a damnable mountain, which was so high and steep that none of our men dared to overtake one another on the mountain path. Horses fell over the precipice, and one beast of burden dragged another down. As for the knights, they stood about in a great state of gloom, wringing their hands because they were so frightened and miserable, not knowing what to do with themselves and their armour, and offering to sell their shields, valuable breastplates and helmets for threepence or fivepence or any price they could get. Those who could not find a buyer threw their arms away and went on.[43]

Finally, around 10 October 1097, the First Crusade reached Marash, at the head of the Amouk valley and the route towards Antioch and northern Syria. Upon their approach, the town's Muslim garrison fled, and Marash's Armenian governor Thatoul, who had until then ruled as a Turkish client, offered the Franks a warm welcome. Lavish markets were set up, from which the crusaders could purchase all manner of supplies and provisions to soothe away memories of the Anti-Taurus.[44]

The First Crusade had survived the crossing of Asia Minor, albeit with major losses – perhaps half of those who had left Europe had been lost to battle, disease and starvation.[45] No other crusade would manage this feat, though many tried. Sheer bloody-minded perseverance, the help of allies and a healthy dose of luck enabled the armies of this first expedition to succeed. Now, however, the Franks faced the greatest challenge of the crusade.

BALDWIN'S COLD-BLOODED AMBITION

While the rest of the crusade prepared to march on Antioch, Baldwin of Boulogne left to find his fortune. Having abandoned Cilicia at the behest of his Armenian confidant Bagrat, he briefly rendezvoused with the Frankish host at Marash. In mid-October his English wife, Godwera, died from an illness, but if Baldwin felt any great grief it did not long distract him from his purpose. After the frustrations and disappointments of Cilicia, he decided to break away from the crusade, putting aside his vow to march to the Holy Land. Bagrat promised rich pickings to the east, and Baldwin saw an opportunity to carve out a new Levantine lordship around the River Euphrates. If he succeeded, the resultant territory might benefit the crusade, acting as a buffer state and foraging centre, but on this occasion there can be little doubt that Baldwin was acting primarily out of self-interest. His resources were extremely limited – he left Marash in the company of no more than a hundred knights – but this was balanced by his ruthless ambition and political acumen.[46]

At first, Baldwin was also able to capitalise on the awe that the western knights of the crusade inspired in Armenians and Turks alike. Playing off their fear of the main Frankish host, he was able to intimidate local Turkish garrisons into capitulation or flight. The towns of Tell Bashir and Ravendan fell into his hands, as their Armenian populations gratefully accepted 'liberation'. He could, by the end of 1097, claim control of a swathe of territory running east to the Euphrates. Baldwin had begun to make his mark. He initially rewarded Bagrat with the lordship of Ravendan, but their friendship soon wore thin. The exact cause of the dispute is unclear – Bagrat may have been plotting to assert his independence – but, for whatever reason, Baldwin declared him a traitor and, when he fled, had him hunted down and dragged before him in chains. Baldwin then had his former ally brutally tortured, at one point threatening to have him 'torn limb from limb while yet alive' unless he confessed his plans.[47]

Baldwin's conquests did not go unnoticed. To the east of the Euphrates, Thoros, the Armenian ruler of Edessa, was having trouble holding on to power. Distrusted by Edessa's populace because of his close links with the Byzantines, and threatened with aggression from his Turkish neighbour, Balduk of Samosata, Thoros needed a new weapon in his arsenal. Impressed by Baldwin's ferocious reputation, he proposed an alliance. Edessa was one of the great cities of Mesopotamia, a fitting capital for Baldwin's new lordship, so in February 1098 he set out across the Euphrates with a small force of knights, his eye open for any opportunity. En route, he only narrowly evaded a large raiding party from Samosata, but on approaching Edessa he enjoyed a rapturous welcome. One of his followers recalled that 'Passing by Armenian towns, you would have been amazed to see them coming humbly to meet us, carrying crosses and banners, and kissing our feet and garments for the love of God because they had heard we were going to protect them from the Turks.'[48]

Thoros may initially have planned to employ Baldwin as a mercenary, but when the Frank actually arrived to such widespread acclaim he quickly decided to formalise their relationship. Although married, Thoros had no children, so he elected to adopt Baldwin as his son and heir. Baldwin duly submitted himself to the necessary, if somewhat bizarre, public ritual: both men were stripped to the waist;

Thoros then embraced Baldwin, 'binding him to his naked chest', while a long shirt was placed over both of them to seal the union.

Thoros soon looked to exploit this adoption. Within a week, Baldwin and his Frankish troops were dispatched at the head of an Armenian force to deal with the threat from Samosata. Although he was unable actually to capture the town, Baldwin succeeded in garrisoning a nearby fort, largely neutralising the immediate threat posed by Balduk. On his return to Edessa, Baldwin discovered that a group of Edessene nobles were plotting to assassinate Thoros and elevate him in his adopted father's place. Our view of Baldwin's reaction, and the degree of his complicity in what followed, depends on which source we trust. According to one Latin contemporary, 'Baldwin refused with every objection to undertake such a crime.' But an Armenian living in Edessa at the time recorded that 'they persuaded him to accede to their evil designs and promised to deliver Edessa into his hands; Baldwin approved of their vicious plot'.[49]

We do know that in early March 1098 Edessa's population turned on Thoros. Terrified, he sought the sanctuary of his citadel. He realised that he could no longer rule the city but, still hoping to negotiate his escape and that of his wife, he turned to Baldwin. The crusader duly swore the most solemn of oaths, his hands placed upon Edessa's most sacred relics, promising to protect the life of his father, and was allowed into the citadel. But, on the very next day, he let the mob into the fortress. Wild with bloodlust, they seized Thoros and 'threw him down from the top of the ramparts into the midst of a raging crowd' which ripped him to pieces and then paraded the remains of his body throughout the city. It was in this manner that Baldwin of Boulogne became ruler of Edessa. Even his own chaplain could muster only this terse defence of Baldwin's actions: 'The [Edessenes] wickedly plotted to slay their prince because they hated him and to elevate Baldwin to the palace to rule the land. This was suggested and it was done. Baldwin and his men were much grieved because they were not able to obtain mercy for him.'[50]

Complicit or not, Baldwin had blood on his hands, but he quickly asserted an iron grip over Edessa and its environs. Within months, Balduk of Samosata had been subdued, becoming a client ruler, while another nearby town, Sorogia, was conquered and entrusted to one of Baldwin's Frankish lieutenants. In the space of less than half a year, with just a handful of men, Baldwin had established the first crusader state in the Near East – the county of Edessa.[51]

BEFORE THE WALLS OF ANTIOCH

The crusaders arrived in Syria, on the northern borders of the Holy Land, in the late summer of 1097. Jerusalem, their ultimate goal, was nearly within their grasp. It was tantalisingly close, perhaps only a month's journey to the south. Unfortunately for the crusaders, a massive obstacle stood in their way: Antioch, one of the greatest cities of the Orient, guarded the route south to Palestine. The Latins laid siege to this city, entering into one of the most brutal, gruelling and prolonged military engagements of the Middle Ages. The crusade stalled in northern Syria for one and a half years, and at this moment, more than any other, its future lay tortuously balanced between utter annihilation and miraculous success. The very concept of crusading was tested to breaking point in the fires of this conflict and ultimately emerged more powerfully and permanently forged.

Even in the eleventh century Antioch was an ancient city. Founded 300 years before the birth of Christ, in the aftermath of Alexander the Great's conquests, and named for one of his generals, Antiochus, it rapidly became a vital conduit of trade between East and West. At its height, Antioch was the third city of the Roman Empire, with a population in excess of 300,000. Alongside its economic and political importance, the city also had an impressive

spiritual pedigree, being revered in Christian tradition as the site of
the first church founded by St Peter, chief of the apostles. Antioch
thrived until the sixth century CE, its magnificence enhanced by a
massive building programme under the Emperor Justinian, which
saw the entire city enclosed within a formidable defensive wall by 560.
Around this time, however, a series of disasters befell the region: Syria
has always been prone to tectonic activity and Antioch was rocked by
three major earthquakes in this period; the outbreak of plague and a
city-wide fire caused further damage; it was sacked by the Persians and
finally conquered by the Arabs in 638. Under the Muslims, Antioch's
power was eclipsed by that of two neighbouring cities – Aleppo and
Damascus. Then, in 969, the Byzantines reconquered the city,
restoring some of its former glory. For more than a century it was a
cornerstone of the Byzantine world, the lynchpin of the empire's
eastern frontier. But in the inevitable ebb and flow of power Greek
dominion over northern Syria waned with the coming of the Seljuq
Turks, and Antioch fell once more into Muslim hands in 1085. By the
end of the eleventh century, then, Antioch was steeped in a
labyrinthine history, its walls echoed with the grandeur of a former
age, its streets were commanded by Turks but peopled by a
cosmopolitan mixture of Greek, Armenian and Syrian Christians,
Arabs and Jews.[1]

When Antioch fell to the Turks, the Seljuqs of northern Syria
enjoyed a short-lived period of unity. Malik Shah seized control of
Baghdad and, through sheer military ferocity and shrewd political
manipulation, bludgeoned the region into submissive unity. His
death in 1092 was followed by a succession crisis and the rapid
fragmentation of Muslim power. By the time the crusaders arrived in
1097, the political makeup of the region was incredibly complex.
Shah's son was embroiled in a struggle for control of Baghdad, while
his nephews, Ridwan of Aleppo and Duqaq of Damascus, fought over
Syria and contested control of Antioch. The city itself was governed
by a wily and ambitious Turcoman named Yaghi Siyan. One
contemporary described his memorable appearance: 'His head was of

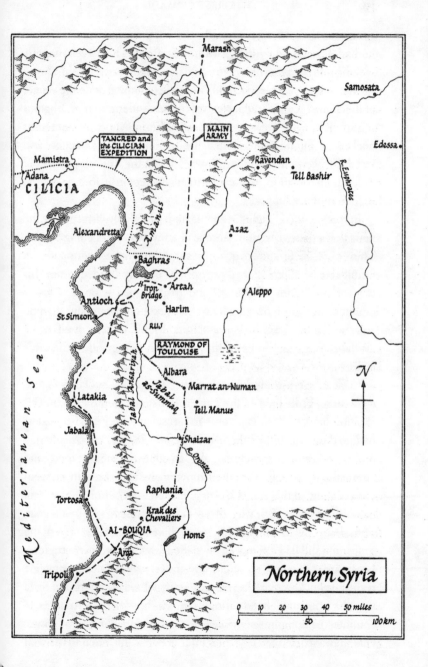

TANCRED and
the CILICIAN
EXPEDITION

MAIN
ARMY

Marash

Samosata

Mamistra

Edessa

Adana

CILICIA

Ravendan

Tell Bashir

R. Euphrates

Alexandretta

Azaz

Baghras

Iron
Bridge

Artah

Aleppo

Antioch

Harim

St Simeon

RUJ

RAYMOND OF
TOULOUSE

Albara

Marrat an-Numan

Jabal as-Summaq

Latakia

Tell Manus

Jabal Ansariyah

Jabala

Shaizar

R. Orontes

Tortosa

Raphania

Krak des
Chevaliers

AL-BOUQIA

Homs

Arqa

Tripoli

N

Northern Syria

Mediterranean Sea

0   10   20   30   40   50 miles

0   50   100 km

enormous size, the ears very wide and hairy, his hair was white and he had a beard which flowed from his chin to his navel.' Eagerly seeking any opportunity to achieve autonomy, Yaghi Siyan vacillated between Aleppo and Damascus, clutching on to the veneer of independence. Seljuq power was further undermined by religious schism: while the Turks were almost all Sunni Muslims, numerous pockets of Shi'ite Arabs dotted the region. In short, faction and instability weakened northern Syria, leaving the Turkish garrison of Antioch in isolation, without immediate recourse to any potent, unified military support.[2]

In this situation, Yaghi Siyan was understandably disturbed by the news that a massive western European army was approaching his city. They were an unknown quantity so, although he commanded a formidable, well-provisioned garrison, he quickly decided to send his two sons – Shams ad-Daulah and Muhammad – on a series of diplomatic missions begging for military aid from Damascus, Aleppo and the city of Mosul in Mesopotamia. In the interests of safety, he also chose to expel some of the Christians living within the city's walls.

In fact, the crusaders themselves were at first unsure of how to deal with Antioch. In light of the city's international reputation and its location on the pilgrimage route to Jerusalem, the Frankish leaders had no doubt heard of its fame even before leaving Europe, and had probably learned something of its strategic significance and approximate strength from the Emperor Alexius. The princes seem to have decided that Antioch must be taken even before they set foot in northern Syria. But why, given that the crusade's ultimate goal, Jerusalem, lay to the south? More than a year later, when the expedition still had not moved on to the Holy City, ordinary crusaders began to ask the same question. The answer was dictated by strategic reality: Antioch exercised so potent a stranglehold over northern Syria that it would have been virtually impossible for the crusaders to continue their pilgrimage in safety if it had remained in enemy hands. Had they bypassed the city, their lines of communication to the west would have been cut, their forces isolated and surrounded. With Antioch secured, the way would be open for resupply and reinforcement by further waves of European crusaders and the Byzantine army, upon which the Franks were depending.[3]

So the question was not whether Antioch should be taken, but how. The matter was hotly debated in a council of leaders in mid-October 1097. Some advocated a cautious policy of distant investment, whereby the Franks would take up a fortified position north of the city, perhaps at Baghras, a former Byzantine stronghold that now lay in ruins. From this position, they could police the region in relative safety, harassing the Antiochene garrison, hampering their lines of supply but avoiding direct confrontation. Having sat out the approaching winter, and with their ranks swelled by expected reinforcements, the crusaders could move to tighten the noose, squeezing Antioch into submission. This policy was probably promoted by the Byzantine Taticius – a similar strategy had worked for the Greeks in 969 and he certainly recommended this approach in January 1098. In the end, however, those in favour of more direct and immediate action, including Raymond of Toulouse, won the day. Perhaps fearing that their army might break up during a long, inactive winter, the princes agreed to attempt a close siege of the city. Perhaps in the knowledge that this would be no easy task, they each swore an oath not to desert the siege.[4]

The princes actually showed considerable strategic foresight on their march south to Antioch, taking care to seize its key satellite defences to the north and south before the siege began. Raymond of Toulouse had earlier sent a contingent under Peter of Roaix to secure the Ruj valley, one of the two southern approaches to Antioch. From Baghras the main army could have taken a direct route south to Antioch, but instead they went east around the Lake of Antioch to secure the fertile plains north-east of the city. Robert of Flanders was dispatched with 1,000 troops to capture Artah, a fortified town that lay some twenty-two kilometres from Antioch, on the intersection of ancient Roman roads from Marash, Edessa and Aleppo. As one contemporary noted, Artah was 'the shield of Antioch' – the region's most important fortress – and no army could possibly hope to invest Antioch with impunity if Artah remained in enemy hands. As it was, no crusader attack was necessary. Robert's approach was enough to spark a revolt among the town's Armenian population, its Turkish garrison fled to Antioch and the Franks were welcomed.

To make their final advance on Antioch, the crusaders needed to cross the Orontes, the great Syrian river that divided the region north to south. This could be done with ease only about twelve kilometres north of Antioch, at the Iron Bridge. A contemporary who wrote about the crusade, but never visited the Levant, imagined that it was given this imposing name because of its remarkable metal construction: 'On each side of the bridge two towers overhung, made indestructible by iron and perfectly adapted for defence.' This sounds impressive, but in reality the name probably came from a distortion of the river's local moniker – the Farfar – that became, in Latin, Pons Ferreus (Iron Bridge). The crossing may have been defended by twin forts and the stone bridge itself was certainly strongly built – it survived intact until 1972. When the Franks arrived it was guarded by up to 700 troops, but they were soon overwhelmed on 19 October 1097 by a crusader vanguard of 2,000 men under Robert of Normandy. At last, the road lay open to Antioch itself.[5]

The crusaders were deeply shocked and intimidated by their first glimpse of the city. Stephen of Blois noted in a letter to his wife, 'We found the city of Antioch very extensive, fortified with incredible strength and almost impregnable.' Another crusader believed that it could never be captured by outside enemies 'if the inhabitants, supplied with bread, wished to defend it long enough'. Having faced innumerable obstacles and travelled thousands of kilometres to reach this point, they suddenly realised that Antioch was virtually invulnerable. Visiting modern Antioch – now named Antakya – one can gain a real sense of the city's size and strength in the eleventh century, and the extraordinary nature of its topography and fortifications. At first sight the modern city, a bustling Turkish outpost on the disputed border with Syria, might seem unremarkable, but a careful eye and some dogged exploration can reveal its medieval magnificence. The city lies at the foot of two craggy mountains – Staurin and Silpius – and, until modern expansion, was hemmed in to the west by the Orontes river. In the sixth century these natural features were enhanced by a remarkable construction programme that enclosed the entire city within a massive defensive wall – almost five kilometres in length, two metres thick and up to twenty in height – running from the Orontes straight up Staurin's and Silpius' precipitous slopes. One Latin contemporary wrote that 'this wonderful city' was defended by walls 'built with most enormous rocks and towers, reckoned to number 360'. The whole defensive system was topped off by an imposing citadel, perched 500 metres above the city, near the summit of Mount Silpius. The mountain sections of these fortifications survive to this day. Following their line on foot requires determination and a head for heights, but drives home two important points: constructing them must have been an incredible labour; attacking them would have been virtual lunacy. Raymond of Toulouse's chaplain perfectly summed up the task facing the crusaders: 'This city extends two miles in length and is so protected with walls, towers and defences that it may dread neither the attack of machine nor the assault of man even if all mankind gathered to besiege it.'

By the late eleventh century these defences may not have been in pristine condition, but they were still extremely formidable. Antioch had six main gates, each of which was given a nickname by the crusaders. The north-eastern road from the Iron Bridge entered Antioch at the St Paul Gate, near the apostle's shrine that had been built into the slopes of Staurin. Next, going anti-clockwise, stood the Dog Gate, the Gate of the Duke and, where the walls eventually reached the Orontes, the Bridge Gate. The latter was crucial because it controlled the only bridge over the river and, therefore, access to the roads from Alexandretta and the port of St Simeon. To the extreme south lay the St George Gate, giving access to the road to the major port of Latakia, and finally, to the east, in a narrow rocky canyon between Silpius and Staurin, stood the formidable Iron Gate, which is still standing today.[6]

This rather convoluted description is necessary because Antioch's complex geography directly shaped events over the next nine months, dictating Latin and Muslim strategy. The crusaders seem to have rapidly decided against any attempt at a direct assault. They had neither the materials nor the craftsmen to build the siege engines and ladders needed to overcome such a heavily fortified site. The obvious alternative was an attrition siege, which was becoming an increasingly important staple of military confrontation across medieval Europe. For both aggressor and defender, this potentially long-drawn-out process was governed not so much by combat as by logistics and morale. In a classic situation, the besieging force would attempt to cut off their target city from any possible outside aid or avenue of supply, hoping to starve them into submission. The defenders, for their part, would strive to outlast their enemy, particularly if the besiegers' lines of resupply were themselves weak. They might also hold out hope for reinforcement by a major force, leaving the besiegers trapped between two fronts. Demonstrations of cruelty and ruthlessness by both parties, designed to intimidate the enemy and sap their morale, were a further tactic in this slow, grinding process.[7]

Once we understand the nature of this style of warfare, and the extent of Antioch's fortifications, we can begin to appreciate the mammoth scale of the crusaders' task. The city had a sizeable Turkish garrison, perhaps numbering 5,000 men, plentiful stores of food and a ready supply of water. The sheer length of Antioch's walls meant that a full encirclement was virtually impossible. The north-western gates of St Paul, the Dog and the Duke could be invested with some measure of security, because forces might be placed before each and still maintain close contact with one another. The problem came with enlarging this cordon. If the Latins wanted to block the Bridge and the St George gates, they would have to cross the Orontes some

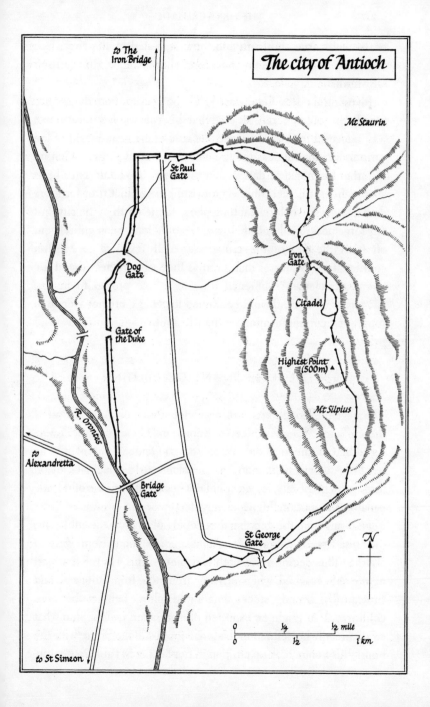

The city of Antioch

to The
Iron Bridge

Mt Staurin

St Paul
Gate

Dog
Gate

Iron Gate

Citadel

Gate of
the Duke

Highest Point
(500m)

Mt Silpius

R. Orontes

to
Alexandretta

Bridge
Gate

St George
Gate

N

to St Simeon

0   ¼   ½ mile
0   ½   1 km

twelve kilometres upstream and, now separated by the river, face complete isolation from the main force should the Muslim garrison sally forth.

Investing the Iron Gate would have been even more dangerous. One Latin contemporary recalled that this 'gate was left free, since it was inaccessible to the besiegers because of the great height of the surrounding mountains, and the narrowness of its paths'.[8] What no historian has noted to date is that the Iron Gate could have been approached. It is accessible via a twisting gorge that runs for more than a kilometre before reaching plains to the north of the city, but any force positioned outside this gate would have been entirely cut off from the rest of the crusaders, wholly exposed to Muslim counterattack. So it was that, even as the siege progressed and the Latin encirclement tightened, this sixth gate proved to be too dangerous to blockade and continued to act as a crucial avenue of supply and communication for the Muslims.

THE SIEGE OF ANTIOCH BEGINS

The siege of Antioch began on 20 October 1097, with the arrival of the crusaders' vanguard, led by Bohemond. One of his followers noted that on the 'next day, Wednesday 21 October, the main army reached Antioch about noon, and we established a strict blockade on three gates of the city, for we could not besiege it from the other side because a mountain, high and very steep, stood in our way'.

Realising from the start that they could not encircle the entire city, the crusaders concentrated their initial efforts upon its north-western quarter. This decision was both expedient – this was the first part of the city reached when arriving from the Iron Bridge – and strategically sound, since it allowed close contact between contingents. As might be expected, the crusaders divided into what could broadly be defined as 'national' groups. Bohemond, with the bulk of his troops, took up position in front of the St Paul Gate, while the remaining southern Italian Normans, including Tancred, camped behind in support. Next, going anti-clockwise, were the northern French, including Robert of Normandy, Robert of Flanders, Hugh of Vermandois and Stephen of Blois. Raymond of Toulouse, Adhémar of Le Puy and the remaining southern French blockaded the Dog Gate, while Duke Godfrey of Bouillon camped before what became known as the Gate of the Duke. Finally, Taticius and the Byzantine contingent camped some distance from the walls, presumably to act as a reserve force.[9]

These initial dispositions may not have been solely dependent upon strategic concerns. The crusaders were accustomed to operating on the principle of 'right by conquest', that is, whoever took possession of property first had the legal right to its possession. Even at the start of the siege, the Latins were probably aware that access to a major gate might allow rapid entry into the city, if and when it fell, and that this factor would determine the distribution of spoils and perhaps even title to Antioch itself. It is, therefore, no real surprise to find that Bohemond, whose ambitions regarding Antioch would soon become apparent, was the first to arrive at the city. Nor, perhaps, should we imagine that gallantry alone inspired his decision to undertake the potentially perilous blockade of the St Paul Gate, the most important of Antioch's portals to be invested at this stage. As in so many campaigns and wars, the protagonists probably harboured plans for the city's division, or even retention, long before its walls ever came into view.

The crusaders may have come prepared for immediate battle, but their arrival was actually followed by a surprising lull in events:

The hostile Turks within Antioch were so frightened that for almost fifteen days they did not harass any of our men. Soon we were ensconced in the neighbourhood, where we found vineyards everywhere, pits filled with grain, apple trees heavy with fruit for tasty eating, as well as many other healthy foods. Although they had wives in Antioch, the Armenians and Syrians would leave the city under pretence of flight and would come to our camp almost every day. They slyly investigated us, our resources, and our strength and then reported on all they had seen to the accursed Antiochians.[10]

In these first, tentative two weeks, Yaghi Siyan was probably trying to assess the crusaders' intentions – would they attempt a frontal assault, seek to blockade the city or simply wish to negotiate a safe passage south? He may also have been trying to buy time in which his appeals for aid might bear fruit. One crusader, Raymond of Aguilers, writing years later and in full knowledge of how difficult the siege would become, wistfully recalled these easy days: 'Those who stayed in camp enjoyed the high life so that they ate only the best cuts, rump and shoulders, scorned brisket, and thought nothing of grain and wine. In these good times only watchmen along the walls reminded us of our enemies concealed within Antioch.'[11]

However, once it became clear that no concerted attack was imminent, the Turkish garrison soon began to adopt a policy of cautious harassment. A Latin eyewitness noted that, 'after the Turks had found out about us, they began to emerge gradually and to attack . . . wherever they could lay ambush for us'. These attacks took three main forms. First, the garrison would use the Iron Gate to access Mount Staurin, where, from an elevated position of impunity, they could rain down missiles upon the crusaders besieging the St Paul Gate; one eyewitness wrote that arrows often 'fell into my Lord Bohemond's camp, and a woman was killed by a wound from one of them'. The Muslims also made frequent use of the unblockaded Bridge Gate to gain access to the plains to the west of Antioch. Mounted archers would then bombard the crusaders camped on the opposite bank of the Orontes. Such troops were difficult to counter:

partly because they were lightly armed with bows and were very agile on horse-back, and partly because they could race back across their aforementioned bridge. Because of their encampment near the banks of the river, Raymond and Adhémar bore the brunt of the raids. These hit and run attacks cost the above leaders all of their horses because the Turks, unskilled in the use of lances and swords, fought at a distance with arrows and so were dangerous in pursuit or flight.[12]

One of Antioch's satellite fortresses, Harim, also remained in Muslim hands. From this fortification, perched on the edge of a spine of rocky hills known as the Jabal Talat, about fifteen kilometres east of the city, and commanding an excellent view of the road to the Iron Bridge, the Turks began to send out skirmishing forces to pick off any stray Latins. By the second week of November, with the initial abundance of food almost waning, the crusaders really began to feel the pressure of these harassing attacks. For their siege to succeed they needed to limit Muslim mobility, containing the garrison within the city's walls as far as possible, and to free up their own lines of supply. One of their first actions, designed to assert greater control over the Antiochene plain, was to fashion a makeshift bridge over the Orontes opposite the Gate of the Duke. Before this, 'they had crossed over from one bank to another on a sluggish boat, watching anxiously'. Now they gathered together all the small boats they could find and lashed them together with rope to form a rudimentary crossing point. This was not a perfect solution and, in particular, mounted knights found it difficult to negotiate this Bridge of Boats at speed. While rushing to one of the frequent skirmishes that took place on the plains, the knight Henry of Esch became so exasperated with the delay that he decided to try to swim his horse across the Orontes. Weighed down by his armour and shield, 'the very deep waters closed over his head. Nevertheless, with God protecting him he reached dry land alive and still sitting on his horse.'[13]

The Bridge of Boats may have been a rather ramshackle affair, but, as the siege continued, it gave the crusaders a crucial advantage: access to the sea. The crossing allowed them to set up a more secure line of contact with Antioch's nearest port, St Simeon, named in honour of the fifth-century Christian hermit who had for decades lived near Aleppo, in isolation atop a stone pillar. From this point onwards the Mediterranean proved to be a vital lifeline for the crusaders, a conduit of contact, supply and reinforcement. Overland the journey to Europe might take months; by sea, under the most favourable conditions, it could be completed in two weeks. Indeed, naval contact actually allowed crusaders to send letters back to their homelands. We know that the crusaders benefited enormously from naval aid – in fact one could argue that the expedition would have failed without it – but our sources seem strangely reluctant to discuss it in any detail. In strategic terms, St Simeon was certainly as important as either Artah or the Iron Bridge, yet we have no clear account of the port's conquest or occupation. The Provençal crusader Raymond of Aguilers tells of a fleet that left England as soon as 'news of the crusades launched in the name of God's vengeance' arrived. It 'dared to sail through the strange and vast surface of the Mediterranean [and] after great trials arrived at Antioch [St Simeon] and Latakia in advance of our army'. Unfortunately this story is not confirmed by any other source. An Anglo-Norman fleet may have seized both of these ports, or perhaps Raymond's account represents a garbled recognition that Anglo-Saxon mercenaries were employed in Byzantine fleets. St Simeon was certainly in Latin hands by mid-November, and this opened the possibility of regular maritime contact with Greek-held Cyprus, and from there access to the rest of the Byzantine Empire and even western Europe. Around this time, the papal legate Adhémar made contact with the Greek patriarch of Jerusalem, now in exile on Cyprus, and together they drafted a letter of appeal to the West. In the months to come Adhémar's policy of détente with the Byzantines bore fruit in the form of much-needed supplies.[14]

On 17 November, thirteen Genoese ships carrying men and supplies landed at St Simeon. Their arrival seems so well timed as to suggest that the crusaders did indeed lay some plans for logistical support before their departure from Europe. They brought vital craftsmen and materials with which to tighten the blockade of Antioch. After sitting in council, the crusade's leaders decided to use these resources to build a siege fort on the slopes of Mount Staurin, close to the Gate of St Paul. This rather rough-and-ready fortification, which became known as Malregard, effectively secured the northern quadrant of the blockade and protected the besieging troops from harrying attacks.[15]

Around the same time the crusaders decided to deal with the garrison of Harim, who, in the words of one eyewitness, 'were daily killing many of our men who were going back and forth from our army'. Something had to be done, because these attacks were hampering the increasingly important task of foraging for supplies. It would seem, however, that at this point the Franks did not actually know where these Muslims troops were coming from, so Bohemond was chosen to lead a small reconnoitring expedition. He was probably expected to locate the Muslim camp rather than actually eliminate it. Had Bohemond been a less astute commander, this little venture could easily have ended in disaster. Knowing that he had limited manpower, and that he would be traversing unknown territory, he decided to employ cautious tactics. He divided his knights into two groups, sent the first out to search the craggy slopes of the Jabal Talat, and held the second in reserve. The plan appears to have been to locate the Muslim troops, use the first force to draw them out and, by means of a feigned retreat, lead them to where Bohemond lay waiting in ambush. In practice it worked brilliantly: although two knights were killed during the first engagement near Harim, the Muslims were then drawn into the trap. One of Bohemond's followers recalled that 'The barbarians fell upon our men because they were few, yet [the Franks] joined battle in good order and many of our enemies were killed.' Had Bohemond led his entire force into the hills he might have been caught unawares, but, as all of his troops appear to have been mounted knights, he adopted a classic Muslim tactic, that of the false retreat, to make use of this extra mobility. Harim may not have fallen, but its threat had been neutralised, and Bohemond had, once again, proved that he had a flair for military command.[16]

It was in the aftermath of this expedition that we first hear of the crusaders employing terror and intimidation as facets of their siege strategy. When Bohemond returned to Antioch, we are told that: '[Those] whom we captured, were led before the city gate and there beheaded, to grieve the Turks who were in the city.' Just as at Nicaea, the crusaders were keen to use every opportunity to impress their martial ferocity upon the garrison they were besieging. The intended message was clear: the Latins were militarily superior, willing to use extreme ruthlessness to achieve their goals, and would carry out even more terrible acts of savagery when Antioch fell unless the city chose to surrender. Such tactics were, of course, not the sole preserve of the Franks. By mid-November the Muslim garrison was just as willing to carry out atrocities. Fulcher of Chartres recalled: 'Alas! how many Christians, Greeks, Syrians and Armenians, who lived in the city, were killed by the maddened Turks. With the Franks looking on, they threw outside the walls the heads of those killed with their catapults and slings. This especially grieved our people.'

The Muslims regularly dragged the Greek Christian patriarch of Antioch, who had until then lived peacefully in the city, up to the battlements, hung him upside down from the walls and beat his feet with iron rods, in sight of the crusaders. Any captured Latin could expect comparable treatment. Adelbaro, archdeacon of Metz, was caught 'playing a game of dice' with a young woman in an orchard near the city. He was beheaded on the spot, she, taken back to Antioch, repeatedly raped and then killed. The following morning their heads were catapulted into the crusader camp.[17]

These acts may appear to be utterly barbaric by modern standards, but they were a staple feature of medieval warfare and became a consistent theme of the siege of Antioch. In viewing such events, we must try to temper our instinctive judgement with an awareness that in the eleventh century war was governed by medieval, not modern, codes of practice. Within the context of a holy war, in which the Franks were conditioned to see their enemy as sub-human, Christian piety prompted not clemency but, rather, an atmosphere of extreme brutality and heightened savagery.

THE BATTLE FOR FOOD

By the last week of November, however, hunger rather than bloodlust began to dominate the minds of the crusaders. By this point the abundance of food and drink enjoyed upon arrival at Antioch had been exhausted. This predicament was exacerbated by the onset of winter. The crusaders were shocked to discover that, not only did it rain in northern Syria, it might even snow. In a letter to his wife, Stephen of Blois complained: 'Before the city of Antioch, throughout the whole winter we suffered for our Lord Christ from excessive cold and enormous torrents of rain. What some say about the impossibility of bearing the heat of the sun throughout Syria is untrue, for the winter there is very similar to our winter in the West.'

For the next four months, the crusaders became utterly obsessed with the struggle against starvation and the elements. In the past historians have argued that the crusaders suffered at Antioch because, through logistical incompetence, they had made no preparations for a prolonged winter siege. Recent research indicates, however, that they struggled in spite of their best efforts to organise efficient lines of supply. We have already seen that the Franks made some preparations even before the siege began, establishing a foraging centre in Cilicia and forging friendships with Armenian Christians during their march around the Amanus mountains. Once in the region of Antioch, they opened the possibility of maritime supply at St Simeon, and by the end of December they had gained access to the larger port of Latakia, which lay some sixty kilometres to the south and offered even better access to Cyprus. The crusaders probably occupied Latakia for a time, but, once again, the details of crusader contact with the port are unclear. Even with these two ports, naval communication and supply were not always reliable through the winter months.[18]

The Franks also made a concerted effort to subdue the region surrounding Antioch when they first arrived in northern Syria. One crusader noted that at the start of the siege 'regional castles and nearby cities fell to us largely because of fear of us and a desire to escape Turkish bondage'. By March 1098 Stephen of Blois boasted that 'there are 165 cities and fortresses throughout Syria which are in our power'. This process may not always have been driven by the interests of the greater good – individuals or groups of knights did on occasion leave the siege on private plunder hunts – but over time the domination and exploitation of the Antiochene district became increasingly structured. Each crusader contingent concentrated its foraging efforts on a different sector, channelling supplies back to troops at the siege front. Raymond of Toulouse's men, for example, focused their attention on the Ruj valley, while the southern Italian Normans following Tancred exploited the region around Harim. But even this relatively organised logistical framework could not keep pace with the demands of such a huge army. An Armenian Christian contemporary recalled that in the bleak winter months:

> The princes [of Cilicia] sent whatever provisions were needed to the commander of the Franks. Likewise the monks of the Black Mountains assisted them by sending provisions, and all the faithful acted benevolently towards the Franks. Nevertheless, because of the scarcity of food, mortality and affliction fell upon the Frankish army to such an extent that one out of five perished and all the rest felt themselves abandoned and far from their homeland.[19]

According to a Latin observer, by mid-December the level of suffering was such as to require more direct action: 'The people of God began to run short of rations. With hunger growing daily more severe, and the army dying from want, especially the humble people, wretched groans and laments assailed [Adhémar] and all the princes. So, they conferred about these problems and how the people could be nourished.'

The plan concocted by this council was to send a major foraging expedition into the countryside, under the command of Bohemond and Robert of Flanders. The hope was that such a large force would be able to pillage for desperately needed supplies with relative impunity. This scheme was a calculated gamble, because such a large-scale deployment weakened the crusaders' hold on Antioch. Unbeknown to the crusaders, it was an even more risky roll of the dice, because at the same time Duqaq of Damascus was marching towards Antioch at the head of a large Muslim relief force. After two months, he had chosen that very moment to rescue Yaghi Siyan.[20]

On 28 December 1097, after making a rather grim attempt to celebrate the Feast of the Nativity, Bohemond and Robert of Flanders set out from Antioch with around 400 knights and a larger, but unspecified, number of infantrymen. We have no eyewitness account of this expedition, so our knowledge of its progress is, at best, patchy. The crusaders probably took a route south and then east of the city, through the Ruj valley and on to the plateau known in Arabic as the Jabal as-Summaq. This fertile upland area offered promising pickings, and for a few days they set about gathering all the food they could carry. By the night of 30/31 December, as they camped near the town of Albara, they must have felt that their mission was almost fulfilled. They had, however, made a desperately dangerous error. Either through the confusion of joint command or through straightforward neglect, Bohemond and Robert had failed to post scouts throughout the region. They were, therefore, completely oblivious to the fact that a major Muslim army from Damascus was only a few kilometres away. Duqaq had finally been moved to action by Shams ad-Daulah's entreaties for aid and, in mid-December, had set out for Antioch in the company of his formidable atabeg (general) Tughtegin and his ally the emir of Homs. The Provençal crusader Raymond of Aguilers believed that their troops numbered 60,000, but this must surely be an exaggeration, and it is unlikely that Duqaq could have raised more than 10,000 men. Even so, this was a considerable force and, had it reached Antioch unhindered, the entire future of the crusade might have been put in jeopardy.

As it was, chance intervened, and the paths of the two armies crossed. In the early morning of 31 December, perhaps while the crusaders were still in camp, Duqaq's army appeared and immediately sought to encircle their enemy. The stunned Franks must have been terrified by this sudden turn of events. Had Bohemond and Robert not taken decisive action, the entire force might have been annihilated. The exact course of the ensuing battle is unclear. Robert seems to have rallied his knights in a frontal attack against the first wave of Muslim troops. Meanwhile, Bohemond held his force in reserve, and was therefore able to head off Duqaq's attempts to surround the crusaders. In the chaotic fighting that followed, both princes broke through the Muslim lines, scattering many of Duqaq's men. With much of the Damascene army in disarray, Bohemond and Robert decided to retreat to safety rather than risk pursuit. The mounted crusader knights had escaped, but in their haste they left their slower-moving infantry and all their gathered supplies at the mercy of the remaining Muslim troops. In the end, neither Latin nor Muslim won a clear victory in this battle, both suffered casualties and parts of each army were forced from the field, but it was enough to convince Duqaq to return home. From the crusaders' point of view, the whole expedition had been a débâcle. Almost their entire infantry had been lost to death or imprisonment and the whole purpose of their venture – the gathering of food – had been thwarted. Robert of Flanders seems to have returned over the next few days to harry stragglers from Duqaq's force, regaining some supplies, but nowhere near enough to feed the entire army back at Antioch. Some contemporary chroniclers tried to put a brave face on events, others passed over it in silence, but it was obvious to all that the crusaders had been caught unawares and almost defeated.[21]

At the same time, the main crusading army back at Antioch had also suffered a damaging attack. On learning of the foraging expedition's departure, either through direct observation or via Armenian Christian spies, Yaghi Siyan decided to mount a counter-offensive from within the city. The besieging force was considerably weakened at this point. Not only were Bohemond and Robert of Flanders missing, Robert of Normandy was also absent, perhaps visiting Latakia, and Duke Godfrey was laid low with illness. On 29

December a Muslim force rushed out of the Bridge Gate and raced towards the Bridge of Boats and the Provençal camp. Raymond of Toulouse responded by crossing the Orontes in force, with both knights and infantry, and at first things seemed to go well. The Turks turned tail and fled across the Antiochene plain, and Raymond gave hot pursuit back towards the Bridge Gate. In fact, the Provençals had been drawn into a trap. It seems likely that the initial Muslim attack was simply designed to lure the crusaders across the river. Once the Franks reached the Bridge Gate, 'the Turks regrouped and launched a counterattack by way of the bridge and lower ford'. Suddenly, the Latins were surrounded by a much larger force, and their attack abruptly turned into a rout. The race back to the Bridge of Boats was utterly chaotic:

Frankish knights, who stopped to fight, found themselves grabbed by the fleeing [crusader] rabble, who snatched their arms, the manes and tails of their horses, and pulled them from their mounts. The Turks hurriedly and pitilessly chased and massacred the living and robbed the dead. In the running fight from their bridge to ours, the Turks killed up to fifteen knights and around twenty footmen. The standard bearer of the Bishop of Le Puy and noble young man, Bernard of Béziers, lost their lives, and Adhémar's standard was taken.[22]

The level of casualties suffered in this engagement was not disastrous, but the defeat was a serious blow to Latin morale. Throughout the crusade, and in medieval warfare in general, princes used personalised banners or standards, often bold and colourful in design, to group and control their forces. These banners were prized possessions, symbols to be followed into battle. They might be raised over buildings or even cities to demonstrate rights to captured property, and surrendered enemies might themselves huddle around their captor's banner to avoid being randomly butchered. In the customs of war the loss of one's banner was a sure sign of defeat; the capture of Adhémar's standard – which depicted the Virgin Mary – was, therefore, both humiliating and deeply depressing. In the following weeks, the Turkish garrison delighted in taunting the Franks by flying the captured banner from Antioch's walls. Taken together, the rout at the Bridge Gate and the events of the Foraging Battle also raised worrying doubts about the ability of mounted knights and crusader infantry to co-operate effectively in battle. The events of late December must have strained the bonds of trust between these two forces, and they certainly prompted the crusade's leaders to reassess their battle tactics in the coming months.[23]

THROUGH THE EYE OF THE STORM

With the advent of the New Year, 1098, the crusader forces were reunited. They had survived two dangerous tests, but their material position at Antioch had not improved. Most of them were already hungry, exhausted and depressed, and the next month brought absolutely no respite. Instead, their conditions of living became increasingly unbearable – death through starvation, illness or battle not simply a possibility, rather a probability – and for the first time fear began seriously to weaken their ranks.

Within Antioch, the Turkish garrison also must have felt the pinch, but with three of the city's gates still open, and with access to much closer allies, they appear to have been far more successful at gathering supplies. In February, the crusader Anselm of Ribemont remarked in a letter: 'The city is supplied to an incredible extent with grain, wine, oil and all kinds of food.' Outside, however, events seemed to conspire against the crusaders. First, the local population began to exploit Latin hunger:

The Armenians, Syrians and Greeks learned that our foraging forces had come back destitute. Consequently, they scoured the countryside, buying grain and other foodstuff which they carried to camp where great famine gripped the besiegers. They sold an ass for eight hyperoi, which is worth 120 solidi in denarii. Despite this market, many crusaders died because they did not have the money for such inflated prices.[24]

The exact value of these prices cannot be calculated, but it is obvious that they were exorbitant. Under these conditions wealth and social status became determinants of life. The poor were of course the first to suffer, but many that had reached Antioch with some riches intact now found themselves destitute. Some were saved by the leaders' charity. Writing to his wife in March 1098, Stephen of Blois remembered the torment of these months: 'Many have already exhausted all their resources in this very holy passion [the siege]. Very many of our Franks, indeed, would have met a temporal death from starvation, if the clemency of God and our money had not succoured them.' Even though these acts of generosity saved some, starvation and suffering were still widespread:

At that time, the famished ate the shoots of beanseeds growing in the fields and many kinds of herbs unseasoned with salt; also thistles, which, being not well cooked because of the deficiency of firewood, pricked the tongues of those eating them; also horses, asses, camels, dogs and rats. The poorer ones even ate the skins of the beasts and seeds of grain found in manure.[25]

On top of all this, a series of natural phenomena – including a comet and an aurora – were experienced in northern Syria and interpreted by the crusaders as miraculous signs of God's displeasure. One Frank recalled that 'at that time, we saw an astonishing glow in the sky, and, in addition, we felt a great movement of the earth, which made us all quake. Many also saw a certain sign in the shape of a cross, whitish in colour, advancing toward the East in a straight path.'[26]

In the face of such unpromising conditions, the crusaders began to panic. Profound adversity sometimes clarifies and crystallises the human heart, and we can learn a great deal about the crusaders' mindset and motivation by exploring how they sought to rationalise their predicament. They were confronted by one central question: if they were fighting a holy war in the name of God, why was their Lord allowing them to suffer and die? Their answer, or at least that of the clergy, was that mainstay of medieval Christianity – sin. Fulcher of Chartres, himself a chaplain, offered this explanation: 'We believed that these misfortunes befell the Franks, and that they were not able for so long a time to take the city, because of their sins. Not only dissipation, but also avarice, or pride, or rapaciousness corrupted them.' If God was punishing the crusaders for their sins, then, the clergy believed, the only solution was to purify the army by whatever means possible. Adhémar of Le Puy began to advocate a return to righteousness through extreme austerity and Christian ritual, urging 'the people to fast three days, to pray, to give alms, and to form a procession; he further ordered the priests to celebrate masses and the clerks to repeat psalms.' The efficacy of a fast among those who were already starving may seem dubious, but the formula of imposed physical denial and intense liturgical observance was believed to be a tried-and-tested recipe for success. It was one to which the crusaders would return.[27]

The process of purification also had more unpleasant sides. One particularly regrettable feature of medieval Christian dogma was the belief that women were essentially agents of sin. This extraordinary concept can be traced back to St Augustine of Hippo, the late-fourth- and early-fifth-century architect of the Just War theory whose enormously influential theological writings continue to shape Christianity to this day. Unfortunately for womankind, Augustine had, like many saints, been quite a philanderer before he turned to God. Once he had dedicated his life to the Church, however, he decided, rather uncharitably, that women had seduced him into sin, and indeed that they were in essence corrupt and dangerous. Perhaps most notably, he contributed to a reinterpretation of the story of Man's fall from Eden, focusing blame upon Eve rather than the serpent. By the eleventh century, then, women could be portrayed as temptresses, agents of evil. It is in this context that we must try to understand one crusader's dispassionate observation that, in January 1098, 'After holding council, [the Franks] drove out the women from the army, both married and unmarried, lest they, stained by the defilement of dissipation, displease the Lord.' The near-contemporary writer Albert of Aachen recorded a more general list of measures and prohibitions:

> All injustice and wickedness was to be cut out from the army, no one was to cheat a Christian brother; no one was to commit theft; no one was to take part in fornication or adultery. If anyone should disobey this order, they would be subject to most severe penalties if caught, and thus God's people would be sanctified from filth and impurity.

It seems, however, that Albert believed that transgression was inevitable, because he went on to record:

> When indeed many of the pilgrims disobeyed the decree they were severely sentenced by the appointed judges: some were put in chains, other flogged, others shaved and branded for the correction and improvement of the whole army.
>
> In that place a man and woman were caught in the act of adultery and they were stripped in the presence of all, their hands were tied behind their backs and they were severely whipped by strikers and rods, and were forced to go round the whole army so that when their savage wounds were seen the rest would be deterred from such and so wicked a crime.[28]

Many sought to combine this rigorous programme of purification with more direct, practical action. It became common for large groups of men, 200 to 300 at a time, to set off on wide-ranging foraging expeditions. Most of these were probably unsanctioned by the crusade leadership, but they were certainly not the preserve of the lower classes. Ludwig, the archdeacon of Toul, once a relatively wealthy cleric, decided, when his money ran out, to lead 300 other clerics and lay people in search of food. Unfortunately for them, spies reported their departure to the Antiochene garrison; 600 Turks were sent out of the Iron Gate to ambush them, and Ludwig and all his followers were butchered.[29]

Even with all the efforts to restore 'purity' and morale, it is not surprising that some crusaders considered desertion when faced with such levels of suffering. Thousands of kilometres from home, adrift among enemies, many must have believed that the entire expedition was close to complete collapse and annihilation. Often, those who left to forage in outlying areas chose not to return to the siege. Even well-known crusade figures were not immune. Towards the end of January 1098, two leaders of the former People's Crusade, the charismatic preacher Peter the Hermit and the knight William the Carpenter, lord of Melun, stole away from the siege in the dead of night. They appear to have travelled on from Constantinople in Bohemond's army, because when the flight was discovered it was Tancred who was sent after them:

> [He] caught them and brought them back in disgrace. William spent the whole night in my Lord Bohemond's tent, lying on the ground like a piece of rubbish. The following morning, at daybreak, he came and stood before Bohemond, blushing for shame. Bohemond said to him, 'You most loathsome of all men whom the earth has to bear, why did you run off in such a shameful way?'[30]

William evidently had a reputation for desertion – he was known to have fled during an earlier expedition against the Moors in Spain – but, even so, most of the army begged Bohemond to be lenient, perhaps because they understood only too well the fear that had afflicted him. In the end, both William and Peter returned to the crusade without further punishment, having sworn an oath to persevere in the siege. The crusade leadership evidently judged them to be too valuable as figureheads for the poor, talismans of morale, for their escape or banishment to be acceptable. Indeed, in the months to come, Peter went on to play a more active role in events.[31]

The crusaders were less sympathetic in their response to another significant departure. Since leaving Constantinople, the Franks had been accompanied by the Greek guide and adviser, Taticius. At the end of January, he announced his intention to travel back into Asia Minor in search of supplies and reinforcements for the siege. The crusaders had, since their arrival at Antioch, been expecting to be reinforced by the Byzantine emperor Alexius Comnenus. At the time, Taticius' proposal was probably accepted, his promises believed. Apparently, he even left all his possessions behind in camp as evidence of his determination to return. He and his men duly set off and eventually rendezvoused with the emperor, but, for reasons that will become clear, Taticius never returned to the siege of Antioch. This betrayal shocked the Franks, and, writing with the benefit of hindsight, most crusader sources were deeply critical of the Greek guide's conduct. Raymond of Toulouse's chaplain wrote: 'Under the pretence of joining the army of Alexius, Taticius broke camp, abandoned his followers, and left with God's curse; by this dastardly act, he brought eternal shame to himself and his men.'[32]

Around this time, Bohemond himself may have considered leaving the army. According to the Provençal crusader Raymond of Aguilers, who, it must be said, was not particularly fond of Bohemond, he 'threatened to depart' because of the suffering of his troops and his own poverty. Raymond went on to state, 'we learnt afterwards that he made these statements because ambition drove him to covet Antioch', and noted that, in order to maintain Christian unity, 'All the princes with the exception of the Count [Raymond of Toulouse] offered Antioch to Bohemond in the event it was captured. So with this pact Bohemond and the other princes took an oath they would not abandon the siege of Antioch for seven years unless it fell sooner.'

Raymond may have confused this promise of full rights to the city with later events, and no other contemporary source recorded these negotiations, but it is possible that Bohemond was already angling for a guaranteed share of Antioch's spoils in early 1098.[33]

That January the crusade reached its lowest point to date. One of Bohemond's followers, who lived through this terrible period, explained the Frankish predicament, conveying an immediate sense of their despair:

> We were thus left in direst need . . . The Turks were menacing us on the one hand, and hunger tormented us on the other, and there was no one to help us or bring us aid. The rank and file, with those who were very poor, fled to Cyprus, Asia Minor or into the mountains. We dared not go down to the sea for fear of those brutes of Turks, and there was no road open to us anywhere.[34]

With this in mind, Simeon, the Greek patriarch of Jerusalem, with the support of Bishop Adhémar, wrote a heartfelt letter of appeal to all the Christians of western Europe. His insistent message is a sure indication of how many crusaders had been lost to death or desertion. What the Franks needed now was more manpower: 'Come to fight in the army of the Lord . . . Bring nothing with you except only what may be of use to us. Let only the men come; let the women, as yet, be left. From the home in which there are two, let one, the one more ready for battle come.' In particular he sought to goad any who had taken a crusading vow but not yet left for the East with the threat of excommunication. Of course, he was not above using deception to encourage recruitment. In spite of all the suffering at Antioch, he still described the Holy Land as 'flowing with milk and honey'; he also maintained that the hardest section of the campaign was over.[35]

Through all of January 1098 only one faint glimmer of hope briefly illuminated the crusaders' cause. During one of the minor skirmishes outside Antioch that were a daily feature of the siege, the Franks captured a young, high-ranking Muslim nobleman. Learning that his family commanded one of the city's towers, they sought to negotiate secret access to the tower in return for his release. A dialogue was established and the scheme might have come to fruition had Yaghi Siyan not discovered the plot and relieved the family members of their command. Showing a complete absence of clemency, the crusaders responded by hauling their bedraggled prisoner, who had already suffered severe torture, before the walls, where he was summarily decapitated in full sight of the Muslim garrison. Their plan had failed on this occasion, but a potential weakness in the city's defences – betrayal – had been exposed.[36]

A NEW ENEMY CONFRONTED

In the first days of February news arrived that a fresh Muslim army was approaching Antioch. This time it was Ridwan of Aleppo who had chosen to lead around 12,000 men to relieve Yaghi Siyan, and was now camped at Harim. By this point, the surprise encounter with Duqaq of Damascus back in December must have alerted the crusaders to the need for better local intelligence. They had perhaps improved their network of scouts and local informers; certainly they had a little time to plan for Ridwan's arrival, but they still faced the very real possibility of being crushed between Antioch's garrison and the Aleppan army. In the face of this new threat, the Latins had three overwhelming concerns, born out of the experiences and depredations of the previous months. They were, above all, desperately short of horses. Concern for their mounts had already been evident during the troublesome crossing of Asia Minor, but, through the winter of 1097–8, the crusaders became wholly fixated upon the wellbeing of their horses. When eyewitnesses described the struggles to find supplies, they almost invariably went on to comment on the excessive cost of horse feed: '[The Franks] endured the sight of their horses wasting away from starvation. Straw was scarce and seven or eight solidi did not buy an adequate amount of grain for one night's provender for one horse.'

One of Bohemond's main justifications for his threat to leave the siege in January had been that he was sick of watching 'his men and horses dying from hunger'. Indeed, our sources give the impression that horses were valued almost as much as men. There were two reasons for this: from a practical military standpoint, the crusaders knew that their most powerful weapon in battle was the mounted knight – the medieval equivalent of a tank; to the individual, a horse conveyed status, indeed one could not effectively maintain the position of knight without a mount. In early 1098, horses were precious commodities. A strange incident amid the chaotic fighting outside Antioch on 29 December was indicative: in the heat of battle a group of knights suddenly turned from the fray, deserting the infantry; but their flight was not inspired by cowardice; instead, they were racing to be the first to catch a single riderless horse which had been spotted leaving the field. Knights soon became reluctant to fight in skirmishes for fear that their horses might be killed, their status lost. In response, the crusader princes, led by Raymond of Toulouse, established a common war chest from which knights could claim funds to replace mounts lost in battle. Funded by the crusader 'confraternity', this arrangement was another example of practical economic co-operation among the crusade leadership. Even so, new horses could be bought only if they were available, and by February they were extremely scarce. It was said that the Provençals could muster only a hundred, and that even these were 'scrawny and feeble'; in the whole army there were at best a thousand knights who still had mounts. Many of these would not have been fully fledged warhorses, and we know that some knights even rode into battle on mules and donkeys. The first question, then, that faced the crusaders when they heard of Ridwan's approach was how to make best use of their limited cavalry.[37]

Two other related matters needed to be resolved: the experience of recent months had demonstrated that a single overall commander was needed in full-scale pitched battles; it was also apparent that, in the heat of a mêlée, proper co-ordination between infantry and cavalry was extremely difficult to achieve. The crusader princes duly held an urgent council on 8 February to discuss these matters and their response to Ridwan's approach. They decided to divide their forces to cover two fronts. Seven hundred knights under the command of Bohemond, Robert of Flanders and Stephen of Blois would ride out to meet Ridwan. Meanwhile, the remaining princes would maintain the siege with the entire infantry. A division of manpower was obviously necessary, but such a radical separation of cavalry and foot is quite revealing. One Latin eyewitness argued that 'this decision came because it was likely that the unfit and timid ones in the ranks of the footmen would show more cowardice than bravery if they saw a large force of Turks'.

This may not be entirely accurate, given that a fair proportion of the infantry must, by this time, have been made up of experienced knights who had now lost their horses. In fact, the division probably had more to do with strategy. Freed of the encumbrance of slow-moving footsoldiers, the cavalry could potentially move with greater precision and speed. The Franks had clearly learned from experience, adopting and adapting the Turkish penchant for mobile, horse-based warfare. The princes probably made a further innovation, electing Bohemond as overall commander of the expeditionary force.[38]

The crusaders were facing an immense challenge: to repel some 12,000 Muslims with under 1,000 troops of their own. The sheer imbalance of these forces makes one wonder whether the Frankish sources exaggerated the severity of their predicament, but, for once, even the Arabic sources confirm that the Aleppan army was numerically superior. How, then, could the crusaders possibly hope to prevail against such odds? Looking back on the battle, one crusader argued that God had miraculously multiplied the number of Latin knights from 700 to 2,000 as the fighting began. In reality, the crusaders might have risked drawing more men from the siege to create a larger combined force, but they chose to rely upon divine support and superior tactics rather than sheer weight of numbers. Their plan was both inspired and audacious. They could have fought a defensive battle, centred around the Iron Bridge, but this would have relied upon grinding attrition and, win or lose, would have been extremely costly in terms of manpower. Instead, outnumbered twelve to one, they decided to go on the offensive.

In a direct reversal of their experiences in the Foraging Battle, they sought to use surprise to their advantage. They set out from Antioch, under the cover of darkness, on the night of 8 February, advancing rapidly along the road to the Iron Bridge. In a sense, they were trying to set up a large-scale ambush and, having taken the initiative, they were able to choose their point of attack. The ground they selected probably lay on the approach to the Iron Bridge, but its exact location cannot be determined with any certainty. It does seem that they hoped to limit the possibility of long-range encirclement by hemming in the Muslim forces on ground flanked by natural obstructions, so they may well have chosen a point between the River Orontes and the foothills behind Antioch. Indeed, the main force of knights may themselves have taken limited cover behind a low hill.

On the morning of 9 February, scouts were carefully deployed and returned with news that Ridwan was marching straight down the road from the Iron Bridge, with two detachments of troops thrown ahead of his main force. The crusaders had one chance for success. They could not hope to prevail in a long-drawn-out engagement; instead they had to rely upon shock tactics and the judicious use of the main weapon, the cavalry charge. Under these conditions timing was paramount. If they deployed their full force immediately the brunt of their charge might be absorbed by Ridwan's vanguard, leaving the main Muslim army free to close and partially encircle the Franks. Instead, in a masterful piece of generalship that was probably the brainchild of Bohemond, they divided their forces into six squadrons. When Ridwan appeared, five of these were deployed against the Aleppan vanguard, while the sixth, under Bohemond, waited in reserve. One eyewitness described these first minutes of battle: 'The din of battle arose to heaven, for all were fighting at once and the storm of missiles darkened the sky.' Knowing that they were heavily outnumbered, these knights must have been terrified, but they played a crucial tactical role. Their shock attack drew Ridwan's main force forward into the heart of the battle. His massed troops now began to push the crusaders back, and the Aleppans most likely felt that victory was at hand. In fact, this was the moment for which Bohemond had prepared. Now, with the Muslims bunched together in one force, he launched his sixth squadron in a ferocious cavalry charge. The author of the *Gesta Francorum*, who was almost certainly in the midst of Bohemond's troops, wrote an impassioned description of this attack:

> So Bohemond, protected on all sides by the sign of the Cross, charged the Turkish forces, like a lion which has been starving for three or four days, which comes roaring out of its cave thirsting for the blood of cattle . . . His attack was so fierce that the points of his banner were flying right over the heads of the Turks. The other troops, seeing Bohemond's banner carried ahead so honourably, stopped the retreat at once, and all our men in a body charged the Turks, who were amazed and took flight. Our men pursued them and massacred them right up to the [Iron Bridge].[39]

The fate of the entire crusade had been gambled on Bohemond's ability to break the massed Aleppan ranks with a perfectly timed, crushing cavalry charge. With one bold manoeuvre he changed the course of the battle, throwing Ridwan's army into a chaotic rout. The crusaders pursued them as far as Harim, capturing horses and supplies. Within hours the remaining Turks had torched the castle and fled eastwards. The expeditionary force had won a spectacular victory. Meanwhile, back at Antioch, the infantry had successfully repelled a series of attacks from the city's garrison. In the wake of these triumphs, the crusaders sought to press home their advantage: 'With the battle and booty won, we carried the heads of the slain to camp and stuck them on posts as grim reminders of the plight of their Turkish allies and of future woes of the besieged.'[40]

In these desperate winter months the crusaders had, through a combination of luck and military genius, survived encounters with two large Muslim relief armies. Had the forces of Damascus and Aleppo combined against them, the outcome would surely have been different. But the fractured world of Muslim Syria led Duqaq and Ridwan to act in isolation, their mutual hatred of one another overcoming any common impulse to repel the crusaders from the gates of Antioch.

By pure coincidence, on or around 9 February, the crusaders received a very different kind of Muslim visitation that allowed them further to exploit the rifts within Islam. An embassy arrived by ship from the Fatimid caliphate of Egypt, ruled at this time by the Vizier al-Afdal. This delegation may well have been sent in response to contacts established by the crusaders after Nicaea and on the advice of the Emperor Alexius. The pathological hatred that divided the two main arms of the Islamic faith – the Sunni Turks of Abbasid Baghdad and the Shi'a Fatimids – meant that the Egyptians had absolutely no intention of opposing the crusaders' siege of Turkish Antioch. Indeed, like many Muslims of the time, they may have misunderstood the Franks' intentions and aspirations to reconquer Jerusalem, believing them to be part of a limited Byzantine campaign.

This was extremely fortunate for the crusaders because, of all the Muslim powers of the Levant, Egypt alone had a navy capable of hampering the Franks' precious maritime connections with Byzantium and the West. The Fatimids were, for the time being, prepared to enter into a pact of neutrality; for their part, the Latin princes were, in the interests of survival, willing to forget the brutal, undifferentiated abhorrence of Islam demanded by crusader rhetoric. Indeed, Stephen of Blois showed no embarrassment when writing to his wife that 'The Emperor of Babylon [al-Afdal] also sent Saracen messengers to our army with letters, and through these he established peace and concord with us.' These envoys appear to have stayed in the crusader camp for almost a month and, when they left, were accompanied by Frankish ambassadors. This rather startling episode must have been common knowledge within the crusade and indicates that, even in the midst of their trials at Antioch, the Franks were not, as we might have expected, inspired by blind religious or ethnic hatred.[41]

The crusaders had endured a terrible winter outside the walls of Antioch. Thousands had died from cold, disease, hunger and battle; others had fled; those that remained must have been changed by the experience. The sheer horror of this period clearly etched itself into the memory of those who later wrote about the crusade, but they seem to have rationalised the experience in different ways. From most eyewitnesses one senses that the crusaders were terribly weakened by these months – left utterly exhausted and in constant fear. Fulcher of Chartres, who did not witness the siege in person, took a different view. In his mind, the crusaders had walked through a burning fire of purification to emerge cleansed of sin and ever more assured in their purpose. This might sound like the romanticised imaginings of a distant observer, but there may be more than an element of truth in Fulcher's words. In July 1098, Anselm of Ribemont, a crusader knight who had lived through the Antiochene winter, wrote that the Franks were strengthened by their ordeal: 'Growing stronger and stronger, therefore, from that day our men took counsel with renewed courage.'

The crusaders had, in some awful sense, been cleansed. The weak had died; the fearful had fled; those ineffective in battle had been slain. Now a smaller, but tougher and more experienced core remained. Some 100,000 crusaders had left Europe; now, at best, 30,000 survived, and the siege of Antioch was far from over.[42]

6

TIGHTENING THE SCREW

The first days of March 1098 marked an end to the trials of winter and a change in the crusade's fortunes. On 4 March an English fleet arrived at St Simeon bearing supplies, building tools and craftsmen. These new resources were invaluable, but we know very little about the men who brought them to the Levant.* Just as with the Genoese fleet that arrived in November 1097, we are really left to guess whether these English ships were part of a calculated supply system or simply a chance arrival. Certainly the eyewitness crusader sources did not remark that the fleet had been long awaited or expected, but, planned or otherwise, its cargo promised to turn the tide of the siege of Antioch.[1]

---

*As we have seen, the exact nature of the English naval contribution to the crusade is unclear – these sailors may have come from England itself, or they may have been Byzantine mercenaries. The matter is further confused by the fact that two prominent Norman chroniclers recorded that Edgar the Ætheling, heir to the throne of England, commanded this fleet. Given that Edgar was still embroiled in a dispute over the succession to the Scottish throne in late 1097, this may be unlikely, if not entirely impossible. We do know that an Italian crusader named Bruno of Lucca travelled east with this fleet, because his fellow citizens were so proud of his adventures that they recorded his journey in a celebratory letter addressed, rather grandly, to every single Christian on earth.

Up to this point the crusaders' encirclement of the city could at best be described as partial. They had blockaded three gates in its north-west quadrant, but the Bridge Gate, the Gate of St George and the less accessible Iron Gate remained unguarded. Efforts had been made to police the roads leading from the Bridge Gate to St Simeon and Alexandretta, but supplies continued to reach the Muslim garrison. Worse still, for the crusaders, their most important line of supply – that leading to St Simeon – was exposed to frequent attack. For the Latins to have any hope of starving the Antiochene garrison into submission, their cordon would have to be tightened and the Bridge Gate area controlled. The arrival of the English fleet offered an opportunity to do just that. As soon as they heard of its appearance, the crusader princes held a council to discuss the best use of these new resources and decided to build a siege fort, similar to the one they had constructed on the slopes of Mount Staurin, in front of the Bridge Gate. This was a risky business on the exposed dead ground between the gate and the Orontes river, so rather than start from scratch they chose to fortify an abandoned mosque that stood on a small hill close to the Bridge Gate.

Before this could happen, the newly arrived craftsmen and materials needed to be fetched from the coast. It is a testament to the value of these commodities and to the potential danger of the journey that two of the crusade's most powerful princes, Bohemond and Raymond of Toulouse, with sixty knights and at least 500 infantry (although we cannot be sure of the total number of infantry), were sent to St Simeon to act as escorts.[2]

The return journey took them three days, and in their absence Yaghi Siyan harassed the remaining crusaders with a number of minor sorties. Bohemond's and Raymond's return journey from the coast was particularly perilous because, laden with tools and building materials, they moved at a slower pace. It probably took them the best part of two days to cover the thirty kilometres from St Simeon, and along the way they allowed gaps to appear in their marching order. This was quite a serious failure of generalship on their part –

marching forces that break formation are inevitably vulnerable to attack – and perhaps indicates a lack of co-ordination between the two leaders. As they neared Antioch, around 7 March, a section of the crusader line, probably infantry, was attacked. The Antiochene garrison had laid an ambush. One eyewitness described the crusaders' abject terror as they were surrounded by screaming Muslim horsemen, fighting much as they had months earlier in the Battle of Dorylaeum:

> The Turks began to gnash their teeth and chatter and howl with very loud cries, wheeling round our men, throwing darts and loosing arrows, wounding and slaughtering them most brutally. Their attack was so fierce that our men began to flee over the nearest mountain or wherever there was path. Those who could get away quickly escaped alive, and those who could not were killed.[3]

The death toll from this initial engagement – some 500 infantry but, surprisingly, only two knights – indicates the continuing lack of cohesion between mounted and foot troops, and, perhaps, the ability of horsemen to escape danger more quickly. This rout could have spelled disaster for the Franks, but Bohemond – who seems to have been commanding the rearguard – rushed forward with re-inforcements, Godfrey of Bouillon led further troops into the fray from the main crusader camp, and a ferocious battle ensued on the ground in front of the Bridge Gate. At this point Yaghi Siyan likewise poured in more troops, and one Latin eyewitness recalled that he closed the Bridge Gate behind them, 'thereby demanding his soldiers to win the fight or perish'. But with the added weight of Godfrey's reinforcements, the crusaders began to gain the advantage. The Muslim troops panicked, turning in headlong flight back towards the Bridge Gate, which Yaghi Siyan now tried to rush open in desperation:

> They fled swiftly across the middle of the bridge to their gate. Those who did not succeed in crossing the bridge alive, because of

the great press of men and horses, suffered there everlasting death with the devil and his imps; for we came after them, driving them into the river or throwing them down, so that the water of that swift stream seemed to be running red with the blood of Turks, and if by chance any of them tried to climb up the pillars of the bridge, or to reach the bank by swimming, he was stricken by our men who were standing all along the river bank.[4]

Modern historians writing on the crusade have tended to downplay the significance of this battle, but to the Franks it seems to have marked an important turning point. Almost every contemporary Latin account provides a detailed description of these events, in language drawn from a grand palette of crusading rhetoric. At points this even outstrips the glorification lavished upon the earlier victories over Duqaq of Damascus and Ridwan of Aleppo. The crusaders who died in the initial Muslim ambush were celebrated as martyrs – 'Our knights or footsoldiers suffered martyrdom, and we believe that they went to heaven and were clad in white robes and received the martyr's palm' – a deliberate contrast to those Muslim dead who, it was claimed, would suffer in hell at the hands of 'imps'. Those who then prevailed in the Frankish counterattack were said to have 'invoked the name of Jesus Christ and, being assured of the journey to the Holy Sepulchre . . . joined in battle with one heart and mind'. To the Latin writers, they were 'knights of the true God, protected on all sides by the sign of the Cross', who held a religious service to give thanks to God as soon as the battle ended. This pious style of description is not unique; indeed throughout the expedition contemporary Latin writers were determined to drive home their belief that the Franks were engaged in a profoundly sacred campaign, fought in God's name and under his direction. What is remarkable is that such a wealth of religious imagery should be squandered on what would appear to be a relatively insignificant battle. We know that skirmishes between the crusaders and the Antiochene garrison took place outside the walls almost daily. The battle of 7 March brought no sudden end to the siege, perhaps it even had no immediately identifiable strategic impact upon its progress, and this is probably why it has effectively been ignored by modern historians. Why, then, was it so important to the crusaders themselves, so impressive a victory that many of the native Christian women still living in Antioch were supposedly prompted to come to 'windows in the walls, and when they saw the wretched fate of the Turks they clapped their hands secretly'?

The crusaders did claim to have inflicted heavy casualties upon their enemy: twelve 'emirs' or commanders were said to have fallen in the battle, 'together with 1,500 more of their bravest and most resolute soldiers, who were the best in fighting to defend the city'. If accurate, these figures would represent a serious weakening of a garrison that had probably numbered 5,000 at best. Estimates of overall Latin casualties vary between 1,000 and the strangely precise figure of 2,055, so losses on each side may well have been almost equal.

In fact, the real significance of the Bridge Gate battle lay in its impact upon morale. During the five months that they had lain encamped around Antioch, the crusaders had survived two major battles against the forces of Damascus and Aleppo, but, to date, this engagement represented perhaps their most decisive victory over the city's garrison itself. Yaghi Siyan had gambled upon deploying a large force to catch Bohemond and Raymond of Toulouse in isolation, but had failed. Eyewitnesses emphasise that this defeat and its aftermath had a marked effect upon the Muslim garrison's state of mind: 'The survivors no longer had the will to howl and gabble day and night, as they used to do . . . henceforth they had less courage than before, both in words and works.' The opposite was true for the crusaders. Those who had survived the horrors of winter and won the recent battle against Ridwan of Aleppo seem to have felt that this latest success presaged a change in the balance of fortune. Raymond of Toulouse's chaplain celebrated the precious booty and much-needed horses captured after the fray: 'Some [crusaders] running back and forth between the tents on Arabian horses were showing their new riches to their friends, and others, sporting two or three garments of silk, were praising God, the bestower of victory and gifts, and yet others, covered with three or four shields, were happily displaying these mementoes of their triumph.'[5]

Even more importantly, the crusaders had succeeded in bringing their prized cargo of tools, materials and craftsmen to Antioch. But, before work began on the new siege fort, a particularly macabre episode took place. At dawn on 8 March the Antiochene garrison stole out of the city to bury their dead in the grounds of the very mosque that the crusaders were planning to fortify. The Franks responded with chilling barbarity:

> Together with them [the Muslims] buried cloaks, gold bezants [coins], bows and arrows, and other tools the names of which we do not know. When our men heard [this] they came in haste to that devil's chapel, and ordered the bodies to be dug up and the tombs destroyed, and the dead men dragged out of their graves. They threw all the corpses into a pit, and cut off their heads and brought them to our tents so that they could count the number exactly, except for those that they loaded on to four horses belonging to the ambassadors of the emir of Cairo and sent to the sea-coast.[6]

We can interpret this action in a number of ways: as a coldly calculated atrocity, part of the ongoing game of siege and intimidation; or, as Raymond of Aguilers would have us believe, the isolated action of the poor rabble, 'excited by the sight of Turkish spoils'. We should recognise, however, that Raymond, perhaps because of his status as a chaplain, appears to have been more acutely aware than other eyewitnesses that the crusaders might be criticised for particularly extreme acts of barbarity, and tends to attribute them to the base and faceless 'poor'. In any case, we can be in no doubt that the cemetery's desecration added to the Muslim garrison's despair. One Latin contemporary noted: 'The sight of this action caused the Turks to be dejected and grief-stricken almost to death, and daily they did nothing but weep and wail.' They were far from broken, but they must have felt that the crusaders were finally gaining the upper hand.[7]

The Franks were now in a position to blockade the Bridge Gate and, around 10 March, work began on fortifying the abandoned mosque. They did not set out to construct a technically sophisticated or even permanent fortress. Even cowed by recent events, the Antiochene garrison might rally to attack the Franks before the fortification was complete, so the crusaders needed an easily erected makeshift fort. For three days a mass effort was made and the princes themselves joined in by helping to carry stones. With a detachment of archers watching the Bridge Gate for any sign of Muslim attack, the crusaders dug a double ditch around the mosque, put up a rough stone-and-lime-mortar curtain wall within this perimeter, and finally raised two improvised rock towers beside the mosque itself.

By 14 March the new stronghold had been completed and named La Mahomerie, the old French for the Blessed Mary, Christ's mother. Although it had been built by a communal effort, its command was now conferred solely upon Raymond of Toulouse. His chaplain took great care to explain why his lord accepted this onerous and expensive task:

> Debate ensued over the choice of a prince as guardian of the new fort, since a community affair is often slighted because all believe it will be attended to by others. While some of the princes, desirous of pay, solicited the vote of their peers for the office, the count, contrary to the wishes of his entourage, grabbed control, partly in order to excuse himself from the accusation of sloth and partly to point the way of force and wisdom to the slothful.[8]

The chaplain went on to explain that, because Raymond had, since the preceding summer, been periodically incapacitated by illness, a rumour had spread among the crusaders that 'he was willing neither to fight nor to give'. With his standing increasingly eclipsed by other princes, and even his own people, the Provençals, beginning to doubt him, Raymond agreed to command La Mahomerie, we are told, in order to reinstate his good name. But Raymond of Aguilers' rather desperate attempts to explain this decision give off the distinct aroma of propaganda. He probably conceded that Raymond of Toulouse's act was not entirely selfless to forestall more damaging questions about his hero's motivation. One issue had begun to burn in Raymond of Toulouse's mind: who would win possession of Antioch when the city finally fell? Before March 1098 Raymond had not made an outstanding contribution to the siege and so could not claim the city on the basis of having orchestrated its fall. He did, however, still possess a relative abundance of one increasingly scarce resource: money. While other princes expected to be paid to organise the defence of La Mahomerie, Raymond offered to meet all expenses out of his own purse. In effect he bought exclusive rights to the siege fort. Why? The laws of war – which granted ownership by 'right of conquest' – had already influenced Bohemond's decision to secure access to the Gate of St Paul at the start of the siege. Now Raymond followed suit by blockading the city's other major portal, the Bridge Gate. Both were now set for a race into Antioch when the city fell.[9]

Towards the end of March 1098 Yaghi Siyan rallied his troops' flagging spirits sufficiently to launch a surprise dawn attack out of the Bridge Gate, testing the strength of La Mahomerie. Raymond of Aguilers, probably camped within the fort by this time, recalled with some horror that their position was almost overrun. In his opinion, it was the miraculous hand of God that saved the Provençals: 'On the preceding day a torrent of rain drenched the fresh earth and thus filled the fosse around [La Mahomerie]. As a result . . . the strength of the Lord hindered the enemy.'

In fact, the crusade princes must have known that the siege fort could never withstand a sustained, full-scale assault – a fortification thrown up in three days was not intended for such a purpose. Instead, in the event of an attack, La Mahomerie was designed to provide Raymond of Toulouse's troops just enough protection to allow

Frankish reinforcements to be sent across the Bridge of Boats. Raymond of Aguilers remembered that the dawn attack was thwarted in just such a way: 'The noise of combat attracted our forces, and as a result the fort was saved.' Antioch's Bridge Gate may not have been sealed, but control of the traffic before it was now in the crusaders' hands.[10]

With the Bridge Gate guarded, the Muslim garrison took to using the city's last major gate, that of St George, but with the increased Latin control over the area even this became precarious. One Latin eyewitness gleefully reported that a group of crusaders, probably Provençals, captured 2,000 horses – surely an exaggeration – that had been led out of the Gate of St George to pasture on the slopes of Mount Silpius. Even so, the crusaders soon took steps to blockade this final gate. In the first week of April the council of princes appointed Tancred, Bohemond's nephew, to fortify and man a monastery next to the gate in return for 400 marks of silver, one-quarter of which came directly from Raymond of Toulouse. This payment is quite revealing. In the *Gesta Francorum* – written by an anonymous southern Italian Norman whom we would expect to be a partisan supporter of his countryman – Tancred is actually reported to have said he would do the job, but only 'if I may know what reward I shall have'. This self-serving attitude was probably the result of both his acquisitive nature and his status in the second, poorer rank of the crusader aristocracy. In fact, Tancred benefited from the arrangement all around, because within days of taking up his post he captured an Armenian and Syrian trade caravan bound for Antioch's St George Gate, seizing 'corn, wine, barley, oil and other such things'.[11]

From early April 1098 the crusaders tightened the noose around Antioch. Their cordon was not perfect – it was still possible for some limited supplies to be brought into the city via the Iron Gate – but the balance had tilted in the besiegers' favour. Throughout the preceding winter they had struggled to gather enough food to survive, while the Antiochene garrison received regular supplies. Now, with the tables turned, the crusaders could forage in relative safety and enjoyed

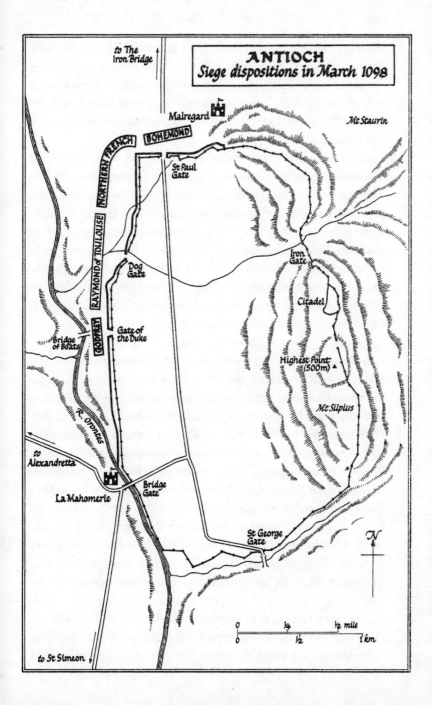

ANTIOCH
Siege dispositions in March 1098

to The Iron Bridge

Malregard

Mt Staurin

NORTHERN FRENCH
BOHEMOND

St Paul Gate

RAYMOND of TOULOUSE

Dog Gate

Iron Gate

Citadel

GODFREY

Bridge of Boats

Gate of the Duke

Highest Point (500m)

Mt Silpius

R. Orontes

to Alexandretta

La Mahomerie

Bridge Gate

St George Gate

N

to St Simeon

0   ¼   ½ mile

0   ½   1 km

secure lines of communication with St Simeon, and it was the turn of Yaghi Siyan and his men to suffer. The crusaders' lot was further improved when lavish gifts of horses and weapons arrived from Baldwin of Boulogne, now established as ruler of Edessa, and, in May, by the return of other crusaders who had manned outlying forts and foraging centres.[12]

The Provençal crusader Raymond of Aguilers made an intriguing observation about this period in a casual aside during a description of Frankish visions. He revealed that at this point in the siege the Latin priest Evremar travelled south to the Muslim city of Tripoli, where he supposedly spent some time 'keeping body and soul together'. The idea that the crusaders might, even in the midst of the struggle to overcome Antioch, be able to travel freely through Islamic territory and even benefit from Muslim hospitality suggests that the lines of inter-religious conflict may not have been as clearly drawn during the expedition as historians once supposed.[13]

Very little is known about the progress of the siege through the remainder of April and May. Even eyewitness sources pass over the period in little more than one or two lines. We can, however, make tentative attempts to piece together some events. The strain within Antioch certainly seems to have been mounting. One Latin contemporary, Peter Tudebode, recalled that around this time Yaghi Siyan sought to ransom a recently captured crusader named Rainald Porchet. He was dragged up on to the city's walls and ordered to negotiate a suitable payment from his Latin comrades below or face death. Tudebode provided a heavily dramatised account of Rainald's reaction, in which he refused to plead for his release, rejected Siyan's last-ditch offer to repudiate Christianity and become a Muslim, and met his subsequent death by decapitation in prayer. The aftermath of this 'martyrdom' was even more ferocious:

Then [Yaghi Siyan], in a towering rage because he could not make Rainald turn apostate, at once ordered all the [captive crusaders] in Antioch to be brought before him with their hands bound behind their backs . . . He ordered them stripped stark naked, and as they stood in the nude he commanded that they be bound with ropes in a circle. He then had chaff, firewood, and hay piled around them, and finally as enemies of God he ordered them put to the torch. The Christians, those knights of Christ, shrieked and screamed so that their voices resounded in heaven.[14]

Tudebode told this story as a powerful example of Christian piety in the face of Muslim cruelty, but, if true, it may also indicate a significant hardening in the psychological battle between besieger and besieged. By massacring his remaining Latin captives, Yaghi Siyan was throwing away potential ransom money. But cold calculation rather than blind rage may have prompted his action. He probably thought that his failure to secure any payment for Rainald demonstrated that the crusaders, believing Antioch's fall to be imminent, would now refuse to pay any further ransoms. By callously butchering prisoners, however, he virtually guaranteed that the remaining crusaders would be baying for Muslim blood, putting an end to any hopes among his faltering garrison for a peaceful surrender. The message to his men was simple: if you want to live, you will have to fight.

By May, the garrison's nerve seemed to be failing. The crusader knight Anselm of Ribemont recorded in a letter that around 20 May an offer of surrender was received from the city. He wrote that the Muslims went 'so far as to receive some of our men among them, and several of their men came out to us'. However, these Latins, including a member of Hugh of Vermandois' contingent, Walo II of Chaumont-en-Vexin, constable to the king of France, were then killed inside Antioch. Anselm believed the whole affair had been a 'trap', but it is quite possible that a section of the Muslim garrison was actually trying to orchestrate an unsanctioned surrender to Hugh's men, only for Yaghi Siyan to discover the affair and slaughter the crusader envoys.[15]

THE TRAITOR WITHIN

This plot may have been foiled, but by late spring there were other disaffected elements within the city. By April, or early May at the latest, Bohemond had established a secret line of communication with an Antiochene named Firuz. Acting alone, or at the head of a very small group of conspirators, Firuz would change the course of history. In many ways, his actions alone determined the fate of the First Crusade. But, for a man of such significance, Firuz is a remarkably shadowy figure. Mentioned by almost every contemporary account of the crusade, his story is slightly different in each telling. His identity, motivation, the very details of how his conspiracy worked, are all veiled in mystery.

Our best guess is that Firuz was an Armenian resident of Antioch who had adopted the Muslim faith. A number of sources describe him as having been a relatively wealthy armour-maker, but we can be certain that during the crusader siege he helped guard the city's walls. He seems to have commanded at least one tower on the south-eastern walls rising above the Gate of St George, not too far from Tancred's siege fort. As such, he had control over a relatively isolated stretch of Antioch's defences. The means for his betrayal are therefore comparatively clear, but what of motive and opportunity? One crusade chronicler would have us believe that Firuz was persuaded to act by three successive visions of Christ. According to a twelfth-century Muslim writer based in Damascus, he turned to the crusaders because Yaghi Siyan had confiscated his wealth and property. Firuz may well have been disenchanted with Antioch's ruler, but in all likelihood his actions were chiefly inspired by simple greed. One southern Italian crusader admitted frankly that Bohemond bribed him with lavish promises of 'riches and great honour', while another contemporary believed that Bohemond promised to make Firuz the equal of Tancred in power and wealth.

But how was contact with Firuz first established? The explanation of the Byzantine princess Anna Comnena, written decades later in

Constantinople, appears at first sight to be wonderfully improbable –
Firuz, she wrote, simply 'used to lean over the walls' and chat with
Bohemond. It is perhaps not entirely impossible that the first
connection was made when Firuz hailed Tancred's men stationed
nearby, but communication is more likely to have been initiated and
maintained via Armenian traders passing in and out of the city.[16]

However their link was formed, by mid-May at the latest
Bohemond had in principle persuaded Firuz to give the crusaders
access to his section of the walls.* But Bohemond was not content
simply to orchestrate Antioch's fall – he wanted to ensure that it fell
into his acquisitive hands and, to that end, he was more than willing
to put his own interests before those of the crusade. Without revealing
his arrangement with Firuz, he came to a council of the princes,
apparently saying:

> Most gallant knights, you see that we are all, both great and small,
> in dire poverty and misery, and we do not know whence better
> fortune will come to us. If, therefore, you think it a good and proper
> plan, let one of us set himself above the others, on condition that
> if he can capture the city or engineer its downfall by any means, by
> himself or by others, we will agree to give it to him.[17]

Knowing that he now held the key to Antioch's downfall, Bohemond
was trying to trick his fellow princes into confirming an agreement
that would guarantee his rights to the city. We cannot doubt that his
scheme was utterly self-serving given that it is reported in full by his
supporter, the author of the *Gesta Francorum*. To Bohemond's
annoyance, however, the rest of the crusade leaders flatly refused his
proposal, maintaining that Antioch must be divided equally among

---

*In a rather garbled account, Albert of Aachen recorded that an Armenian – also,
rather strangely, named Bohemond – acted as a go-between with Firuz, but noted
that it was generally believed in the crusader camp that Bohemond had chanced to
capture Firuz's son earlier in the siege and now coerced him to action.

all. At this point, around the middle of May, there was as yet no sense of urgency or panic in the crusader camp. The tide of the siege had turned in their favour, progress was being made, other ploys – such as that involving Walo of Chaumont-en-Vexin – were being pursued. In short, when Bohemond first came to the negotiating table the crusaders were not desperate. That was about to change.[18]

Back in October 1097, when the crusaders first approached Antioch, Yaghi Siyan had sent his youngest son, Muhammad, east to negotiate support from Baghdad and the rulers of Mesopotamia. This may well have been followed up by further entreaties in March 1098. One Latin chronicler invented a graphic but fanciful account of this embassy, in which Yaghi Siyan's envoys first sought to demonstrate the severity of their situation and the depth of their despair: 'They took their hats off and threw them to the ground, they savagely plucked out their beards with their nails, they pulled at and tore their hair out by the roots with their fingers, and they heaved sighs in great lamentations.'

The sultan of Baghdad was so impressed by this demonstration of despair that he supposedly 'summoned magicians, prophets and soothsayers of their gods and asked about future victory'. Once assured of propitious omens, he ordered a massive relief force to be mustered and placed under the command of his supporter, Kerbogha, the atabeg of Mosul, a figure simply characterised as 'a dreadful man'.[19] The lengthy description of these events may well be pure fiction, but it is representative of two prevalent themes running through most contemporary Latin accounts. Just as there was not one dominant Christian leader of the First Crusade, so the Latin expedition faced a series of Muslim enemies rather than a single foe. Lacking an obvious, primary antagonist, many Latin observers singled out Kerbogha as the crusade's most dangerous opponent, styling him, to some extent at least, as their anti-hero. Kerbogha tends, therefore, to be the subject of more speculative, even fantastical, characterisation than any other Muslim leader. In one extraordinary passage, the author of *Gesta Francorum* even went so far as to record a lengthy, but entirely fabricated, conversation between Kerbogha and his mother, in which she warned him not to fight the crusaders because they were protected by the Christian God, predicting that 'If you join battle with these men you will suffer very great loss and dishonour, and lose many of your faithful soldiers, and you will leave behind all the plunder which you have taken, and escape as a panic-stricken fugitive.'

All in all, Kerbogha comes across in the Latin sources as an arrogant but formidable general. Perhaps more importantly, observers in the crusader camp believed that he was the officially appointed representative of the Seljuq sultan of Baghdad – in the *Gesta Francorum* he is described as 'commander-in-chief of the army of the sultan of Persia'. In a sense he is portrayed as the sanctioned champion of Islam, leading the finally united might of Syria and Mesopotamia:

Kerbogha had with him a great army whom he had been assembling for a long time, and had been given leave by the khalif, who is the pope of the Turks, to kill Christians . . . [He had] collected an immense force of pagans – Turks, Arabs, Saracens, Paulicians, Azymites, Kurds, Persians, Agulani and many other people who could not be counted.[20]

Kerbogha stood at the head of this intimidating, if rather bewildering, array of troops, but his image as the 'official' leader of Sunni resistance to the crusade is deeply misleading. If we piece together the evidence provided by the limited corpus of Arabic sources for these events, a strikingly different picture emerges. Kerbogha had risen to power in Mosul, far to the east in Mesopotamia, on the back of his reputation as an astute and merciless military commander, and although he was the sultan of Baghdad's ally, he was not his puppet.

Kerbogha harboured his own ambitions for northern Syria, and the advent of the First Crusade presented the perfect opportunity for their realisation. Under the cloak of a sacred struggle to annihilate the ravening Frankish horde, he hoped to occupy Antioch and large swathes of Syria. If successful, he himself might be able to challenge for power in Baghdad. Kerbogha spent six months carefully laying the military and diplomatic foundations for his campaign, piecing together an immensely intimidating coalition of Muslim forces. Drawn from across the Abbasid world, armies were committed from Damascus, Harran, Homs, Mardin, Samosata and Sindjar, among other places. Most came not from religious duty or deep-felt hatred of the crusaders, but rather out of fear of Kerbogha. They knew that he might one day lead the Seljuq world, and they chose now to be his ally rather than his enemy. Only Ridwan of Aleppo resisted the call to arms, staunchly refusing to renounce his independence.

Some allies joined Kerbogha at Mosul, others marched directly to a rendezvous at Antioch, but, once gathered, the Turkish host was massively powerful. An Armenian from Edessa estimated their number at 800,000 cavalry and 300,000 infantry; one Muslim chronicler simply described Kerbogha's army as 'uncountable'. These must have been gross exaggerations, but Kerbogha probably commanded in excess of 35,000 men. So long as the campaign went well, Kerbogha could expect to retain the 'loyalty' of this massive composite army. But should his generalship falter, should the façade of his inexorable ascent towards pre-eminence begin to crumble, then their obedience might weaken.[21]

Rumours that a huge Muslim army was gathering reached Antioch in the second half of May 1098. The crusader princes decided to investigate the matter more fully, dispatching scouting parties under the likes of Reinhard of Toul and Drogo of Nesle, east to Artah, south to the Ruj and north towards Cilicia. Their surveillance confirmed the princes' worst fears: 'They saw the [Muslim] army swarming everywhere from the mountains and different roads like the sands of the sea, marvelling at their infinite thousands and totally unable to count them.'[22]

On 28 May the first scouts returned to Antioch with their dreadful news. It now seemed that, after eight months camped outside the city walls, the exhausted, bedraggled Franks would be crushed between Antioch and Kerbogha's advancing army. Knowing what a devastating effect this revelation would have on crusader morale, the princes decided to keep the news secret for the time being and met to discuss the situation in an emergency council on 29 May. Facing battle on two fronts and probable extermination, all the princes, with the likely exception of Raymond of Toulouse, now agreed to Bohemond's earlier proposal, apparently stating: 'If Bohemond can take this city, either by himself or by others, we will thereafter give it to him gladly, on condition that if the emperor come to our aid and fulfil all his obligations which he promised and vowed, we will return the city to him as it is right to do.'[23]

This partial compromise allowed them to meet Bohemond's demands while still paying lip-service to their oaths to the Emperor Alexius. With this agreement in place, Bohemond finally revealed his relationship with Firuz. Historians have often argued that the Latins were incredibly fortunate that Kerbogha chose to besiege Edessa for three weeks in May before moving on to Antioch, because this bought the crusaders enough time to orchestrate the Firuz scheme. In reality it is very likely that Bohemond had already established communications with Firuz in the preceding months. He certainly had the means to orchestrate the city's betrayal at the council held earlier in May, but held back because he was not promised his desired reward. This reveals two important points: Bohemond was focused above all else upon securing the right to rule Antioch; and Kerbogha's delay at Edessa did not save the crusade, it merely postponed the moment at which Bohemond sprang his carefully crafted plan.[24]

In the following days the final preparations were made with Firuz, and his son was smuggled out of the city to act as a hostage in Bohemond's camp. The plan agreed between Bohemond and Firuz was relatively straightforward. On the evening of 2 June a large detachment of crusaders – both cavalry and infantry – would march off in plain view of the Muslim garrison, only to return under cover of darkness. The knights would retrace their steps and then make the rest of the way on foot, while the infantry would be led by one of Firuz's co-conspirators through the mountains. Both groups would then rendezvous at the walls above the Gate of St George. Having completed this diversionary manoeuvre, a small detachment of troops would scale the walls near Firuz's tower, overwhelm any immediate resistance and then rush to open the city's gates.

A high degree of secrecy surrounded the whole scheme. One crusade chronicler remarked that 'Bohemond's plan was not common knowledge' among the crusaders, and some Provençals seem to have been surprised by the course of events on 2/3 June. Since Armenians moving amid the Franks had earlier been believed to be spying for the Muslim garrison, it would have made sense not to broadcast Bohemond's plan throughout the army.* One might suspect that Bohemond tried to keep his plans secret to ensure that his men were able to seize key sections of the city. In reality, however, the plan must have been widely agreed by the princes in order to ensure a rapid and co-ordinated response as soon as the walls were breached. Even with a traitor co-operating inside the city, Bohemond's scheme was still desperately dangerous. Without an immediate and overwhelming deployment of crusaders into the city once the gates were opened, the isolated advance troop might well be butchered and the opportunity lost. Bohemond certainly seems to have co-ordinated his movements with Raymond of Toulouse and Adhémar of Le Puy, and to have agreed that, once the first breach was made, Godfrey of Bouillon and Robert of Flanders would lead a direct attack on Antioch's citadel.[25]

One prince who did not play any part in Bohemond's scheme was Stephen of Blois. He probably attended the council on 29 May, but

---

*Tancred's biographer, Ralph of Caen, who wrote about a decade after the event, would even have us believe that his hero had no idea that the attack would take place. This seems improbable given that Tancred commanded the siege tower not far from Firuz's section of wall, but can perhaps be explained by Ralph's desire to excuse Tancred's failure to play a significant role in these events.

he seems to have decided that, in the face of Kerbogha's approach, the crusaders' prospects for survival were bleak. Early on 2 June he announced that he was ill and, in the company of many of the crusaders from Blois-Chartrain, withdrew north over the Belen Pass to Alexandretta. He never returned, although, as we shall see, he was to have a profound effect on the crusade's later progress. The shocking impact of Stephen's departure, which even at the time must have been construed by many as a desertion, was rendered even more significant by the fact that the other princes had, in the early months of 1098, chosen him to act as the expedition's 'commander-in-chief'. This title probably meant that Stephen had chaired crusader councils. The desertion of one of the crusade's most powerful leaders at the very moment when its fate hung in the balance did not augur well for the Latins' prospects and the crusader camp was gripped by an atmosphere of fear and anticipation on 2 June.[26]

That evening one of Bohemond's followers, a man bearing the rather odd nickname of 'Bad-crown', summoned the troops that would make the diversionary departure. Everything went to plan, and at roughly 3 a.m. on 3 June some 700 crusaders gathered on the slopes above the Gate of St George. A sizeable group under the command of Godfrey and Robert of Flanders carried on towards the citadel while the rest stayed with Bohemond. They waited until the night-watch carrying lanterns passed by atop the walls and then rushed forward to contact the traitor within. To their immense relief Firuz was there. He lowered a rope to which the crusaders attached their oxen-hide ladder, which was then duly hauled up and secured to the battlements. Sixty men were due to climb up in the advance party, but they were absolutely terrified. One Latin contemporary recalled that 'their hearts were struck with fear and very great doubt and each of them was reluctant and very much against being the first in and climbing the walls'. Many would have known the recent fate of Walo of Chaumont-en-Vexin and his men when they were betrayed in the city. Mounting the ladder they had no real idea whether or not they were heading into a trap.

The *Gesta Francorum*, whose author followed Bohemond to the foot of the walls, provides palpable evidence of the dangers involved. He described how Bohemond encouraged his men, saying: 'Go on, strong in heart and lucky in your comrades, and scale the ladder into Antioch, for by God's will we shall have it in our power in a trice,' but then shrewdly decided not to join the first wave of attack himself. Eventually, men began to climb. A knight from Chartres named Fulcher (not to be confused with his namesake, the crusade chronicler), the son of Fulcher fitz-Gerard, a canon of Notre Dame de Chartres, was the first to mount the walls. But now, in their panicked desperation not to be caught in mid-climb, too many crusaders rushed up the ladder and, overburdened, it toppled, killing some and injuring others:

> The people of God shook with horror at this, thinking all these things had happened by Turkish trickery, and that now all those sent in had undoubtedly perished. No sound, no outburst was heard in the city nor on the ramparts, even though those who fell made a great noise. Lord God raised a strongly blowing wind that night. [Firuz], obedient to the vow he had made to Bohemond concerning the betrayal of the city, once again let down the rope to draw up the ladder.[27]

At last, the remaining men reached the wall top and the most dangerous moment of the entire assault. Speed and silence were essential, for had the general alarm been raised the entire attack might have been thwarted. Amazingly, the crusaders managed to kill the patrolling watchmen and the sleeping guards of the nearest three towers 'without an outcry' being made, although in their haste they did mistakenly hack to death Firuz's own brother. Back on the ground Bohemond's remaining troops became impatient. The author of the *Gesta Francorum*, who was in among this group, vividly recalled that 'there was a [postern] gate not far from us to the left, but it was shut and some of us did not know where it was, for it was still dark. Yet by fumbling with our hands and poking about we found it, and all made a rush at it, so that we broke it down and entered.'[28]

Up to this point the attack had been based on stealth and silence. Now, suddenly, that changed. With the breach made, Bohemond sounded bugles so that by prearranged signal Godfrey and Robert would know to begin their attack on the citadel. All at once, Bohemond's men began shouting and screaming to terrify the Antiochenes, calling out their rallying cry, 'God's will! God's will!' again and again. Every eyewitness account remarks on the abrupt and overwhelming outburst of noise. One remarked that 'at this moment the shrieks of countless people arose, making an amazing noise throughout the city'. Another reported: 'The crusaders killed all whom they met, and at daybreak they cried out in such terrifying screams that the whole city was thrown into confusion and women and children wept.'[29]

In those crucial first minutes the combination of surprise, the confusion of darkness and fear of the crusaders' unrestrained brutality paralysed the defenders. As soon as he was within the city, Bohemond ordered his banner, blood red in colour, to be raised from the walls near the top of Mount Silpius. His intention was clear – to stake an unquestionable claim to the city – but, according to one eyewitness, his act had a more immediate impact: 'Now as dawn broke our standards flew atop the southern hill of Antioch. Panicked by the sight of our troops on the overhanging hill, some of the Antiochenes rushed through the gates while others leaped from the walls. The Lord threw them into such chaos that not a single one stood and fought.'[30]

At the same time, some of the native Christians still living within the city decided to turn on the Muslim garrison and began opening the city's remaining gates. This chaotic reaction to Bohemond's assault sealed Antioch's fate. Had Yaghi Siyan moved quickly to staunch the breach in the south-eastern quarter and maintain a tight guard over the city's other gates, he might have averted disaster. As it was, with the way open, the remaining crusaders began pouring into the city. What followed was a chaotic and bloody massacre, fuelled by eight months of suffering, starvation and stored aggression. Although some pockets of Muslim resistance remained, these were quickly overwhelmed. In the half-light of dawn the slaughter was indiscriminate: 'They were sparing no Muslim on the grounds of age or sex, the ground was covered with blood and corpses and some of these were Christian Greeks, Syrians and Armenians. No wonder since [in the darkness] they were entirely unaware of whom they should spare and whom they should strike.' After the city had fallen an eyewitness noted: 'All the streets of the city on every side were full of corpses, so that no one could endure to be there because of the stench, nor could anyone walk along the narrow paths of the city except over the corpses of the dead.'[31]

The Muslim garrison had only one success. In the first wave of fighting Godfrey and Robert of Flanders failed to break into Antioch's formidable citadel. With panic sweeping the rest of the city, Yaghi Siyan's son rallied what few troops he could find and struggled up the slopes of Mount Silpius to find refuge in the fortress. Isolated high above the city, the citadel remained in Muslim hands. Yaghi Siyan himself proved less cool-headed. Believing the citadel to have fallen already, he took flight, perhaps out of the Iron Gate, with his personal bodyguard. He managed to get some distance from the city, but was then thrown by his horse and left for dead by his men. A few hours later, his battered body was discovered by an Armenian butcher who promptly decapitated it and presented the head to the crusaders.[32]

After eight tortuous months of ineffective military investment, the crusaders finally overcame Antioch's fortifications by means of intrigue and bribery. Once within the city they unleashed a ferocious wave of carnage before which the Muslim garrison could not stand. Repellent as it was, the appalling violence perpetrated by the Latins during the sack of Antioch did in fact improve the crusade's prospects of success. Their willingness to butcher the city's garrison gave them a reputation for absolute ruthlessness, and in the coming months other Muslim cities on the road to Jerusalem considered negotiating with the Latins rather than face wholesale destruction.

Perhaps inevitably, the crusaders' bottled-up bloodlust was matched only by their hunger for booty. Indeed, one contemporary recalled that, once inside Antioch, 'our rabble wildly seized everything that they found in the streets and houses. But the proved soldiers kept to warfare, in following and killing the Turks.' The truth was that most of the city's resources had been exhausted:

> [The crusaders] patrolled the city looking for provisions, but they discovered few. They found many purple garments of different kinds, also pepper and very many spices, the gentiles' clothes and tents, gaming pieces and dice, also some money but not much. No wonder, for during the long siege, the many thousands of gentiles assembled in that place had used it all up.[33]

Raymond of Toulouse did, however, capitalise upon his position in front of the Bridge Gate. When fighting began on 3 June his men overran this entrance and seized all the buildings in the area, including the Bridge Gate itself and the Palace of Antioch. Thus, while Bohemond raised his banner above the city, Raymond simultaneously established a powerful Provençal foothold in Antioch. It looked as though Bohemond was not going to claim possession of the city quite as easily as he had hoped.[34]

The crusaders had stolen and battled their way into Antioch, but their success came not a moment too soon. On the very next day, 4 June, Kerbogha's army began to arrive; the crusaders were soon surrounded. Suddenly the besiegers had become the besieged.[35]

TO THE EDGE OF ANNIHILATION

In June 1098 the First Crusaders found themselves ensnared in a bizarre predicament. Having spent some eight months battling to gain entry to Antioch, they now suddenly found themselves trapped within its walls. The advance scouts from Kerbogha's immense army began to arrive outside Antioch. They soon struck an early blow against the crusaders. The Muslim scouting party, made up of 300 cavalry, initially made a cautious approach, sending ahead a detachment of thirty men to reconnoitre the city. The sight of this seemingly isolated force approaching Antioch proved too much to resist for Roger of Barneville, a powerful southern Italian Norman knight renowned for his martial prowess and skill as a negotiator. In a moment of foolhardy bravery he charged out against them with only fifteen of his most capable men and, when the Muslims fled, raced on in pursuit. In spite of all his military experience, Roger had been lured into a fatal error of judgement and fallen foul of the Muslims' favourite tactic – the feigned retreat. As he was drawn away from the safety of the city, the remainder of the Muslim scouting force suddenly poured out of a hidden valley. The Latin chronicler Albert of Aachen described how Roger, facing odds of twenty to one, turned tail, making a desperate break for the city:

The Turks on galloping horses drove on the fleeing [crusaders], until Roger drew near the town-wall and almost escaped across the shallows of the Orontes with his men. But luck was against him and in full view of all those who were standing around the ramparts the noble champion was beaten by a Turkish soldier on a faster horse. An arrow pierced his back and penetrated his liver and lung, and so he slipped from his horse and breathed his last.

In full sight of the cowed and horrified onlookers within Antioch, his body was decapitated and his head stuck on the end of a Muslim spear as a trophy of victory. Albert of Aachen imagined this scouting party gleefully reporting to Kerbogha that the crusaders would offer little resistance. Roger's body was recovered and buried with full honours by Adhémar of Le Puy and all the princes in the doorway of the St Peter's basilica. Even so, the crusaders saw the death of so prominent a knight as a dreadful omen. One of their number remarked that with the loss of this 'most illustrious and beloved knight ... sorrow and fear gripped our people'. Their ultimate nightmare had come to fruition – thousands of kilometres from home, already exhausted by months of battle and suffering, they were about to be surrounded by an overwhelming force from which there was seemingly no escape.[1]

The crusaders quickly decided that they were in no position to meet this new threat in a full-scale battle, as they had done with Ridwan's army in February. Kerbogha's force was much larger – outnumbering their own by as much as two to one – and, more importantly, the crusaders themselves were now critically short of cavalry, having run out of horses. Albert of Aachen believed that this explained why the Franks failed to respond when Roger of Barneville was ambushed:

Hardly 150 horses remained to the [crusaders], and those were enfeebled by shortage of fodder; the Turks' horses, however, were fat and not worn out. As many as 400 Turkish horses were found and captured in the city of Antioch, which they had not yet begun to tame for riding to their custom, or taught to turn about in pursuit of the enemy and urge on with spurs.[2]

Under these circumstances, the princes chose to fall back on Antioch's immense fortifications and took up defensive positions within the city. On 5 June Kerbogha's main army reached the Iron Bridge, the key crossing of the River Orontes, twelve kilometres north of the city. The crusaders had left a garrison to protect the bridge, but it was quickly overrun and slaughtered. Only the Frankish commander was spared, left in chains to rot in one of the bridge's towers.[3]

The way forward to the city now lay open, but Kerbogha continued to exercise caution. He chose to establish his main camp some three kilometres north of Antioch, at the junction of the Orontes and its smaller tributary, the Kara Su – giving himself time to assess the city's defences and make contact with the Muslims still holding its citadel. Almost immediately, his attention turned to La Mahomerie, the siege fort built by the crusaders in front of Antioch's Bridge Gate. The Franks seem to have abandoned their two other forts – Malregard and Tancred's Tower – but were determined to retain control of the strategically crucial zone around La Mahomerie. During their own attempts to besiege the city this area had proved to be a vital battleground, and now it controlled access to the crusaders' sole surviving line of supply, the road to St Simeon. For the next three days Kerbogha set about testing Frankish resolve, throwing 2,000 men against the siege fort's makeshift defences. For some reason the job of resisting this vicious onslaught fell to Robert of Flanders, even though Raymond of Toulouse had, before the fall of Antioch, jealously guarded his position as commander of La Mahomerie. Now Robert made a valiant attempt to hold on to the fort with just 500 men, and for three days he resisted wave after wave of Muslim attack. Eventually though, on the night of 8/9 June, with the futility of his position clear, he moved his troops back into the city under cover of darkness and set fire to La Mahomerie, destroying the fort to prevent it falling into enemy hands.[4]

In this same period, Kerbogha made contact with Yaghi Siyan's son, Shams ad-Daulah, now in command of Antioch's citadel. There may, at first, have been some brief discussion between these two about rights to the city, but ad-Daulah quickly realised that he was in no position to negotiate. Kerbogha put one of his own commanders in control of the citadel and, around 8 June, began massing forces in and around the fortress on the eastern, more gentle slopes of Mount Silpius. Further troops were deployed to blockade the Gate of St Paul in the north of the city. By 10 June Kerbogha was ready to unleash an almighty assault upon the crusaders. The Franks themselves had spent months struggling to overcome Antioch's defences, but Kerbogha now had one tremendous advantage – control of the citadel. From this position he could threaten the entire length of the walls running atop Mount Silpius and, even more significantly, he might gain access to the small path that wound its way down to the main city below. The crusaders were exhausted, outnumbered, isolated and horseless, but, even so, had they had possession of the citadel they might have had some slender hope of holding out against Kerbogha. As it was, they knew that there would be no long-drawn-out rerun of their own siege. This struggle would instead be swiftly settled by bloody combat.

The citadel's overwhelming strategic significance was not lost on Bohemond – from the first moment of Antioch's fall on 3–4 June he had concentrated his efforts upon gaining a foothold on Mount Silpius. He rejected the idea of mounting a frontal assault on the citadel itself from within Antioch after taking one look at its fortifications. True to its name, this stronghold was designed to resist attack both from outside the city and from within. Even today, with its walls crumbling in disrepair, a line of formidable towers can be seen, defiantly facing the city below. By the time Kerbogha took control of this fortress, Bohemond had, however, established a camp opposite and to the south, along the ridge of Mount Silpius. Muslim and Latin were left facing each other across a small rocky valley, which can also be clearly seen today. From his position, Bohemond had control of a large section of the city walls and a series of towers from which he might hope to police the path leading down to Antioch. Of course, just as Antioch's huge size had presented problems to the crusaders as besiegers, now it posed similar difficulties to them as defenders. From 8 June, with Kerbogha gathering the bulk of his forces around the citadel, Bohemond seems to have been joined by Robert of Normandy and Robert of Flanders, but the Franks could ill afford to spread themselves too thinly – Godfrey stayed below in the city to defend the Gate of St Paul, while Raymond divided his time between fighting at the citadel and defending the Bridge Gate.[5]

On 10 June the crusaders, realising that Kerbogha was almost ready to launch an attack via the citadel, decided to make a pre-emptive strike. Using a small postern gate further south along the ridge of Mount Silpius they deployed a force to harry Kerbogha's camp. This rather audacious attack seems to have caught the Muslims off guard, and, aided by the element of surprise, the crusaders managed to drive them into a retreat. Overjoyed by their apparent success, some Latins merrily began to loot the camp, only to be overrun by Kerbogha's counterattack. Caught in the open, those who could made a chaotic flight back to the postern gate, but, as one Frankish eyewitness recalled, this 'was so terribly strait and narrow that many of the people were trampled to death in the crowd'. This ill-judged foray beyond the walls left the crusaders frightened and demoralised, but much worse was to come. Kerbogha now launched a combined offensive. His troops poured out of the citadel towards Bohemond's upper camp and along the path to the city, and at the same time others, approaching from outside, attacked the city walls running south of the citadel. Forced to fight on two fronts, the crusaders were stretched to the limit: 'The Turks strained with might to overrun and expel us from their route because descent into Antioch was possible only through our mountain. From morning until evening the fight raged with ferocity the like of which has never been reported.'[6]

What shocked the crusaders most was that, with such vast reserves of manpower, Kerbogha was able to unleash a seemingly unending stream of attackers. For two days the fighting raged without pause from dawn till dusk. A crusader who lived through this terror remarked that 'a man with food had no time to eat, and a man with water no time to drink'. The sheer, brutal intensity of this struggle sent some crusaders over the edge. One Latin eyewitness recalled that 'many gave up hope and hurriedly lowered themselves with ropes from the wall tops; and in the city soldiers returning from the encounter circulated widely a rumour that mass decapitation of the defenders was in store. To add weight to the terror, they too fled even as some urged the undecided to stand fast.'

Soon, panic spread throughout the city and even well-known knights began to desert:

While this was going on, William of Grandmesnil [Bohemond's brother-in-law], Aubré his brother, Guy Trousseau and Lambert the Poor, who were all scared by the battle of the previous day, which had lasted until evening, let themselves down from the wall secretly during the night and fled on foot to the sea, so that both their hands and their feet were worn away to the bone. Many others, whose names I do not know, fled with them. When they reached the ships which were in St Simeon's Port they said to the sailors, 'You poor devils, why are you staying here? All our men are dead, and we have barely escaped death ourselves.' When the sailors heard this they were horrified, and rushed in terror to their ships and put to sea. At that moment the Turks arrived and killed everyone whom they could catch. They burned those ships which were still in the mouth of the river and took their cargoes.

Given the unrelenting ferocity of Kerbogha's attacks and the nature of the crusaders' overall predicament, it is not surprising that many chose to flee. On 11 June another rumour spread through the army suggesting that the princes themselves were preparing to flee towards the coast, and the crusade leaders were able to calm their troops only by each swearing an oath not to abandon Antioch. One Provençal crusader noted that, 'even then only the closing of the gates of Antioch by orders of Bohemond and Adhémar prevented wholesale evacuation'.[7]

Those who stayed somehow managed to hold their ground on Mount Silpius for four long days. In part they survived through sheer, bloody-minded determination and martial skill: Bohemond was in the thick of the fighting and at one stage he was surrounded and had to be rescued by Robert of Flanders and Robert of Normandy; later a southern Italian knight, known only as Mad Hugh, managed to defend a tower on the walls single-handedly, breaking three spears in the process. Even so, the casualty rate was high – among the dead was Peter Tudebode's brother, lost to a wound received during the fighting. On 12 June the shortage of manpower up on Silpius became so desperate that Bohemond took the curious step of ordering buildings in the south-western quarter of the city, where he believed some crusaders were hiding, to be set alight. The fire got out of hand, almost reaching the Basilica of St Peter and the Church of St Mary, but it did apparently prompt some to join the fighting.[8]

A distinctly medieval mixture of piety and superstition also began to figure in the unfolding of events. On 11 June a priest named Stephen of Valence came to the princes gathered at the top of Silpius, claiming to have received a vision of Christ and the Virgin Mary in which the crusaders were admonished for their sins and charged to purify themselves for five days. The Provençal chaplain Raymond of Aguilers, impressed by the priest's story, recounted how 'Stephen reported the above vision to an assembly [of crusaders], swore upon the cross to verify it, and finally signified his willingness to cross through fire or throw himself from the heights of a tower if necessary to convince the unbelievers.' This story does not seem to have had a massive or immediate effect upon morale, but it does foreshadow the powerful, almost fevered tide of ecstatic spirituality that was about to grip the crusaders. Then, on the night of 13/14 June, with the Frankish resistance close to collapse, a strange light was seen in the heavens. One of Bohemond's followers recalled: 'There appeared a fire in the sky, coming from the west, and it approached and fell upon the Turkish army, to the great astonishment of our men and of the Turks also. In the morning the Turks, who were all scared by the fire, took flight in panic.'[9]

Seen as a divine portent, this phenomenon, probably a comet, heartened the crusaders and unnerved the Muslims. But Kerbogha's decision to redeploy his troops on 14 June was based on sound strategic judgement and not prompted simply by superstition. Having tried to break through the crusader lines for four days, he now elected to spread his forces more evenly, throwing a wider, enclosing net around the city. A substantial force was left in the citadel, the guard on the Gate of St Paul was strengthened and now, for the first time, a concerted effort was made to blockade the Bridge Gate and the Gate of St George. A crusader in Antioch at the time wrote that from this point on 'the Turks besieged the city on all sides, so that none of our men dared to go out or come in except by night and secretly'. Kerbogha may have failed to smash his way into Antioch, but now he would squeeze the crusaders into submission.[10]

With the city surrounded and communications with St Simeon severed, the crusaders were effectively cut off from the outside world. For the next two weeks the second siege of Antioch entered a new phase. Intermittent skirmishing continued: Godfrey lost 200 men during one attempt to raid the Muslim camp outside the Gate of St Paul; Tancred, whom one Latin contemporary described as a 'very fierce knight who could never have enough Turkish bloodshed' later made a stealthier attack out of the same gate with ten men and proudly returned with the heads of six slain Muslims. There were many other acts of individual 'heroism'. At one point, Henry of Esch, who almost drowned in the Orontes during the first siege of Antioch, spotted a group of Muslims setting ladders against an unmanned tower near the Iron Gate. He immediately rushed into the breach with only two men – his relatives Franco and Sigemar of Mechela –

in support, and was able to hold off the enemy long enough for reinforcements to arrive. Henry survived the encounter unscathed, but Franco received 'a very severe and scarcely curable wound to the head', while Sigemar was 'pierced through the belly with a sword to its hilt'. Meanwhile, on the slopes of Mount Silpius, the princes took the opportunity presented by the relative lull in fighting to throw up a crude defensive wall of stones and mortar between their upper camp and the citadel, which they then patrolled day and night.[11]

In reality, after 14 June, Kerbogha adopted a strategy of containment, and as a result a more insidious and debilitating threat began to unman the crusaders – starvation. They had already endured terrible shortages of food through the preceding winter, but now, stranded in a city which had already been stripped of resources by an eight-month siege, they faced a new level of suffering. One Frankish eyewitness recounted:

> The blasphemous enemies of God kept us so closely shut up in the city of Antioch that many of us died of hunger, for a small loaf cost a bezant, and I cannot tell you the price of wine. Our men ate the flesh of horses and asses; a hen cost fifteen shillings, an egg two, and a walnut a penny. All things were very dear. So terrible was the famine that men boiled and ate the leaves of figs, vines, thistles and all kinds of trees. Others stewed the dried skins of horses, camels, asses, oxen or buffaloes, which they ate.[12]

Another contemporary was appalled by the stories of misery told by those who lived through these days:

> With the city thus blockaded on all sides, and the [Muslims] barring their way out all round, famine grew so great amongst the Christians that in the absence of bread they . . . even chewed pieces of leather found in homes which had hardened or putrefied for three or six years. The ordinary people were forced to devour their leather shoes because of the pressure of hunger. Some indeed,

1. In the Middle Ages, Christians believed that Jerusalem – the crusaders' ultimate goal – lay at the centre of the world, reflecting the city's immense spiritual significance. This thirteenth-century map, like all maps of this age, thus depicted the Holy City as the 'navel of the world'.

2. In *c.* 1130 the sculptor Giselbert completed his masterpiece, *The Last Judgement*, the arch above the entrance of the Cathedral of St Lazare, Autun. No visitor could have avoided this striking reminder of the agony experienced by the Damned – in this detail, the tortured moment of judgement at the Weighing of Souls, and the death of a strangled sinner – which transforms the theoretical dangers of Sin into graphic reality.

3. Before the Council of Clermont, Pope Urban II toured southern France priming his supporters to ensure that the launch of the First Crusade met a warm welcome. Here (CENTRE LEFT) he consecrates a new altar at the hugely influential monastery of Cluny.

4. Then, as the Council of Clermont was drawing to a close on 27 November 1095, Urban preached his momentous sermon initiating the First Crusade.

Some of Europe's most powerful princes responded to Urban's call to arms

5. A nineteenth-century French artist imagines Adhémar of Le Puy (dressed in red robes) declaring Raymond of Toulouse as leader of the Provençal crusaders after the preaching at Clermont. Raymond, resplendent in white, gazes heavenward in contemplation of his imminent glory.

6 & 7. Godfrey of Bouillon sets out on the First Crusade (LEFT). This nineteenth-century statue in Brussels (RIGHT) reflects his popularised reputation as the expedition's 'hero'.

8 & 9. The crusading message was also spread across western Christendom by charismatic preachers like Peter the Hermit. (ABOVE) Peter leads a contingent of the People's Crusade, while (BELOW) he is granted an audience with the Byzantine Emperor Alexius Comnenus.

10. The Byzantine Emperor Alexius I Comnenus (1081–1118), here depicted in a twelfth-century Greek mosaic, was the most powerful Christian ruler on earth. Having expected the arrival of a few hundred Western mercenaries, he had to deal with the influx of some 100,000 crusaders bent on the recovery of Jerusalem. Alexius' astute management of the Crusade's crossing of his empire demonstrated his political acumen, but the expedition's eventual conquest of Syria and Palestine soured relations between Byzantium and the West.

11. The immense land walls of the Greek capital, Constantinople, would have reinforced the power and wealth of Byzantium in the minds of the crusaders.

12. Upon crossing into Asia Minor and the fringes of the Islamic world, the crusaders' first target was the ancient city of Nicaea. During its siege the Franks catapulted the heads of slain Muslims into the city to intimidate the garrison.

13 & 14. The first pitched battle between the crusaders and Muslim troops took place at Dorylaeum on 1 July 1097. The chaotic struggle, in which mounted Seljuq Turkish archers sought to adopt encirclement tactics, shocked the Franks – one terrified eyewitness later recalled how the 'Turks began, all at once to howl and gabble and shout . . . screaming like demons'. Later medieval artists sought to convey the sheer confusion of this encounter.

15. The imposing city of Antioch, built on the side of Mount Silpius, was entirely enclosed within massive walls, sections of which were built on dizzying slopes. Between October 1097 and June 1098 the First Crusaders sought to breach these seemingly impregnable fortifications.

16 & 17. Here, two surviving sections of the wall plunge down the side of the mountain.

18. Of Antioch's six major gateways only the Iron Gate (LEFT), built in a rocky chasm, remained open for the duration of the crusader siege.

19. High above the city, atop Mount Silpius, stood the citadel of Antioch (BELOW). Built to withstand attack both from outside the city and from within, no force could claim true dominion of Antioch without possession of this fortress.

20. Near dawn on 3 June 1098 crusaders mounted a ladder lowered by the renegade Firuz as Bohemond looked on. By this act of betrayal, Antioch fell to the Franks. This is one of a series of dramatic engravings of the crusade by the nineteenth-century French artist Gustave Doré.

21. The great battle of Antioch on 28 June 1098 was the turning point of the entire crusade. Against all the odds, the besieged Franks fought their way out of the city and overcame Kerbogha of Mosul's massive army. Later tradition held that Adhémar of Le Puy (LEFT) carried the Holy Lance into the fray, where its 'miraculous' power ensured victory.

22. The fortified town of Marrat an-Numan fell to an expeditionary force of crusaders in December 1098 but, isolated on the plains of Syria, these Franks soon ran out of food, prompting some to resort to cannibalism.

23. In late January 1099 the First Crusaders overwhelmed the hill-fort of Hisn al-Akrad. Over the next two centuries the Hospitallers refortified the site, creating Krak des Chevaliers, perhaps the most impressive castle of the medieval age.

The city of Jerusalem

24. The Dome of the Rock, lying within the Temple Mount complex, is revered to this day by Christians and Muslims alike.

25. The Tower of David, Jerusalem's citadel.

26. The city's imposing walls.

27. St Stephen's Gate.

28. To defeat Jerusalem's formidable defences, the First Crusaders spent weeks building siege weapons – depicted here with some imagination by Doré. The city fell on 15 July 1099 after a brief but brutal assault.

29. After the sack of Jerusalem the crusaders came, still covered in their victims' blood, to give thanks to God in the Holy Sepulchre – the site of Christ's death and resurrection.

30. Having captured the Holy City, the crusaders still had to meet one final threat – the armies of Egypt gathering on the coast at Ascalon. Here, after securing victory on 12 August 1099, Godfrey of Bouillon returns in triumph to the Holy Sepulchre, bearing the captured sword and standard of the Egyptian vizier, al-Afdal.

filled their wretched bellies with roots of stinging nettles and other sorts of woodland plants, cooked and softened on the fire, so they became ill and every day their numbers were lessened by death. Duke Godfrey, as they say who were there, paid out fifteen marks of silver for the flesh of a miserable camel; for a she-goat it is testified beyond doubt that his steward Baldric gave three marks to the seller.[13]

The First Crusade had now reached its nadir. Tormented by the constant threat of a full-scale Muslim assault, too terrified to contemplate a counterattack yet weakened day by day by death and hunger, a crisis in morale left the Latin army utterly paralysed within Antioch. All the eyewitness sources indicate that total defeat seemed both inevitable and imminent.[14] It was under these conditions that one of the expedition's most extraordinary and intriguing episodes took place – an event that would appear to provide a direct insight into the crusaders' state of mind.

THE HOLY LANCE OF ANTIOCH

On the evening of 10 June a bedraggled peasant from Provence named Peter Bartholomew came, unbidden, to seek an audience with Bishop Adhémar of Le Puy and Count Raymond of Toulouse. In the private interview that followed Peter related a remarkable tale, stating that he had, since 30 December 1097, been visited by 'two men clad in brilliant garments' on no fewer than five separate occasions. He described these apparitions, saying: 'The older one had red hair sprinkled with white, a broad and bushy white beard, black eyes and an agreeable countenance, and was of medium height; his younger companion was taller, and fair in form beyond the sons of men.'

These were, he believed, visions of St Andrew the apostle, accompanied by Christ. Peter described the progress of these apparitions in considerable detail. They had begun at the end of 1097 when an earthquake shook Antioch, and continued – as Peter's travels took him across northern Syria in search of food – in locations as diverse as Edessa, Mamistra and St Simeon. Quite apart from anything else, Peter's story indicates the lengths to which some crusaders were forced to go to forage for supplies. Peter had, he said, received his final vision that very day, as he sat 'dejected and listless' on a rock, having barely escaped alive from the fighting beyond the city walls on the top of Mount Silpius. From his very first appearance, St Andrew had had one very specific message to give Peter. Christian tradition held that, at the time of his crucifixion, Jesus' body had been pierced in the side by a spear wielded by the Roman soldier Longinus, which became known as the Holy Lance. This most sacred relic, St Andrew revealed, was now buried in the Basilica of St Peter, the main church of Antioch itself. In his earliest vision, back when the city still lay unconquered, Peter, still clad in his nightshirt, had been miraculously spirited past Muslim guards into the midst of the basilica and shown the Lance's exact resting place. Peter was charged with revealing the relic's location to the crusader princes so that it might be recovered once Antioch fell, and then used as a standard, for, the apostle said, 'he who carries this lance in battle shall never be overcome by the enemy'. But, Peter claimed, he had been too frightened and intimidated to tell his story, even though St Andrew returned again and again to castigate him for his inactivity. Now, finally, in the crusade's darkest hour, he had decided to come forward.[15]

Fantastical as Peter's tale may sound today, saintly visions and empowered relics were firmly established elements in the Christian cosmology of the eleventh century. Western European society had been conditioned to believe that saints – the sanctified dead – could act as intercessors in heaven for ordinary Christians living on earth, petitioning God for aid on their behalf and appearing through visions and miracles to manifest his divine will on earth. The physical remnants of these venerated Christians' lives – including parts of their body and objects that they had touched – were deeply revered. These relics were tangible foci of sanctity, mobile powerhouses of spiritual authority and intervention. Where a relic went, so the presence of the saint followed and thus, also, the power of God. Of all the relics in the Christian world, an item from Christ's own life was considered to be the most precious and powerful, so the potential significance of the Holy Lance was immeasurable. We should not for one minute imagine that belief in the efficacy and reality of this seemingly eccentric ideological framework was limited to the credulous poor. Kings, counts, popes and bishops venerated saints and their relics. Bishop Adhémar brought a small piece of wood, which he believed had been part of the cross upon which Christ was crucified, with him on crusade; Raymond of Toulouse carried a chalice that had belonged to St Robert of Chaise-Dieu, a celebrated holy man and founder of a Benedictine monastery. The crusaders had also been picking up new relics throughout their journey. A priest in Robert of Flanders' contingent actually stole an arm of St George from a Byzantine monastery. When he died the relic eventually found its way into the possession of Robert himself, who then became so devoted to the saint that he began styling himself 'the son of St George'.[16]

Peter Bartholomew's revelations about the location of the Holy Lance came at a time when spiritual fervour was near boiling point – as one eyewitness remarked in mid-June, 'now reported revelations of our comrades became rife' – but at first his story met with a rather mixed reception. Even Raymond of Aguilers, chaplain to the count of Toulouse, and the firmest advocate of the Lance's authenticity and power among the eyewitness crusader writers, admitted that at the end of their interview 'The Bishop [Adhémar] considered the story fraudulent, but the count immediately believed it and placed Peter Bartholomew in the custody of his chaplain, Raymond [of Aguilers].'[17]

In many ways, Bishop Adhémar's scepticism was quite under-standable. The Latin Church and its clergy certainly accepted that saints might appear in visions and manifest miracles through their relics, but they were also keen to validate the authenticity of such stories very carefully. Such proof was, of course, not easy to come by. Often the decision to accept or condemn was made on the basis of the visionary's social status and his willingness to swear a sacred oath in support of his story. On this basis, Peter – a poor servant in the employ of the Provençal knight William Peyre of Cunhlat – started off at a disadvantage in comparison, for example, to the priest Stephen of Valence, although one source does record that, like the latter, 'Peter came forward and swore the whole story was quite true.' The real problem, as Adhémar must have known, was that a Holy Lance was already sitting in the relic collection of the Byzantine emperor in Constantinople. According to Greek tradition, the Lance had been discovered in Jerusalem by St Helena in the early fourth century, and then brought to Constantinople some 400 years later. Naturally, therefore, Adhémar greeted Peter's tale with caution.[18]

Even so, by the time Kerbogha began redeploying his forces to encircle Antioch on 14 June, Raymond of Toulouse had decided that a search for the Lance must be made. Raymond of Aguilers, who played an intimate part in these events, wrote a feverishly detailed account of what took place:

> On [14 June] twelve men and Peter Bartholomew collected the appropriate tools and began to dig in the church of the Blessed Peter, following the expulsion of all other Christians. The bishop of Orange, Raymond of Aguilers, author of this work, Raymond of [Toulouse], Pons of Balazun, and Farald of Thouars were among the twelve. We had been digging until evening when some gave up hope of unearthing the Lance. In the meantime, after the count had gone to guard the citadel, we persuaded fresh workers to replace the weary diggers and for a time they dug furiously.
>
> But the youthful Peter Bartholomew, seeing the exhaustion of our workers, stripped his outer garments and, clad only in a shirt and barefooted, dropped into the hole. He then begged us to pray to God to return His Lance to the crusaders so as to bring strength

and victory to His people. Finally, in His mercy, the lord showed us his Lance and I, Raymond, the author of this book, kissed the point of the Lance as it barely protruded from the ground. What great joy and exultation then filled the city.[19]

In physical terms, the relic 'discovered' by Peter was probably little more than a small shard of metal, but, initially, most First Crusaders wholeheartedly accepted its authenticity. Adhémar may have continued to harbour some doubts, but among the majority of the princes and throughout the massed ranks of the army the Lance enjoyed a rapturous reception. One Latin eyewitness recalled that 'across all the city there was boundless rejoicing', while another Frankish chronicler remarked that a 'great euphoria seized the city' as the native Greek, Armenian and Syrian population of Antioch rushed to join the celebrations. The discovery of such an extraordinarily powerful relic, coming at the very moment at which the crusade had seemed to face certain annihilation, was interpreted by many as an irrefutable indication of God's renewed support for the expedition.

Traditionally, modern historians have drawn a clear, almost unwavering, connection between the Lance's discovery and the events that followed, arguing that, from the edge of defeat, the crusaders were galvanised into action by the Lance's electrifying impact. With morale rejuvenated, they elected to pursue a bold, aggressive and extremely dangerous strategy – to break out of the city and confront Kerbogha's army head on. Hans Eberhard Mayer, one of the greatest living authorities on the crusading movement, has written: 'The immediate effects of the discovery were enormous. The army's morale was raised and all were united in the urgent determination to break the blockade and destroy Kerbogha.'[20]

This approach does have a solid basis in evidence – in short, we believe that the crusaders were directly inspired to act by the Holy Lance because that is precisely what they tell us. Later that year, on 11 September 1098, the crusader princes declared in a letter to the pope: 'We were so comforted and strengthened by [the Lance's] discovery and by so many other divine revelations that some of us who had been discouraged and fearful beforehand, then became courageous and resolute to fight, and encouraged each other.'[21]

The *Gesta Francorum*, written by an anonymous southern Italian Norman crusader, has done even more to shape our opinion. Widely circulated and often copied in the Middle Ages, this eyewitness account has come to exert an almost inescapable influence over our own modern reading of the First Crusade. Crucially, the anonymous author of this text, having just described the unearthing of the Holy Lance, recorded that 'from that hour we decided on a plan of attack, and all our leaders forthwith held a council'.[22] From these words, one is almost left imagining the crusaders – their zealous blood boiling with battle hunger – sprinting from the Basilica of St Peter, straight out of the city gates and into combat. But this impassioned image is deeply misleading. The Holy Lance was discovered on 14 June 1098, yet the crusaders did not go into battle until 28 June. Two whole weeks separate these events.

Precise evidence for the period is lacking, but a reconstruction of this shadowy hiatus can be attempted. The crusaders would have been in no mood to hang around because food was, day by day, becoming scarcer in the city and many Franks were beginning to starve. It also seems unlikely that the crusaders would have needed two weeks to prepare for battle, given that they had, back in February of that same year, defeated Ridwan of Aleppo with just a few days' notice. Peter Bartholomew did issue a series of proclamations after having received a new visitation from St Andrew and Christ during the night of 15/16 June. These included the recommendation that all crusaders 'turn from sin to God and offer five alms because of the five wounds of the Lord'. Raymond of Toulouse, who organised the collection of these donations, amassed quite a fortune as a result. The Franks were also instructed to celebrate the discovery of the Lance on 21 June, although we have no idea how widely this was observed. Even so, no particular or dramatic event prevented the crusaders from going to battle.[23]

We can then explain the delay of two weeks that followed 14 June only by accepting that, while the discovery of the Holy Lance certainly bolstered Frankish morale, it was not enough to convince them to go immediately into battle against such terrible odds. This would mean that the unearthing of the relic was not the key turning point in the second siege of Antioch, much less a watershed in the fortunes of the entire crusade. To understand when and why the Franks decided to risk battle on 28 June we must consider other factors.

The crusaders had, since late 1097, been expecting Byzantine reinforcements to arrive at Antioch, possibly under the command of the Greek emperor himself, Alexius I Comnenus. For their part, the Byzantines had been busy trying to exploit the damage done by the crusaders to Seljuq power in Asia Minor. In the early spring of 1098 Alexius sent a fleet, under the command of his brother-in-law John Doukas, into the Mediterranean to mop up pockets of Turkish resistance along the west coast at Smyrna and the city of Ephesus, once a grand Roman metropolis. John then made a break inland, overrunning the famous spring-town of Hierapolis, before making camp at Philomelium. By early June, Alexius had marched an army from Constantinople to rendezvous with John. This two-pronged sweep brought much of the south-west quarter of Asia Minor back under Byzantine control.

According to his daughter and biographer Anna Comnena, Alexius was then at last ready to march on Antioch to be reunited with the Franks. But this was not to be. Around 20 June a rather forlorn group of travellers arrived out of the east at Philomelium. After deserting his comrades at Antioch on 11 June and taking ship from St Simeon, William of Grandmesnil landed at Alexandretta. There he found another deserter, Stephen of Blois, who, on the basis of William's story and his own surveillance of Kerbogha's army, decided that the time was ripe for quitting the perils of northern Syria. Together they set sail for Tarsus, and from there continued their journey overland, only to come across Alexius at Philomelium. Not surprisingly, they painted a grim picture of events at Antioch, apparently telling the emperor that 'the Franks had been reduced to a position of the utmost danger; in fact, they swore on oath that the collapse was complete'. The Latin sources that recounted this meeting imagined Count Stephen making even more dire predictions: 'I tell you truly that Antioch has been taken, but the citadel has not fallen, and our men are all closely besieged, and I expect by this time they have been killed by the Turks. Go back, therefore, as fast as you can, in case they find you and your followers.'

In truth, Alexius may never have planned to make an immediate move to Antioch – from his perspective it made more sense to hold his ground in Anatolia and advance to claim Antioch only once the crusaders had done the hard work of securing its downfall – but now he faced a clear choice. Naturally, his absolute priority was the safety of Constantinople and the empire. If the crusaders had already been overrun then he could do little for them. If he set off for Antioch only for the city to fall while he was en route his army might well be caught by a resurgent wave of Turkish aggression and obliterated. With the First Crusade on the brink of collapse, the risks involved in making a headlong rescue attempt were simply too great. Despite voluble protestations from a group of Latin mercenaries within his army – among them Bohemond's own brother, Guy – the emperor made his choice. An immediate evacuation of the entire area was ordered, and a scorched-earth policy set in motion, so that any advancing Muslim force would be unable to forage for food. With the fields of Anatolia aflame, Byzantium turned its back on the crusaders.[24]

We cannot be certain that news of Alexius' decision reached the Franks in Antioch before 28 June. Albert of Aachen believed that it did, writing that 'the terrible news of the emperor turning back and his army dispersing sped across the ramparts of Antioch and afflicted the pilgrims' hearts with great grief and shook much of the boldness from their spirits'. But Albert was not an eyewitness and his chronology could well be at fault. A messenger would literally have had to sprint back to northern Syria for it to be possible. Even so, as the days of June slipped by and Kerbogha's iron grip around Antioch tightened, the Franks must have begun to give up hope of reinforcement.[25]

If this reading of events is correct, then by the fourth week in June the crusaders were in desperate straits – weak with starvation, surrounded by enemies and abandoned by their allies. It is in this context that we must examine the strange and seemingly incongruous events of 24 June. On around that date, the crusader princes sent two envoys into the midst of Kerbogha's camp. They chose as ambassadors Peter the Hermit, disgraced deserter and demagogue to the masses, and an interpreter named Herluin. At least three eyewitnesses, actually in Antioch at the time, recorded that Peter carried a bold message of extraordinary defiance. Even though it was they, the Franks, who were trapped, seemingly powerless, within Antioch, Peter reportedly confronted Kerbogha with an ultimatum, saying, 'Our leaders, as one man, require you to take yourselves off quickly from the land which belongs to God and the Christians, for the Blessed Peter converted it long ago to the faith of Christ by his preaching. But they give you permission to take away all your goods . . . whithersoever you may choose.'[26]

Not surprisingly, Kerbogha simply laughed in their faces, warned that death or captivity awaited unless they surrendered immediately and converted to Islam, and sent the envoys back to Antioch empty handed. In reality, the crusade princes would have known that such unrealistic demands were virtually guaranteed to be rejected out of hand. Of course, our sources were not really trying to portray this as an episode of serious negotiation, but rather to show the crusaders as wildly defiant in the face of extreme adversity. Perhaps this was the truth of the matter – the envoys' mission may simply have been a propaganda exercise. Other Latin writers who were not present at Antioch presented the embassy in slightly more realistic terms:

They announced to the Turks through a certain Peter the Hermit, that unless they peacefully evacuated the region which at one time belonged to the Christians, they would surely begin war against them. But, if they wished it to be done otherwise, war could be waged by five or ten or twenty, or by 100 soldiers chosen from each side, so that with not all fighting at the same time, such a great multitude would not die, and the party which overcame the other would take the city and kingdom freely without controversy. This was proposed, but not accepted by the Turks, who, confident in their large numbers and courage, thought that they could overcome and destroy us.[27]

This suggestion of a champions' trial by battle is intriguing, not least because Fulcher seems to imply that, even in this crusading context, the avoidance of excessive bloodshed was morally desirable. Nonetheless, it was still basically an unrealistic proposal, because Kerbogha had no reason to risk giving up his numerical superiority. In fact, if we accept the testimony of the crusader sources, we must conclude that the princes were not here engaging in genuine diplomacy. Peter's embassy could then be variously explained as a morale-boosting exercise, a spying mission to gauge the strength and disposition of Kerbogha's forces or perhaps simply a delaying tactic.

Only in less partisan, non-Latin sources do we receive any hint that something much more serious might have been going on behind the scenes. Matthew of Edessa, an Armenian Christian near-contemporary, described what he believed happened in June 1098:

[Kerbogha's] army arrived [at Antioch]. Being seven times larger than the Frankish force, their troops violently besieged and harassed it. Then the Franks became threatened with a famine, because provisions in the city had long become exhausted. More and more hard-pressed, they resolved to obtain from Kerbogha a promise of amnesty on condition that they deliver the city into his hands and return to their own country.

A later Arabic source would seem to corroborate this story, recording that 'after taking Antioch, the Franks camped there for twelve days without food. The wealthy ate their horses and the poor ate carrion and leaves from the trees. Their leaders, faced with this situation, wrote to Kerbogha to ask for safe conduct through his territory, but he refused, saying: "You will have to fight your way out."'[28]

This evidence has been widely discounted by historians on the assumption that the crusaders, their morale buoyed up on a rising wave of pious fervour after the discovery of the Holy Lance and already committed to battle, would never have seriously considered seeking terms of surrender. But, in fact, the decision to take the risk of sending Peter the Hermit on an embassy to Kerbogha makes more sense if we accept that he was dispatched to explore the real possibility of negotiating a surrender. On 24 June the crusader princes found themselves trapped in a corner – isolated and exhausted, their armies had finally been brought face to face with the spectre of defeat and extermination. They had marched across the known world not to conquer Antioch but to recover the Holy City of Jerusalem and perhaps now, in desperation, their leaders, at least, were prepared to consider any option that might allow them to reach Palestine alive. Had they given up Antioch, but been permitted to leave northern Syria, this still might have been possible.[29]

When Kerbogha, from his position of strategic dominance, refused to accept anything short of unconditional surrender, that door closed. The crusaders were left with a clear choice: fight or face death or captivity. Albert of Aachen, who based his account on the personal recollections of men who lived through the second siege of Antioch, recorded:

> The Christian people were besieged and began to suffer from shortage of supplies and lack of bread. They did not have the strength to suffer these things any longer, so great and small consulted together, saying it was better to die in battle than to perish from so cruel a famine, growing weaker from day to day until overcome by death.[30]

As the last days of June approached, the crusaders did, without doubt, make a profoundly courageous decision – to face Kerbogha's horde in open battle. Looking back with hindsight, the partisan crusade writers may well have judged it inappropriate to record that before this they contemplated surrender.

The controversial suggestion that the Franks were not primarily or directly inspired to fight Kerbogha by the discovery of the Holy Lance is potentially unsettling, because it threatens to undermine a cornerstone in our accepted image of the First Crusaders. The remarkable impact of the Holy Lance has long been held up as a fundamental proof of their overwhelming religious devotion. Historians have argued that it was only the inspirational power of the crusaders' faith – their unshakeable conviction that they were acting with divine sanction – that stirred them from anxious slumber. If the Franks did indeed spend much of the period between 14 and 28 June in an agony of fearful indecision, and perhaps even sought to negotiate the surrender of Antioch, then we are left looking at a subtly different species of crusader: one for whom spiritual devotion was still an extremely powerful motivating force, but perhaps not an all-conquering inspiration. Blind, ecstatic faith did not send the crusaders running into battle. Instead, with all other options exhausted, trapped in an intolerable predicament, their strength failing, they decided to place their trust in their God and risk everything in one last-ditch effort.

THE GREAT BATTLE OF ANTIOCH

By 25 June 1098 the crusade leaders had made their choice. They elected to pursue a bold, aggressive and extremely dangerous strategy – to break out of the city and confront Kerbogha's army head on. Bohemond was elected temporary commander-in-chief of the entire army. Raymond of Aguilers put this down to 'the Turkish threat, the illness of Count Raymond and Adhémar and the flight of Stephen of Blois', but in reality Bohemond may have been chosen primarily because he had a proven track record as a general. The Franks also decided to undertake a regime of spiritual purification before going to battle: 'Three days [were] spent fasting and in processions from one church to another, our men confessed their sins and received absolution, and by faith they received the body and blood of Christ in communion, and they gave alms and arranged for masses to be celebrated.'[31]

On 28 June 1098 they were ready to fight, and at first light they began marching out of the city while clergy lining the walls offered prayers to God. The crusaders staked the fate of the entire expedition upon this desperate strategy, yet historians have only recently begun to provide a convincing explanation for the astounding outcome of the battle that followed.[32] In choosing to confront Kerbogha the Franks faced a number of immense obstacles. They were proposing to engage a numerically superior and largely cavalry-based enemy, albeit one that was divided into those actually encircling Antioch and Kerbogha's main army encamped about a kilometre to the north and east of the Orontes river. In contrast, the rather tattered crusading force – perhaps numbering 20,000 including non-combatants – was now mainly infantry based. Virtually every single horse brought from Europe had died during the arduous journey to northern Syria and the long siege of Antioch. By June 1098, the crusaders could muster no more than 200 steeds trained for war, and many were reduced to riding into battle on pack animals. The German Count Hartmann of Dillingen, who had helped to design a strange siege engine at Nicaea, was said 'to have ridden a donkey to the battle and held merely a Turk's round shield and sword on the day'.[33]

Even princes had trouble finding a decent mount on 28 June – Godfrey of Bouillon was given one by Raymond of Toulouse, while Robert of Flanders actually had to beg to collect enough money to purchase his. Those horses that were available were in a feeble state. In the preceding weeks many crusaders had sought to sustain themselves by drinking blood drawn from their steeds. Now on the eve of the battle, in a determined attempt to ensure that they did not simply collapse in the midst of the fighting, Bishop Adhémar ordered every crusader in possession of a mount to feed it with every scrap of grain they could muster. For the majority, though, no steed, however poor, could be found, and so hundreds of knights were forced to fight on foot. One Latin contemporary bemoaned this fact, remarking that 'our knights had been forced to become footmen, weak and helpless', but this development was not a complete disaster. The crusaders had been reduced to a battle-hardened core – their army was dominated by an increasingly elite infantry force of well-armed, ferocious knights. The power of the crusading army had not been broken, but reshaped into a different type of weapon – one that fought on foot rather than from horseback. The Franks could no longer rely upon the force of a heavy cavalry charge to carry the day.[34] What was needed now was a general capable of adjusting his battle-tactics to the tools at hand, and that commander was Bohemond.

He faced a seemingly insurmountable task. First, the crusaders would have to break through the Muslim cordon surrounding Antioch and avoid being cut to pieces during what would inevitably be a painfully slow, piecemeal deployment outside the city. There was every possibility that the first wave of crusaders might be stopped in its tracks and decimated before the full weight of the Frankish army could even get out of the city. Once arrayed on the plains of Antioch, they would then, somehow, have to overcome the enemy. On the face of it, the odds were not in their favour. Kerbogha did, however, have a few potential problems of his own. In order to encircle Antioch he had been forced to disperse his troops quite widely, making it difficult to concentrate his resources quickly in one place. More importantly, while the crusaders enjoyed the bond of a desperate common cause and the experience of fighting side by side for months, Kerbogha's massive army was cobbled together from disparate elements. Drawn from cities across northern Syria and held together only by a veneer of unity, this force needed an extremely firm hand to guide it. One Muslim chronicler believed Kerbogha lacked this quality: 'Thinking that the present crisis would force the Muslims to remain loyal to him, [Kerbogha] alienated them by his pride and ill treatment of them. They plotted in secret anger to betray him and desert him in the heat of battle.' Should the Muslim host face a crisis, these deeply submerged fractures might bubble to the surface with disastrous consequences.[35]

Bohemond's battle plan was outstanding, its execution exceptional. The Bridge Gate was chosen as the sally-point, placing the Latins on the western bank of the Orontes. This limited the number of enemy troops initially encountered because the physical barrier of the river hampered any approach by the besieging Muslim forces stationed at the other gates. Hugh of Vermandois was selected to lead a squadron of archers in the first wave of attack out of the gate. He rushed headlong across the bridge, unleashing an intense volley of arrows that beat back the first line of Muslim troops. The way out of the city now lay open. Bohemond's plan was to deploy his remaining forces on to the plain of Antioch in the immediate wake of Hugh's shock attack, throwing his infantry to the front, and then close with the mounted enemy, to cut down their ability to manoeuvre or use missile weapons.

In order to move through the Bridge Gate with relative speed and to present their full weight of arms to the enemy as rapidly as possible, Bohemond laid down a masterful plan of action. To provide cohesion even in the midst of battle the army was divided into four clear-cut contingents: the northern French under Robert of Normandy and Robert of Flanders; Godfrey of Bouillon commanding the Lotharingians and Germans; and Adhémar of Le Puy leading out the southern French. As in earlier battles, Bohemond himself held the final, largest group – here mostly made up of southern Italian Normans – in reserve, so that he could meet any sudden threat or plug gaps that might appear in the crusader lines. Only Raymond of Toulouse, once again complaining of illness, was left in the city with 200 men to hold back any assault from the citadel. Before they left the city 'heralds scurried through Antioch urging each man to fight with his leader' so that each group might hold its formation. Once the Bridge Gate was cleared, the first contingent – the northern French – marched in column behind Hugh's force and then deployed to his left. Each division followed suit, fanning out leftwards in a rough semi-circle. We should not imagine this manoeuvre taking place with the precision of a Roman legion, rather that it was rough and ready, but extremely effective. The disposition of these troops was the finest expression of Bohemond's military genius, but even with all his careful planning, the crusaders might have been crushed as they exited the city had Kerbogha reacted differently.[36]

As soon as the Bridge Gate was opened, Kerbogha, encamped some kilometres to the north, was alerted by the raising of a black flag above the Muslim-held citadel. At this moment he was presented with a critical tactical decision: to deploy his main force immediately, attacking the crusaders while they debouched from the city; or to wait and then meet them in a full-scale pitched battle on his own ground. In these crucial first minutes Kerbogha hesitated, undecided. Looking back on the battle, the crusaders simply could not understand why Kerbogha failed to react. One later reflected that 'he could have blocked them', but was distracted because he was in the midst of 'playing at chess within his tent'. The princes themselves later recalled in a letter to the pope that, as they marched out of Antioch, 'we were so few that [the Muslims] were assured that we were not fighting against them, but were fleeing'.[37]

Writing many years later, the Muslim chronicler Ibn al-Athir invented the following discussion between Kerbogha and his advisers to explain events: 'The Muslims said to Kerbogha: "You should go up to the city and kill them one by one as they come out; it is easy to pick them off now that they have split up." He replied: "No, wait until they have all come out and then we will kill them."'[38] Ibn al-Athir roundly condemned this strategy, but, although it is easy with the benefit of hindsight to criticise such a sluggish response, Kerbogha was plagued by reasonable doubts about the wisdom of rushing into battle. Catching the crusaders in mid-deployment might well have led only to short-lived skirmishing, followed by a Latin retreat within the city and a return to stalemate. It was in Kerbogha's interests to bring the siege to a rapid conclusion. What he wanted was a full-scale confrontation.

In the end, however, Kerbogha made the worst of all decisions. With the chance for a rapid strike gone, he should have held his ground for battle; instead he chose to make a rather panicked, tardy advance. His timing was disastrous, for just as his men approached Antioch the tide of the battle began to turn.

The crusaders, having forced their way on to the Antiochene plains, almost immediately faced a counterattack from the Muslims who had been guarding the Bridge Gate, and this was quickly followed up by troops rushing from their positions before the Gates of St Paul and the Duke. Then, perhaps most dangerously of all, the crusaders were attacked from the rear by a force coming from the blockade of the Gate of St George. At this decisive moment, facing encirclement in open battle, the crusaders held their ground. Reinhard of Toul was dispatched with a squadron of northern French and Lotharingians to act as rearguard. He met the attack coming from the south-east with such ferocity that his opponents fled the field, setting light to the battleground to cover their escape. Reinhard's infantry suffered massive casualties, but the rear had held. At the same time, the Franks at the front line held formation as Muslim attacks swirled around them:

As was their custom, they began to scatter on all sides, occupying hills and paths, and, wherever they could, they wished to surround us. For they thought they could kill all of us in this manner. But our men having been trained in many battles against their trickery and cleverness, God's grace and mercy so came to our aid that we, who were very few in comparison to them, drove them all close together. Then with God's right hand fighting with us, we forced them so driven together to flee, and to leave their camps with everything in them.[39]

Unable to break the crusaders' resolve, the first wave of attackers – those who had been blockading Antioch – began to panic. With the Franks advancing to press home their advantage, these Muslims turned tail and fled. At that same moment, Kerbogha arrived at the head of his secondary force and ran straight into his own routed comrades. Now in headlong retreat, they shattered the formation of his troops, and soon the entire Muslim army was thrown into disarray. At this moment a commanding, charismatic general might have been able to save the day, but Kerbogha was not up to the challenge. He failed to rally his army, and one by one the contingents that had followed him to Antioch cut their losses and fled the field. In the end, the shock of a sharp, powerful attack and the unwavering solidity of the crusader formation exposed deep-seated fractures within the Muslim army. After only a brief engagement Kerbogha was forced into retreat and ignominious defeat. Disgraced, he returned home to Mosul. One Muslim chronicler wrote in shock: 'The Franks, though they were in the extremity of weakness, advanced in battle order against the armies of Islam, which were at the height of their strength and numbers, and they broke the ranks of the Muslims and scattered their multitudes.'[40]

Although the Latins had killed only a fraction of his army, the threat posed by Kerbogha had been neutralised. His main camp was overrun and thoroughly ravaged by jubilant crusaders: 'The enemy left his pavilions, with gold and silver and many furnishings, as well as sheep, oxen, horses, mules, camels and asses, corn, wines, flour and many other things of which we were badly in need.' One Latin chronicler reported that, 'when their women were found in the tents, the Franks did nothing evil to them except pierce their bellies with their lances'. This comment seems extraordinarily callous, but its author was actually trying to tell us that these women were not raped. In the opinion of this clerical writer, slaughter carried out in the name of God was infinitely preferable to the heinous sin of fornication with dehumanised 'infidels'.[41]

Within hours the Muslim garrison of Antioch's citadel surrendered and the whole city was at last truly and safely in Latin hands. The significance of the Great Battle of Antioch cannot be overstressed. It was, without doubt, the single most important military engagement of the entire expedition. The crusaders had, throughout June 1098, faced the very real possibility of annihilation. The Muslim army was both larger and better equipped than that of the Latins, containing a sizeable cavalry element. The crusaders took an enormous, but arguably necessary, risk in meeting this force. Zealous conviction, gifted generalship and a healthy dose of luck brought them victory against all the odds. To contemporary writers, this achievement was so extraordinary that it could only be explained as a miracle. They argued that the Franks had been saved from certain defeat by only one thing: direct, palpable intervention by the hand of God. Numerous 'miracles' were recorded. Raymond of Aguilers recorded that 'in the beginning of the march out to battle the Lord sent down upon all His army a divine shower, little but full of blessing. All those touched by this were filled with all grace and fortitude and, despising the enemy, rode forth as if nourished on the delicacies of kings. This miracle affected our horses no less.' An eyewitness, who actually fought in the battle, added:

> there came out of the mountains, also, countless armies with white horses, whose standards were all white. And so, when our leaders saw this army, they were entirely ignorant as to what it was, and who they were, until they recognised the aid of Christ, whose leaders were Ss George, Mercurius and Demetrius. This is to be believed, for many of our men saw it.[42]

The crusaders certainly did fight the battle in an atmosphere of fervent spiritual conviction. As they marched out to fight, priests lined the walls of Antioch reciting blessings. Others, carrying crosses, marched out in the very midst of the troops, 'chanting and praying for God's help and the protection of the saints'. Raymond of Aguilers himself carried the Holy Lance in among the southern French contingent led by Bishop Adhémar, and it was said that Kerbogha was literally paralysed by the sight of the relic. Religious devotion did have a huge effect on the outcome of the battle. With their resolve reinforced by Christian ritual, empowered by a powerful sense of divine sanction, the crusaders' nerve held even as they were surrounded by the enemy. A less devout or desperate force might have broken, but, bound together by their steadfast resolve, these men kept formation and so won the day.[43]

After immense sacrifice and suffering, the crusaders were at last in possession of Antioch. For nine months the city had stood like an impenetrable wall before them, barring their way forward. Now, finally, the road south was open and the Holy City of Jerusalem beckoned.

8

DESCENT INTO DISCORD

In the first days of July 1098 the crusaders could look upon their achievements with some satisfaction. They had just won a seemingly miraculous victory in the Battle of Antioch. That city was now conquered and pacified. Jerusalem, their ultimate goal, lay only three weeks' hard march to the south. No overwhelming obstacles stood in their way. After the brutal sack of Antioch and spectacular defeat of Kerbogha, those Muslim-held cities and towns that did stand on the road to Jerusalem were now terrified of the Franks and unlikely to offer serious resistance.

Many crusaders must have felt that the end of their pilgrimage was almost in sight. They were wrong. The Holy City may have been only weeks away, but no crusader was to see its walls for more than a year. Ironically, in that interval, thousands of Latins who had had the strength and fortune to survive the testing journey from Europe and the savage ordeal of Antioch's siege fell victim to disease, hunger and small-scale fighting, never to reach Palestine. At a time when the crusade seemed on the verge of success, the entire expedition stalled, fragmented and almost dissolved.

DELAY AND DISSIPATION

On 3 July a council of crusader princes made a fateful pronouncement: 'They dared not enter into the land of the pagans, because in summer it is very dry and waterless, and so they decided that they would therefore wait until the beginning of November.' Judging their troops to be exhausted and their lines of supply extended, they chose to delay any attempt to march south towards Jerusalem until 1 November. The Provençal crusader Raymond of Aguilers, for one, did not approve: 'We believe that, if the Franks had advanced, not one city between Antioch and Jerusalem would have thrown a rock at them, so frightened and weakened at this time were the Saracen cities following the defeat of Kerbogha.' He may have been right, but in truth the crusaders were immobilised by more fundamental and far-reaching problems.[1]

The contest for Antioch

The princes were now confronted by an inescapable question: what to do with the city of Antioch. Back in the spring of 1097 almost all the crusader princes had sworn an oath at Constantinople promising to return any former Byzantine territories that they might capture to the Emperor Alexius. Antioch was at the top of the wish-list of cities that Alexius was hoping to recover in this way. However, just before the city fell to the crusaders, Bohemond convinced his colleagues to guarantee possession of Antioch to whomever could engineer its capture. Therefore, in July 1098 there were two claimants to the city – Alexius and Bohemond. Modern historians have often cast the latter as the villain of this contest, arguing that in the struggle for Antioch Bohemond revealed his true character. Driven by greed and ambition, he was determined to possess the city, no matter what the cost.

In part, this is an accurate picture. In his defence, one could argue that someone would have to stay behind to govern Antioch after the crusaders had gone to such lengths to capture it. Bohemond had long believed he was the only man for the job. He had harboured designs on Antioch ever since the crusade arrived in northern Syria, and perhaps even earlier. Back in October 1097, at the start of the siege, he had taken up position before one of Antioch's most important gates, that of St Paul, ensuring his troops quick access to the city once it fell. Speed was of the essence, because the crusader princes had agreed to observe the rule of 'right by conquest' – that is, whoever was first to take possession of property or territory was deemed to have legal rights of ownership. When towns or cities fell crusaders literally sprinted in to grab whatever they could. Bohemond's priorities were further demonstrated by his management of the Firuz affair, as he revealed the renegade's existence only once the promise of Antioch had been made. Then, as soon as its defences were breached, Bohemond rushed to have his blood-red banner raised above the city as proof of his claim.[2]

Perhaps most significantly, Bohemond managed to take possession of Antioch's citadel in the immediate aftermath of the battle against Kerbogha. This was a crucial step because, as the crusaders had discovered, the city was really untenable without control of its fortress. Bohemond was, however, almost beaten to this prize by another crusader – his increasingly vocal rival Raymond, count of Toulouse. While his fellow princes were marching out of Antioch to do battle with Kerbogha on 28 June, Raymond, suffering from another of his frequent bouts of illness, remained within the city to guard against an attack from the citadel. Feigned or not, his infirmity put him in an excellent position to receive the citadel's surrender. According to one eyewitness, he tried to do just that:

> When the emir who was in charge of the citadel saw Kerbogha and all the others fleeing from the battlefield before the Frankish army, he was much afraid, and he came in a great hurry to ask for a Frankish banner. [Raymond], who was there keeping watch outside the citadel, ordered his own banner to be delivered to the emir, who took it and was careful to display it upon his tower.

Unfortunately for Raymond, when this 'emir' – one of Kerbogha's lieutenants named Ahmad ibn-Marwan – discovered that the banner he had received was not Bohemond's he promptly sent it back, 'and just then the noble Bohemond came up and gave him his own banner, which he accepted with great joy'. Together they agreed terms of surrender, Bohemond garrisoned the citadel with his own men and Ahmad voluntarily converted to Christianity.[3] If true, the story of Raymond's rejection would indicate that, at least in the minds of the conquered Muslims, Bohemond offered better prospects of protection. The exchange of a banner did, after all, represent a reciprocal agreement, whereby the victor laid claim to spoils while taking custody and responsibility for those captured. Above all, the citadel's garrison was hoping to avoid being butchered in an uncontrolled sack. Although Raymond could claim some legal right to the fortress because his banner had been raised first, Bohemond had the advantage of possession. With his men firmly ensconced in the citadel Bohemond was in no mood to budge.

Raymond was, however, not without his own foothold within the city. When Antioch fell on 3 June, he capitalised on the siege position he had held in front of the Bridge Gate, seizing the gatehouse itself and the nearby governor's palace. Then, after Kerbogha was defeated, Raymond moved to reoccupy the ruined siege fort of La Mahomerie. By the start of July he had carved out a cohesive Provençal enclave within Antioch. With possession of the Bridge Gate he controlled the roads to St Simeon and Alexandretta, two of the city's primary lifelines to the outside world. Bohemond might use the citadel to claim lordship of Antioch, but Raymond was poised to destabilise and even emasculate his position.[4]

The lines of confrontation had been drawn. Whether self-serving or pragmatic, Bohemond's intentions were fairly transparent. He wanted to rule Antioch. Raymond's objectives are harder to pinpoint. On the surface he appears as an honourable advocate of justice, a man whose determination to uphold the promises made to Alexius prompted him to become the upholder of Byzantine interests. In fact,

Raymond had been the only prince who refused to show the emperor full subservience at Constantinople. The count's newfound pro-Byzantine inclinations after the Great Battle of Antioch were actually fuelled, first and foremost, by his own ambition. In supporting Alexius' claim, Raymond weakened Bohemond and earned himself a valuable new ally. By these steps, Raymond sought to forge his own path towards wealth and power.[5]

An intense debate transfixed the princes at the start of July. Bohemond argued that the Byzantines had failed to reinforce the crusaders at Antioch, thereby forfeiting any rights to the city. His position was strengthened once news eventually arrived of the Greeks' decision to turn back from Philomelium. Raymond, on the other hand, maintained that the oath to Alexius still held and thus Antioch belonged to the emperor by right. Faced with this difficult choice, the remaining princes prevaricated. On the surface they offered to uphold the Byzantine claim. Hugh of Vermandois and the lesser prince Baldwin of Hainault were dispatched on an embassy to Constantinople, 'asking [Alexius] to come and take over the city and fulfil the obligations which he had undertaken towards them'. But behind the scenes the princes showed tacit support for Bohemond's position, ceding him control of those sections of Antioch that they had defended during the second siege. At this crucial juncture the council of princes failed to take decisive action. Instead they abdicated responsibility: if the emperor arrived with his army he could have Antioch; if not, the city was Bohemond's. Had they succeeded in reaching a more proactive decision at this point, the expedition might still have been able to begin the journey towards Palestine after a few months' rest. As it was, the first faltering steps down the road of delay and dissipation had been taken.[6]

Even so, measures were taken at the start of July to bring a modicum of order to Antioch. The crusaders set about the laborious process of restoring, and in some cases reconsecrating, the city's many Christian churches. Chief amongst these was the Basilica of St Peter, where the Holy Lance had been unearthed. They began 'cleans[ing] the basilica, which the Turks had profaned with their sacrilegious rites, from all defilement and rebuilt with every decoration the altars which had been overturned'. According to one Latin source, a magnificent fresco of Christ adorning the interior of the basilica, the centrepiece of its decoration, had remained untouched throughout the Muslim occupation. It was said that a Turk had climbed up to deface the image but, through a miracle, had fallen to his death – after this, we are told, no Muslim was brave enough to try again.[7]

With the restoration of Antioch's churches under way, the obvious next step was the reinstatement of its Christian clergy. This raised a rather delicate dilemma. The head of the Christian faith at Antioch – the patriarch – had for centuries been Greek, and so too had been the majority of the city's clergy. The Greek patriarch John IV the Oxite had remained in the city throughout the first siege, enduring public torture and abuse at the hands of the Muslims. When the city fell, he was set free. Now the expectation was that he would be reinstalled at the head of the Antiochene Church. The crusade had, after all, been preached, at least in part, to bring aid to the eastern Churches. The problem with this was that the presence of a powerful Greek cleric in Antioch gave the Byzantines a firm foothold in the city. It might prove very difficult for a Latin Catholic crusader, such as Bohemond, to hold on to Antioch against the Byzantine emperor's wishes with a Greek bishop living right under his nose. As it was, at the start of July John IV was confirmed as patriarch, probably at the absolute insistence of Adhémar of Le Puy, who had maintained close links with the Greek Church throughout the crusade. Unsure of whether the emperor would actually arrive to repossess Antioch, John settled for control of ecclesiastical affairs and made no attempt to interfere in Antioch's political future. For the time being at least, an uncomfortable compromise was achieved.[8]

The crusade is reshaped

The battle between Bohemond and Raymond for control of Antioch was compounded by, and connected to, a wider problem. The crusade now faced a full-scale crisis of leadership and direction. Having agreed to delay any march on Jerusalem until November, and with envoys dispatched to Constantinople, the princes had to decide how to prevent the fragmentation and dissolution of their armies during four months of inactivity. Up to this point the expedition had just about been held together by the common goal of Antioch's capture. Without a new, immediate focus the entire venture threatened to lose direction. Worse still, the crusaders had to be fed, but with Antioch now in Latin hands the surrounding region could no longer be treated as enemy territory and ravaged at will, and the Franks were running out of new places to raid. The council of princes came up with a partial solution. Each contingent would retire to the foraging centres used during the first siege of Antioch, so that the demand for resources might be spread across northern Syria. Bohemond and the southern Italians split their time between Antioch and Cilicia to the north-west. Raymond of Toulouse and the southern French based themselves in the Ruj valley to the south-east of Antioch, while Godfrey of Bouillon and many of the northern French headed for the environs of Edessa.

At the same time, the very makeup and fabric of these contingents were altering. Through the horrors of the preceding months, death, desertion and poverty worked to break down the intricate web of ties that had bound the crusaders to one another. Bonds of family, lordship and vassalage were severed. In this atmosphere of instability many crusaders sought, over the summer of 1098, to forge new allegiances, realigning themselves with new lords and new causes. In early July the princes issued a general proclamation at Antioch, stating, 'If there were any poor man, lacking gold and silver, who wished to take service with them and stay on, they would gladly enrol him.' This process prompted a piecemeal revolution in the structure and distribution of power within the crusade. Many prominent knights, such as Drogo of Nesle and Reinhard of Toul, who had both led scouting parties to watch for Kerbogha's arrival in May, now took their retinues to Edessa in search of work: '[They] came with their

fellow soldiers, some on horseback, others on foot, to the state of
Edessa to earn rewards for military service from Baldwin, who had
been made duke [there], spending some time with him. For they had
suffered the utmost difficulty and become impoverished by the long
expedition.'[9]

Those who, like Baldwin of Boulogne, had reserves of wealth, were
now in a position to assemble a swarm of new followers. Other
leading knights began to take more entrepreneurial measures to
ensure their survival. Around 17 July, Raymond Pilet, who had up
until this point served in Raymond of Toulouse's army, 'took into his
service many knights and footsoldiers' and set off south from the Ruj
on a semi-independent expedition. His goal seems to have been fairly
straightforward – to conquer towns and amass booty. He marched into
the Jabal as-Summaq, the plateau region to the south-east of Antioch,
in which Bohemond and Robert of Flanders had sought to forage
back in December 1097. On that occasion the crusaders had run into
a large army from Damascus. To begin with, at least, Raymond Pilet
enjoyed greater success. The Syrian Christian inhabitants of a small
fortress, Tell Mannas, surrendered to him, and from this base he set
about plundering the region. A week later another local fortress, this
one manned by Muslims, fell to a frontal assault and was looted. One
crusader recalled: '[Raymond's men] captured all the peasants of the
district and killed those who would not be christened, but those who
preferred to acknowledge Christ they spared.' This seems to be one
of the first occasions since the pogroms of Rhineland Jews that the
First Crusade edged towards becoming a war of conversion. There is
a relatively short distance between forced apostasy and Raymond
Pilet's offer to accept Christianity or die.[10]

So far, Raymond's venture had been remarkably successful, but
now he became somewhat over-ambitious. He was approached by a
group of Syrian Christians from the region's largest town, Marrat an-
Numan, a site of considerable commercial and strategic value given
its position on the ancient Roman road connecting Aleppo to the
southern city of Damascus. They encouraged him to launch an attack

on Marrat's Muslim garrison, and, with his confidence buoyed by recent victories, Raymond decided to oblige them, setting off from Tell Mannas on 27 July. Marrat lay barely half a day's march away, but Raymond seems to have grossly underestimated the level of resistance he would encounter and therefore brought only a small supply of water with him – a terrible mistake in the burning heat of the Syrian summer. Upon arrival, instead of finding a feeble garrison that might be quickly overcome, Raymond was confronted by a sizeable, belligerent force of Aleppan troops rushing out of Marrat to meet him. Suddenly he had a real battle on his hands:

> [The enemy] went on attacking our men all through the day, and their onslaught lasted until evening. The heat was unspeakable, and our men could not endure such fearful thirst, for they could find no water to drink, so they wanted to get back safely to their castle. The Syrians and poor pilgrims, for their sins, got into a blind panic and began to retreat in a hurry.

Raymond Pilet's assault turned into a rout, and we are told, grimly, that 'many of our people gave up their souls to God' in the chaos that followed. Among the dead was Arnold Tudebode, another relation of the contemporary crusade chronicler Peter Tudebode. Raymond's expedition may have ended in failure – after a few days his battered force returned to the Ruj – but it had pointed to the possibility of future conquests in the region.[11]

Meanwhile, back at Antioch, disaster struck. Even though most crusaders had dispersed across northern Syria, a large number, especially the poor, remained in Antioch. Adhémar of Le Puy, papal legate and spiritual shepherd of the crusade, chose to remain with them. This proved to be a fateful decision. In the last days of July a mysterious but deadly illness began to spread uncontrollably throughout the city.

A most deadly plague struck Antioch, by which a countless

multitude of the Christian army, as many noble leaders as of the common crowd, were taken. In this fatal scourge the reverend Bishop [Adhémar] was the first to be struck down and ended his life on the 1 August. Nobles and lesser people wept over him with overwhelming grief and agreed to bury him in the Basilica of St Peter itself, in the same place that the Lord's Lance was found.[12]

This epidemic – probably an outbreak of typhoid – gripped the city throughout August and began to spread to outlying regions. In a deadful twist of fate, a large group of Latin reinforcements arrived in northern Syria at just that moment. Fifteen hundred German crusaders from the region of Regensburg had taken ship from Europe to join the latter stages of the expedition to Jerusalem. When they landed at St Simeon they were immediately exposed to the disease, which raced through their ranks like wildfire. Having travelled thousands of kilometres to reach the Levant, all 1,500 were dead within days of setting foot on its shores. Other fatalities included Henry of Esch, who had survived fierce fighting during the second siege of Antioch. In recognition of his heroism, he was buried with full honours in the doorway of St Peter's basilica.[13]

Bishop Adhémar's death was a severe and untimely blow to the expedition. He had never been the crusade's outright leader, and he had certainly been unable to resolve the dispute over Antioch, but his presence had had an unmistakable impact upon the overall progress of the campaign. His conciliatory attitude towards the eastern Churches had brought the crusaders much-needed assistance from the Greeks and, in particular, from Byzantine Cyprus. As the pope's official representative he possessed the authority to guide the expedition with a steadying hand. Now, just as the crusade seemed to be losing its way, that placatory presence was removed.[14]

WHO WILL LEAD?

Through the summer of 1098, with the bitter dispute over Antioch unresolved and the setback of Adhémar's death, it became increasingly obvious that the crusade lacked decisive leadership. The committee rule of the council of princes that had functioned in the face of threats from the likes of Kerbogha was failing. The time seemed ripe for one individual to step forward, seize the reins of command and drive the crusade on to Jerusalem. Three men could fill this post: Bohemond of Taranto; Godfrey of Bouillon; and Raymond of Toulouse.

The candidates

Bohemond was perhaps the most obvious choice. He had proved his qualities as a military leader time and again over the preceding months, and had in June been made temporary commander-in-chief of the entire crusade. As the architect of Antioch's fall and Kerbogha's defeat, he was powerfully positioned to assume the mantle of leadership. But Bohemond's ambitions lay elsewhere. Antioch, rather than Jerusalem, was paramount in his mind – his goal was to retain possession of the city already captured rather than direct the advance on the Holy City. By mid-July, it was blatantly obvious where the full force of Bohemond's attention lay. Within a few days of the victory over Kerbogha, Mediterranean shipping began once again to move freely through St Simeon, bringing the crusaders badly needed supplies. Bohemond shrewdly realised that if he were to hold on to Antioch he must immediately secure lines of communication and support beyond the confines of northern Syria. Once the Byzantines saw that he had no intention of honouring the oath to Alexius and returning the city, the naval aid that they had siphoned through Cyprus and Latakia – the large port to the south of Antioch – would dry up.

With this in mind, Bohemond sought to purchase assistance from other quarters. The only Christian powers capable of challenging the

Greeks' domination of the Mediterranean were the Italian merchant cities of Venice, Pisa and Genoa. Bohemond chose to negotiate first with the Genoese, granting them property in Antioch and trading rights in return for their support. On 14 July they had documents – what would technically be known as charters – drawn up specifying the details of their agreement, copies of which survive to this day. As we have already seen, these charters, which at first sight might appear to be rather dull and formulaic, are actually rich mines of information. Typically in this type of material, the person ceding rights or property – the donor – opens by identifying himself with a lavish list of titles and honours. This 'address clause' offers an insight into how donors saw themselves or wished to be seen. Significantly, in his charter Bohemond identified himself simply as 'the son of Robert Guiscard, duke of Apulia'. His decision to make no claim to be ruler of Antioch, nor use of the title 'prince' – which he would later adopt – tells us that, at this point, Bohemond was unsure of his position. He was manoeuvring to gain power, but was not yet in a position to claim it. As one near-contemporary observed, while Raymond of Toulouse continued to hold the Bridge Gate and Palace of Antioch, Bohemond could be nothing more than the city's partial-ruler or 'half-prince'.[15]

Around the same time, Bohemond looked to cement his connection with Cilician Armenia to the north. Tancred, his nephew, had established a southern Italian Norman foothold there in the early autumn of 1097. During the summer of 1098 Bohemond paid a lengthy visit to the region, probably basing himself at the town of Mamistra, on the eastern reaches of the Cilician plain. The fertile soil of this region made it an economic goldmine – for now Bohemond could use Cilicia to feed his troops, and in years to come its fisheries and textile industry could be expected to bring him great wealth – but of even greater import was its strategic value. One reason the crusaders sent an expedition to occupy the region back in September 1097, even before they arrived at Antioch, was to open the most direct route from Asia Minor to northern Syria for later waves of Byzantine and Frankish reinforcements. Now, the last thing Bohemond wanted was an open road running between Byzantium and Antioch, so he reaffirmed his foothold in Cilicia to create a buffer zone between himself and the Greeks.[16]

From July 1098 onwards, Bohemond was more interested in securing northern Syria than leading the crusade to Jerusalem. An alternative candidate for that honour was Godfrey of Bouillon, duke of Lower Lotharingia. As summer waned into autumn, his stock rose among the crusaders. In part this was a function of the support offered by his brother, Baldwin of Boulogne, a man otherwise preoccupied with the consolidation of his own hold over the city of Edessa, more than 150 kilometres north-east of Antioch. Back in March, Baldwin had given Godfrey rights to the income and produce of Tell Bashir, a town on the road to Edessa. By summer, Godfrey had garnered rights to exploit a second, neighbouring town, Ravendan. One commentator estimated, rather wildly, that Tell Bashir alone brought in 500,000 gold bezants per annum, a princely sum. In July, Godfrey moved to the region and, perhaps as a result of his increased prosperity, attracted a considerable number of new followers.[17]

His reputation was further bolstered when Omar of Azaz, a local Muslim ruler, chose to approach him for assistance. The chronicler Albert of Aachen, who admired Godfrey, provided a colourful explanation of this episode. According to his account, a knight in Godfrey's retinue – Fulbert of Bouillon – was ambushed and killed by troops from Azaz while travelling with his wife to Edessa. While Fulbert was decapitated, his wife, 'because she was greatly pleasing to the eye on account of her beautiful face, was taken prisoner', and was soon forced to wed one of Omar's lieutenants. Azaz was at that time subject to Ridwan of Aleppo, but the advent of the First Crusade weakened his hold over the region and Omar saw his chance to make a break for independence. Albert of Aachen implies that Omar chose to seek an alliance with Godfrey because Fulbert's widow had described the duke as the leading figure among the Franks.

In reality, Omar may well have turned to him simply because he was the closest option – Azaz lay on the old Roman road between Tell Bashir and Antioch – but his approach does at least demonstrate that the Franks had been incorporated into the sphere of Levantine power-politics, and that the boundaries of Latin–Muslim enmity were blurring. In early September, with Azaz facing imminent attack from Ridwan of Aleppo, Omar urgently dispatched a Syrian Christian envoy to Godfrey to make an urgent appeal for aid, and followed this up with the offer of his own son as hostage. When Godfrey finally agreed, news was carried back to Azaz by carrier pigeon. Godfrey duly led a relief force towards Azaz and quickly frightened off the Aleppan army. Realising that Godfrey stood to gain a new ally in northern Syria, Raymond of Toulouse and Bohemond rushed from Antioch to get in on the act, but they were too late. As far as Omar was concerned, Godfrey had saved the day, and he lavished gifts on him, among which was a richly decorated set of armour, 'marvellously inlaid with gold and silver'. Omar seemed to have made a wise decision – by allying himself to the new power in Syria he had won freedom from Aleppo – but within a year the tide had turned. His son died in the crusader camp, probably through illness rather than treachery, and, when the crusaders moved to the south, Omar was suddenly isolated. Taken captive by Aleppan troops and dragged before Ridwan, he pleaded for clemency, swearing lifelong obedience. Unmoved, Ridwan promptly had him executed.[18]

Godfrey of Bouillon's reputation may have been growing in the second half of 1098, but there remained one crusader whom he could not, as yet, hope to eclipse. Raymond of Toulouse took the most purposeful strides towards pre-eminence in the aftermath of the Great Battle of Antioch. From the very earliest days of the crusade's inception, Raymond had thought of himself as the natural choice to become its secular leader, but throughout the first and second sieges of Antioch long bouts of illness had prevented him from playing a consistently high-profile role in events. His infirmity was doubtless linked to his advanced years – being in his mid-fifties, he would have been classed as elderly by medieval standards – but, nevertheless, in the minds of many he was deemed not to have been pulling his weight.

In the summer of 1098, with Bohemond having removed himself from the race, Raymond's natural advantages – the gravitas brought by his age and experience, and his broad base of support among the southern French – were amplified and consolidated by two further factors. As we have seen, in the aftermath of the second siege, the complex web of allegiance and alliance that enswathed the First Crusade was restructured. As one of the richest crusader princes, Raymond was perfectly placed to reap the benefits of this process. His wealth bought him hundreds, perhaps even thousands of new followers, as well as support from some surprising quarters. Around this time, the anonymous author of the *Gesta Francorum*, a man who had so far spent the entire expedition in the company of Bohemond, seems to have begun travelling with the southern French and, from this point on, a subtle shift in his presentation of Raymond's character can be detected.[19]

The full significance of Raymond's connection to the Holy Lance also became apparent in this period. From the start, he had taken every opportunity to establish an intimate link between himself and the relic. Having played a central role in its discovery, he now became the Lance's protector and advocate. His partisan supporter, Raymond of Aguilers, took pains to emphasise this relationship. When the Lance was uncovered he wrote that St Andrew appeared to Peter Bartholomew saying: 'Behold God gave the Lance to the count, in fact, had reserved it for him alone throughout the ages, and also made him leader of the crusaders on the condition of his devotion to God.'[20]

This does not mean that, once the Lance was discovered, all the crusaders suddenly accepted Raymond of Toulouse's pre-eminence or authority. But this extract reflects the type of propaganda circulating about Raymond from July 1098 onwards. He wanted the Franks to believe that his connection to the Lance made him the obvious choice to become leader – he certainly seems to have thought this himself. His case became all the more powerful once Kerbogha was defeated. To the crusaders, their victory in the Great Battle of Antioch was so astounding, so utterly extraordinary, that it could only be explained by the intervention of divine agency. It was God's will, manifested through the power of the Holy Lance, which had brought them success. Thus was it that – in the summer of 1098, rather than in the destitution of the second siege – the full power of the crusaders' belief in the Lance began to mature. Raymond's patronage of the Lance may have affected the balance of power among the princes. Robert of Flanders, who had had no particular link to the Provençal camp before this point, now allied himself with Raymond. This was probably a function of the count's position as protector and advocate of the Lance, because Robert is known to have been a staunch devotee of the relic, founding a religious house in its honour upon his return to Europe.[21]

Raymond managed the cult surrounding the relic with what, at times, appears to be almost ruthless efficiency. The support of Peter Bartholomew was central to this process. His popularity and influence was rising day by day, in tandem with that of the Lance he had uncovered. Whether through conscious design or unconscious impulse, the messages contained in Peter's continuing visions became increasingly audacious and outspoken in their support of his patron Raymond's political cause. This was never more apparent than in the startling manipulation of Adhémar of Le Puy's memory. Within forty-eight hours of the bishop's death on 1 August, Peter Bartholomew 'received' his first vision of Adhémar's spirit. In life, the papal legate had always been sceptical about the Holy Lance's authenticity, a damaging blow to the relic's cult. In death, Raymond and Peter set about appropriating Adhémar's legacy to reverse this trend. It can be no coincidence that when the bishop was buried in the Basilica of St Peter, the spot chosen for his interment was the very hole from which the Holy Lance had been drawn. This was the definitive physical intermingling of their two cults and a powerful step towards the reconfiguration of Adhémar's persona.

Peter's visions then began to relay the bishop's 'words' from beyond the grave. It turned out, of course, that Adhémar had been wrong all along. Now, at last, he realised that the metal shard discovered by Peter truly was a piece of the Holy Lance – but how he had suffered to reach this realisation. In his vision, Peter heard from Adhémar that after death his soul had been sorely punished for the sin of having doubted the Lance: 'Following the uncovering of the Lance, I sinned deeply and so was drawn down to hell, whipped most severely, and as you can see my head and face were burned.' He was saved from damnation only by an act of faith – the three *denarii* he had given as alms to the Lance – and the cleansing power of a devotional candle lit in his memory. Adhémar went on to say, through Peter, that he was quite happy with his resting place in Antioch.

> Bohemond said that he would carry my body to Jerusalem. For his sake he shall not move my corpse from its resting place because some of the blood of Christ, with whom I am now associated, remains there. But if he doubts my statements, let him open my tomb and he shall see my burned head and face.[22]

With this U-turn in his stance on the Holy Lance, Adhémar's spirit became the perfect mouthpiece for the promotion of Count Raymond's political agenda. Indeed, in the first vision, he promised to return regularly to 'offer better counsel than I did in life'. His initial instructions were all in Raymond's favour. He swelled the count's army by entrusting all his former followers to him and then suggested that 'the count and his chosen ones [should] select a bishop in my place' to act as the new spiritual leader of the crusade, although Raymond was ultimately unable to implement this instruction.

The alliance between Raymond and Peter Bartholomew – prince and prophet – was a powerful one, but Peter was a potentially dangerous bedfellow. In a few short weeks he had been catapulted out of impoverished obscurity to become a demagogue to the crusader masses. As time went on, this newfound power went to his head, his character became increasingly unstable, his pronouncements more wide-ranging and outlandish. After his first vision of Adhémar, Peter reported another visitation from St Andrew. Scattered among the now familiar rhetoric regarding Raymond's power and connection to the Lance were additional, potentially more disturbing messages. According to Peter, St Andrew did not want Antioch to be returned to the Greeks, suggesting that they would 'desecrate' the city. Instead, he said, a Latin patriarch should be appointed and Antioch retained by the crusaders. This explosive message did not sit comfortably alongside Raymond's new pro-Byzantine policy and the 'official' line that he was only showing an interest in Antioch on the emperor's behalf.

Raymond almost certainly nursed his own dreams of ruling Antioch and did everything in his power to retain a foothold in that great city. In mid-summer he even made an abortive attempt to provoke a full-scale riot against Bohemond in the city streets. But in many ways the dispute over Antioch acted as a costly distraction from Raymond's main ambition – to lead the crusade.[23]

An impasse is reached

By summer's end the crisis within the crusade was no closer to resolution. Hugh of Vermandois and Baldwin of Hainault, dispatched as ambassadors to Alexius, were attacked by Turks while recrossing Asia Minor. Baldwin was lost and Hugh's journey severely delayed.[24] By the time he reached Constantinople to tell the full story of Kerbogha's defeat, autumn had set in and it was too late in the year for the emperor to march on Antioch. Although no Byzantine representative appeared to claim the city, Raymond of Toulouse continued to oppose any suggestion that Bohemond should be given sole possession. As yet no crusade leader held sufficient power or influence to reinvigorate or redirect the expedition. Facing this stalemate, the princes turned back to Europe for aid. On 11 September they wrote a joint letter to Pope Urban II in Rome outlining the course of the expedition to date and relating the grievous news of Adhémar's death. This missive implored Pope Urban II to come to Antioch and lead the crusade on to Jerusalem in person:

Since you initiated this pilgrimage and by your sermons have caused us all to leave our lands . . . we [now] beg you to come to us and urge whomsoever you can to come with you. For it was here [in Antioch] that the name of Christian first originated . . . Therefore what in the world would seem more proper than that you, who are the father and head of the Christian religion, should come to the principal city and capital of the Christian name and finish the war, which is your project, in person . . . For if you come to us and finish with us the pilgrimage that you inaugurated the whole world will be obedient to you.[25]

This heartfelt appeal for spiritual leadership and military reinforcement played upon Antioch's link to St Peter, the foundation of the Christian Church, and Pope Urban's own responsibilities and ambitions. But another, more subtle message is also interlaced within this petition. Bohemond, the chief architect of this letter, wove his own self-serving agenda into the text. By stressing Antioch's Christian heritage and the 'global' power that ecclesiastical control of the city would bring to the papacy, he hoped to lure Urban into Latinising the Church in northern Syria, thus ending Bohemond's problems with the Greek patriarch and Byzantine influence. The letter thus contained a startling clause that seems wholly at odds with the crusade's avowed mission to aid eastern Christians: 'We have subdued the Turks and the pagans; but the heretics, Greeks and Armenians, Syrians and Jacobites, we have not been able to overcome . . . Use us, your obedient sons, [to] eradicate and destroy by your authority and our strength all heresies of whatever kind.'[26]

Preoccupied in Europe, Urban II was not tempted by this uncompromising image of Latin expansionism, and by 1 November, the Feast of All Saints, neither Roman pope nor Greek emperor had arrived in Syria to resolve the crusaders' quandary. As agreed, all the princes reassembled at Antioch at the start of the month to plan the next stage of the expedition, but the intractable division between Bohemond and Raymond remained. Even after days of negotiation in the Basilica of St Peter no solution could be reached. Bohemond, perched in his citadel, dominated the city, but Raymond clung on to his foothold around the Bridge Gate with unshakeable tenacity. Neither Godfrey, nor either of the two Roberts, nor any other prince possessed the will or authority to impose a settlement. Raymond's chaplain summarised the impasse, writing that, 'divided by contradictions, the princes became so violent that they almost took up arms. As a result the journey [to Jerusalem] and all matters pertaining to it and the care of the poor were postponed.'[27]

By mid-November all attempts at arbitration broke down and the princes began, once again, to disperse. This time, no date for reassembly was set – it looked as though the entire expedition was doomed simply to fizzle out. The indecision of autumn 1098 was lamentable. Bohemond's greed, Raymond's obstinacy and the feeble ineptitude of their colleagues looked set to cost the crusade dearly. While a focused and purposeful force might have used the autumn to reach Jerusalem, the First Crusaders now faced an unnecessary second winter of aimless delay and vulnerability to attack or starvation in northern Syria. This prospect did not sit well with the mass of crusaders, and popular discontent began to bubble to the surface:

The people, on seeing this princely fiasco, began to suggest first privately and later publicly: 'It is obvious that our leaders, because of cowardice or because of the oath to Alexius, do not wish to lead us to Jerusalem . . . If the Antiochene quarrel continues, let us tear down [the city's] walls; then the era of princely goodwill existing prior to its capture will return with its destruction. Otherwise, we should turn back to our lands before hunger and fatigue exhaust us.'[28]

As yet, such protests failed to sway the princes, but the will of the crusader masses could not be ignored for ever.

ON TO THE PLAINS OF SYRIA

The stark winter months that followed the impasse of early November 1098 have been widely misunderstood by modern historians. They have suggested that, with stalemate reached, the quarrel over Antioch temporarily fell dormant. It is argued that, instead, the crusaders concentrated on the need to forage for food or even made preliminary attempts to continue the march to Jerusalem. In reality, the bitter contest for control of Antioch burned on as fiercely as ever, as did the struggle to become the crusade's outright leader, but the battleground upon which these disputes were played out moved south.[29]

Throughout the summer, Raymond of Toulouse had sought to destabilise Bohemond's hold over the citadel of Antioch and to amass a wide-based platform of popular support through the agency of the Holy Lance. By autumn, he realised that nothing short of outright warfare would pry the city from the tightening grip of the southern Italian. For a leading prince to make such a blatant break with the fraternal ethos of crusading was unacceptable, so, finding the way blocked in one direction, Raymond elected to fight on new ground. If he could not actually oust Bohemond from Antioch, he would instead attempt to make the city untenable. The first step towards this had already been taken – Raymond had a strong foothold within Antioch that hampered Bohemond's access to the sea. To add to this, the count now set about expanding and consolidating the Provençal enclave to the south of Antioch. From this power-base Raymond hoped to hamper Bohemond's lines of supply and compromise Antioch's strategic integrity. Bohemond might keep his seat in the city, but, if Raymond had his way, he would not be sitting comfortably.

The contest moves south

With all this in mind, Raymond turned his gaze south to the plateau region known as the Jabal as-Summaq. Geographically, this was a natural choice, an extension from the Provençal base of operations in the neighbouring Ruj valley. In strategic terms, dominion over this fertile region offered wealth through trade and farming, and control over one of the two southern approaches to Antioch. In fact, Raymond's expansion into the Jabal as-Summaq had begun even before the assembly in early November. Around 25 September 1098 he had led an expeditionary force against the ancient town of Albara. His chaplain, Raymond of Aguilers, accompanied him and later described how the town fell after a short but fiercely fought assault: 'Here [Raymond] slaughtered thousands, returned thousands more to be sold into slavery at Antioch, and freed those cowardly ones who surrendered before the fall of Albara.'

Raymond of Aguilers may have exaggerated the size of the town's population, but he seems to have been singularly unimpressed by Albara itself. The Provençal army cannot all have been so unmoved, for the medieval town of Albara was built alongside a much larger, vastly imposing late-Roman settlement. Even today one can walk out of the small, unremarkable modern town, pass through cherry orchards and find oneself in the midst of an amazingly well-preserved sixth-century community, with startling stone mausoleums topped by pyramidal roofs. So striking are these structures that local legend has it they were built by giants. In fact, Albara is only one of many abandoned, now almost forgotten, Roman 'Dead Cities' scattered across this part of the Syrian landscape, shards of a lost, classical age. It is still possible to walk through these hills and literally stumble across uncatalogued, uninhabited but largely intact late-Roman watchtowers. The effect on the crusaders as they moved through this mysterious, deserted landscape must have been unsettling.

Raymond of Toulouse may have seized Albara with relative ease, but he took great care to ensure that the town remained in Provençal hands. First 'he restored the town to the Christian faith', converting its mosque into a church. More significantly, he decided to install a priest from his army, Peter of Narbonne, as the first Latin bishop of Albara. Peter was later consecrated by the Greek patriarch of Antioch, but his appointment was a clear sign that even Raymond – now a Byzantine ally – wanted the territories he captured to follow the Latin creed. Bishop Peter's task, however, was as much military and political as it was spiritual. He was generously endowed with 'one-half of Albara and its environs' and was instructed to 'hold [the town] even unto death'. With this wealth Peter was later able to keep a garrison of seven knights and thirty foot soldiers under the command of another of Raymond of Toulouse's followers – William Peyre of Cunhlat, the former master of Peter Bartholomew – and this quickly grew to seventy infantry and sixty or more knights. The first bastion of Raymond's Provençal enclave had been established.[30]

After the Antiochene assembly failed to restore peace in early November, Raymond renewed his interest in the Jabal as-Summaq. Around 23 November 1098 he and Robert of Flanders set out for the region from Antioch, taking the road via Rugia and Albara. Their destination was Marrat an-Numan, the region's most prized settlement in both strategic and economic terms, and the site of Raymond Pilet's humiliating defeat the previous summer. If his experience was anything to go by, Raymond of Toulouse could expect Marrat to put up much stiffer opposition than Albara. This may be why he chose to launch his campaign with the assistance of his new ally Robert of Flanders. Together they arrived at Marrat on 28 November. Sensing that Raymond was on the brink of establishing his own, potentially threatening power-base in the Jabal as-Summaq, Bohemond decided that he could no longer bide his time in Antioch, and so rushed off in pursuit, reaching Marrat by the end of November. His intention was not so much to hamper Raymond's attack as to prevent the Provençals from seizing sole rights to the region.[31]

The siege of Marrat an-Numan

First, of course, the crusaders had to engineer Marrat's fall – no simple task. Although this 'wealthy and heavily populated' town lay on an undulating upland plain and so lacked natural defences, it was fully enclosed within a defensive wall and surrounded by a dry moat. At first its populace, remembering the ease with which Raymond Pilet's attack had been thwarted, were scornful of the crusader threat. One Provençal eyewitness recalled, 'the haughty citizens railed at our leaders, cursed our army, and desecrated crosses fixed to their walls to anger us. We were so enraged by the natives that we openly stormed the walls.'

This first attack did not go well. Some Franks reached the town walls, but they carried only two scaling ladders which were 'short and fragile'. With no way into Marrat, the 'leaders saw that they could do nothing and that they were labouring in vain' and so ordered the retreat. Even with the combined force of Raymond, Robert and Bohemond's troops, the crusaders were still ill prepared to prosecute full-scale siege warfare. Realising that a new approach was needed, the three princes met in council. Marrat demanded a different type of strategy from that adopted at Antioch. The town was small enough for a close-encirclement siege to be attempted, but starving the enemy into submission would inevitably be a long-drawn-out process, one during which the crusaders themselves were just as likely to run short of food. Indeed, with winter reaching its height, their lines of supply soon began to show signs of strain. Within a week the crusaders' food supplies started to dwindle. One Latin eyewitness remarked: 'It grieves me to report that in the ensuing famine one could see more than ten thousand men scattered like cattle in the field scratching and looking, trying to find grains of wheat, barley, beans or any vegetable.'[32]

At the same time, discipline was flagging. Peter Bartholomew, who had accompanied Raymond into the Jabal as-Summaq, accused the army of a whole host of sins, including 'murder, pillage, theft and adultery', and prescribed a series of cleansing 'spiritual preparations', the offering of prayers and the giving of alms.

Under these conditions the princes needed to bring their investment of Marrat to a swift resolution. The Muslim garrison refused their offers for a negotiated surrender, so the crusaders decided to adopt an aggressive, assault-based siege strategy. This style of warfare had particular requirements for both attacker and defender. The crusaders' primary aim was to overcome Marrat's defences, for once a breach had been achieved they could bring their numerical superiority to bear within the confines of the town. The goal of the Muslim garrison was to use any and all means available to stop the enemy getting access to the walls. Luckily two chroniclers of the crusade, Raymond of Aguilers and the anonymous author of the *Gesta Francorum*, were present at Marrat and lived through the siege that followed. By combining their vivid accounts with the surviving Arabic evidence a richly detailed picture of the military techniques emerges.

To ease their approach, the crusaders began by filling in sections of the dry moat. The town walls themselves might be overcome in two ways – by forcing them to collapse or by climbing over them. The crusaders pursued both lines of attack. Sappers were deployed to undermine the walls. In its most advanced form sapping involved digging and then collapsing tunnels beneath a wall to undermine its stability. The crusaders had employed this time-consuming technique at Nicaea, but at Marrat they seem to have used a quicker, more basic approach. The defensive methods used by the Muslim garrison – we hear that they 'hurled stones from catapults, darts, fire, hives of bees, and lime upon our men who had sapped their walls' – suggest that the crusaders were out in the open, simply running to the foot of the walls and trying to pry out or smash the masonry to cause a collapse.

For the most part, however, the crusaders, and in particular the Provençals, concentrated their efforts on finding the means actually to mount the walls of Marrat. Trees from a nearby wood were cut down to produce larger, sturdier ladders, but the decisive step was the construction of a formidable siege tower:

> Raymond [of Toulouse] caused a wooden siege tower to be built, and it was strong and lofty, so engineered and constructed that it ran upon four wheels. On the top storey stood many knights and Everard the Huntsman, who blew loud blasts on his horn, and underneath were armed knights who pushed the tower up to the town wall, over against one of its towers. When the pagans saw this they immediately made an engine by which they threw great stones upon our siege tower, so that they nearly killed our knights. Moreover, they threw Greek fire upon the siege tower, hoping to burn and destroy it, but this time God would not let it burn, and it was higher than all the town's walls.[33]

During an attack the crusaders, for their part, 'threw great stones down upon those standing on the city wall' and, when close enough, used spears to harry the enemy and long iron hooks to drag their tower right up to the wall. This impressive siege tower took nearly ten days to build, and was an expensive project even for Raymond, but, once completed, it made a huge difference to the crusaders' prospects. On 11 December a full-scale assault was launched and, tellingly, the crusaders opted to attack Marrat from at least two different directions at once. Raymond's siege tower – packed full of Provençal knights, among whom was William V, count of Montpellier – was pushed up to the walls. Behind it 'stood the priests and clerks, clad in the holy vestments, beseeching God to defend his people'. Horrified by the threat of the tower, the Muslim garrison concentrated its efforts towards repelling this attack. This proved fatal. On the other side of town another Provençal detachment had simultaneously attacked the wall, this time with scaling ladders, and facing weakened resistance they prevailed. Gulpher of Lastours, an Aquitainian knight who had joined Raymond's contingent, was the first to mount the wall, but his success nearly turned to disaster:

The ladder broke at once under the weight of the crowd who followed him, but nevertheless he and some others succeeded in reaching the top of the wall. Those who had gone up cleared a space around them. Others found a fresh ladder and put it up quickly, and many knights and foot soldiers went up it at once, but the Saracens attacked them so fiercely, from the wall and from the ground, loosing arrows and fighting hand to hand with spears, that many of our men jumped off.[34]

Hard pressed as they were, some crusaders managed to hold their ground on the wall. Once again the Muslim garrison was forced to switch priorities, pulling troops away from other sections of the wall to shore up this breach. In the ensuing respite sappers, on the other side of town, 'protected by the siege tower, were undermining the town's defences' when, suddenly, a section of the wall collapsed and 'panic-stricken [the garrison] fled into the town'. As the crusaders began pouring on to its walls, Marrat lay on the brink of capture, but the breakthrough came too late in the day to be immediately conclusive – 'night ended the fight and left some towers and parts of the city in Saracen control. Already in possession of the upper hand, the princes decided not to risk the chaotic uncertainty of urban combat in the dark, and, having encircled the town with their knights 'to cut off any escapees', they settled down to await dawn. The poorer crusaders who had accompanied Raymond, Robert and Bohemond were not so patient. With the backbone of Marrat's resistance broken their minds turned to the possibility of plunder: 'Because starvation had made them [desperate, they] carried the fight to the besieged in the shades of the night. Thereby the poor gained the lion's share of booty and houses in Marrat while the knights, who awaited morning to enter, found poor pickings.'[35]

The fall of Marrat presents a clear distillation of the crusaders' darker impulses – their single-minded greed and cold-blooded brutality. The town's sack was always going to be about one thing – plunder – and the Franks were prepared to go to virtually any lengths to get it. The princes certainly did not choose to wait for daylight to facilitate a more controlled, peaceful surrender from the Muslim garrison. They held off until 12 December so that they might overrun the town more safely and strip it of loot more efficiently. Bohemond attempted to negotiate the surrender of Marrat's leaders, instructing them through an interpreter that if they gathered with their families in a specified 'palace which lies above the gate, he would save them from death'. But this act had nothing to do with clemency. Bohemond did not carefully orchestrate the safe capture of Marrat's aristocracy to offer them security or preferred treatment. He simply wanted them in one place so that he might rob them more easily. We hear from one eyewitness that 'Bohemond took those whom he had ordered to enter the palace, and stripped them of all their belongings, gold, silver and other valuables, and some of them he caused to be killed, others to be taken to Antioch and sold as slaves.'[36]

The sheer ferocity of Marrat's sack was intensified by the poorer crusaders' night-time scavenging. As day broke on 12 December, the knights, frustrated that they had been beaten to the best booty, unleashed their anger on the town's populace in a mad scramble to gather up what was left:

Our men all entered the city, and each seized his own share of whatever goods he found in houses or cellars, and when it was dawn they killed everyone, man or woman, whom they met in any place whatsoever. No corner of the town was clear of Saracen corpses, and one could scarcely go about the streets except by treading on their dead bodies.[37]

One medieval Arabic writer later estimated the Muslim dead at 10,000, an exaggeration, but one that indicates the perceived severity of the slaughter. Some Muslims escaped immediate death by hiding in caves underneath the town, but the crusaders went to almost perverse lengths to get at them and their riches:

The Christians filched all the goods above ground, and, driven by hopes of Saracen wealth underground, smoked the enemy out of their caves with fire and sulphur flames. When the plunder in the caves proved disappointing, they tortured to death the hapless Muslims in their reach. Some of our men had the experience of leading the Saracens through the streets, hoping to locate spoils of war, only to find their captives would lead them to wells and then suddenly jump headlong to their deaths in preference to revealing goods owned by them or others. Because of their intransigence all submitted to death. Their corpses were thrown into swamps and areas beyond the walls, and so Marrat yielded little plunder.[38]

Of course, the conquest of Marrat was not just about amassing moveable treasure. Raymond of Toulouse had come south to expand his Provençal enclave, cement his domination of the Jabal as-Summaq and destabilise Bohemond's grip over northern Syria. Bohemond, for his part, had followed Raymond to prevent him taking sole possession of Marrat. With the town captured, the princes were presented with one overriding question: who had the right to claim Marrat? Having been responsible for constructing the campaign's decisive weapon – the siege tower – Raymond saw himself as the chief architect of Marrat's fall and naturally believed he deserved full rights to the town. In contrast, the Provençals argued, Bohemond and his men had been 'only half hearted in pressing the siege . . . more of a hindrance than a help'. Even so, during the sack Bohemond, acutely attuned as always to the exigencies of the right of conquest, raced along the walls posting men to occupy as many towers as possible. Raymond's followers may have seized most of the town itself, but Bohemond controlled the greater part of its defences.

Thus from 12 December a complex stalemate was achieved. Raymond could not claim sole lordship of Marrat while Bohemond retained control of his towers. The mirror image of this predicament existed at Antioch, where Bohemond's rule was challenged by Raymond's possession of the Bridge Gate and Palace. The true, underlying significance of the entire expedition to Marrat emerged once negotiations towards a settlement began. Apparently, Bohemond stated bluntly: 'I shall agree to nothing with Raymond unless he cedes the Antiochene towers to me.' Bohemond had come to the Jabal as-Summaq in search of a bargaining tool with which to break the deadlock at Antioch, but when Raymond proved utterly unwilling to relinquish his foothold in that city, it became clear that, far from being resolved, the quarrel between them had instead only intensified.[39]

THE FALTERING PATH

The Feast of the Nativity passed at Marrat in miserable inactivity. Most crusaders, from knights to the poorest peasants, were becoming increasingly disgruntled. Once the meagre spoils of the recent sack had been exhausted, hunger once again began to threaten. As far as the mass of crusaders was concerned, the expedition would survive only if it began moving south with a rejuvenated unity of purpose, towards Jerusalem. Popular pressure was growing within both the Provençal and southern Italian Norman camps, for the princes to put aside their differences and focus instead upon the interests of the crusade. Both Raymond and Bohemond were facing the real possibility of open rebellion or desertion.

Many Provençals believed Raymond should strike out for Jerusalem regardless of what the other crusade princes might do. They wanted him, 'the recipient of the Holy Lance . . . to make himself leader and lord of the army', but they warned that, if he were not willing to restart the expedition, he should 'hand over the Holy Lance to the masses, and they would continue the march to Jerusalem under the Lord's leadership'. The threat was obvious – do something to solve the crisis or risk losing popular support. To the masses, Raymond's prestige had been boosted through his association with the Holy Lance, their totem of success and divine sanction, but his role as its guardian also conveyed a new burden of heightened expectations. If Raymond did not prove himself to be unswervingly dedicated to the Lance's cause – that of the crusade – then the prestige he had gained might actually do him more harm than good.

Under this acute pressure, Raymond took two steps to appease his followers. In the last days of December he announced his intention to march south towards Jerusalem in just over two weeks. Bohemond, having already expressed his refusal to recommence the expedition before Easter 1099, decided to leave for Antioch a few days later. With no deal brokered with the Provençals, Bohemond chose to withdraw his troops from Marrat, deeming it impossible to maintain safely such an isolated foothold in the Jabal as-Summaq. After this, Raymond performed a further exercise in public relations, announcing a second general council of the crusader princes to discuss the expedition's resumption, this time to be held at Rugia, the Provençal base. By these two steps Raymond reasserted his ascendancy among the princes. On the surface at least he seemed to be taking the moral high ground in the dispute with Bohemond, and the call to council at Rugia rather than Antioch conveyed an obvious underlying message about his dominant authority.

The truth was, however, that even in the first days of January 1099 Raymond was still trying to fulfil both of his goals – territorial gains in northern Syria and leadership of the crusade. With his popular critics temporarily assuaged, he began to consolidate his hold over Marrat. Together with Peter of Narbonne, the newly appointed bishop of Albara, he set about 'Christianising' the town – converting mosques and erecting crosses – and 'determining both the number and choice of personnel' for its Frankish garrison. Raymond may have been preparing to march south towards Jerusalem, but he still had every intention of holding on to his carefully constructed enclave in the Jabal as-Summaq and of continuing to challenge Bohemond's position in Antioch.[1]

Around 4 January 1099 the princes gathered at Rugia for one

last-ditch attempt to resolve the dispute over Antioch, but, not surprisingly, neither Bohemond nor Raymond would agree to budge an inch. Raymond's next outlandish act probably explains why he bothered to call the abortive council in the first place. With all the princes gathered together, he sought to buy their support. His chaplain recalled that 'Raymond offered Godfrey and Robert of Normandy 10,000 solidi apiece, 6,000 to Robert of Flanders, 5,000 to Tancred, and proportionately to others,' a considerable investment. He may have dressed this up as financial sponsorship of the crusading ideal, but in essence Raymond was trying to purchase confirmation of his status as leader of the expedition with hard cash. In fact, only two of the four named princes seem to have taken the bait at this point. From mid-January Robert, duke of Normandy and his men joined forces with the southern French. More surprisingly, so too did Tancred. Bohemond's nephew had been gradually moving out of his uncle's shadow since the summer of 1097. Now he made a full break and seems actually to have entered service with Raymond.

Godfrey, meanwhile, maintained his neutrality and Robert of Flanders, who had followed Raymond into the Jabal as-Summaq, now seems to have broken with the Provençal camp. Perhaps disillusioned by Raymond's acquisitiveness, Robert returned to Antioch with Bohemond. All the same, Count Raymond came out of the council of Rugia in a strengthened position. He may not yet have been acknowledged as the crusade's outright leader, but he was now the dominant force within the expedition.[2]

Not everything went Raymond's way in the first week of January 1099. While he was occupied at Rugia, events at Marrat took an unexpected and shocking turn. The lines of supply sustaining the Provençal presence there had always been tenuous, but with the advent of the New Year they collapsed. The poor, who had already endured a hungry Christmas, were now left destitute. Suddenly it seemed that the horrors of starvation that had ravaged the Franks one year earlier outside Antioch had returned. Now at Marrat, without princely guidance, the most destitute crusaders went to appalling lengths to alleviate their hunger. Some, desperate to find money wherever they could, 'ripped up the bodies of the [Muslim] dead, because they used to find coins hidden in their entrails'. Others took even more savage steps: 'Here our men suffered from excessive hunger. I shudder to say that many of our men, terribly tormented by the madness of starvation, cut pieces of flesh from the buttocks of Saracens lying there dead. These pieces they cooked and ate, savagely devouring the flesh while it was insufficiently roasted.' Another account that is perhaps even more disturbing asserted that, 'food shortage became so acute that the Christians ate with gusto many rotten Saracen bodies which they had pitched into the swamps three weeks before. This spectacle disgusted as many crusaders as it did strangers.'

This cannibalism at Marrat is among the most infamous of all the atrocities perpetrated by the First Crusaders. These acts were so extreme that, in contrast to the usually offhand contemporary descriptions of violence, both key sources here show real dismay and revulsion. To the men writing about the crusades, some forms of violence – holy war carried out in the name of God – were acceptable, while all others deserved condemnation. On this occasion the line of acceptability was crossed. The division between glorification and censure, the exaltation of wholesale massacre and denunciation of cannibalism, might appear arbitrary, perhaps even simplistic, when today the very notion of religious warfare might be considered an abomination. But, on the question of Christian violence, the moral and spiritual code that governed medieval European society differed vastly from that which prevails today. Thus, before judging the nature of crusading violence, we must remember that in the Middle Ages, an era of endemic savagery, warfare was regulated by a particular, medieval sense of morality.

Terrible as it is to acknowledge, the horrors perpetrated at Marrat did have some positive effects on the crusaders' short-term prospects. News of the Franks' brutality soon reached nearby Muslim towns and cities. One crusader noted that 'the infidels spread stories of these and other inhuman acts of the [crusaders], but we were unaware that God had made us an object of terror'. This, combined with tales of the Latin sack of Antioch, was enough to convince many Muslim commanders and garrisons that the crusaders were bloodthirsty barbarians, invincible savages who could not be resisted. In the coming months, most quickly decided that it would be better to accept costly and humiliating truces with the Franks rather than face them in battle.[3]

The mob back at Marrat had another surprise for Raymond of Toulouse when he returned from Rugia around 7 January. In his absence, Peter of Narbonne had begun preparations to garrison the town 'with knights and footmen from the army'. But, when news of this plan spread through the masses and it became clear that despite his promises Raymond had every intention of retaining Marrat and perpetuating the dispute with Bohemond, open rebellion broke out. The poor made a startling demonstration of civil disobedience. To prevent any further delays or arguments, they started pulling down Marrat's walls and fortifications, stone by stone, intending to leave it defenceless and untenable:

> Thereupon, even the sick and weak, arising from their beds and hobbling along on sticks, came all the way to the walls. An emaciated person could roll back and forth and push [stones] from the walls. The bishop of Albara and Raymond's friends, exhorting and pleading against such vandalism, went about the town, but those who had scrambled from the walls and hidden at their approach were quick to resume their work as soon as the guards passed by them.[4]

In reality, the mob may well have done serious damage to Marrat's walls but could hardly have razed its defences to the ground in such a short space of time. More significant for Raymond was the unmistakable message carried in their actions: no longer could he contest the domination of northern Syria with Bohemond while also playing the role of an idealised crusade leader dedicated to the recapture of Jerusalem. The time had come for one path to be chosen and Raymond took the road to the Holy City. Putting the needs of the crusade first, he made no attempt to refortify Marrat, effectively turning his back on the Jabal as-Summaq, for the time being at least.

Over the next few days Raymond led forceful raids south towards the nearby town of Kafartab in search of badly needed food for the poor. By 13 January his army had just enough supplies to march out of the region. As a powerful reminder of his renewed dedication to the crusade, Raymond chose to leave Marrat in religious procession: 'On the appointed day the count, his clerics, and the bishop of Albara departed and trudged along barefooted, calling out for God's mercy and the saints' protection, as flames set by the departing Christians mounted the ruins of Marrat. In the rear marched Tancred with forty knights and many footmen.'

Within two days they were joined by Robert of Normandy. After countless months of delay, dispute and distraction the expedition had at last resumed its journey south towards Jerusalem. The First Crusade looked set to enter its final act.[5]

TALKING TO THE ENEMY

The expedition had now reached a turning point. Raymond's decision to march south out of the Jabal as-Summaq proved so popular that he seemed set to become the unquestioned leader of the entire crusade. But he still faced some thorny problems. His dispute with Bohemond lay unresolved and the schism between them was now probably irreparable, but two other princes, Godfrey of Bouillon and Robert of Flanders, still remained at Antioch with their armies. Without their strength and support, Raymond had little hope of forcing his way through to Palestine and Jerusalem. He also had to determine a strategy for the journey ahead.

Eighteen months earlier the crusaders had crossed Asia Minor with relative speed by, for the most part, avoiding confrontation. With the exception of Nicaea, they had not sought to capture nor garrison most of the settlements passed. Upon reaching Syria, however, the expedition had been brought to a standstill by the Latins' determination to seize Antioch and its environs. Now a choice had to be made: the road to Jerusalem was littered with Muslim towns and cities; if the crusaders sought to conquer each and every one their progress south would be interminably slow. But there was an alternative: with the Muslim world of Syria thrown into disarray by Kerbogha's defeat at Antioch and cowed by the recent brutality at Marrat, there was every possibility that the crusaders might make a rapid, purposeful advance on Jerusalem, negotiating advantageous, even profitable, truces with local Islamic rulers as they went.

For Raymond of Toulouse, this approach had one major flaw – it failed to reward his smouldering territorial ambitions. It appeared that Raymond had turned away from the squabble over Antioch, recommitting himself to the crusading ideal, refocusing upon Jerusalem. But actually he had, at the very least, left a Provençal garrison at Albara and probably harboured plans to consolidate his hold over the Jabal as-Summaq at a later date. As the crusade began moving south, it soon became clear that Raymond had not been cleansed of his desire for conquest, and soon he was once again torn between his two conflicting passions – the power of leadership and rewards of territorial gain. He may have been poised to lead the crusade in January 1099, but his actions in the first four months of that year would determine once and for all whether he could retain that position.

In the early weeks of the march south from Marrat, it seemed that Raymond had resolved to focus on the march to Jerusalem. Even before leaving the Jabal as-Summaq the crusaders began to receive delegations from nearby Muslim powers, and for the time being Raymond was happy to negotiate truces. His chaplain remarked: 'News of the resumption of the crusade caused nearby rulers to send Arab nobles to Raymond with prayers and many offerings and promises of future submission as well as free and saleable goods.'

The first settlement to offer terms was Shaizar, an imposing fortress perched on a rocky spur above a bend in the Orontes river and held by the Banu Munqidh, an Arab family who had long railed against the Seljuq domination of Syria. Being less than heartbroken over the defeats suffered by the Turks at Antioch, and judging the Franks to be the new pre-eminent power in the region, the Munqidhs quickly offered safe passage through their lands and 'to sell them horses and food'. Their approach was perfectly understandable – simply put, they were hoping to get the crusaders out of their lands as quickly and peacefully as possible to protect Shaizar from assault and destruction. The crusaders' reaction is more problematic. In earlier phases of the expedition our Latin sources presented the crusaders as brutal xenophobes, possessed of a seemingly psychopathic hatred of Islam, conditioned by papal rhetoric and popular preaching to view all Muslims as sub-human. Now 'suddenly' the Franks were willing to negotiate with the 'enemy', albeit on this occasion from a dominant and exploitative position.

The truth is that the crusaders were, when it suited their purposes, willing to adopt a more pragmatic approach to their dealings with Islam. This was not simply dependent upon the ethnic or religious background of the Muslims encountered. While some crusaders were conscious of the differences between Seljuq Turks, Arabs and Egyptians, this did not dictate their attitude, as negotiation took place with all three groups. This adaptable outlook is unlikely to have been the preserve of the 'enlightened' aristocracy, as no popular outcry within the crusader host is recorded. Eyewitness Latin accounts of the expedition, written on the whole by clergymen, are reluctant to admit the full extent of this 'diplomatic' contact. Their monochromatic presentation of relations with Islam may have blinded us to some of its subtler nuances. The First Crusaders were capable of compartmentalising their feelings towards the Muslims of Syria and Palestine. They could sheath the sword of holy war when necessary.[6]

The détente with Shaizar soon brought benefits for the crusaders. On the second day travelling through Munqidh territory their hunger

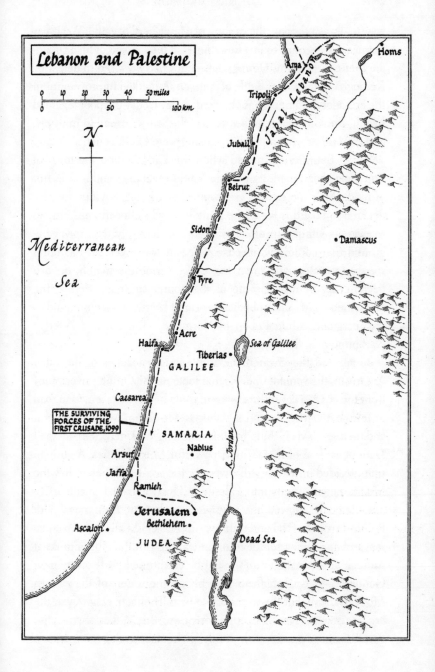

Lebanon and Palestine

0 10 20 30 40 50 miles
0   50   100 km

N

Mediterranean
Sea

Homs

Arqa

Tripoli

Jubail

Beirut

Sidon

Tyre

Jabal Lebanon

• Damascus

Acre
Haifa

GALILEE

Sea of Galilee

Tiberias •

Caesarea

THE SURVIVING
FORCES OF THE
FIRST CRUSADE, 1099

SAMARIA
Nablus
•

Arsuf

Jaffa

R. Jordan

Ramleh

Jerusalem •
Bethlehem •

Ascalon •

JUDEA

Dead Sea

was finally assuaged by the capture of a large herd of cattle. Wealthier Latins were also able to buy fresh horses at the markets of Shaizar and another nearby town, Homs, whose emir had been led to defeat by Kerbogha in the Great Battle of Antioch. A marked improvement in the crusaders' prospects was observed as 'day by day the poor regained health, the knights became stronger, the army seemed to multiply, and the farther we marched the greater were God's benefits'.

These bounties continued when the Latins found the town of Raphania abandoned, its 'gardens full of vegetables and houses full of food'. After the rigours experienced at Marrat, Raymond wisely decided to take this leg of the journey slowly, allowing his army to recover its vitality. In all, they spent ten leisurely days traversing ground that could have been covered in two. Even so, Raymond sought to protect and order his forces during the march, once it became apparent that some of the poorer stragglers were being ambushed by Muslim robbers. Raymond himself took command of the rearguard, while Robert of Normandy, Tancred and Peter of Narbonne held the vanguard.[7]

Finally, as they neared the south-eastern reaches of the Jabal Ansariyah, the verdant uplands that separate the Orontes river valley from the coast, a definitive choice of route had to be taken. One road to Jerusalem struck inland, heading to the east of Mount Lebanon and then south via Nablus, but this would have taken the crusade past Damascus, one of Syria's most powerful Muslim cities. A council soon decided instead to strike west for the coast and then follow the Mediterranean south into Palestine. This route had one massive advantage: it allowed the crusaders to benefit from naval aid. Reinforcements, food and military supplies could all be received by sea, and rapid channels of communication with the other Franks at Antioch and the Byzantines might be established via the Venetian, Genoese and English fleets now plying the waters of the eastern Mediterranean. For this approach to be fully effective, however, the crusaders would have to occupy ports along the southern Syrian and Palestinian coast to allow ships safe anchorage.[8]

The road towards the coast took the crusaders through the beautiful fertile valley of al-Bouqia, and here again they spent time gathering supplies. To the south the valley rises into the snow-capped peaks of the Lebanese mountains, but to the north it is overlooked by the foothills of the Jabal Ansariyah, where today still stands perhaps the greatest fortification to be wrought by human hand in any age – Krak des Chevaliers. Situated on a steep-sided promontory, and thus rendered almost impregnable on three sides, Krak was constructed by the Latin Knights of St John, the Hospitallers, through the twelfth and thirteenth centuries. Pouring vast sums of money into the project, employing the finest architects and masons, they created an almost flawless expression of medieval castle technology. Today Krak survives as the most perfectly preserved monument of the crusading age, its vast twin walls enclosing a complex system of defences, with space to billet 2,000 troops. Back in 1099 only a small, relatively rudimentary fortification – Hisn al-Akrad – stood where Krak would later be built. Even so, with their stronghold positioned high above the al-Bouqia valley, its garrison felt protected enough to unleash a series of skirmishing attacks upon the crusaders as they passed on 28 January. Enraged by their audacity, Raymond set off to launch a frontal assault on the castle. He made little headway and at one point was almost killed when separated from his men, but the sheer ferocity of the Frankish attack terrified the Muslims. On the following morning the crusaders awoke to find the fortress abandoned, as 'only the spoils of war and a ghost castle awaited us'. With food once again in plentiful supply, they passed a further two weeks in al-Bouqia.

News of this latest Latin success against a fortification that had been considered impregnable sent further shock waves through the local Muslim world. The emir of Homs rushed to confirm his treaty with Raymond, sending gifts of horses and gold. Fakhr al-Mulk ibn-Ammar, the Arab emir of Tripoli, one of the great coastal cities to the south, was similarly impressed. Like the Banu Munqidh of Shaizar, his family had for years clung on to independence from Seljuq Turkish rule and was more than willing to purchase safety from the passing crusader army. The emir duly sent Raymond ten horses, four mules and some gold as gifts to open negotiations for a truce.[9]

Up to this point, Raymond of Toulouse had enjoyed considerable success. In his first month as nominal leader of the expedition the army had made slow but sustainable progress south. For once, his men were well fed and in good spirits, and Raymond's position and status seemed increasingly secure. But he was actually facing a real crisis. Riding the wave of earlier crusader successes, the count had reached the coast with a relatively small army. Even with the support of Robert of Normandy and Tancred, he commanded, at best, 5,000 combatants. By February 1099, his army had reached the limit of military viability: to march any further south without reconnecting with the other crusading forces would be an extremely risky proposition, inviting death and destruction. In a sense Raymond had taken a gamble when he marched south from Marrat. He had hoped that this move would galvanise the other princes still at Antioch, forcing them to rejoin an expedition that was now under his direction. Raymond's piecemeal progress to the coast had given them plenty of time to catch up. But, as he neared Tripoli, there was still no sign of Godfrey, Bohemond or Robert of Flanders. They had called his bluff.

THE SIEGE OF ARQA

It was against this background that Raymond made perhaps his most ill-fated decision of the entire crusade. Unable to continue the march south in safety, he elected to bide his time in the region around Tripoli, directing his men to besiege the nearby town of Arqa on 14 February 1099. Raymond's motives for pursuing this course of action are far from clear. Strategic necessity cannot have been paramount in his mind, as Arqa presented no obvious threat or obstacle to the crusaders' progress. In reality, a number of interlocking factors probably inspired his decision. The prospect of waiting idly for the arrival of his fellow crusading princes threatened to dent Raymond's prestige and prompt the gradual disintegration of his indolent army. At the same time, his acquisitive eye may already have settled upon Tripoli, either as a potential conquest or simply as a source of revenue. The crusaders' formidable reputation had so cowed local Muslim rulers that they were now prepared to buy peace with hard cash, and an attack on Arqa might force the price up. A Provençal crusader recalled: '[On returning from Tripoli our envoys] persuaded Raymond that its emir would in four or five days give him gold and silver to his heart's content if he laid siege to Arqa, a strongly defended place.'[10]

The siege of Arqa appeared to offer a perfect opportunity to provide the army with gainful employment, intimidate and exploit Tripoli and, should things go well, perhaps even act as the first stepping-stone towards a full-scale conquest of the region. Unfortunately for Raymond, Arqa proved instead to be a terrible stumbling block. If Raymond began the investment believing the town would soon capitulate he was deeply mistaken. Looking back with dismay upon the siege, one eyewitness gave a grim estimate of Arqa's strength: 'This castle was full of an immense horde of pagans, Turks, Saracens, Arabs and Paulicians, who had made its fortifications exceedingly strong and defended themselves bravely.'[11]

At first the crusaders seemed to be in control of events. Even before Arqa was encircled, Raymond looked to secure access to the coastline and naval communication by dispatching two of his followers, Raymond Pilet and Raymond, viscount of Turenne, at the head of a small expeditionary force. They came first to the port town of Tortosa, lying one day's hard march to the north of Tripoli, but found it strongly garrisoned. The anonymous author of the *Gesta Francorum*, now travelling with Raymond of Toulouse's contingent, wrote: 'when night fell they withdrew into a corner where they encamped and lit many fires so that it might appear that the whole host was there. The pagans were terrified and fled secretly in the night, leaving the town full of provisions. It also has an excellent harbour.'

On the heels of this wily success, another port further north up the coast, Marqab, quickly decided to offer terms of surrender, erected Raymond of Toulouse's banner and accepted a Latin garrison. These coastal footholds opened up the possibility of naval support to some extent, but there was no port in the immediate vicinity of Arqa, which in any case lay some kilometres inland, to allow a consistent line of communication to be established. Greek and Venetian ships were forced to anchor along the coastline, disgorge their cargoes of 'grain, wine, barley, pork and other marketable goods' and then sail off to the safety of the northern ports.

Once the siege of Arqa had been established, Raymond's troops also led foraging parties into the environs of Tripoli itself. At first the city put up some resistance, but its defensive force was annihilated, causing the stream that runs into Tripoli to run red with Muslim blood. Terrified, the city and many of the surrounding settlements agreed to raise Raymond's banner as a prelude to their seemingly inevitable capitulation.[12]

On the margins, therefore, the siege of Arqa seemed to be progressing at an acceptable pace. The problem arose at Arqa itself: the town simply refused to fall. Very little precise evidence about the siege survives, but we do know that the Muslim garrison made effective use of defensive projectile weapons. Possessing at least one large catapult, they were able to rain deadly missiles down upon the crusaders. Pons of Balazun, a close friend of Raymond of Aguilers and co-author of the early sections of his chronicle, was killed by one such rock. Anselm of Ribemont, who wrote at least two detailed letters describing his experiences on the expedition, was struck on the head by another and died. It was widely rumoured within the army that Anselm had had a premonition of his impending demise. It was said that on the very morning of his death he awoke,

summoned priests to him, confessed his omissions and sins, invoked God's mercy and told them of the imminence of his death. While they stood shocked by the news, since they saw Anselm hale and hearty, he explained: 'Don't be astonished; listen to me. Last

night I saw Lord Engelrand of St Pôl, who lost his life at Marrat,
and I, fully conscious, enquired, "What goes here? You were dead,
and behold now you are alive." Lord Engelrand replied, "Those
who die in Christ's service never die."'

Engelrand supposedly went on to assure Anselm that he too would
find a place in heaven when he was killed on the morrow. Assured of
his salvation, Anselm apparently prepared for his death with good
cheer.[13] This story may have served to reinforce the conviction among
the crusaders that those killed in battle en route to Jerusalem were
martyrs destined for heavenly paradise, but it could not cancel out the
harsher reality that confronted the Franks at Arqa. The lives of good
men were being lost in a siege that seemed to be hopeless.

The crusaders spent three long, frustrating months investing Arqa,
with little or no return. In this time other events overtook them. As
winter waned, an embassy from al-Afdal, vizier of Fatimid Egypt,
arrived. Following Byzantine advice, the crusaders had established
contact with the Fatimid Muslims of Egypt back in 1097, and in
March 1098 had sent envoys to Cairo to discuss the possibility of
mutual co-operation against the Seljuq Turks of Syria and Palestine.
Now at last they had returned in the company of Fatimid envoys
bearing al-Afdal's response.

In the intervening year much had changed. Capitalising on the
disarray within the Seljuq world that followed Kerbogha's defeat at
Antioch, the Fatimids had, in August 1098, attacked and overthrown
the Turkish rulers of Jerusalem. Suddenly the crusaders' chief goal,
the Holy City, had a new master – al-Afdal. Initially, all seemed well.
The crusader envoys to the Fatimids were able to visit Jerusalem in
peace. But by 1099 al-Afdal was in close correspondence with the
Byzantine Emperor Alexius, who revealed that a Graeco-Frankish
alliance was in tatters and disclosed what he knew about the
diminishing size of the crusader army. From this oasition of relative
strength, al-Afdal had become less receptive to the Latins'
proposals. They offered to hand over any former Fatimid territories

they captured from the Turks and to divide equally any other land obtained with Egyptian aid. In return, the crusaders had one 'simple' request – they wanted Jerusalem. Al-Afdal's response reveals that he was no longer interested in a military alliance with the Franks, but was now simply intent upon formulating a truce that might forestall a crusader invasion of Palestine. It also demonstrates that he had severely underestimated the Latin commitment to the recovery of Jerusalem. His offer – to allow small groups of unarmed crusaders to visit the holy sites of Jerusalem as pilgrims – was flatly refused. All possibility of a negotiated peace evaporated and the lines of confrontation were drawn.[14]

As the first weeks of spring arrived, there was still no sign of a breakthrough at Arqa, nor of the arrival of the remaining crusader forces. Bohemond, Godfrey and Robert of Flanders were still occupied in the north. When Raymond had marched south from Marrat, in mid-January, Bohemond had seized his chance at Antioch. Judging the count to be too preoccupied to intervene, he moved to expel all Provençal troops from the city, overwhelming and absorbing Raymond's enclave around the Bridge Gate. It is not known whether any blood was shed in the process, but one thing was now clear. Among the Latins at least, Bohemond had become the acknowledged master of Antioch and it was extremely unlikely that he would immediately abandon his hard-fought conquest in favour of continuing the pilgrimage to Jerusalem. Around 1 March he accompanied Godfrey and Robert as far as Latakia, which was still in Greek hands at this point, but he soon turned back towards Antioch. In spite of Bohemond's actions, no division between the Byzantines and the crusaders was apparent – all three princes were able to move through Latakia with impunity – suggesting that, as yet, Bohemond had not openly refused to return Antioch to the emperor.[15]

A short day's march south of Latakia, Godfrey and Robert came to the small coastal fortress of Jabala, to which they duly laid siege. They were still engaged in this venture when, around the start of April, Peter of Narbonne, the new bishop of Albara, arrived from Arqa bearing an urgent message from Raymond of Toulouse. A rumour was abroad in Syria that the Seljuqs of Baghdad had gathered a new army and were, even now, marching on Raymond's position. In essence, the count was now begging for his colleagues to reinforce him:

> When they heard this news [Godfrey and Robert] made a treaty with the emir [of Jabala] at once and agreed with him on terms of peace, receiving a tribute of horses and gold, and so they left the [fortress] and came to our help; but the threatened attack did not come, so the said counts encamped on the other side of the river and took part in the siege of Arqa.[16]

One Latin source, written decades later, accused Raymond of inventing the Seljuq threat in order to finally bring Godfrey and Robert of Flanders south, and this is quite possible. Godfrey was reluctant to involve himself in the siege of Arqa, but by the end of March it still seemed that Raymond might realise his dream of leading the reunited crusade south to Jerusalem as its unquestioned commander-in-chief. In reality, the full consequences of his entanglement with Arqa were about to become clear.[17]

Raymond began the siege of Arqa with two ambitions: to buy time to reunite the crusade under his own banner; and to lay the foundation for territorial domination of the region around Tripoli. Just as at Antioch and the Jabal as-Summaq, he failed to focus exclusively upon one goal. Now, with the arrival Godfrey and Robert of Flanders, the expedition was as ready as it would ever be to attempt the march on Jerusalem. Indeed, with the recent collapse of negotiations with the Fatimids, speed of action was even more essential. If the Franks struck south immediately they might be able to break through to Jerusalem before the Egyptians had time to organise an effective defence. But Raymond was unwilling to relinquish his hopes for Arqa and Tripoli. Rather than move on when no progress was being made, he persisted and day by day, week by week, allowed his competence and integrity as the expedition's leader to become intricately intertwined with the fate of Arqa.

From one perspective, at least, the siege was proving to be a resounding success – it filled the crusader princes' coffers to the brim. By 1 April local Muslim powers were practically fighting for the opportunity to offer the most generous terms in return for peace and safety:

> The emir of Tripoli offered us 15,000 gold pieces of Saracen money plus horses, she mules, many garments, and even more such rewards in succeeding years. In addition the lord of Jabala, fearful of another siege, sent our leaders tribute of 5,000 gold pieces, horses, she mules, and an abundant supply of wine. Now we were well provisioned because many gifts from castles and cities other than Jabala were sent to us.[18]

With so much wealth pouring in, it was decided to further refine the system governing the distribution of booty by setting up a special fund which saw one-tenth of all spoils put into a communal kitty. Even though only a quarter of this was eventually dispersed among the 'poor and infirm', it still made a marked difference to their standard of living. As his lands back in Europe lay on the border with Iberia, Raymond of Toulouse would have been aware that for much of the eleventh century the Christians of northern Spain had grown rich on the tribute extracted from their Muslim neighbours to the south in what amounted to little more than protection racketeering. As time went on this system had become so profitable that the Christian kings of Léon-Castile had actually become reluctant to overthrow their ever-weakening Islamic 'enemies' for fear of losing valuable revenue.

A similar reluctance seems to have taken hold of Raymond in the latter stages of Arqa's investment. If the town fell he would either have to follow up his threats and assault Tripoli itself or move on south, but so long as the siege continued and the local Muslim world remained cowed, he could reap a rich harvest. Unfortunately for Raymond, cracks soon started to appear in this comfortable arrangement. A number of lesser crusade figures became increasingly greedy and each, hoping to establish his own tribute network, 'dispatched messengers with letters to Saracen cities stating that he was the lord of the crusaders'. The emir of Tripoli also started to wonder why he was paying so much money to protect himself from the Franks when they were not even able to capture Arqa. The crusaders countered the first signs of this questioning with a brutal raid against Tripoli, of which Raymond of Aguilers happily reported: '[Afterwards] the land stank of Muslim blood, and the aqueduct [which ran into the city] was choked with their corpses. It was a delightful sight as its swirling waters tumbled the headless bodies of nobles and rabble into Tripoli.' For the time being a rebellion had been averted, but the precarious balance between threat and exploitation could not remain in place for ever.[19]

In this context, two events sealed the fate of Raymond of Toulouse and the siege of Arqa. Ever since Peter Bartholomew had 'discovered' the relic of the Holy Lance of Antioch, in June 1098, and Raymond had endorsed his story, the count's status and prestige had grown alongside that of the visionary. With Adhémar of Le Puy's death the Provençals had begun promoting Peter as the expedition's new, popular spiritual leader. Given Peter's unpredictability, Raymond's patronage of him was always going to be as risky as it was empowering, but as the months progressed Peter's visions and pronouncements became ever more fantastical.

This reached a peak after 5 April 1099 when Peter Bartholomew came forward claiming to have witnessed a new vision of Christ, St Peter and St Andrew. The message he bore to the crusaders was utterly extraordinary. According to his story, the Lord had proclaimed the existence of many sinners among the crusading ranks and instructed Peter to root them out in the following manner: Raymond of Toulouse was to call forth the entire army and have them 'line up as if for battle or for a siege'. Peter would then 'miraculously' find the crusaders arrayed in five ranks. The Latins in the first three ranks would be devoted followers of Christ, but the remainder were those polluted by sins ranging from pride to cowardice. Peter actually came forward saying that God had instructed him to oversee the immediate execution of any crusader found wanting in this bizarre selection process.

Not surprisingly, there was an almighty uproar once Peter's story had been broadcast throughout the army. Antagonisms, resentments and jealousies towards the upstart prophet that had been held in check by his widespread popularity now bubbled to the surface. Outside the Provençal contingent, crusaders may have harboured nagging doubts about the authenticity of Peter's revelations, but in the tide of zealous veneration for the Holy Lance that followed the seemingly miraculous victory over Kerbogha they had thought better of openly challenging the visionary. Peter's claims after 5 April were so outlandish, his recommendations so extreme, that for many his spell was broken. At last doubts were openly expressed, and their mouthpiece was Arnulf of Chocques, chaplain to Robert of Normandy. Already 'a respected man because of his erudition', Arnulf was unswervingly ambitious and must have realised that by discrediting Peter Bartholomew he himself might be lifted to prominence. He publicly challenged the validity of Peter's visions and, by association, the authenticity of the Holy Lance. Bartholomew's bluff had been called, but even in the face of these accusations he refused to back down, offering instead to prove his integrity through an ordeal.[20]

Ordeals played an important if infrequent role in medieval systems of justice. Our popular modern perception – that brutal trials by fire or water were the mainstay of the legal system during the Middle Ages – is far from the truth. In reality, ordeals were used only as a last resort and, in particular, when an individual's moral character could not be vouched for within society. In such cases, where an oath could not be trusted, the accused might undergo some form of trial, usually under the supervision of the clergy. This might involve holding on to a red-hot iron or placing one's hand in a cauldron of boiling water.

Again, contrary to modern misconceptions, it was not generally expected that the defendant would emerge totally unscathed even if innocent. Instead, the wounds of the accused would be bound and inspected some days later, with any sign of infection being taken to indicate guilt.[21]

By April 1099 Peter Bartholomew must himself have been totally convinced of the Holy Lance's authenticity and his own role as God's messenger, because he chose to undergo a particularly harsh and hazardous trial by fire, reportedly saying: 'I not only wish, but I beg that you set ablaze a fire, and I shall take the ordeal of fire with the Holy Lance in my hands; and if it is really the Lord's Lance, I shall emerge unsinged. But if it is a false Lance, I shall be consumed by fire.'

Peter underwent four days of fasting to purify his soul before the test. Then on Good Friday, before a massive crowd of crusaders, dressed in a simple tunic and bearing the relic of the Holy Lance, he willingly walked into an inferno – blazing 'olive branches stacked in two piles, four feet in height, about one foot apart and thirteen feet in length'. Contemporary authors provide very different accounts of what happened to Peter in those flames. Raymond of Aguilers, an eyewitness, but also a steadfast champion of the Holy Lance and its discoverer, believed that he emerged unscathed:

Peter walked through the fire, and his tunic and the Holy Lance which was wrapped in the most exquisite cloth, were left unsinged. As he emerged Peter waved to the crowd, raised the Lance, and screamed out, 'God help us.' Whereupon the crowd seized him, seized him I say, and pulled him along the ground. Almost everyone from the mob pushed and shoved, thinking Peter was nearby and hoping to touch him or snatch a piece of his clothing. The mob made three or four gashes on his legs in the tussle, and cracked his backbone. We think that Peter would have died there if Raymond Pilet, a renowned and courageous knight, had not with the aid of numerous comrades charged the milling mob, and at the risk of death snatched him from them. But we cannot write more because of our anxiety and distress.[22]

It is not inconceivable that Peter was trapped and injured by a hysterical riot – charismatic spiritual figures were often mobbed by ecstatic crowds in the Middle Ages. Indeed, in the early thirteenth century a frail and sickly St Francis of Assisi made his last journey in the company of a bodyguard, because it was feared that if he died on the road his body would otherwise be ripped apart by relic hunters. Even so, Raymond of Aguilers admitted that Peter suffered some 'trivial burns on his legs' during the trial.

The northern French crusade chronicler Fulcher of Chartres, who was not present at Arqa, was much more sceptical:

The finder of the Lance quickly ran through the midst of the burning pile to prove his honesty, as he had requested. When the man passed through the flames and emerged, they saw that he was guilty, for his skin was burned and they knew that within he was mortally hurt. This was demonstrated by the outcome, for on the twelfth day he died, seared by the guilt of his conscience.

However they were inflicted, there was no escaping the fact that within two weeks Peter Bartholomew died from the injuries received on the day of his ordeal. His Provençal supporters saw to it that he was buried on the site of his trial, but for most crusaders his reputation had been irredeemably tarnished. The true efficacy of the Holy Lance was now doubted, its cult widely criticised, even ridiculed.[23]

At the same time, grievous damage was done to Raymond of Toulouse's reputation. Having ridden on the back of the Lance's cult, he now suffered a severe reversal at its refutation. Then, just as his claim to lead the crusade was faltering, a second dilemma emerged. Around 10 April ambassadors from the Byzantine emperor Alexius I Comnenus arrived at Arqa. They had come to protest loudly Bohemond's retention of Antioch and the contravention of the oaths given at Constantinople. Offering 'large sums of gold and silver' as an enticement, they instructed the crusaders to wait for Alexius himself to arrive on 24 June, 'so that he could journey with them to Jerusalem'.

This news prompted the emergence of a definite rift within the expedition. Raymond, who had been pursuing a policy of détente with the Greeks, now argued that Alexius' arrival would only strengthen the crusaders' chances of reaching Jerusalem. While they waited the Franks could concentrate on finally overcoming Arqa and thus avoid a harmful blow to their martial reputation. The majority, however, distrusted the emperor's intentions or, indeed, doubted whether he would ever actually make the journey to Arqa. By mid-April a fully fledged stalemate had been reached, with neither side willing to budge. The dispute became so heated that the clergy declared a period of fasting, prayers and alms-giving in the hope that God would then return peace to the expedition.[24]

Raymond of Toulouse was in a desperate fix. He still enjoyed considerable support, but even some Provençal crusaders were beginning to lose faith. Around this time, Tancred, whose support Raymond had earlier bought with the handsome gift of '5,000 solidi and two thoroughbred Arabian horses', broke ranks with the count and transferred his allegiance to Godfrey of Bouillon. Sensing that the aura that had surrounded the Holy Lance was now shattered, Raymond made a calculated decision: no longer able to rely upon the power gained from association with one relic cult, he cynically resolved to 'create' another. In order to replace the totemistic energy of the Lance, Raymond looked once again to appropriate the memory of Adhémar of Le Puy. In life the bishop had carried a relic of the True Cross – a small piece of wood believed to have been part of the cross upon which Christ was crucified – and on his death this had found its way to the port of Latakia. Raymond now dispatched Adhémar's brother, William Hugh of Monteil, on an urgent mission to Latakia to recover the relic. Raymond's plan was not bluntly to forsake the Holy Lance, but rather initially to augment and then gradually replace its cult with that of Adhémar's cross. This scheme was not wholly successful, for when William Hugh duly returned with the relic in hand Raymond's own entourage became so imbued with crusading zeal that they too wanted only to make an immediate departure for Jerusalem.[25]

Ultimately, Raymond manoeuvred himself into a corner. He allowed his capability as a leader to be too closely equated with success at Arqa. As the crusaders' siege of the town foundered, the double blows of Peter Bartholomew's death and the widespread unpopularity of Raymond's pro-Byzantine stance left the count reeling. With even his own men demanding a resumption of the march south, he was forced to concede. In the first week of May, Raymond finally agreed to leave Arqa unconquered and continue the journey to Jerusalem.

As the march began, the crusaders were pleasantly surprised to find that the southern Levantine climate affected seasonal change. One writer observed: 'We were eating spring beans in the middle of March and corn in the middle of April.' With an earlier harvest they hoped to find plentiful supplies on their journey through Palestine. Once the decision was reached, the siege of Arqa was promptly abandoned. The crusaders passed through Tripoli in peace and by 16 May they were at last set on the road to Jerusalem.[26]

The pilgrimage to the Holy City was now in its final stage, but the crusade would never again be dominated by Raymond of Toulouse. The count had, for a time, held sway over the expedition, even coming close to standing as its unchallenged leader, but the débâcle at Arqa was a watershed in his career. From now on he would have to share power and prestige with his fellow princes.

10

THE HOLY CITY

The siege of Arqa ended in failure, but it at least prompted all the remaining armies of the First Crusade to mass in one place. On 16 May 1099, after long months of delays and prevarication, the expedition set out at an almost breakneck speed towards Jerusalem. From this point on the expedition was to maintain an almost unwavering focus upon its ultimate goal – the conquest of the Holy City. In part the crusaders' haste was born out of a desire to avoid any further distractions or interruptions, but they must also have known that every day saved in the advance on Jerusalem meant less time for the Fatimids to organise their defences. Having consulted Maronite Christians living in Lebanon about possible routes into Palestine, and perhaps relying upon the skills of an elderly Muslim guide supplied by the emir of Tripoli, the crusaders took a bold step, opting for the coastal road. This direct approach had the distinct advantage of speed and the continued possibility of naval support, but in strategic terms it was a considerable gamble. At a number of points the coastal route passed through narrow gaps between the sea and mountains, passages that could be effectively closed by even a relatively small defending force. The crusaders took the chance on getting through before the Fatimids set up blockades.

On the first day out of Tripoli the Franks had to follow a rugged, narrow path around a precipitous promontory that juts dramatically into the sea and is today known locally as Raz ez-Chekka – the Face of God. Practically reduced to marching in single file, the crusaders were dangerously exposed, but they met no resistance. By the evening of 19 May they had successfully negotiated two further trouble spots – 'a cliff where the path is very narrow and we expected to find our enemies lying in ambush' and the crossing of the Dog river, the effective border with Palestine – bypassing settlements at Batrun and Jubail to reach Beirut. So far not a blow had been struck. The next day the expedition reached the town of Sidon, whose garrison attacked a group of Franks foraging for food, but these Muslims were quickly beaten back by a group of mounted knights.[1]

One crusade chronicler recalled that, while camped near Sidon, a number of crusaders were killed by the bite of an extremely venomous variety of 'fiery' snake. Locals apparently gave the Franks tips on how to counteract these attacks, suggesting that 'a man who was bitten should lie at once with a woman, a woman with a man, and thus they would be released from all the swelling and heat of the poison'. Another more practical, if not particularly restful, recommendation involved banging stones together or pounding shields through the night so that 'they could sleep in safety from the snakes, which [would be] terrified by this noise and clamour'. The Franks enjoyed two days of rather fitful rest at Sidon. They had adopted a sensible marching strategy – pushing hard for two to three days to cover ground at speed and then allowing the army to recover – thus limiting the amount of time spent in potentially exposed marching formation. Using this approach they followed the coastline south passing Tyre, Acre and on to Caesarea, where they spent four days celebrating Pentecost. The Latins met with no opposition, although a knight, Walter of La Verne, and his men disappeared during a foraging trip – it was assumed that they had been ambushed by a Muslim raiding party. For the most part, the towns they passed were happy to see them go in peace, and the crusaders were in no mood to dally.[2]

Finally, on 30 May, the Franks broke inland at Arsuf and made a beeline for Jerusalem. By 3 June they had reached the major town of Ramleh, the last potential barrier to their advance. Robert of Flanders went ahead in the company of the knight Gastus of Bederez to reconnoitre, but they found the town entirely deserted. Terrified by the crusaders' approach, its Muslim garrison had fled the previous night. Positioned on the main route between Jerusalem and the coast, Ramleh was a site of considerable strategic importance, and with the famous Christian Basilica of St George – said to house the saint's body – lying on its outskirts, it also had spiritual significance. To secure Frankish possession of the town and pay due reverence to St George who the crusaders hoped would be their 'intercessor with God and faithful leader', the princes created a Latin bishopric of Ramleh. Just like the bishopric instituted at Albara, this was no ecclesiastical restitution or conversion, but rather an innovation, a brand new episcopal see with combined military and clerical responsibilities. On this occasion, however, no Provençal from Raymond of Toulouse's camp was chosen as bishop. Instead, it was Robert of Rouen, a northern French crusader, who was elevated and provided with a garrison, 'paid tithes and endowed with gold, silver and horses' – a move that confirms Raymond's weakened status.[3]

On 6 June the crusaders loaded up the plentiful grain supplies discovered at Ramleh and set off for Jerusalem. By the end of the day they had reached Qubeiba, just sixteen kilometres west of the Holy City. That night a delegation of eastern Christians from Bethlehem arrived in the crusader camp, begging for the Latins to free them immediately from Islamic rule. Tancred and Baldwin of Le Bourcq, a member of Godfrey's contingent, were immediately dispatched at the head of a hundred knights. Riding through the night, passing the distant shadow of Jerusalem in the half-light of dawn, they reached Christ's birthplace and were received as deliverers with an emotional welcome, culminating in a Mass at the Church of the Nativity. Tancred soon returned to join the main army, but not before taking the liberty of raising his own banner above Bethlehem. Riding north,

Tancred found his comrades ranged before the walls of Jerusalem. Many, unable to wait a moment longer, had set out from Qubeiba in the middle of the night. Now, at last, their extraordinary journey was at an end.[4]

THE SIEGE OF JERUSALEM

For close on three years the crusaders had marched across the face of the known world, enduring terrible suffering, to reach the most sacred Christian city on earth. Jerusalem was, in their eyes, the centre of the cosmos, the city where Christ had lived, died and been resurrected. Many crusaders believed that if only the earthly city of Jerusalem could be recaptured, it would become one with the heavenly Jerusalem, a Christian paradise. Not surprisingly, many wept openly when the long-sought objective of their pilgrimage finally came into view on 7 June 1099.[5]

Fatimid incompetence had allowed the Franks to cover more than 300 kilometres from Tripoli to Jerusalem in less than a month. Had the Egyptians attempted even a limited defence of Palestine, the crusade could have been stopped in its tracks. As it was, the Fatimids either misjudged the Franks' intentions or grossly underestimated their ability to march at speed, because the crusade was allowed to advance virtually unchallenged. The Latins did pay a price for the rapid, almost headlong, pace of their approach. Leaving cities such as Beirut and Acre unconquered in their wake, the crusaders had now placed themselves in a position of extreme isolation, with no network of communication or logistical support to fall back on. They had not even had time to occupy Jaffa, the port closest to Jerusalem. With their nearest allies hundreds of kilometres distant, well aware that before long the Fatimids would launch a massive counterattack, the crusaders had still raced to Jerusalem. It was a move of the utmost daring, at once expedient and visionary. Knowing that they lacked the manpower or resources to overcome all Palestine, the Franks chose to make a last-ditch strike at its heart, but they would probably never have taken such an immense gamble if not possessed by pious conviction, a steadfast belief in the force of divine protection. In the cold light of strategic reality, failure to secure the almost immediate capture of Jerusalem would leave the stranded expedition facing extermination.

In the context of this 'all or nothing' strategy, the crusader siege of Jerusalem was never going to resemble the earlier investment of Antioch. There was no time to establish an encirclement siege and await the piecemeal collapse of the city's resistance. Instead, only one realistic approach presented itself – a full-scale frontal assault on Jerusalem's mighty walls.

Of all the cities encountered by the First Crusaders, none could exceed the historic and spiritual resonance of Jerusalem. Across 3,000 years of human settlement, the passing of countless generations, this city became inseparably entwined with the genesis and essence of three religions. This was the epicentre of Christianity, the site of Jesus' Passion. But it was also the seat of the Israelites – the first city of Judaism – and the third holiest city in the Islamic world, deeply revered as the site of Muhammad's ascent to heaven. Jerusalem's spiritual stature was matched by its imposing physical presence. Today, any visitor to the Old City of Jerusalem, at the heart of the sprawling modern metropolis, will gain a palpable sense of the breathtaking sight that confronted the crusaders, for its massive stone walls, reconstructed under the Ottomans, follow the line of Jerusalem's eleventh-century fortifications almost exactly.

Some four kilometres long, up to fifteen metres high and three metres thick, enclosing an area of approximately eighty-six hectares, Jerusalem's main walls presented a prodigious obstacle to any attacker. To the east and west these worked to reinforce natural defences, as the Judaean hills fell away steeply into the Qidron–Josaphat and Hinnon valleys. To the north and south-west, where flatter ground made it possible to approach the walls, they were reinforced by a secondary outer wall and a series of dry moats. This circuit of fortifications – shaped like a lopsided rectangle – was pierced by five major gates, each guarded by a pair of towers and punctuated by two major fortresses. In the north-western corner stood a formidable stronghold, the Quadrangular Tower, while midway along the western wall rose Jerusalem's ancient citadel, the Tower of David. One Latin chronicler described the latter's awe-inspiring construction: 'The Tower of David is built of solid masonry up to the middle, constructed of large square stones sealed with molten lead. If it were well supplied with rations for soldiers, fifteen or twenty men could defend it from every attack.'[6]

Within Jerusalem, the Fatimid governor, Iftikhar ad-Daulah, commanded a sizeable garrison, which had recently been reinforced by an elite troop of 400 Egyptian cavalrymen. On hearing of the crusaders' approach, Iftikhar had taken further steps to hamper their assault, expelling many of the eastern Christians living in Jerusalem and poisoning or blocking all the wells outside the city. In contrast, within Jerusalem itself, the Muslim garrison could rely on numerous cisterns to supply uncontaminated water.[7]

Any assault upon Jerusalem would inevitably be a bloody affair, but for most crusaders the rewards far outweighed the risks. Within its walls lay a prize beyond measure: the Church of the Holy Sepulchre. It was to liberate this, the most sacred site on earth – where Christ had died on the cross and arisen reborn – that they had left their homes in Europe and faced the horrors of the journey east. A Latin chronicler imagined Tancred's emotions early in the siege when, visiting the Mount of Olives, he was at last able to overlook Jerusalem: 'He turned his gaze towards the city, from which he was now separated only by the Valley of Josaphat, [and saw] the Lord's Sepulchre . . . Drawing a great sigh, he sat down on the ground, and would willingly have given his life there and then, just for the chance to press his lips to that [most holy church].'[8]

The Latins arrived with a small but battle-hardened force of around 1,300 knights and 12,000 'able-bodied men'. From the start of the siege, however, the rift within the army was obvious. The crusader

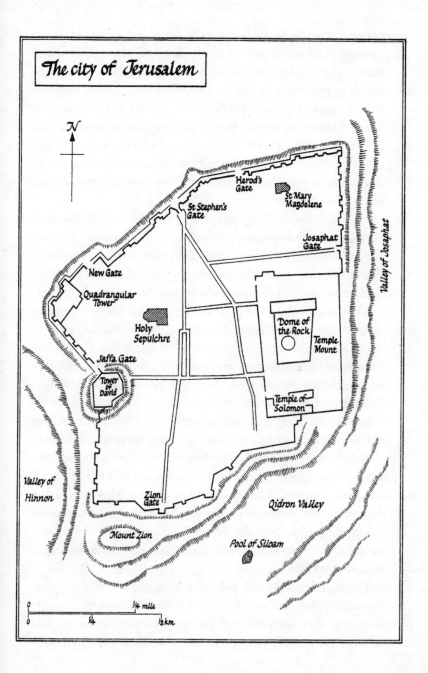

The city of Jerusalem

N

Herod's Gate
St Mary Magdelene
St Stephen's Gate
Josaphat Gate
New Gate
Quadrangular Tower
Holy Sepulchre
Dome of the Rock
Temple Mount
Jaffa Gate
Tower of David
Temple of Solomon
Valley of Josaphat
Valley of Hinnon
Zion Gate
Qidron Valley
Mount Zion
Pool of Siloam

0   ¼ mile
0   ¼   ½ km

host was effectively divided in two: the largest group, including Godfrey of Bouillon, Robert of Flanders and Tancred, moved to besiege the city from the north, taking up positions between the Quadrangular Tower and St Stephen's Gate; meanwhile, Raymond of Toulouse and the southern French at first set up camp before the Tower of David, but quickly moved to a more threatening but exposed position before the Zion Gate. This formation had obvious strategic advantages, forcing the Muslim garrison to prepare for an attack on two fronts, but it was also symptomatic of a deep-seated fracture among the crusaders.

After Raymond of Toulouse lost control of the expedition at Arqa, his popularity plummeted. Raymond did receive some support from another visionary, Peter Desiderius, who sought to fill the void left by Peter Bartholomew's death, but, by the start of Jerusalem's siege, military and spiritual authority had gravitated towards another prince. Godfrey of Bouillon had long been respected for his Christian devotion and martial prowess. With Raymond's decline, Godfrey stepped forward to become the crusade's leading prince. His position was consolidated by the support of Arnulf of Chocques, the cleric who had helped to discredit Peter Bartholomew and the Holy Lance. Sensing the need for a new spiritual 'totem' to inspire and unify the Frankish host, Arnulf had a golden cross bearing the image of Christ made and encouraged a cult following to grow up around it. Godfrey duly became the patron and protector of this new 'standard' and, although it never achieved the same popularity as the Holy Lance, the cross did add to his aura of authority. Robert of Normandy, who had supported Raymond of Toulouse in the first half of 1099, changed sides, taking up a position to the north of Jerusalem, and Raymond soon became so isolated that even Provençal crusaders began defecting to Godfrey's camp.[9]

Having taken up their positions around the city, the crusaders launched their first direct assault on 13 June. The Provençal crusader Raymond of Aguilers believed that the princes were spurred into action by the prophecies of a hermit encountered on the nearby

Mount of Olives, promising victory if the offensive was continued throughout the day. In fact, the intense and ever-mounting pressure to overcome the city with speed was probably enough to prompt such a hasty frontal attack. The crusaders' problem was that the region immediately around Jerusalem was devoid of woodland, and without timber it was impossible to prepare an adequate supply of siege tools. One story has it that Tancred found a small stack of wood hidden away in a cave, into which he had stumbled to relieve himself during a particularly painful bout of dysentery. This was enough to construct a single large scaling ladder, with which Tancred, now recovered, rushed forward to assault Jerusalem. An eyewitness later recalled the frustrations of this attack: 'We did indeed destroy the curtain wall, and against the great wall we set up one ladder, up which our knights climbed and fought hand to hand with the Saracens with swords and spears. We lost many men but the enemy lost more.'

Luckily for Tancred, he had not been the first man up the scaling ladder. That unfortunate honour had been seized by a knight from Chartres, Raimbold Creton, who had fought atop Mount Silpius during the second siege of Antioch. Ascending the walls, 'He had [just] seized the top of the battlements with his left hand, when suddenly an enemy sword, of the sort that can only be lifted with two hands, fell on him. Moving at lightning speed the blade sliced through his forearm, almost completely severing his hand.'[10]

Raimbold survived this dreadful wound, but the crusaders, unable to gain a foothold on the walls, were eventually forced to retreat. It was obvious to all that without careful preparation the Holy City would not fall. Thus, on 15 June, Raymond and the other princes put aside their disputes long enough to settle upon a course of action – no further assault would be attempted until the necessary weapons of siege warfare could be constructed. But the crusaders lacked the tools, timber and craftsmen needed to build siege towers, catapults and battering rams.[11]

As the princes considered their next move, a further crisis began to grip the army. Although they arrived with the harvest stored at

Ramleh and suffered no severe food shortages, in the middle of a
scorching Palestinian summer, adrift among the arid Judaean hills,
the crusaders soon began to feel the effects of thirst. With all the
surrounding wells poisoned or collapsed, the only local water source
was the Pool of Siloam, a small lake fed by an intermittent spring at
the foot of Mount Zion, but this lay within bowshot of the city. Even
so, when the pool filled every three days, many would still brave
Muslim arrows for a meagre drink:

> When [the spring] gushed forth on the third day the frantic and
> violent push to drink the water caused men to throw themselves
> into the pool and many beasts of burden and cattle to perish there
> in the scramble. The strong in a deadly fashion pushed and shoved
> through the pool, choked with dead animals and filled with
> struggling humanity, to the rocky mouth of the flow, while the
> weaker had to be content with the dirtier water.

The Franks were soon forced to range further afield in search of
water, but this brought its own attendant dangers:

> We suffered so badly from thirst that we sewed up the skins of oxen
> and buffaloes, and we used to carry water in them for the distance
> of nearly six miles. We drank the water from these vessels although
> it stank, and what with foul water and barley bread we endured
> great distress and affliction every day, for the Saracens used to lie
> in wait for our men by every spring and pool, where they killed
> them and cut them to pieces.

The worst water, taken from 'filthy marshes', reportedly contained
leeches, which were often accidentally swallowed by the poorest
crusaders in their rush to gulp down what they could, causing an
agonising death.[12] These water shortages troubled the Franks
throughout the siege of Jerusalem, but help in another quarter was at
hand.

On 17 June news arrived in the crusader camp that six ships, most originating in Genoa, had docked at Jaffa, the nearest port to Jerusalem. Unbeknown to the Franks, Jaffa's Muslim garrison had abandoned its ramshackle defences – 'one intact tower of a badly ruined castle' – leaving the port deserted. Thus the Genoese had been able to find mooring, but now requested an escort from their fellow Latins. Three squadrons were immediately dispatched: twenty knights and fifty footsoldiers under Geldemar Carpenel, a member of Godfrey of Bouillon's contingent; a further fifty knights under the Provençal Raymond Pilet; and a last group under William of Sabran, who had marched to Jerusalem with the Provençal contingent. En route to Jaffa they ran into a Fatimid patrol, 600 men strong, near Ramleh. Geldemar's troops, in the vanguard, caught the brunt of the fighting and, heavily outnumbered, they suffered numerous casualties. Only when Raymond Pilet raced forward with re-inforcements were the Fatimids beaten back.

Lucky to be alive, the crusaders arrived at Jaffa, 'where the sailors joyously received them with bread, wine and fish'. They seem to have celebrated in some style, because, 'happy and heedless', they neglected to post any seaward lookouts. As dawn broke the following day, the sailors awoke to find their ships surrounded by a large Fatimid fleet. Forced to abandon their vessels, they escaped with the crusaders just before the port was overrun. Fortunately for this now heavily laden party, the return journey to Jerusalem passed without incident. Even though the fleet itself had been lost, its cargo and crew were an enormous boost for the crusade's fortunes. Among the Genoese sailors were many gifted craftsmen, including William Embriaco, and they brought with them 'ropes, hammers, nails, axes, mattocks and hatchets, all indispensable'. All the evidence suggests that the crusaders had not anticipated the fleet's arrival, but it would be incredible, almost miraculous, if such a timely boon had been wholly unplanned.[13]

In the days that followed, local Christians advised the Franks on the location of nearby forests, so wood could be procured. Robert of

Normandy and Robert of Flanders soon returned with the first train of timber-laden camels. In five days, the crusaders' condition had been utterly transformed – everything was now in place for the construction of siege weapons to begin. But, even here, the continued division among the Latins was in evidence. Raymond of Toulouse appointed William Embriaco to head the building programme on Mount Zion, but to the north of the city Godfrey employed the skills of the experienced campaigner Gaston of Béarn, who until now had been a dedicated devotee of the Provençal camp. By this stage, Raymond's high-handed behaviour had evidently begun to alienate even his closest allies.[14]

The bad blood between the princes soon boiled over into open confrontation. In what seems like an act of extraordinary folly, given the urgent need for a concerted effort to overthrow Jerusalem quickly, the crusaders began to squabble over who should rule the Holy City if and when it was captured:

> We now called a meeting because of the general quarrels among the leaders and specifically because Tancred had seized Bethlehem. There he had flown his banner over the church of the Lord's Nativity as if over a temporal possession. The assembly also posed the question of the election of one of the princes as a guardian of Jerusalem in case God gave it to us.[15]

Not only were the princes unable to agree upon a candidate, but the Latin clergy now vociferously maintained that it would be wrong and sinful to raise a king over the Holy City, God's patrimony. They believed that Jerusalem should be preserved as a spiritual realm, governed by the Church, and simply protected by a temporal military ruler bearing the lesser title of 'advocate' or protector. Just as at Antioch, the crusaders' acquisitive minds had become fixated upon the spoils of war – power, territory and plunder – long before the battle itself was won. Now, however, far from bringing a voice of reason and conciliation, the clergy themselves were caught up in the midst of the wrangling. This dispute raged on unresolved until the assault was launched. The open rift between Raymond of Toulouse and Tancred was temporarily patched up in the final days before battle commenced, but, given the level of Frankish factionalism, it is remarkable that they were able to co-ordinate and launch any sort of attack at all.[16]

Two overriding emotions empowered their efforts – desperation and devotion. Having endured such an immense struggle simply to reach Jerusalem, and now facing the palpable threat of Fatimid counterattack, most crusaders were driven by an unshakeable determination to conquer the Holy City and complete their pilgrimage to the Holy Sepulchre. Without such an inspirational goal, or such impending danger, the expedition might well have been ripped apart by division. As it was, the crusaders' spiritual fervour and survival instinct coalesced, providing just enough impetus to hold the few remaining threads of Frankish unity in place.

For three weeks in late June and early July, the crusaders applied themselves with furious energy to the task at hand. Both Godfrey's and Raymond's supporters threw themselves into an intense construction programme. In the former, Gaston of Béarn supervised the building work, while the princes 'attended to the hauling of wooden materials'. Meanwhile, William Embriaco acted as foreman in the Provençal camp, with Peter of Narbonne, bishop of Albara, overseeing the procurement of materials. By this stage, Raymond of Toulouse was losing popular support at a damaging pace. With more and more crusaders transferring their allegiance to Godfrey's faction, Raymond was forced to pay those who remained with funds from his treasury just to get them to work, and to make up the shortfall in manpower with Muslim captives. Elsewhere in the crusader host, only skilled artisans and craftsmen were paid from a communal fund, while everyone else 'laboured, built and co-operated' through day and night, 'gladly turn[ing] their shoulders to the task'.[17]

The crusaders set out to construct the finest siege weapons available in the eleventh century, using cutting-edge military technology.

At the heart of their assault strategy were two fearsome siege towers; three storeys tall and constructed upon wheeled platforms, these were designed to be pushed up against a wall, thus allowing a large number of attackers to access its ramparts in relative safety. To protect the tower and its passengers from arrows, rocks and fire, the entire structure was covered in wattles of interwoven branches and thick animal hide. Godfrey's tower had a further technological refinement: it could be rapidly dismantled into portable sections and then reconstructed in a new position. The crusaders built an array of other siege weapons: a massive battering ram with an iron-clad head 'of horrendous weight and craftsmanship', shielded from above by a wattle roof; a number of large-scale *mangonellae* (catapults); numerous scaling ladders; and a series of portable wattle screens under which troops could approach the walls. To the south of the city, Raymond adopted a novel approach to the daunting task of filling the dry moat protecting the walls around the Zion Gate: 'Our leaders discussed how they should fill the ditch, and they had it announced that if anyone would bring three stones to cast into that pit he should have a penny. It took three days and nights to fill it.'[18]

At the same time, within Jerusalem, the Fatimid garrison was not idle. They could see only too well where the Franks were preparing to strike. Their own mangonels were brought to the walls to be in firing range once an assault began. They also took elaborate steps to protect threatened sections of wall from bombardment or battering. One Latin eyewitness described how 'they brought out sacks of straw and chaff, and ships' ropes of great size and closely woven, and fixed them against the walls and ramparts, so that they would cushion the attack and blows of the mangonel'.[19]

As preparations for the attack continued at a furious pace, tension inevitably mounted and both sides were soon engaged in a secondary war of intimidation, designed to sap the enemy morale and their will to fight. This followed the pattern of terrorisation and abuse experienced in the earlier sieges of Nicaea and Antioch. During a foraging expedition in late June, Baldwin of Le Bourcq, Baldwin of

Boulogne's second cousin, captured 'a very noble [Muslim] knight, a bald-headed man, of outstanding stature, elderly and corpulent'. The crusaders were evidently impressed by this 'wise, noble' figure for the princes 'frequently enquired about his life and customs' and sought to persuade him to convert to Christianity. When he declined, however, they made an example of him: 'He was brought out in front of the Tower of David to frighten the guards of the citadel and was beheaded by Baldwin's squire in full view of all.'

Later, a Fatimid spy was caught outside ferrying messages in and out of Jerusalem. After interrogation, the Latins sought to terrify the enemy by throwing him back into the city, as they had done with other victims in previous sieges. On this occasion, however, the captive was still alive: 'He was put into the catapult, but it was too heavily weighed down by his body and did not throw the wretch far. He soon fell on to sharp stones near the walls, broke his neck, his nerves and bones, and is reported to have died instantly.' For their part, the Muslim garrison resorted to insulting the Christian faith: 'To arouse the Latins' anger, they fixed crosses [on top of the walls] in mockery and abuse, upon which they either spat, or they did not shrink from urinating upon them in full view of everyone.'[20]

By early July, in this atmosphere of hatred and expectancy, the crusaders' military preparations were nearing completion. Around this time, the visionary Peter Desiderius came forward claiming to have received a new message from Adhémar of Le Puy. Apparently, the dead legate had, in a vision, prescribed a series of purifying rituals designed to purge the crusaders of sins and restore them to a state of unity, thus bringing about a return of God's favour. One Latin eyewitness recalled that after a council of princes and clergy had approved these measures,

> an order went out that on [8 July] clergymen with crosses and relics of saints should lead a procession with knights and the able-bodied men following, blowing trumpets, brandishing arms, and marching barefooted. We gladly followed the orders of God and

the princes, and when we marched to the Mount of Olives we preached to the people on the spot of Christ's ascension after the Resurrection . . . A spirit of forgiveness came over the army and along with liberal donations we implored God's mercy.[21]

The Fatimid garrison showed little respect for these rituals, and when the procession later passed close to the walls near the Mount Zion they peppered the crusader ranks with arrows, wounding clergy and laymen alike, and arousing Frankish bloodlust.[22] Finally, at the end of the second week of July, with their preparations complete, the crusaders were ready to unleash their rage.

THE FINAL ASSAULT

On 14 July 1099, as the first light of dawn reddened the sky, horn-calls resounded through the crusader camps, announcing the start of the long-awaited attack upon Jerusalem. But, as the Muslim garrison braced itself for the first onslaught, it suddenly became apparent that the Franks had pulled off a spectacular strategic coup. Godfrey and his allies, ranged before Jerusalem's northern walls, had for the last three weeks been building their siege tower in front of the city's Quandrangular Tower. The Fatimids had naturally responded by readying themselves for an attack in that area, strengthening that section of the walls and concentrating troops there. This was just what the crusaders had hoped for – all along, their conspicuous preparations had been a ruse. In the middle of the night of 13/14 July the Franks set about breaking down the siege tower into its constituent parts, portaging them almost one kilometre to a position east of St Stephen's Gate, and then re-erecting the entire structure. This was an incredible technical accomplishment and an awesome feat of physical endurance, but the rewards were considerable:

The Saracens were thunderstruck next morning at the sight of the changed position of our machines and tents ... Two factors motivated the change of position. The flat surface offered a better approach to the walls for our instruments of war, and the very remoteness and weakness of this northern place had caused the Saracens to leave it unfortified.[23]

On the northern front, the crusaders' first priority was to break through the outer curtain wall at this new strike point – without this they would have no hope of reaching the main walls. As the battle cry went up they unleashed the first wave of missiles from three mangonels, bombarding the inner walls and ramparts. This barrage might have done some damage to these physical defences, but the real purpose of this attack was to deter the Fatimid garrison from mounting an effective counterattack. Under this covering fire, the Franks deployed their massive battering ram, which, even mounted on a wheeled platform, was enormously cumbersome. As the day wore on, the Franks struggled to inch the ram forward, finally bringing it to bear against the curtain wall: 'It was driven on by the strength of an incredible number of men, and with a heavy charge it weakened and overthrew the outer walls ... [creating] an enormous breach.'[24]

At the point where the crusaders struck, the curtain wall had been raised only a few metres in front of the main city walls, and the momentum of the battering ram's last mighty charge actually sent it crashing through into these much taller, more formidable defences. An almost comically chaotic scene followed. Fearing that the main walls would now be severely damaged, the Fatimids poured 'fire kindled from sulphur, pitch and wax' down upon the ram, setting it alight. In panic, the crusaders hastily mustered their meagre supplies of water, putting out the fire. However, it soon became clear that the breach in the curtain wall was so confined, and the space between this outer defence and the main walls so restricted, that it would be virtually impossible to manoeuvre the charred remains of the battering ram out again. This was a potential disaster for the Franks, because with the breach blocked their siege tower could not be effectively deployed. So it was that in a bizarre reversal of tactics, the crusaders returned to set light to their own ram, while Muslims vainly sought to preserve its obstructive mass, pouring water from the ramparts. Eventually, the Franks prevailed and the wooden ram was destroyed. By day's end, the northern Franks had succeeded in penetrating the first line of defence, opening the way for a frontal assault on the main walls.[25]

To the south of the city on Mount Zion, the Provençals had enjoyed less success. The Fatimids had apparently feared that the brunt of the crusader assault would come on this front – unprotected as it was by any outer wall – because they had deployed the majority of their mangonels to the south. With a restricted battleground, Raymond of Toulouse had been unable to change his point of attack at the last minute and thus met ferocious resistance. One crusader, who witnessed the assault first hand, remembered the horror of this confrontation in vivid detail:

First we began to push our [tower] against the walls and then all the hellish din of battle broke loose; from all parts stones hurled from [catapults] flew through the air and arrows pelted like hail . . . As the machines [of war] came close to the walls defenders rained down upon the Christians stones, arrows, flaming wood and straw, and threw mallets of wood wrapped with ignited pitch, wax and sulphur, tow, and rags on the machines. I wish to explain that the mallets were fastened with nails so that they stuck in whatever part they hit and then burned. These projectiles . . . kindled fires which held back those whom swords, high walls, and deep ditches had not disconcerted.[26]

The Provençal tower never reached the walls and was eventually pulled back to safety. On balance, by the end of the first day the crusaders had made some progress, but many Franks were shocked by the sheer intensity of the fighting, and almost everyone was exhausted by the bone-crunching effort involved. One eyewitness recalled that 'with the coming of night, fear settled down on both camps'.[27]

At dawn on 15 July the assault recommenced. To the south, the Provençals continued to suffer under an almost continuous defensive bombardment. Even the Latin chroniclers were impressed by the Fatimids' determination, remarking that 'the defenders fought against our men with amazing courage, casting fire and stones'. Once more Raymond's siege tower was laboriously driven on towards the city walls, but eventually, under a dreadful hail of missiles, it began to collapse and burn. Those Franks that could do so scrambled out in fear of their lives, abandoning the wreckage, which was now in such a damaged state that Raymond of Toulouse was unable to persuade any crusader to enter it again. For one and a half days the Provençals had struggled in the face of overwhelming odds, making little or no progress, and were left stricken with 'fatigue and hopelessness'. But their efforts were not wasted. The crusaders' decision to assault Jerusalem on two fronts may have owed more to factionalism than to calculated strategic planning, but its effect was the same. Forced to defend the northern and southern walls, the Fatimid garrison stretched its resources to breaking point, and while the defenders held their ground against the Provençals, they were enjoying far less success against Godfrey and his allies.[28]

As the second day of the assault began on the northern front, under cover of a renewed bombardment the crusaders began to push their huge siege tower, on top of which Godfrey had placed the golden cross 'standard', towards the breach in the curtain defences and on to the main walls. This three-storey structure, some sixteen metres in height and filled with men – including, on the top floor, Godfrey of Bouillon himself – was immensely heavy, slow-moving and unwieldy. Moving the tower up to the walls was a hazardous process because once in range of the Fatimid mangonels its ponderous bulk presented a perfect target. One Latin chronicler noted: 'The Saracens defended themselves from the Franks and, with slings, hurled firebrands dipped in oil and grease at the tower and at the soldiers who were in it. Thereafter death was present and sudden for many on both sides.'[29]

Given the tightly packed streets and buildings within Jerusalem, the Fatimid garrison was able to deploy their mangonels only on or beside the main walls. This meant they could not adjust the range of their heavy bombardment to strike those who managed to get close to the city. The first stage of the siege tower's deployment was essentially a slow but deadly race, in which the defenders sought to destroy the structure with every missile they could muster, and the crusaders pushed on as fast as possible, hoping to slip under the curtain of fire. This was a high-risk manoeuvre, and at one point during the advance Godfrey was nearly killed: 'A stone flying randomly hit a certain soldier who was standing at [Godfrey's] side hard on the head. His skull was broken and his neck shattered and he was killed instantly. The duke, who narrowly missed so sudden a blow, fought back fiercely with his crossbow against the citizens and those manning the mangonels.'

In the end, the crusaders prevailed, perhaps in part because they had prepared the siege tower so diligently. The wattle screens tied around the structure managed to deflect many of the Fatimids' stone missiles, and the defenders had no better luck using fire: 'From time to time they hurled on to the panels protecting the engine pots vomiting flames . . . [but they] were covered with slippery skins and did not hold the flames or live coals thrown onto them, but at once the fire slipped from the skins, fell to the ground and went out.'[30]

Once the crusaders succeeded in pushing the tower through the gap in the curtain wall the nature of the fighting changed. Both sides now exchanged frantic volleys of smaller-scale missile weapons, including slings and flaming arrows. The immense height of the siege tower now gave the Franks a significant advantage – at this point the main city walls were about fourteen metres high – allowing Godfrey and his men in the top storey to rain down a stream of suppressing fire upon the defenders. In desperation, with the tower now perhaps less than a metre from the walls, the Fatimids deployed a 'secret' weapon.

They unleashed a peculiar form of flammable missile, akin to Greek fire, that produced a flame 'which could not be put out by water', hoping that this finally would burn the siege engine to the ground. Luckily for the crusaders, local eastern Christians – presumably those exiled from Jerusalem – had forewarned them of this mysterious fire and revealed how to deal with it. Although impervious to water, the fire could be extinguished by vinegar, and so, having shrewdly stored a supply in wineskins inside the tower, the Franks countered the attack almost immediately.[31]

As midday approached Godfrey's assault reached its turning point. If the crusaders could keep up the momentum of attack and actually force their way on to the battlements of Jerusalem, then the tide of battle would turn in their favour. Suddenly, in the midst of fierce fighting, the crusaders realised that a nearby defensive tower and a portion of the city walls were on fire. Whether through the use of flaming catapult missiles or fire arrows, the Franks had succeeded in setting light to the main wall's wooden sub-structure. This fire 'produced so much smoke and flame that not one of the citizens on guard could remain near it' – in panic and confusion the defenders facing the crusaders' siege tower broke into retreat. Realising that this breach might last only few moments, Godfrey hurriedly cut loose one of the hide-covered wattles protecting the tower and fashioned a makeshift bridge across to the ramparts. The first crusader to mount the walls of Jerusalem was Ludolf of Tournai, closely followed by his brother Engelbert. These two were quickly joined by a rush of crusaders, including Godfrey, and once a foothold had been established scores of Franks rushed forward to mount the walls with scaling ladders.[32]

As soon as Godfrey and his men had achieved this first dramatic breach, the Muslim defence of Jerusalem collapsed with shocking rapidity. Terrified by the crusaders' savage reputation, those stationed at the northern wall turned and fled in horror at the sight of the Franks mounting the walls. Soon the entire garrison was in a state of chaotic rout. Raymond of Toulouse was still struggling on Mount

Zion, his troops close to collapse, when the incredible news of the breach arrived. Suddenly Muslim defenders on the southern front, who only moments before had been fighting with venom, began to desert their posts. Some were even seen jumping from the walls in terror. The Provençals wasted no time in rushing into the city to join their fellow crusaders. Their long-cherished dream had been realised – Jerusalem had been conquered.[33]

BLOODY VICTORY

The sack of Jerusalem on 15 July 1099 is one of the most extraordinary and horrifying events of the medieval age. Over the course of three years the Latins had, through force of arms and power of faith, forged a route across Europe and the Near East. In the long-imagined moment of victory, with their pious ambition realised, they unleashed an unholy wave of brutality throughout the city, surpassing all that had gone before. The Provençal crusader Raymond of Aguilers joyfully reported:

> With the fall of Jerusalem and its towers one could see marvellous works. Some of the pagans were mercifully beheaded, others pierced by arrows plunged from towers, and yet others, tortured for a long time, were burned to death in searing flames. Piles of heads, hands and feet lay in the houses and streets, and men and knights were running to and fro over corpses.[34]

Many Muslims fled towards the Temple Mount, where some rallied, putting up futile resistance. One Latin eyewitness remembered how 'all the defenders fled along the walls and through the city, and our men went after them, killing them and cutting them down as far as Solomon's Temple, where there was such a massacre that our men were wading up to their ankles in enemy blood'.

Some prisoners were taken – indeed Tancred and Gaston of Béarn

reportedly gave their banners to a group huddled on the roof of the
Temple of Solomon – but even these were later slaughtered by other
crusaders. As the massacre on the Temple Mount was taking place,
other Franks ranged through the city at will:

> After a very great and cruel slaughter of Saracens, of whom 10,000
> fell in that same place, they put to the sword great numbers of
> gentiles who were running about the quarters of the city, fleeing in
> all directions on account of their fear of death: they were stabbing
> women who had fled into palaces and dwellings; seizing infants by
> the soles of their feet from their mothers' laps or their cradles and
> dashing them against the walls and breaking their necks; they were
> slaughtering some with weapons, or striking them down with
> stones; they were sparing absolutely no gentile of any place or
> kind.[35]

Of Jerusalem's Muslim inhabitants, few other than the Fatimid
commander, Iftikhar ad-Daulah, and the remnants of the elite
Egyptian cavalry force seem to have survived the general carnage.
When Godfrey overran the northern walls they made a break for the
Tower of David, riding at speed through the city's narrow streets.
Once there, they hastily abandoned their precious horses and locked
themselves within the confines of the citadel. Even so, they quickly
thought better of trying to hold out against the crusaders, negotiating
terms of surrender with Raymond of Toulouse.[36]

The sack of Jerusalem was not simply characterised by dreadful
brutality. In the midst of all this violence, the crusaders' minds quickly
turned to thoughts of spoils. Conditioned by the customs of war and
accustomed to long years of survival through plundering, the Franks
now gave free rein to their acquisitive instincts. One eyewitness
remarked that 'our men rushed around the whole city, seizing gold
and silver, horses and mules, and houses full of all sorts of goods'.
Tancred, for one, was said to have rushed into the Temple of
Solomon, grabbing all the gold, silver and precious stones that he

could carry. In fact, the crusaders' pillaging seems to have been remarkably methodical:

> After this great massacre, they entered the homes of the citizens, seizing whatever they found in them. It was done systematically, so that whoever had entered the home first, whether he was rich or poor, was not to be harmed by anyone else in any way. He was to have and to hold the house or palace and whatever he had found in it entirely as his own. Since they mutually agreed to observe this rule, many poor men became rich.[37]

Later, once the first rush of looting had died down, some Franks went to such disgusting lengths to sate their avaricious impulses that even their fellow crusaders were astounded: 'How astonishing it would have seemed to you to see our squires and our footmen, after they had discovered the trickery of the Saracens, split open the bellies of those they had just slain in order to extract from the intestines the bezants which the Saracens had gulped down their loathsome throats while alive.'[38]

The crusaders had apparently come to Jerusalem alight with a pious passion to do God's work, but a modern observer might be forgiven for imagining that no flame of Christian devotion could possibly continue to burn amid such a storm of greed and violence. Not so. For the sack of Jerusalem proves one thing beyond contestation – in the minds of the crusaders, religious fervour, barbaric warfare and a self-serving desire for material gain were not mutually exclusive experiences, but could all exist, entwined, in the same time and space. So it was that, fresh from bloodthirsty slaughter and rapacious plundering, the Franks suddenly turned their hands to acts of worship and devotion. In a moment that is perhaps the most vivid distillation of the crusading experience, they came, still covered in their enemies' blood, weighed down with booty, 'rejoicing and weeping from excessive gladness to worship at the Sepulchre of our Saviour Jesus'. This was the task for which they had marched thousands of kilometres– to 'liberate' the most sacred place on earth, the supposed site of Christ's crucifixion and resurrection, to give thanks to God in the Holy Sepulchre of Jerusalem. A Latin contemporary rejoiced in recounting that 'going to the Sepulchre of the Lord and his glorious Temple, the clerics and also the laity, singing a new song unto the Lord in a high-sounding voice of exultation, and making offerings and most humble supplications, joyously visited the Holy Place as they had so long desired to do'.

All the eyewitness Latin accounts record this remarkable scene of devotion. None seems to find it incongruous. It is easy, when considering the First Crusade, to imagine the motives and emotions of its participants in modern terms, to suppose, with what we might term informed cynicism, that they, and the contemporaries who wrote about them, simply cloaked the expedition in a patina of spirituality and fervent piety so as to excuse and justify their actions. There was certainly nothing noble or praiseworthy about the Frankish sack of Jerusalem, but it demonstrates that many crusaders were driven on, not simply by bloodlust or greed, but also by an authentic and ecstatic sense of Christian devotion. The crusaders had come to the Levant as armed pilgrims. Now at last, against massive odds and at horrific cost in terms of human suffering, they had 'freed' the Holy Land in the name of Christianity.[39]

I I

AFTERMATH

Jerusalem's fall on 15 July 1099 left the Holy City awash with blood, its streets littered with mutilated corpses, the air heavy with the putrid stench of death. So great had the massacre been that the sheer weight of Muslim bodies left rotting in the mid-summer sun threatened to overwhelm the Latins with disease. The princes soon ordered that the city be cleared, and the handful of Muslim survivors were forced into grim labour: '[They] dragged the dead Saracens out in front of the gates, and piled them up in mounds as big as houses. No one has ever seen or heard of such a slaughter of pagans, for they were burned on pyres like pyramids, and no one save God alone knows how many there were.' Only the Fatimid commander, Iftikhar ad-Daulah, and his troops escaped. They alone negotiated terms of surrender that were actually upheld. Having turned over the Tower of David to Raymond of Toulouse, the count escorted them out of the city with safe passage to the nearest Egyptian stronghold, the southern port of Ascalon.[1]

THE RULE OF JERUSALEM

On 17 July, with the smell of blood still thick in their nostrils, the crusader princes met in council to discuss the fate of their hard-won prize. In the weeks and months leading up to the sack of Jerusalem the Latin expedition had been almost ripped apart by a fractious leadership struggle. The right to rule the Holy City now became the focus of this friction. Raymond of Toulouse, once the crusade's prospective leader, had lost so much support because of the débâcle at Arqa and his continued patronage of the widely discredited Holy Lance that he was now eclipsed by Godfrey of Bouillon. Having played an instrumental role in the capture of Jerusalem, Godfrey could in some sense claim right of conquest. But the clergy continued to resist the idea that this most sacred of cities might be ruled by a secular king. Yet, in the absence of the late Greek patriarch Simeon, only recently deceased, the Church had no obvious candidate to promote. On 22 July a compromise was reached: Godfrey was elected ruler, but rather than styling himself as outright king, he adopted the less assertive title of 'Advocate of the Holy Sepulchre', implying a position of protector, subordinate to the Church.[2]

Outmanoeuvred, Raymond of Toulouse was enraged. When Godfrey invited him to vacate the Tower of David he stubbornly refused, saying that he planned to stay in residence at least until Easter. The lessons learned at Antioch a year earlier had taught him that possession of such a significant citadel might still enable the rule of Jerusalem to be contested. But his intransigence proved profoundly unpopular, even antagonising many of his own followers who were now starting to think of the journey back to Europe. In the face of intensifying protests, Raymond turned to his old ally, Peter of Narbonne, the recently elevated Latin bishop of Albara, ceding him control of the Tower so that the matter could be put to proper arbitration. Yet even Peter now decided that the tide of political fortune had turned and swiftly betrayed Raymond, opening the citadel to Godfrey's men without a fight. By the end of July, Raymond and his remaining southern French supporters had been thoroughly neutralised. Leaving Godfrey in full possession of Jerusalem, the count set out to visit the River Jordan and then established a camp at the nearby town of Jericho.[3]

In his absence, a new patriarch of Jerusalem was elected. The man chosen was the Norman French crusader Arnulf of Chocques, who had risen to prominence as a vocal opponent of the Holy Lance. His elevation on 1 August 1099 marked a definitive turning point in the course of the First Crusade. One year after the death of the papal legate Adhémar of Le Puy, the commanding influence of the southern French had evaporated and Rome's policy of co-operative deference to the Byzantine Church was in tatters. The creation of a Latin patriarch was an open attack on Greek rights, although as yet Arnulf stopped short of actually ostracising the Orthodox clergy. He did, nonetheless, rapidly earn a rather unsavoury reputation. It was widely rumoured that his election had been uncanonical given the low ecclesiastical status from which he was raised. He was also said to have been a rapacious womaniser and a popular subject of lewd camp stories. Arnulf also demonstrated a particular proclivity for religious intolerance. Rather than embrace eastern Christian sects like the Armenians, Copts, Jacobites and Nestorians – the self-same 'brethren' that the crusaders had been nominally charged to protect – the new patriarch oversaw their expulsion from the Church of the Holy Sepulchre. In a bitter revelation, these eastern Christians soon discovered that they had in fact been better off under Muslim rule than they were in a 'liberated' Jerusalem.[4]

Against this background of crude bigotry, Arnulf sought to cement his position through the cultivation of a new relic cult. Soon after the city's fall, stories began to circulate that a piece of the True Cross, an artefact of extraordinary potency, was hidden somewhere in the city. The story of its discovery around 5 August is confused. Most contemporary sources agree that this relic – a rather battered silver and golden crucifix believed to contain a chunk of wood from the actual cross upon which Christ had died – had been concealed by the indigenous Christian population of Jerusalem to keep it from their Muslim masters, the secret of its location being known only to a select few. It is, however, impossible to confirm that the cult surrounding this relic actually predates 1099. The exact site of its supposed resting place and the method of its recovery are even less clear. According to one source, a crafty Syrian willingly volunteered the information, but another text suggests that Arnulf practically had to torture the locals before they would reveal the spot. Similarly, the True Cross is variously described as being uncovered 'in a secluded corner of the Church of the Holy Sepulchre . . . concealed within a silver case' or 'in a humble and dusty place in an abandoned house'. But, in spite of all this uncertainty, there is no question that, once unearthed, this relic was seized upon by Arnulf, its cult widely promoted by special celebratory services in the Holy Sepulchre. He was determined to use this new remnant of Christ's life finally to eradicate any lingering memory of the Holy Lance and to legitimate the new Latin order in Jerusalem.[5]

The last battle

The First Crusaders had brought Latin rule to the secular and spiritual realm of Jerusalem, but one dreadful danger still threatened to obliterate their achievement. The Fatimid ruler of Egypt, the vizier al-Afdal, was leading a powerful strike force on Palestine to recapture the Holy City. After the inhuman trials involved in securing the crusade's success, little thought was now given to surrender, but, with an Egyptian attack imminent, the Franks did have to decide how to react. They rejected the idea of knuckling down within Jerusalem's fortifications to endure a siege, that stratagem having almost cost them the ultimate price at Antioch. Instead, with characteristic daring, they chose to meet the Fatimids head on in battle.[6]

This type of martial audacity had propelled the expedition across the face of the known world, but before now it had always been married to an empowering, unifying sense of purpose. By the mid-summer of 1099, with the campaign's primary objective achieved, the fire of crusading enthusiasm began to flicker as never before. The gnawing threat of discord had all but shattered the principle of command by council, leaving Godfrey and Raymond in open dispute and Latin resources in a state of sluggish disorder. As the new ruler of Jerusalem sought to rally the crusaders for one last battle, it suddenly looked as though the entire expedition might collapse at the final hurdle.

It was Tancred, patrolling the Palestinian coastline, who procured the intelligence proving that an Egyptian offensive was only days away. In early August he captured a group of advance Fatimid scouts who, under interrogation, revealed that al-Afdal was massing his forces some eighty kilometres south-east of Jerusalem, at Ascalon, the only major port between Palestine and Egypt. Once the news reached Godfrey he realised that the crusaders must unite to survive, but Raymond of Toulouse and, for some inexplicable reason, Robert of Normandy refused his urgent call to arms, claiming that they needed still further confirmation that a Fatimid attack was at hand. Thus on 9 August Godfrey was forced to march out of Jerusalem with only the support of Robert of Flanders. Their troops left the city barefoot, as penitent soldiers of Christ, accompanied by Patriarch Arnulf and the relic of the True Cross, but, without the full weight of Frankish manpower, they looked doomed to annihilation. Reaching Ramleh that night, Godfrey issued one last desperate appeal stating that from this advanced position there was no question that battle would be joined.

Under pressure from their followers, Raymond and Robert relented, setting out on 10 August. Even though it was now widely discredited, the core of the count's Provençal supporters still carried the Holy Lance with them as a totem of victory. Jerusalem was stripped of Latin troops. Only Peter the Hermit was left behind to organise propitiatory prayers among the clergy. There would be no way back from defeat in the coming confrontation. Should the crusader ranks falter, the Holy City would undoubtedly fall back into the hands of Islam.[7]

The Frankish host, patched together by a vague semblance of ideological unity, gathered at Ramleh. It was the sheer lethal force of the ordeals endured by these men on the road to Jerusalem that now enabled them to function as an army. Three long years of hard campaigning had left only the toughest, most able and luckiest warriors alive. Thus a deeply experienced if divided force of elite troops – some 1,200 knights and 9,000 infantrymen – marched south out of Ascalon on 11 August in tightly disciplined formation. Late in the day they captured another group of Egyptian spies who were able to confirm al-Afdal's battle plan and the size and disposition of his forces. The Fatimids had raised a substantial army, perhaps 20,000 strong, with a heavy cavalry at its core and incorporating an array of north African troops, including Bedouins, Berbers and fearsome Ethiopians wielding giant flails capable of eviscerating man and horse in one blow. This force, camped in the fields outside Ascalon, was preparing to march on Jerusalem on the very next day.[8]

Outnumbered perhaps two to one, the crusaders decided that their only hope lay in surprise. They settled down to a night of dread and discomfort a few miles north of the port. Starting out before dawn on 12 August, with Raymond of Toulouse on the right flank, Godfrey on the left and the two Roberts and Tancred holding the centre, they closed distance, and once the Fatimid camp came into sight, charged at pace. Al-Afdal had failed to set sufficient scouts, and in the half-light the Franks fell on their sleeping, stunned enemy. Robert of Normandy drove his knights into the heart of the camp, seizing al-Afdal's personal standard and most of his possessions. Racing along the coastline, Raymond chased many Fatimids into the sea to drown, while elsewhere others rushed back to Ascalon only to be crushed to death as they tried to press through the gates. The Egyptian army never recovered from that first shock attack, and the battle quickly turned into a rout:

In their great fright [the Fatimids] climbed and hid in trees, only to plunge from boughs like falling birds when our men pierced them with arrows and killed them with lances. Later the Christians uselessly decapitated them with swords. Other infidels threw themselves to the ground grovelling in terror at the Christians' feet. Then our men cut them to pieces as one slaughters cattle for the meat market.[9]

Al-Afdal and a few of his officers managed to escape into Ascalon, astonished at being so easily crushed by a force that the vizier had assumed would be a spent rabble. Horrified, he set sail for Egypt. The crusaders secured a rich assortment of treasure and weaponry amid the ruins of the Fatimid camp, 'gold, silver, long cloaks, other clothing and [twelve kinds of] precious stones . . . helmets decorated with gold, the finest rings, wonderful swords, grain, flour and much else'. Al-Afdal's sword alone was later sold for the princely sum of sixty gold bezants. So great was the hoard that not everything could be carried off the field, and so the Latins decided to burn whatever weapons were left behind. Just a few days after anxiously leaving Jerusalem, they made a triumphant return, proudly processing through the city streets. The First Crusaders had survived their last true test.[10]

The cancer of factionalism that had been eating away at the expedition did still inflict its wound. In the wake of the battle, the terrified garrison of Ascalon sought to arrange terms of surrender. But they refused to hand the city over to anyone other than Raymond of Toulouse, the one prince known to have upheld his promise of safe passage during the sack of Jerusalem. Incensed and suspicious, Godfrey interfered, fearful that Raymond might establish an independent enclave on the coast. The negotiations collapsed and Ascalon remained in Muslim hands. A vital opportunity had been missed and, because of the princes' bitter but ultimately petty rivalry, a resurgent Fatimid navy was able to maintain a dangerous foothold on the Palestinian coast for more than half a century.[11]

With the victory in the Battle of Ascalon, the main armies of the First Crusade reached the end of their remarkable journey. Those that survived had witnessed a 'miracle'. The Holy City of Jerusalem had been recaptured against incalculable odds and all the might of Islam had broken on the rock of Latin devotion. Now, as summer waned, the thoughts of most turned to home. In early September 1099 Robert of Normandy, Robert of Flanders and the vast majority of the remaining crusaders set out for Europe, taking ship from Syria to Constantinople and beyond. For the time being at least, Raymond of Toulouse lingered in the northern Levant. Only 300 Latin knights remained in Jerusalem to help Godfrey of Bouillon defend this new outpost of Latin Christendom.[12]

THE CRUSADING EXPERIENCE

Like the participants in any military campaign, the First Crusaders were changed by their experiences. Some found fame, others notoriety; a select few were catapulted to power and influence, but thousands more were left broken and destitute. Many felt they had lived through a miracle and, having been touched by the hand of God, found their faith strengthened. But, whether they remained in the East or returned to the West, all were marked by the scouring wind that was this holy war.

Returning home

Most crusaders returned to western Europe after the capture of Jerusalem and the triumph at Ascalon. News of their success raced ahead of them, spreading like wildfire across Latin Christendom. But one man never learned of the expedition's fate. Pope Urban II, architect of the crusading ideal, died in Rome on 29 July 1099, just two weeks after the fall of the Holy City and before the tidings of victory could arrive.[13]

The return journey to the West proved arduous and expensive, and any booty collected in the closing stages of the campaign was soon spent. Thousands of crusaders limped back into Europe, many exhausted, sick and penniless. But those who had survived to the end were now revered as heroes in Latin society.

Robert of Flanders, for one, was from this point onwards celebrated as 'the Jerusalemite'. He returned to find his country in considerable disarray, but soon turned his hand to restoring order. He maintained an aura of piety until his death in 1111, donating the now famous relic of the arm of St George, carried in his contingent since the crusade had passed through Byzantium, to the monastery of Anchin. A church was duly built there and dedicated to the saint who had 'protected' Robert and his followers through countless dangers.[14]

Robert of Normandy had a less prosperous career after the crusade. He is known to have made a pilgrimage to Mont-St-Michel to give thanks for his survival, but his fortunes waned nonetheless. During his absence in the East, Robert's brother, William Rufus, king of England, died and was succeeded by his ambitious younger sibling, Henry I. After an abortive attempt to seize power in England, Robert was roundly defeated by Henry at the Battle of Tinchebrai in 1106. Captured, he spent twenty-eight miserable years incarcerated in various prisons, among them the Tower of London, until his death in 1134. It was later said that he met with such disaster because he had refused the crown of Jerusalem 'not out of reverence, but out of fear of the work involved'.[15]

A number of prominent crusaders continued to show clear dedication to the ideals of holy war. The southern French lord Gaston of Béarn, who had marshalled the construction of siege engines at Jerusalem, was one of the knights who went on to lend martial expertise to the struggle against the Moors of Spain. Other crusaders sought to express their thanks to God through more peaceful acts of devotion. Rotrou of Perche, who had been one of the first soldiers to brave the walls of Antioch on 3 June 1098, decided to devote himself to the protection and patronage of the Cluniac community at Nogent-le-Rotrou. Some are known to have founded new monasteries, or even to have become monks or priests.[16]

Of course, not all turned aside from the path of violence and dissolution. Before 1095, the northern French brute Thomas of Marle had a reputation for rapacious cruelty. He joined the crusade alongside the notorious Emicho of Leiningen, persecutor of the Rhineland Jews, but managed to find a place in the second wave of armies and survived all the way to Jerusalem. Having completed his pilgrimage, he returned only to gain new renown for his savage lawlessness. Thomas may have been marked by the cross, but he could not switch off the elemental ferocity that had driven him, and many of his comrades, to the gates of the Holy City.[17]

The knight Raimbold Creton from Chartres was another crusader who, at first, seemed to turn his back on spiritual devotion. He came back from the Levant crippled, having lost his hand in the first assault on Jerusalem. Within a few years of his return, he was severely censured by the Church for having beaten and castrated a monk whose servants had been stealing his crops. But, after undergoing fourteen years of penance, Raimbold seems to have been a reformed character.[18]

As far as we know, no one returned from the East laden down with gold and silver, but some did bring back more exotic treasures. Perhaps the most bizarre of these belonged to Gulpher of Lastours, the first Frank on to the walls of Marrat an-Numan in December 1098, who was said to have come home with a pet lion. For most, their 'booty' was in the form of religious relics. The preacher Peter the Hermit returned with a piece of the Holy Sepulchre and a relic of John the Baptist and founded a religious community in France dedicated to their cults. Other crusaders flooded Europe with an array of artefacts, including a single hair from Christ's beard, a whole ball of the Virgin Mary's hair, pieces of the True Cross and the Holy Lance and remnants of numerous saints. Hundreds of crusaders also brought back palm fronds from Jerusalem, symbolic tokens of their completed pilgrimage.[19]

There were, of course, thousands of men and women who turned aside from the path of the crusade, prompted to desert by fear, starvation, illness and exhaustion. As they crept back into Europe, their failure to fulfil their vows earned them the scorn and disdain of Latin society. Among these were Hugh of Vermandois, who never rejoined the crusade after being sent on an embassy to Constantinople, and Stephen of Blois, who had fled from Antioch in the early summer of 1098 and now faced open condemnation from his wife, Adela. The intense, public shame of their supposed cowardice soon spurred these princes, and numerous other 'failed' crusaders like them, to seek redemption by joining a new, 'third wave' of Latin armies heading out to the Holy Land.

Since 1095, Pope Urban had called for more and more recruits to reinforce the First Crusade. Once news of Jerusalem's recapture reached the West, a fresh surge of enthusiasm swept across Europe, as tens of thousands sought to emulate the main expedition's 'heroic' achievements. This campaign, known to history as the '1101 Crusade', aggressively promoted by Urban's successor Pope Paschal, saw recruitment that almost eclipsed that of the first two waves combined. By September 1100, armies of new and old crusaders alike began setting off to defend the Holy Land.

This 'third wave' was joined at Constantinople by none other than Raymond of Toulouse. With his ambitions for Jerusalem thwarted, Raymond had renewed his alliance with the Greek emperor Alexius and travelled to Byzantium still carrying his prized relic of the Holy Lance. He agreed to give the campaign the benefit of his experience and knowledge, but even this was not enough to save the 1101 Crusade from total disaster. The expedition enjoyed neither the luck nor the hard-bitten unity of purpose that had characterised the First Crusade. It was ripped apart by the Seljuqs of Asia Minor, suffering horrific casualties, and those few who did reach the Holy Land achieved nothing of value. Having sought to cleanse their reputations, both Hugh of Vermandois and Stephen of Blois lost their lives in this fruitless endeavour. Raymond of Toulouse survived by the skin of his teeth, but seems to have mislaid the Holy Lance somewhere in Asia Minor.[20]

Settling in the east

After the débâcle of the 1101 Crusade, Raymond of Toulouse elected to remain in the east, joining the ranks of those First Crusaders who settled in the Levant. He soon demonstrated his keen desire to forge a new lordship in the Near East. In his absence, the Provençal enclave, so carefully established in the Jabal as-Summaq in 1098–9, fell under the sway of Antioch. Raymond thus turned his attention to the Lebanese city of Tripoli and its environs. In the years that followed, he battled to subdue the surrounding region and died in 1105 while laying siege to Tripoli itself. The city held out until 1109, but once it fell Raymond's legacy was complete. The county he founded would endure well into the thirteenth century.[21]

To the north, Raymond's old adversary Bohemond of Taranto retained control of his long-cherished prize, the city of Antioch. Bohemond did see fit to complete his pilgrimage to Jerusalem in December 1099 alongside the nascent count of Edessa, Baldwin of Boulogne. But upon his return to Syria the southern Italian Norman had precious little time to relish his achievements. Facing Byzantine aggression to the north in Cilicia and through the southern port of Latakia, as well as renewed Muslim resistance to the east, Bohemond's initial efforts to create an independent Latin principality centred on Antioch were beset on all sides. Then, in the summer of 1100, the fortune that had blessed so many of his enterprises deserted him entirely. Overrun in a petty skirmish, he was taken prisoner by a Muslim warlord in eastern Asia Minor and spent three long years in captivity. Soon after his eventual ransom, he led the combined forces of Antioch and Edessa to a humiliating defeat in the Battle of Harran at the hands of Aleppo and its allies.[22]

By 1105, Bohemond had suffered enough. Having fought so hard for possession of Antioch, he now set sail for the West, effectively turning his back on the Levant. Once in Europe, he convinced a gullible Pope Paschal II to proclaim a new crusade, this time expressly directed towards conquering the Balkans from Byzantium. Having nursed his hatred and resentment of Alexius Comnenus for decades, Bohemond finally had the chance to exact his revenge, but once again fate cheated him. His army was crushed by Alexius outside Durazzo in 1108 and, forced to sign a degrading declaration of surrender, he retired to southern Italy, dying a broken man in 1111.[23]

It fell to Bohemond's nephew, Tancred of Hauteville, to defend Latin Antioch. Having risen to prominence in the course of the crusade, he now showed his true quality. Tancred's relentless ambition and immense martial energy transformed the nascent principality. By the time of his death in 1112, its borders had been expanded and consolidated, the threat posed by Aleppo had been all but neutralised, and Antioch's power and influence could even challenge that of Jerusalem. As it was, the fruits of Tancred's labour were squandered by his successor Roger of Salerno, who, twenty-one years to the day after the astounding victory against Kerbogha, led the Antiochene army to destruction in the evocatively named Battle of the Field of Blood. The principality survived, but never again attained such prominence.[24]

The true jewel of Latin dominion in the Levant was, of course, the city of Jerusalem. Its first protector, Godfrey of Bouillon, had only just begun to consolidate his position when he fell ill and died in the summer of 1100. This champion of the crusading ideal was buried on the very site of Christ's crucifixion. With Godfrey's demise, power passed to his brother, Baldwin of Boulogne. To seize this prize, Baldwin ceded control of the county of Edessa to his cousin and namesake, the crusader Baldwin of Le Bourcq, and raced south to Palestine. He had already demonstrated a capacity for cold-blooded ruthlessness and an ardent hunger for power during the annexation of Edessa. Now there was little question that he would demand full and absolute control of Jerusalem. On 25 December 1100 he was crowned as the first Latin king of Jerusalem.[25]

Arnulf of Choques had by this stage been ousted from power, but the reputation of the True Cross that he helped to 'discover' survived intact and its cult grew apace. Armed with the power of his office and wielding this potent relic, Baldwin carved out the foundations of a mighty realm. The interior of Palestine was subdued through sheer, brutal force. A string of coastal ports was overcome, vital strategic and economic lifelines. Baldwin even initiated the settlement of the inhospitable Jordanian desert. Living until 1118, it was his stable hand that protected the legacy of the First Crusade, shepherding all the crusader states through their first two decades of existence. Baldwin and his fellow Latins had forged an outpost of western Christendom in the heart of Islam that would endure for almost two centuries. The bloody and incessant battle to defend these isolated satellite settlements against a rising tide of Muslim aggression would change the course of history.[26]

CONCLUSION

If we consider the First Crusade as a whole, taking an overarching view of its nature and impact, we are immediately confronted by one simple but utterly overwhelming fact: the expedition succeeded. Against all the odds, its primary goal – the recovery of Jerusalem – was achieved. This sounds like an obvious statement, but the full force and impact of this victory are actually quite difficult to appreciate.

The reasons for the crusade's success are readily apparent. Historians have long appreciated the central significance of the profound religious and political fractures that afflicted Islam at the end of the eleventh century. Had the Muslims of the Near East united in the face of the First Crusade it could not possibly have prevailed. The combined forces of Damascus, Aleppo and Mosul would surely have crushed the Franks outside the walls of Antioch; facing the collective might of the Abbasid and Fatimid caliphates, the Latins could never have mounted the sacred walls of Jerusalem. In the years to come, hundreds of thousands of Franks sought to equal the achievements of these First Crusaders, but in the face of burgeoning Islamic solidarity, none prospered.[1]

However, other contributing factors have, to date, been under-played. The expedition was not quite the ramshackle venture we once imagined. The Latins may not have maintained complex lines of supply on the road to the East, but their campaign does show clear evidence of strategic and logistical forethought. Bohemond took care to provision the gathering armies at Nicaea in 1097, and the crusaders pursued a productive policy of close co-operation with the Greeks. They also made careful preparations before attempting to push into Syria and overcome Antioch, building a network of alliances with indigenous Christians and creating a system of foraging centres. The expedition also benefited immensely from naval support while still at Antioch and then on the road south to Palestine – the arrival of a Genoese fleet at Jaffa in the summer of 1099 transformed the siege of Jerusalem. The precise degree of planning and co-ordination behind these fortuitous encounters is unclear, but Pope Urban II is known to have encouraged the maritime powers of northern Italy to collaborate with the crusaders.

Perhaps the greatest 'miracle' of the First Crusade is that its communal approach to leadership actually worked. Indeed, on the whole, it functioned with remarkable efficiency. The council of princes managed to direct the campaign through a multiplicity of difficulties and, facing severe military threats at Antioch, learned to rely upon Bohemond's martial genius and his capacity for inspir-ational generalship. This command structure did falter in the face of intense personal rivalry, but, fractious as it was, the crusade was still driven on by the unifying vision of Jerusalem.

Intense spiritual conviction empowered the First Crusaders, lending them resolve in the face of extraordinary hardship. But once we attempt to gauge the exact quality and degree of their religious devotion we hit the real complexities arising from their success. Modern historical analysis can offer a rationalisation of their accomplishments, but for contemporaries living in the medieval age one thing alone explained the spectacular triumph of the First Crusade – God's omnipotent will. Throughout Latin Europe the conquest of Jerusalem was seen as definitive proof that the crusading ideal did indeed enjoy divine sanction. The fame and renown of the crusaders' exploits resounded across western Christendom and, almost immediately, the quills of history began to twitch, enshrining the expedition for future generations. Scores of writers – some eyewitnesses, others distant observers, but almost all drawn from an ecclesiastical background – sought to record its events, and the crusade became perhaps the most widely documented phenomenon of its era. Describing what they saw as a miracle, they naturally emphasised the pious devotion of their Frankish protagonists, believing that these crusaders must have burned with zeal for God to guide them to victory. Had the First Crusade failed, we can be sure that we would now know far less about its progress, and the image of its participants as devout soldiers of the faith might be less pronounced.[2]

Documentary evidence predating the conquest of Jerusalem, such as letters and charters, nonetheless confirms that most crusaders were primarily inspired to set out for the Holy Land by personal Christian devotion. The dramatic events of their campaign also indicate that they were imbued with robust and authentic spirituality. But a nuanced analysis of their reactions to events, such as the discovery of the Holy Lance at Antioch, suggests that their piety was not always ecstatic and overpowering. Tempered by the harsh realities of medieval warfare, the Latins fought in the name of Christ but were not immune to despair, depravity and dissolution. The First Crusaders were, for the most part, brutal warriors whose barbaric cruelty and innate avarice were barely contained by the ideals and ethos espoused by the papacy. Their struggle to reconquer Jerusalem was not primarily powered by any passionate allegiance to the Church, nor by a dutiful desire to defend Christendom. They suffered the horrors of the crusade to fulfil an intimate and ultimately self-serving need: to overcome their desperate fear of damnation and emerge, purified, at the gates of heaven.[3]

The success of the First Crusade had other, far-reaching effects. In 1095 Pope Urban II had conceived of the expedition as a one-off. But the conquest of Jerusalem seemed to confirm God's support for the notion of sanctified violence and the efficacy of crusading became widely accepted in the Latin West. The victories in the East established Frankish settlements that needed consolidation and defence, and with the papacy keen to manipulate what it saw as a powerful new weapon and the laity intent upon replicating the First Crusaders' achievements, it is little surprise that more crusades followed. Over the next century a crusading 'movement' gradually emerged, transforming European history. The practice of war was reshaped by the conflict on the Levantine frontier, both in terms of ideology and technology. Patterns of trade and economy altered to accommodate the settlement of the eastern Mediterranean. And the balance of political power shifted as both the Church and temporal rulers sought to harness the devastating force of the crusades. For two hundred years Latin armies set out to defend the Holy Land. None succeeded in re-creating the 'glories' of the First Crusade, but through failure and disillusionment, the fire of holy war was sustained by the memory of that expedition.[4]

The First Crusade's impact upon the relationship between western Christendom and Islam proved the most insidious and destructive. At Clermont, Urban sought to mobilise the armies of the West by creating a grossly distorted image of the Islamic world. Latins were encouraged to believe that Muslims were sadistic, sub-human savages – their natural enemy. In the campaign that followed, the Franks prosecuted an appallingly vicious war against Islam, peppered with unspeakable horrors such as the sack of Antioch and the massacre at Jerusalem. This was extreme violence, even by medieval standards, but we should not imagine that there was a distinct, stark contrast between the degree of brutality meted out by the crusaders in the Levant and the nature of internecine warfare that prevailed in Europe.[5]

The truth is that the papacy's dehumanisation of Islam did not exert an unwavering hold over the minds of the Franks. Even during the course of the expedition to Jerusalem, they demonstrated a more malleable attitude towards Muslims, engaging in extensive negotiations with the Fatimids of Egypt, pursuing limited alliances with Muslim rulers of northern Syria like Omar of Azaz and happily formulating a series of admittedly exploitative truces with the emirs of southern Syria, Lebanon and Palestine. The evidence of this contact is intermittent, and to an extent our Latin sources seem keen to present the crusade as an intense and unbending religious conflict.

In reality, contact may have been continuing on a completely different level. Raymond of Aguilers' assertion that the Latin priest and visionary Evremar went to the Muslim city of Tripoli to rest and recuperate during the latter stages of the siege of Antioch suggests that cross-cultural interaction may actually have been far more common than we know. Arabic sources certainly indicate that the Muslims of the Near East were willing to adopt a pragmatic approach to their dealings with the crusaders, just as they had with the Christian Greeks for generations.[6]

Between 1096 and 1099 the forces of the Latin West and Islam fought each other as enemies. But neither side appears to have truly viewed the other as an 'alien' species for whom they had an inbuilt, genetically encoded hatred. The crusaders' conquest of Jerusalem obviously did nothing to promote inter-religious harmony, but within a decade the Frankish settlements in the East had begun to be gradually incorporated into the political fabric of the Levant. Trade and commerce blossomed, and diplomacy took its place alongside conflict. In 1108, and again in 1115, the Latins even campaigned alongside Muslim allies.[7]

Only when the memory of the First Crusade was appropriated and refashioned in western Europe did the atmosphere of Latin–Muslim antipathy solidify. Unrelenting papal propaganda advanced the ideals of religious intolerance in the course of the twelfth century, and soon those earliest crusaders were being celebrated as much for their brutal attacks on Islamic foes as for the dramatic recapture of Jerusalem. In the Levant, a series of ambitious Muslim warlords, culminating in the mighty Sultan Saladin, seized upon the crimes of the First Crusaders. Demanding revenge, they re-ignited the fires of *jihad*, and under the cover of this ideal set out to unify Islam under their despotic rule. By 1300, the memory of the crusade as a war engendered by fanatical hatred had become embedded in the collective consciousness of western and eastern society. The lines of religious discord hardened; Christendom and Islam had been set on the path to enduring conflict.

GLOSSARY

Abbasids	'Dynasty' at the head of Sunni Islam; centred on Baghdad
Atabeg	Military and governmental office of general
Basilica	Early form of church
Byzantium	Continuator of the eastern Roman Empire
Emir	Semi-independent Muslim ruler
Fatimids	'Dynasty' at the head of Shi'a Islam; centred on Cairo
Fideles beati petri	The faithful/vassals of St Peter; supporters of Popes Gregory VII and Urban II
Franks	Generic term for the First Crusaders
Holy Lance	The spear that pierced the side of Christ while on the cross
Indulgence	Remission of sin in return for participation in the First Crusade
Jihad	Islamic ideal of Holy War
Latins	Generic term for western European Christians
Relic	Physical remnant from the life of a revered Christian
Seljuqs	Turcoman tribesmen who seized control of much of the Near East in the second half of the eleventh century

CHRONOLOGY

1095

1–7 March	Council of Piacenza
July–November	Pope Urban II tours France
18–28 November	Council of Clermont
27 November	Pope Urban proclaims the First Crusade
December–September 1096	Urban carries out an extensive preaching tour across France to publicise the First Crusade
December	Peter the Hermit starts preaching the crusade

1096

March	First contingents of the People's Crusade set out
May–June	Jewish pogroms in the Rhineland
1 August	Peter the Hermit reaches Constantinople
c. 7 August	People's Crusade crosses over to Asia Minor
August–December	Main armies of the crusade set out for the East
21 October	Annihilation of the People's Crusade at Civetos
November–May 1097	Main armies reach Constantinople

1097

February	Godfrey of Bouillon crosses the Bosphorus
May–June	Siege of Nicaea
16 May	First battle against Kilij Arslan
19 June	Surrender of Nicaea
1 July	Battle of Dorylaeum
July–September	Crossing of Asia Minor
September–October	Tancred and Baldwin of Boulogne in Cilicia
c. 10 October	Main army reaches Marash
20 October	Siege of Antioch begins
17 November	Genoese ships arrive at St Simeon
31 December	Foraging Battle against Duqaq of Damascus

1098

January	Attempted flight of Peter the Hermit
	Departure of Taticius
9 February	Battle against Ridwan of Aleppo
February	Fatimid embassy arrives in the crusader camp
4 March	English fleet arrives at St Simeon
10–14 March	Construction of La Mahomerie
2 June	Stephen of Blois leaves Antioch
3 June	Betrayal and sack of Antioch
4–5 June	Kerbogha's army arrives at Antioch
	Second siege of Antioch begins
14 June	Discovery of the Holy Lance
25 June	Peter the Hermit leads an embassy to Kerbogha
28 June	Great Battle of Antioch
1 August	Death of Adhémar of Le Puy
September	Capture of Albara
November–December	Siege of Marrat an-Numan

1099

c. 4 January	Council at Rugia
13 January	Raymond of Toulouse sets out from Marrat
February–May	Siege of Arqa
April	Peter Bartholomew undergoes ordeal by fire
16 May	Main armies set out from Arqa for Jerusalem
3–6 June	Crusade at Ramleh
7 June	First Crusade reaches Jerusalem
13 June	First assault on Jerusalem fails
17 June	News arrives of six Genoese ships docked at Jaffa
15 July	First Crusade captures Jerusalem
12 August	Battle of Ascalon

NOTES

CHAPTER 1: HOLY WAR PROCLAIMED

1. Robert the Monk, *Historia Iherosolimitana*, *RHC Occ.* III, pp. c. 727–8. This quotation is an abridged version of Robert's text. An English translation of Robert's version of Pope Urban II's sermon at Clermont is given in: L. and J. S. C. Riley-Smith, *The Crusades: Idea and Reality, 1095–1274* (London, 1981), pp. 42–5.

2. *Gesta Francorum et aliorum Hierosolimitanorum*, ed. and trans. R. Hill (London, 1962), p. 7.

3. J. M. Powell, 'Myth, legend, propaganda, history: The First Crusade, 1140–c. 1300', *Autour de la Première Croisade*, ed. M. Balard (Paris, 1996), pp. 127–41.

4. A. Becker, *Papst Urban II. (1088–1099)*, Schriften der Monumenta Germaniae Historica 19, 2 vols (Stuttgart, 1964–88); A. Becker, 'Urbain II, pape de la croisade', *Les Champenois et la Croisade. Actes des Ive Journées rémoises, 27–28 novembre 1987*, ed. Y. Bellenger and D. Quéruel (Paris, 1989), pp. 9–17.

5. For further reading on the Franks see: E. James, *The Franks* (Oxford, 1988); P. Geary, *Before France and Germany: The Creation and Transformation of the Merovingian World* (Oxford, 1988).

6. For further reading on Charlemagne and the Carolingians see: R. McKitterick, *The Frankish Kingdoms Under the Carolingians, 751–987* (London, 1983).

7. M. G. Bull, 'Origins', *The Oxford Illustrated History of the Crusades*, ed. J. S. C. Riley-Smith (Oxford, 1995), pp. 13–33. On the use of the term

Franks see: J. S. C. Riley-Smith, *The First Crusaders, 1095–1131* (Cambridge, 1997), pp. 64–5.

8. Bull, 'Origins', pp. 13–15, 19–20; M. G. Bull, *Knightly Piety and the Lay Response to the First Crusade: The Limousin and Gascony, c. 970–c. 1130* (Oxford, 1993), pp. 23–33; J. S. C. Riley-Smith, *The First Crusade and the Idea of Crusading* (London, 1986), p. 3; Riley-Smith, *The First Crusaders*, pp. 27–8.

9. For an introduction to the Christianisation of Europe see: R. Fletcher, *The Conversion of Europe* (New York, 1988); P. Brown, *The Rise of Western Christendom* (Oxford, 1996).

10. For an introduction to medieval Christianity see: B. Hamilton, *Religion in the Medieval West* (London, 1986).

11. For an introduction to monasticism and religious life see: C. H. Lawrence, *Medieval Monasticism: Forms of Religious Life in Western Europe in the Middle Ages* (London, 1984).

12. N. Hunt, *Cluny under St Hugh, 1049–1109* (London, 1967); H. E. J. Cowdrey, *The Cluniacs and the Gregorian Reform* (Oxford, 1970). Cluny is used here as a case study to illustrate the rising significance of monastic reform, a process that was also taking place in other religious houses such as Gorze and Brogne.

13. For further reading on the medieval papacy see: W. Ullmann, *A Short History of the Papacy in the Middle Ages* (London, 1974); C. Morris, *The Papal Monarchy: The Western Church from 1050 to 1250* (Oxford, 1989).

14. Morris, *The Papal Monarchy*, pp. 57–108.

15. On Pope Gregory VII and the Reform Movement see: Morris, *The Papal Monarchy*, pp. 109–33; H. E. J. Cowdrey, *Pope Gregory VII, 1073–1085* (Oxford, 1998); U.-R. Blumenthal, *The Investiture Controversy: Church and Monarchy from the Ninth to the Twelfth Century* (Philadelphia, 1988).

16. F. Duncalf, 'The councils of Piacenza and Clermont', *A History of the Crusades*, ed. K. M. Setton, vol. 1, 2nd edition (Madison, 1969), pp. 220–52.

17. J. Wilkinson, *Jerusalem Pilgrims Before the Crusades* (Warminster, 1977); Riley-Smith, *The First Crusaders*, pp. 25–39; J. France, 'The destruction of Jerusalem and the First Crusade', *Journal of Ecclesiastical History*, vol. 47 (1996), pp. 1–17.

18. To trace the grand sweep of Byzantine history see: G. Ostrogorsky, *History of the Byzantine State*, trans. J. M. Hussey, 2nd edition (Padstow, 1968).

19. On the history of the Christian reconquest of Iberia see: D. Lomax, *The Reconquest of Spain* (London, 1978). On the question of connections between the *reconquista* and crusading see: Bull, *Knightly Piety*, pp. 70–114.

20. On the relationship between Latin Christendom and Islam see: R. W. Southern, *Western Views of Islam in the Middle Ages* (Cambridge, 1962); R. Hill, 'The Christian view of the Muslims at the time of the First Crusade', *The Eastern Mediterranean Lands in the Period of the Crusades*, ed. P. M. Holt (Warminster, 1977), pp. 1–8; J. Flori, 'La caricature de l'Islam dans l'Occident médiéval. Origine et signification de quelques stéréotypes concernant l'Islam', *Aevum*, vol. 66 (1992), pp. 245–56; N. Daniel, *Islam and the West: The Making of an Image* (Edinburgh, 1960); M. Bennett, 'First Crusaders' images of Muslims: The influence of vernacular poetry?', *Forum for Modern Language Studies*, vol. 22 (1986), pp. 101–22; J. Gauss, 'Toleranz und Intoleranz zwischen Christen und Mulsimen in der Zeit vor den Kreuzzügen', *Saeculum*, vol. 19 (1968), pp. 362–89.

21. Lomax, *The Reconquest of Spain*, pp. 68–93; Riley-Smith, *The First Crusade and the Idea of Crusading*, pp. 18–20; Riley-Smith, *The First Crusaders*, pp. 66–7.

22. Riley-Smith, *The First Crusade and the Idea of Crusading*, pp. 13–30; Riley-Smith, *The First Crusaders*, p. 53–6; A. C. Krey, 'Urban's crusade, success or failure?', *American Historical Review*, vol. 53 (1948), pp. 235–50; R. Crozet, 'Le voyage d'Urbain II et ses négotiations avec le clergé de France (1095–1096), *Revue historique*, vol. 179 (1937), pp. 271–310; R. Somerville, 'The French councils of Urban II: some basic considerations', *Annuarium Historiae Conciliorum*, vol. 2 (1970), pp. 56–65; R. Somerville, 'The council of Clermont and the First Crusade', *Studia Gratiana*, vol. 20 (1976), pp. 323–37; R. Somerville, 'The council of Clermont (1095) and Latin Christian society', *Archivum Historiae Pontificae*, vol. 12 (1974), pp. 55–90.

23. F. H. Russell, *The Just War in the Middle Ages* (Cambridge, 1975); C. Erdmann, *The Origin of the Idea of Crusade* (Princeton, 1977); J. T. Gilchrist, 'The Erdmann thesis and canon law, 1083–1141', *Crusade and Settlement*, ed. P. W. Edbury (Cardiff, 1985), pp. 37–45; J. T. Gilchrist, 'The Papacy and the war against the "Saracens", 795–1216', *International History Review*, vol. 10 (1988), pp. 174–97; E. O. Blake, 'The formation of the "crusade idea"', *Journal of Ecclesiastical History*, vol. 21 (1970), pp. 11–31; H. E. J. Cowdrey, 'Cluny and the First Crusade',

Revue bénédictine, vol. 73 (1973), pp. 285–311; H. E. J. Cowdrey, 'The genesis of the crusades: The springs of western ideas of holy war', *The Holy War*, ed. T. P. Murphy (Columbus, 1976), pp. 9–32; H. E. J. Cowdrey, 'The papacy and the origins of crusading', *Medieval History*, vol. 1 (1991), pp. 48–60; H. E. J. Cowdrey, 'Canon law and the First Crusade', *The Horns of Hattin*, ed. B. Z. Kedar (Jerusalem, 1992) pp. 41–8; J. S. C. Riley-Smith, *What were the Crusades*, 3rd edition (Basingstoke, 2002); J. Flori, *La formation de l'idée de croisades dans l'Occident Chrétien* (Paris, 2001).

24. Russell, *The Just War in the Middle Ages*, pp. 16–39.

25. Ibid., pp. 1–39; J. A. Brundage, *Medieval Canon Law and the Crusader* (Madison, 1969), pp. 19–24.

26. I. S. Robinson, 'Gregory VII and the Soldiers of Christ', *History*, vol. 58 (1973), pp. 169–92; Riley-Smith, *The First Crusaders*, pp. 44–52; H. E. J. Cowdrey, 'Pope Gregory's "Crusading" plans of 1074', *Outremer*, ed. B. Z. Kedar, H. E. Mayer and R. C. Smail (Jerusalem, 1982), pp. 27–40; H. E. J. Cowdrey, 'Pope Gregory and the bearing of arms', *Montjoie: Studies in crusade history in honour of Hans Eberhard Mayer*, ed. B. Z. Kedar, J. S. C. Riley-Smith and R. Hiestand (Aldershot, 1997), pp. 21–35.

27. Riley-Smith, *The First Crusaders*, pp. 53–8.

28. H. E. J. Cowdrey, 'Pope Urban II's preaching of the First Crusade', *History*, vol. 55 (1970), pp. 177–88; D. C. Munro, 'The speech of Pope Urban II at Clermont, 1095', *American Historical Review*, vol. 11 (1905–6), pp. 231–42; S. Schein, 'Jérusalem: objectif original de la Première Croisade?', *Autour de la Première Croisade*, ed. M. Balard (Paris, 1996), pp. 119–26; Riley-Smith, *The First Crusade and the Idea of Crusading*, pp. 13–30; Riley-Smith, *The First Crusaders*, pp. 60–75; P. Cole, *The Preaching of the Crusades to the Holy Land, 1095–1270* (Cambridge, MA, 1991), pp. 1–36; A. Fliche, 'Urbain II et la croisade', *Revue d'histoire de l'église de France*, vol. 13 (1927), pp. 289–306; A. C. Krey, 'Urban's crusade, success or failure?', *American Historical Review*, vol. 53 (1948), pp. 235–50.

29. Robert the Monk, p. 727.

30. H. Hagenmeyer, *Die Kreuzzugssbriefe aus den Jahren 1088–1100* (Innsbruck, 1901), pp. 136–7; 'Papsturkunden in Florenz', ed. W. Wiederhold, *Nachrichten von der Gesellschaft der Wissenschaften zu Göttingen*, Phil.-hist. Kl. (Göttingen, 1901), pp. 313–14. English translations of these two letters are given in: Riley-Smith, *The Crusades: Idea and Reality, 1095–1274*, pp. 38–40; Fulcher of Chartres, *Historia*

Hierosolymitana (1095–1127), ed. H. Hagenmeyer (Heidelberg, 1913), pp. 130–8. Two English translations of Fulcher's text are available: *A History of the Expedition to Jerusalem 1095–1127*, trans. F. S. Ryan, ed. H. S. Fink (Knoxville, 1960); E. Peters (ed.), *The First Crusade: The Chronicle of Fulcher of Chartres and other source materials*, 2nd edition (Philadelphia, 1998), pp. 47–101.

31. Guibert of Nogent, *Dei gesta per Francos*, ed. R. B. C. Huygens, Corpus Christianorum, Continuatio Mediavalis, 127A (Turnhout, 1996), pp. 111–17. Guibert's text is translated into English in: *The Deeds of God through the Franks: A Translation of Guibert de Nogent's Gesta Dei per Francos*, trans. R. Levine (Woodbridge, 1996).

32. Fulcher of Chartres, p. 132; Baldric of Bourgueil, bishop of Dol, *Historia Jerosolimitana, RHC Occ.* IV, pp. 12–14. An English translation of Baldric's version of Pope Urban II's sermon at Clermont is given in: Riley-Smith, *The Crusades: Idea and Reality, 1095–1274*, pp. 49–53; Robert the Monk, pp. 728–9; Guibert of Nogent, pp. 111–16. P. Cole, 'O God, the heathen have come into your inheritance (Ps. 78.1): The theme of religious pollution in crusade documents, 1095–1188', *Crusaders and Muslims in twelfth–century Syria*, ed. M. Shatzmiller (Leiden, 1993), pp. 84–111.

33. Fulcher of Chartres, pp. 136–7.

34. A considerable debate surrounds the possibility of a connection between the Peace of God movement and the concept of crusading. See: Bull, *Knightly Piety*, pp. 21–69; H. E. J. Cowdrey, 'The Peace and Truce of God in the eleventh century', *Past and Present*, vol. 46 (1970), pp. 42–67; J. Flori, 'L'église et la guerre sainte de la "Paix de Dieu" à la "croisade"', *Annales ESC*, vol. 47 (1992), pp. 453–66.

35. Guibert of Nogent, pp. 112–13. On the practice of medieval pilgrimage see: J. Sumption, *Pilgrimage: An Image of Mediaeval Religion* (London, 1975).

36. H. E. J. Cowdrey, 'Pope Urban II and the idea of crusade', *Studi medievali*, ser. 3, vol. 36 (1995), pp. 721–42; J. Richard, 'Urbain II, la prédication de la croisades et la définition de l'indulgence', *Deus qui mutat tempora: Menschen und Institutionen im Wandel des Mittelalters. Festschrift für Alfons Becker zu seinem fünfundsechzigsten Geburstag*, ed. E.-D. Hehl, H. Seibert and F. Staab (Sigmaringen, 1987), pp. 129–35.

CHAPTER 2: AFIRE WITH CRUSADING FEVER

1. Riley-Smith, *The First Crusade and the Idea of Crusading*, pp. 13–57;
   Riley-Smith, *The First Crusaders*, pp. 12–20, 43–153; J. S. C. Riley-Smith,
   'The motives of the earliest crusaders and the settlement of Latin
   Palestine, 1095–1100', *English Historical Review*, vol. 98 (1983), pp.
   721–36; Bull, *Knightly Piety*, pp. 250–88; M. G. Bull, 'The roots of lay
   enthusiasm for the First Crusade', *History*, vol. 78 (1993), pp. 353–72; J.
   France, 'Patronage and the appeal of the First Crusade', *The First
   Crusade: Origins and Impact*, ed. J. P. Phillips (Manchester, 1997), pp.
   5–20; B. McGinn, 'Iter Sancti Sepulchri: The piety of the first
   crusaders', *Essays on Medieval Civilization*, ed. B. K. Lackner and K. R.
   Philip (Austin, 1978), pp. 33–72.

2. Riley-Smith, *The First Crusaders*, pp. 44–7, 52, 54–6.

3. Baldric of Bourgeuil, pp. 15–16.

4. Hagenmeyer, *Kreuzzugssbriefe*, pp. 136–7.

5. J. A. Brundage, 'Adhémar of Le Puy: The bishop and his critics',
   Speculum, vol. 34 (1959), pp. 201–12; J. H. and L. L. Hill, 'Contemporary
   accounts and the later reputation of Adhémar, bishop of Le Puy',
   Mediaevalia et humanistica, vol. 9 (1955), pp. 30–8; G. J. de Adhémar-
   Labaume, *Adhémar de Monteil, évêque du Puy, légat d'Urbain II,
   1079–1098* (Le Puy, 1910); H. E. Mayer, 'Zur Beurteilung Adhemars von
   Le Puy', *Deutsches Archiv für Erforschung des Mittelalters*, vol. 16 (1960),
   pp. 547–52.

6. J. H. and L. L. Hill, *Raymond IV, Count of Toulouse* (Syracuse, 1962);
   A. Dupont, 'Raymond IV de Saint-Gilles et son role en Orient pendant
   la Première Croisade (1096–1099)', *Bulletin des séances de l'Académie
   de Nîmes*, vol. 47 (1970), pp. 19–21, 24–6; Riley-Smith, *The First
   Crusaders*, pp. 45–6, 106–7.

7. Hagenmeyer, *Kreuzzugssbriefe*, pp. 136–7; Riley-Smith, *The First
   Crusaders*, pp. 56–60, 75–7; Riley-Smith, *The First Crusade and the Idea
   of Crusading*, pp. 31–3.

8. This analysis presupposes that Urban's controlling measures post-date
   his sermon at Clermont and that these measures were included in the
   narrative accounts of his speech through hindsight. Riley-Smith, *The
   First Crusade and the Idea of Crusading*, pp. 30, 50; Becker, *Papst Urban
   II*, pp. 232–80; Hagenmeyer, *Kreuzzugssbriefe*, pp. 137–8; 'Papsturkunden in Florenz', pp. 313–14; *Papsturkunden in Spanien. I Katalonien*,
   ed. P. F. Kehr (Berlin, 1926), pp. 287–8. An English translation of

this letter is given in: Riley-Smith, *The Crusades: Idea and Reality, 1095–1274*, p. 40.

9. 'Papsturkunden in Florenz', p. 313.

10. J. France, *Victory in the East: A Military History of the First Crusade* (Cambridge, 1994), pp. 26–79; J. France, 'Technology and the success of the First Crusade', *War and Society in the Eastern Mediterranean, 7th–15th Centuries*, ed. Y. Lev, The Medieval Mediterranean, vol. 9 (Leiden, 1997), pp. 163–76; Bull, 'Origins', pp. 18–22. Godfrey of Bouillon's use of the crossbow is mentioned by the crusade chronicler Albert of Aachen. Albert's account is currently only available in Latin as: *Historia Hierosolymitana*, *RHC Occ.* IV, pp. 265–713. A new edition and translation by S. B. Edgington will, however, be published shortly by Oxford Medieval Texts, based on her Ph.D.: 'The *Historia Iherosolimitana* of Albert of Aachen: A critical edition', ed. S. B. Edgington (unpublished Ph.D. thesis, University of London, 1991). I am deeply indebted to Dr Edgington for allowing me access to this work in advance of publication. In view of this I will cite all references to Albert's account by book and chapter so that the new edition can be consulted. An example of Albert's reference to Godfrey's use of the crossbow thus appears as: Albert of Aachen, VI.16.

11. Riley-Smith, *The First Crusade and the Idea of Crusading*, pp. 31–3; Riley-Smith, *The First Crusaders*, pp. 89–90.

12. Anna Comnena, *Alexiade*, ed. and trans. B. Leib, vol. 3 (Paris, 1976), pp. 122–3. The Alexiad has been translated into English in: *The Alexiad of Anna Comnena*, trans. E. R. A. Sewter (Harmondsworth, 1969).

13. William of Malmesbury, *Gesta Regum Anglorum*, vol. 1, ed. and trans. R. A. B. Mynors, R. M. Thomson and M. Winterbottom, vol. 1 (Oxford, 1998), p. 693.

14. Riley-Smith, *The First Crusaders*, p. 45. They were also connected by the bonds of lordship, for when Roger Borsa became the pope's vassal in 1089, Bohemond was technically left as Urban's rear vassal.

15. R. B. Yewdale, *Bohemond I, Prince of Antioch* (Princeton, 1917), pp. 1–33; W. B. McQueen, 'Relations between the Normans and Byzantium, 1071–1112', *Byzantion*, vol. 56 (1986), pp. 427–76; M. Angold, *The Byzantine Empire, 1025–1204: A Political History*, 2nd edition (London, 1997), pp. 129–31; Anna Comnena, vol. 1, pp. 143–68, vol. 2, pp. 7–60; Riley-Smith, *The First Crusaders*, pp. 17–18, 100–1.

16. R. L. Nicholson, *Tancred: A Study of His Career and Work in Their Relation to the First Crusade and the Establishment of the Latin States*

in *Syria and Palestine* (Chicago, 1940). The Latin Ralph of Caen wrote Tancred's biography in the first decade of the twelfth century. It offers a view of the First Crusade from Tancred's perspective: Ralph of Caen, *Gesta Tancredi in expeditione Hierosolymitana*, RHC Occ. III, pp. 587–716.

17. William of Tyre, *Chronique*, ed. R. B. C. Huygens, Corpus Christianorum, Continuatio Mediaevalis, 63, vol. 1 (Turnhout, 1986), p. 427. William of Tyre's history is translated into English in: *A History of Deeds Done Beyond the Sea by William Archbishop of Tyre*, trans. E. A. Babcock and A. C. Krey, 2 vols (New York: 1943).

18. J. C. Andressohn, *The Ancestry and Life of Godfrey of Bouillon* (Bloomington, 1947); P. Aubé, *Godefroy de Bouillon* (Paris, 1985); G. Despy, 'Godefroid de Bouillon, myths et réalités', *Academie Royale de Belgique, Bulletin de la Classe des Lettres et des Sciences Morales et Pollitiques*, ser. 5, vol. 71 (1985), pp. 249–75; Riley-Smith, *The First Crusaders*, p. 96.

19. P. Gindler, *Graf Balduin I. von Edessa* (Halle, 1901); William of Tyre, pp. 454–5.

20. C. W. David, *Robert Curthose, Duke of Normandy* (Cambridge, Mass., 1920); J. A. Brundage, 'An errant crusader: Stephen of Blois', *Traditio*, vol. 16 (1960), pp. 380–95; M. M. Knappen, 'Robert II of Flanders in the First Crusade', *The Crusades and Other Historical Essays Presented to Dana C. Munro by his former students*, ed. L. J. Paetow (New York, 1928), pp. 79–100.

21. Riley-Smith, *The First Crusaders*, pp. 81–105; A. V. Murray, 'Questions of nationality in the First Crusade', *Medieval History*, vol. 1 (1991), pp. 61–73. Historians continue to debate the number of participants on the First Crusade. My estimate has tended to side with the calculations made by J. France, *Victory in the East*, pp. 122–42. For other recent contributions to the field see: B. Bachrach, 'The siege of Antioch: A study in military demography', *War in History*, vol. 6 (1999), pp. 127–46; Riley-Smith, *The First Crusaders*, p. 109; J. S. C. Riley-Smith, 'Casualties and the number of knights on the First Crusade', *Crusades*, vol. 1 (2002), pp. 13–28.

22. Robert the Monk, pp. 729–30; Baldric of Bourgeuil, p. 16.

23. Brundage, *Medieval Canon Law and the Crusader*, pp. 17–18, 30–39,115–21; J. A. Brundage, 'The army of the First Crusade and the crusade vow: Some reflections on a recent book', *Medieval Studies*, vol. 33 (1971), pp. 334–43; Riley-Smith, *The First Crusade and the Idea of Crusading*, pp. 22–3, 81–2.

24. R. Somerville, *The Councils of Urban II. 1. Decreta Claromontensia* (Amsterdam, 1972), p. 74. Baldric of Bourgeuil, p. 15, actually chose to present Pope Urban as seeking to capitalise on Latin greed. In his version of the Clermont sermon, Baldric has Urban promise prospective crusaders that: 'You will get the enemies' possessions, because you will despoil their treasuries.'

25. Riley-Smith, *The First Crusade and the Idea of Crusading*, pp. 34, 39–40.

26. H. E. Mayer, *The Crusades*, trans. J. Gillingham, 2nd edition (Oxford, 1988), pp. 21–3; Riley-Smith, *The First Crusade and the Idea of Crusading*, p. 47; France, *Victory in the East*, pp. 11–16.

27. Baldwin of Boulogne also set out on crusade with his English wife, but she died en route.

28. Riley-Smith, *The First Crusade and the Idea of Crusading*, p. 43; Riley-Smith, *The First Crusaders*, pp. 112, 118.

29. M. G. Bull, 'The diplomatic of the First Crusade', *The First Crusade: Origins and Impact*, ed. J. P. Phillips (Manchester, 1997), pp. 35–54; G. Constable, 'Medieval charters as a source for the history of the crusades', *Crusade and Settlement*, ed. P. W. Edbury (Cardiff, 1985), pp. 73–89.

30. Bull, *Knightly Piety*, pp. 115–203.

31. Ralph of Caen, pp. 605–6.

32. Bull, *Knightly Piety*, pp. 155–281; Riley-Smith, *The First Crusade and the Idea of Crusading*, pp. 31–49; Riley-Smith, *The First Crusaders*, pp. 81–143.

33. Guibert of Nogent, p. 87.

34. Ralph of Caen, p. 606.

35. I have here presented only a small sample of the material relating to crusader preparations and the evidence of pious intent. For a fuller treatment of the subject see: Riley-Smith, *The First Crusade and the Idea of Crusading*, pp. 36–49; Riley-Smith, *The First Crusaders*, pp. 106–43.

36. Guibert of Nogent, p. 121.

37. E. O. Blake and C. Morris, 'A hermit goes to war: Peter and the origins of the First Crusade', *Studies in Church History*, vol. 22 (1985), pp. 79–107; C. Morris, 'Peter the Hermit and the Chroniclers', *The First Crusade: Origins and Impact*, ed. J. P. Phillips (Manchester, 1997), pp. 21–34; M. D. Coupe, 'Peter the Hermit – a re-assessment', *Nottingham Medieval Studies*, vol. 31 (1987), pp. 37–45; J. Flori, 'Faut-il réhabiliter Pierre l'Ermite? (une réevaluation des sources de la Première Croisade)', *Cahiers de civilisation médiévale*, vol. 38 (1995), pp. 35–54; J. Flori, 'Pierre l'Ermite et sa croisades – légende et vérité', *Cahiers de Clio*, vols. 125–26 (1996), pp. 29–39.

38. J. M. B. Porter, 'Preacher of the First Crusade? Robert of Arbrissel after the Council of Clermont', *From Clermont to Jerusalem: The Crusades and Crusader Societies, 1095–1500*, ed. A. V. Murray (Turnhout, 1998), pp. 43–53; Riley-Smith, *The First Crusaders*, pp. 76–7.

39. Albert of Aachen, I.2.

40. Guibert of Nogent, p. 121.

41. William of Tyre, p. 124.

42. Guibert of Nogent, p. 121.

43. M. D. Lambert, *Medieval Heresy: Popular movements from Bogomil to Huss*, 3rd edition (Oxford, 2002), pp. 52–69.

44. Albert of Aachen, I.2–5; William of Tyre, I.11–12, pp. 124–7; Blake and Morris, 'A hermit goes to war', pp. 84–97.

45. Riley-Smith, *The First Crusade and the Idea of Crusading*, p. 34.

46. Albert of Aachen, I.2; Anna Comnena, vol. 2, p. 207.

CHAPTER 3: THE JOURNEY TO BYZANTIUM

1. Riley-Smith, *The First Crusade and the Idea of Crusading*, pp. 49–57; J. S. C. Riley-Smith, 'The First Crusade and the persecution of the Jews', *Studies in Church History*, vol. 21 (1984), pp. 51–72; R. Chazan, *European Jewry and the First Crusade* (Berkeley, 1987); A. S. Abulafia, 'Invectives against Christianity in the Hebrew Chronicles of the First Crusade', *Crusade and Settlement*, ed. P. W. Edbury (Cardiff, 1985), pp. 66–72.

2. Riley-Smith, *The First Crusade and the Idea of Crusading*, pp. 51–2; Mayer, *The Crusades*, pp. 35–41; S. Runciman, 'The First Crusade and the foundation of the kingdom of Jerusalem', *A History of the Crusades*, vol. 1 (Cambridge, 1951), pp. 134–41.

3. Peters, *The First Crusade*: The Anonymous of Mainz, p. 113.

4. Peters, *The First Crusade*: Solomon ben Simson, p. 129.

5. Albert of Aachen, I.26.

6. Peters, *The First Crusade*: Solomon ben Simson, p. 126.

7. J. T. Gilchrist, 'The perception of Jews in the canon law in the period of the first two crusades', *Jewish History*, vol. 3 (1988), pp. 9–24.

8. Peters, *The First Crusade*: Solomon ben Simson, p. 131.

9. R. Chazan, 'The Hebrew First Crusade chronicles', *Revue des études juives*, vol. 133 (1974), pp. 235–54; R. Chazan, *God, Humanity and History: The Hebrew First Crusade Narratives* (Berkeley, 2000); A. S.

Abulafia, 'The interrelationship between the Hebrew chronicles on the First Crusade', *Journal of Semitic Studies*, vol. 27 (1982), pp. 221–39.

10. Peters, *The First Crusade*: The Anonymous of Mainz, p. 115.

11. Ibid., p. 117.

12. Albert of Aachen, I.27.

13. Ibid., I.28–9; France, *Victory in the East*, pp. 88–95.

14. Fulcher of Chartres, p. 163.

15. France, *Victory in the East*, pp. 95–102. On the general question of crusader transport and Mediterranean travel see: M. Bennett, 'Travel and transport of the crusades', *Medieval History*, vol. 4 (1994), pp. 91–101; J. H. Pryor, *Geography, Technology and War: Studies in the Maritime History of the Mediterranean, 649–1571* (Cambridge, 1987).

16. Anna Comnena, vol. 2, pp. 213–15; *Gesta Francorum*, pp. 5–6.

17. Fulcher of Chartres, pp. 163–74; V. Epp, *Fulcher von Chartres: Studien zur Geschichtsschreibung des ersten Kreuzzuges* (Düsseldorf, 1990).

18. Raymond of Aguilers, *Le 'Liber' de Raymond d'Aguilers*, ed. J. H. Hill and L. L. Hill (Paris, 1969), pp. 36–8. Raymond's account is translated into English in: *Historia Francorum qui ceperunt Iherusalem*, trans. J. H. Hill and L. L. Hill (Philadelphia, 1968); J. Richard, 'Raymond d'Aguilers, historien de la première croisade', *Journal des Savants*, vol. 3 (1971), pp. 206–12; *Gesta Francorum*, p. 5.

19. Albert of Aachen, II.1–6. Although not an eyewitness Albert did write a detailed and valuable account of the First Crusade with Godfrey as his central character. For a discussion of Albert's value as a source see: S. B. Edgington, 'The First Crusade: Reviewing the Evidence', *The First Crusade: Origins and Impact*, ed. J. P. Phillips (Manchester, 1997), pp. 55–77; S. B. Edgington, 'Albert of Aachen reappraised', *From Clermont to Jerusalem: The Crusades and Crusader Societies, 1095–1500*, ed. A. V. Murray (Turnhout, 1998), pp. 55–67; S. B. Edgington, 'Albert of Aachen and the *chanson de geste*', *The Crusades and their Sources: Essays Presented to Bernard Hamilton*, ed. J. France and W. G. Zajac (Aldershot, 1998), pp. 23–37; C. Morris, 'The aims and spirituality of the crusade as seen through the eyes of Albert of Aix', *Reading Medieval Studies*, vol. 16 (1990), pp. 99–117; A. A. Beaumont, 'Albert of Aachen and the county of Edessa', *The Crusades and Other Historical Essays Presented to Dana C. Munro by His Former Students*, ed. L. J. Paetow (New York, 1928), pp. 101–38. On Godfrey's contingent see: A. V. Murray, 'The army of Godfrey of Bouillon, 1096–1099: structure and dynamics of a contingent on the First Crusade', *Revue belge de philology et d'histoire*, vol. 70 (1992), pp. 301–29.

20. *Gesta Francorum*, pp. 7–8. On the debate surrounding the centrality of the *Gesta Francorum* as a source for the First Crusade and on the identity of its author see: J. France, 'The Anonymous *Gesta Francorum* and the *Historia Francorum qui ceperunt Iherusalem* of Raymond of Aguilers and the *Historia de Hierosolymitano Itinere* of Peter Tudebode', *The Crusades and Their Sources: Essays Presented to Bernard Hamilton*, pp. 39–69; J. France, 'The use of the anonymous *Gesta Francorum* in the early twelfth–century sources for the First Crusade', *From Clermont to Jerusalem: The Crusades and Crusader Societies, 1095–1500*, ed. A. V. Murray (Turnhout, 1998), pp. 29–42; C. Morris, 'The *Gesta Francorum* as narrative history', *Reading Medieval Studies*, vol. 19 (1993), pp. 55–71; K. B. Wolf, 'Crusade and narrative: Bohemond and the *Gesta Francorum*', *Journal of Medieval History*, vol. 17 (1991), pp. 207–16. On Bohemond's contingent see: Riley-Smith, *The First Crusaders*, pp. 100–1; E. M. Jamison, 'Some notes on the *Anonymi Gesta Francorum*, with special reference to the Norman contingent from South Italy and Sicily in the First Crusade', *Studies in French Language and Medieval Literature presented to Professor Mildred K. Pope* (Manchester, 1939), pp. 195–204; G. T. Beech, 'A Norman–Italian adventurer in the East: Richard of Salerno 1097–1112', *Anglo-Norman Studies, XV: Proceedings of the XV Battle Conference and of the XI Colloquio Medievale of the Officina di Studi Medievali, 1992*, ed. M. Chibnall (Woodbridge, 1993), pp. 25–40.

21. Anna Comnena, vol. 2, p. 208.

22. On the history of Byzantium see: M. Angold, *The Byzantine Empire, 1025–1204: A Political History*, pp. 15–98; P. Charanis, 'The Byzantine empire in the eleventh century', *A History of the Crusades*, ed. K. M. Setton, vol. 1, 2nd edition (Madison, 1969), pp. 177–219. On the debate surrounding the impact of Manzikert see: C. Cahen, 'La campagne de Mantizikert d'après les sources musulmans', *Byzantion*, vol. 9 (1934), pp. 628–42; M. Angold, 'The Byzantine state on the eve of the battle of Manzikert', *Byzantinische Forschungen*, vol. 16 (1991), pp. 9–34.

23. Anna Comnena, p. 109. On Anna Comnena's biography of Alexius *The Alexiad* see: J. France, 'Anna Comnena, the Alexiad and the First Crusade', *Reading Medieval Studies*, vol. 10 (1984), pp. 20–38; J. Chrysostomides, 'A Byzantine historian: Anna Comnena', *Medieval Historical Writing in the Christian and Islamic Worlds*, ed. D. O. Morgan (London, 1982), pp. 30–46; G. A. Loud, 'Anna Komnena and

her sources for the Normans of southern Italy', *Church and Chronicle in the Middle Ages: Essays Presented to John Taylor*, ed. I. Wood and G. A. Loud (London, 1991), pp. 41–57; R. D. Thomas, 'Anna Comnena's account of the First Crusade: History and politics in the reigns of the emperors Alexius I and Manuel I Comnenus', *Byzantine and Modern Greek Studies*, vol. 15 (1991), pp. 269–312; R.-J. Lilie, 'Der erste Kreuzzug in der Darstellung Anna Komnenes', *Varia II: Beiträge von A. Berger et al.*, Poikila Byzantina, vol. 6 (Bonn, 1987), pp. 49–148.

24. On the reign of Alexius Comnenus see: Angold, *The Byzantine Empire*, pp. 115–56; M. Angold, *Church and Society in Byzantium Under the Comneni, 1081–1261* (Cambridge, 1995); M. Mullett, 'Alexios I Komnenos and imperial renewal', *New Constantines: The Rhythm of Imperial Renewal in Byzantium, 4th–13th Centuries. Papers from the Twenty-Sixth Spring Symposium of Byzantine Studies, St Andrews, March 1992*, ed. P. Magdalino (Aldershot, 1994), pp. 259–67.

25. On contact between Byzantium and the West see: P. Charanis, 'Byzantium, the West and the origin of the First Crusade', *Byzantion*, vol. 19 (1949), pp. 17–36; J. Shepard, 'The uses of the Franks in eleventh-century Byzantium', *Anglo-Norman Studies, XV: Proceedings of the XV Battle Conference and of the XI Colloquio Medievale of the Officina di Studi Medievali, 1992*, ed. M. Chibnall (Woodbridge, 1993), pp. 275–305.

26. R.-J. Lilie, *Byzantium and the Crusader States, 1096–1204*, trans. J. C. Morris and J. E. Ridings (Oxford, 1993), pp. 1–7; Duncalf, 'The councils of Piacenza and Clermont', pp. 220–52; D. C. Munro, 'Did the Emperor Alexius ask for aid at the council of Piacenza?', *American Historical Review*, vol. 27 (1922), pp. 731–33; J. Shepard, 'Cross purposes: Alexius Comnenus and the First Crusade', *The First Crusade: Origins and Impact*, ed. J. P. Phillips (Manchester, 1997), pp. 107–29.

27. Anna Comnena, vol. 2, p. 208.

28. *Gesta Francorum*, pp. 2–3.

29. Albert of Aachen, I.15; Raymond of Aguilers, pp. 44–5. Anna Comnena, vol. 2, p. 210, suggests that Alexius actually counselled Peter to wait for crusader reinforcements before crossing the Bosphorus.

30. Albert of Aachen, I.15–16; Anna Comnena, vol. 2, p. 210; *Gesta Francorum*, p. 3; Orderic Vitalis, *The Ecclesiastical History of Orderic Vitalis*, ed. and trans. M. Chibnall, vol. 5 (Oxford, 1975), p. 33.

31. *Gesta Francorum*, pp. 3–4; Albert of Aachen, I.16–17; Anna Comnena, vol. 2, pp. 210–11.

32. Albert of Aachen, I.18–19; Anna Comnena, vol. 2, p. 211.

33. *Gesta Francorum*, p. 4–5; Albert of Aachen, I.19–21; Anna Comnena, vol. 2, p. 211.

34. Albert of Aachen, I.21.

35. Ibid., I.22; *Gesta Francorum*, p. 5.

36. Raymond of Aguilers, p. 38; Fulcher of Chartres, pp. 178–9.

37. Anna Comnena, vol. 2, pp. 206–7, 233. Lilie, *Byzantium and the Crusader States*, pp. 3–28, provides an outline of the initial contact between Alexius and the second wave of crusaders.

38. *Gesta Francorum*, pp. 5–6, 8–11; Raymond of Aguilers, pp. 39–41; Fulcher of Chartres, pp. 171–6; Albert of Aachen, II.7–9; S. Runciman, 'The first crusaders' journey across the Balkan Peninsula', *Byzantion*, vol. 19 (1949), pp. 207–21.

39. Raymond of Aguilers, p. 39.

40. Albert of Aachen, II.10–15.

41. Fulcher of Chartres, pp. 176–7.

42. Ibid., pp. 175–6.

43. Odo of Deuil, *De profectione ludovici VII in Orientam*, ed. and trans. V. G. Berry (New York, 1948), p. 65.

44. Albert of Aachen, II.10–15; Anna Comnena, vol. 2, pp. 220–6.

45. Anna Comnena, vol. 2, p. 226.

46. Albert of Aachen, II.16.

47. Anna Comnena, vol. 2, p. 226; Lilie, *Byzantium and the Crusader States*, pp. 8–28; France, *Victory in the East*, pp. 110–21; J. H. Pryor, 'The oaths of the leaders of the First Crusade to emperor Alexius I Comnenus: fealty, homage, *pistis*, *douleia*', *Parergon*, vol. 2 (1984), pp. 111–41.

48. Anna Comnena, vol. 2, pp. 230–4; *Gesta Francorum*, p. 12; Albert of Aachen, II.18. Regarding the debate over the terms agreed between Bohemond and Alexius see: A. C. Krey, 'A neglected passage in the *Gesta* and its bearing on the literature of the First Crusade', *The Crusades and Other Historical Essays Presented to Dana C. Munro by His Former Students*, pp. 57–78; J. Shepard, 'When Greek meets Greek: Alexius Comnenus and Bohemond in 1097–98', *Byzantine and Modern Greek Studies*, vol. 12 (1988), pp. 185–277.

49. Anna Comnena, vol. 2, p. 234; Raymond of Aguilers, pp. 41–2; Fulcher of Chartres, pp. 177–8; *Gesta Francorum*, p. 13; Albert of Aachen, II.19–20. On the debate surrounding Raymond's relationship with Alexius see: Lilie, *Byzantium and the Crusader States*, pp. 25–6; France, *Victory in the East*, pp. 120–1; J. H. and L. L. Hill, 'The convention of

Alexius Comnenus and Raymond of St. Gilles', *American Historical Review*, vol. 58 (1952–53), pp. 322–7; J. H. Hill, 'Raymond of St Gilles in Urban's plan of Greek and Latin friendship', *Speculum*, vol. 26 (1951), pp. 265–76.

50. Albert of Aachen, II.16; Anna Comnena, vol. 2, p. 233; Raymond of Aguilers, p. 42; Fulcher of Chartres, p. 179.

51. Anna Comnena, vol. 2, pp. 230, 234.

52. C. Hillenbrand, *The Crusades: Islamic Perspectives* (Edinburgh, 1999), pp. 33–50; C. Hillenbrand, 'The First Crusade: The Muslim perspective', *The First Crusade: Origins and Impact*, ed. J. P. Phillips (Manchester, 1997), pp. 130–41; C. Cahen, *Introduction à l'histoire du monde musulman médiévale*, Initiation à l'Islam, vol. 1 (Paris, 1982); C. Cahen, *Orient et Occident aux temps des croisades* (Paris, 1983); P. M. Holt, *The Age of the Crusades: The Near East from the 11th Century to 1517* (London, 1986), pp. 1–22 ; F. Gabrieli, 'The Arabic historiography of the crusades', *Historians of the Middle East*, ed. B. Lewis and P. M. Holt (London, 1962), pp. 98–107.

53. Hillenbrand, *The Crusades: Islamic Perspectives*, pp. 38–40, 439–67, 511–33; France, *Victory in the East*, pp. 145–9; C. Cahen, 'The historiography of the Seljuqid period', *Historians of the Middle East*, pp. 59–78; C. Cahen, 'The Turkish invasion: The Selchükids', *A History of the Crusades*, ed. K. M. Setton, vol. 1, 2nd edition (Madison, 1969), pp. 135–76.

54. Hillenbrand, *The Crusades: Islamic Perspectives*, pp. 89–108; B. Z. Kedar, 'Croisade et jihad vus par l'ennemi: une étude des perceptions mutuelles des motivations', *Autour de la Première Croisade*, ed. M. Balard (Paris, 1996), pp. 345–58.

CHAPTER 4: THE FIRST STORM OF WAR

1. *Gesta Francorum*, p. 13; Fulcher of Chartres, pp. 178–83; Raymond of Aguilers, pp. 42–3; Anna Comnena, vol. 3, p. 7.

2. *Gesta Francorum*, pp. 13–14; Albert of Aachen, II.37.

3. *Gesta Francorum*, p. 14. It is possible that during this interim period attempts were made to negotiate the surrender of Nicaea. Anna Comnena, vol. 3, p. 7, suggests that the crusader forces were divided because of the needs of supply, but even if this were the case the advance group was still exposed.

4. Anna Comnena, vol. 3, pp. 10–11.

5. Ibid., pp. 7–12; Fulcher of Chartres, pp. 185–7; Albert of Aachen, II.23.

6. Raymond of Aguilers, pp. 42–3; Albert of Aachen, II.21; Hagenmeyer, *Kreuzzugssbriefe*, p. 139.

7. On siege dispositions see: *Gesta Francorum*, p. 15–16; Albert of Aachen, II.22–4.

8. Quotation from John Zonoras' *Epitome*, taken from an unpublished translation by R. Macrides and P. Magdalino; Fulcher of Chartres, p. 183.

9. Fulcher of Chartres, pp. 202–3; Murray, 'Questions of nationality in the First Crusade', pp. 61–73.

10. Albert of Aachen, II.32, II.43.

11. *Gesta Francorum*, p. 14; Raymond of Aguilers, p. 43; Albert of Aachen, II.22–24.

12. Anna Comnena, vol. 3, pp. 7–8.

13. Albert of Aachen, II.25–6.

14. *Gesta Francorum*, pp. 14–15; Raymond of Aguilers, p. 43; Hagenmeyer, *Kreuzzugssbriefe*, p. 144; Albert of Aachen, II.26–28; Anna Comnena, vol. 3, pp. 8–9.

15. Anna Comnena, vol. 3, p. 9; *Gesta Francorum*, p. 15; Hagenmeyer, *Kreuzzugssbriefe*, p. 144; Albert of Aachen, II.27–8; Fulcher of Chartres, p. 187; Albert of Aachen, II.34.

16. Fulcher of Chartres, pp. 185–7; Raymond of Aguilers, p. 43; Albert of Aachen, II.29; Hagenmeyer, *Kreuzzugssbriefe*, p. 139.

17. Albert of Aachen, II.30.

18. *Gesta Francorum*, p. 15; Albert of Aachen, II.31.

19. Raymond of Aguilers, pp. 43–4; Albert of Aachen, II.33; *Gesta Francorum*, pp. 15–16.

20. *Gesta Francorum*, pp. 16–17; Raymond of Aguilers, p. 44; Fulcher of Chartres, pp. 187–9; Albert of Aachen, II.32; Anna Comnena, vol. 3, pp. 11–12; Hagenmeyer, *Kreuzzugssbriefe*, pp. 139–40, 144–5.

21. *Gesta Francorum*, pp. 16–18; Raymond of Aguilers, p. 44; Fulcher of Chartres, pp. 188–9; Hagenmeyer, *Kreuzzugssbriefe*, pp. 144–5; Albert of Aachen, II.37. Anna Comnena, vol. 3, pp. 12–16, suggests that Alexius sought to trick the Franks by making it appear that Nicaea fell in battle to Byzantine troops rather than surrendered.

22. Albert of Aachen, II.37; *Gesta Francorum*, p. 17. On the concept of martyrdom in the context of the First Crusade see: H. E. J. Cowdrey, 'Martyrdom and the First Crusade', *Crusade and Settlement*, ed. P. W.

Edbury (Cardiff, 1985), pp. 46–56; J. Flori, 'Mort et martyre des guerriers vers 1100. L'exemple de la Première Croisade', *Cahiers de civilisation médiévale*, vol. 34 (1991), pp. 121–39; C. Morris, 'Martyrs of the Field of Battle before and during the First Crusade', *Studies in Church History*, vol. 30 (1993), pp. 93–104; J. S. C. Riley-Smith, 'Death on the First Crusade', *The End of Strife*, ed. D. Loades (Edinburgh, 1984), pp. 14–31.

23. Hagenmeyer, *Kreuzzugssbriefe*, pp. 139–40, 144–5; France, *Victory in the East*, pp. 165–6.

24. Fulcher of Chartres, pp. 189–90; Anna Comnena, vol. 3, pp. 16–17.

25. *Gesta Francorum*, p. 18; Albert of Aachen, II.38; Hagenmeyer, *Kreuzzugssbriefe*, p. 145.

26. Fulcher of Chartres, pp. 189–91.

27. Ibid., pp. 192–3; *Gesta Francorum*, p. 20. Stephen of Blois noted 260,000 Muslim troops (Hagenmeyer, *Kreuzzugssbriefe*, p. 145). France, *Victory in the East*, pp. 170–85, makes an elaborate, if not always entirely convincing, attempt to locate the battlefield and describes the ensuing conflict.

28. *Gesta Francorum*, pp. 18–20; Fulcher of Chartres, pp. 192–7; Albert of Aachen, II.39–40.

29. Fulcher of Chartres, pp. 194–6; Albert of Aachen, II.39.

30. *Gesta Francorum*, pp. 19–21; Fulcher of Chartres, pp. 197–9; Albert of Aachen, II.41–3; Raymond of Aguilers, pp. 45–6; Hagenmeyer, *Kreuzzugssbriefe*, p. 145; Anna Comnena, vol. 3, pp. 18–19.

31. Ibn al-Qalanisi, *The Damascus Chronicle of the Crusades, Extracted and Translated from the Chronicle of Ibn al-Qalanisi*, trans. H. A. R. Gibb (London, 1932), pp. 41–2; *Gesta Francorum*, p. 21–3; Albert of Aachen, II.40, II.43.

32. *Gesta Francorum*, p. 23.

33. Albert of Aachen, III.1–2. Albert's text has here been abridged.

34. Fulcher of Chartres, p. 88; Riley-Smith, *The First Crusade and the Idea of Crusading*, pp. 64–5.

35. *Gesta Francorum*, p. 22; Albert of Aachen, III.3.

36. T. S. R. Boase, 'The history of the kingdom', *The Cilician Kingdom of Armenia*, ed. T. S. R. Boase (Edinburgh and London, 1978), pp. 1–33; P. Charanis, *The Armenians in the Byzantine Empire* (Lisbon, 1963); J. H. Forse, 'Armenians and the First Crusade', *Journal of Medieval History*, vol. 17 (1991), pp. 13–22; G. Dédéyan, 'Les princes arméniennes de l'Euphratese et l'empire byzantin (fin Xie – milieu XIIe s.)', *L'Arménie et Byzance: Histoire et culture* (Paris, 1996), pp. 79–88.

37. T. S. Asbridge, *The Creation of the Principality of Antioch, 1098–1130* (Woodbridge, 2000), pp. 16–19; France, *Victory in the East*, pp. 190–6.

38. Asbridge, *The Creation of the Principality of Antioch*, pp. 18–23.

39. *Gesta Francorum*, pp. 24–5; Fulcher of Chartres, pp. 206–208; Albert of Aachen, III.3–13; Ralph of Caen, pp. 632–7.

40. Ralph of Caen, pp. 634–9; Asbridge, *The Creation of the Principality of Antioch*, pp. 21–2.

41. Asbridge, *The Creation of the Principality of Antioch*, pp. 22–3.

42. *Gesta Francorum*, pp. 25–7; Asbridge, *The Creation of the Principality of Antioch*, pp. 23–4.

43. *Gesta Francorum*, p. 27.

44. Ibid.; Albert of Aachen, III.27–8.

45. Anselm of Ribemont's first letter to Manasses II archbishop of Rheims makes it clear that the crusader ranks were being thinned out by battle and illness (Hagenmeyer, *Kreuzzugssbriefe*, p. 145).

46. Albert of Aachen, III.17, III.27; Fulcher of Chartres, pp. 205–9; Matthew of Edessa, *Armenia and the Crusades, Tenth to Twelfth Centuries: The Chronicle of Matthew of Edessa*, trans. A. E. Dostourian (Lanham, 1993), p. 168.

47. Albert of Aachen, III.18.

48. Ibid., III.19; Fulcher of Chartres, pp. 208–12; Matthew of Edessa, p. 168.

49. Albert of Aachen, III.20–22; Fulcher of Chartres, pp. 211–14; Matthew of Edessa, pp. 168–9.

50. Albert of Aachen, III.23–4; Matthew of Edessa, pp. 169–70; Fulcher of Chartres, pp. 213–14.

51. Albert of Aachen, III.24–5. On the history of the county of Edessa see: M. Amouroux-Mourad, *Le comté d'Edesse, 1098–1150* (Paris, 1988).

CHAPTER 5: BEFORE THE WALLS OF ANTIOCH

1. On the general history of Antioch see: G. Downey, *A History of Antioch in Syria* (Princeton, 1960).

2. Albert of Aachen, IV.26; C. Cahen, 'The Turkish invasion: The Selchükids', *A History of the Crusades*, ed. K. M. Setton, vol. 1, pp. 135–76; *Introduction à l'histoire du monde musulman médiévale*, Initiation à l'Islam, vol. 1 (Paris, 1982); P. M. Holt, *The Age of the Crusades: The Near East from the 11th Century to 1517* (London, 1986), pp. 9–15; A.-M. Eddé, 'Ridwan, prince d'Alep de 1095 à 1113', *Revue des*

études islamiques, vol. 54 for 1986 (1988), pp. 101–125; Hillenbrand, *The Crusades: Islamic Perspectives*, pp. 47–50.

3. The city of Antioch could also claim special spiritual significance for Christians because, according to tradition, Christ's chief apostle St Peter founded the first Christian church there and acted as its bishop. J. S. C. Riley-Smith, 'The First Crusade and St Peter', *Outremer*, ed. B. Z. Kedar, H. E. Mayer and R. C. Smail (Jerusalem, 1982), pp. 41–63; Asbridge, *Creation of the Principality of Antioch*, p. 211. According to Baldric of Bourgeuil, p. 12, Pope Urban II mentioned Antioch in his sermon at Clermont alluding to the link with St Peter, but this account may have been influenced by hindsight. However, the evidence offered by Fulcher of Chartres, p. 217 and the anonymous author of the *Gesta Francorum*, p. 66 does suggest that the First Crusaders were aware of Antioch's connection with St Peter.

4. Raymond of Aguilers, pp. 46–7; France, *Victory in the East*, pp. 220–2.

5. Asbridge, *Creation of the Principality of Antioch*, pp. 24–7.

6. Hagenmeyer, *Kreuzzugssbriefe*, p. 150; Fulcher of Chartres, p. 217; Albert of Aachen, III.36; Raymond of Aguilers, pp. 47–8; France, *Victory in the East*, pp. 222–4.

7. R. Rogers, *Latin Siege Warfare in the Twelfth Century* (Oxford, 1992), pp. 1–63.

8. Guibert of Nogent, p. 170.

9. *Gesta Francorum*, p. 28; Albert of Aachen, III.38–9; Ralph of Caen, pp. 641–3; France, *Victory in the East*, pp. 224–6.

10. Peter Tudebode, *Historia de Hierosolymitano itinere*, ed. J. H. Hill and L. L. Hill (Paris, 1977), pp. 63–4.

11. Raymond of Aguilers, p. 49.

12. *Gesta Francorum*, p. 29; Raymond of Aguilers, p. 50. Raymond's text has here been abridged.

13. Albert of Aachen, III.40–44; Fulcher of Chartres, pp. 218–19.

14. Raymond of Aguilers, p. 134; Hagenmeyer, *Kreuzzugssbriefe*, pp. 146–9. For further discussion of naval support see: France, *Victory in the East*, pp. 209–20. For a more general discussion of Mediterranean naval activity see: J. H. Pryor, *Geography, Technology and War: Studies in the Maritime History of the Mediterranean, 649–1571* (Cambridge, 1987).

15. Raymond of Aguilers, p. 49; Caffaro di Caschilfellione, *De liberatione civitatum Orientis liber, RHC Occ.* V, pp. 49–50; *Gesta Francorum*, p. 30.

16. Hagenmeyer, *Kreuzzugssbriefe*, pp. 145, 158; *Gesta Francorum*, p. 29; Peter Tudebode, pp. 64–5; Raymond of Aguilers, p. 49.

17. *Gesta Francorum*, p. 29; Fulcher of Chartres, p. 221; Albert of Aachen, III.46.

18. France, *Victory in the East*, pp. 188–96, 206–20.

19. Raymond of Aguilers, p. 48; Hagenmeyer, *Kreuzzugssbriefe*, p. 151; Matthew of Edessa, p. 167; Asbridge, *Creation of the Principality of Antioch*, pp. 27–31.

20. Albert of Aachen, III.50; *Gesta Francorum*, pp. 30–31; Raymond of Aguilers, p. 50; Fulcher of Chartres, pp. 221–4.

21. Albert of Aachen, III.51–2; *Gesta Francorum*, p. 31; Hagenmeyer, *Kreuzzugssbriefe*, p. 158; Ibn al-Qalanisi, p. 43; Kemal ad-Din, *La Chronique d'Alep, RHC Or.* III, p. 580.

22. Raymond of Aguilers, pp. 50–1.

23. *Gesta Francorum*, pp. 32–3.

24. Hagenmeyer, *Kreuzzugssbriefe*, p. 145; Peter Tudebode, p. 68.

25. Hagenmeyer, *Kreuzzugssbriefe*, p. 150; Fulcher of Chartres, pp. 224–6.

26. Fulcher of Chartres, p. 224; *Gesta Francorum*, p. 33; Raymond of Aguilers, p. 54; Albert of Aachen, III.52.

27. Fulcher of Chartres, pp. 222–3; *Gesta Francorum*, p. 34; Raymond of Aguilers, p. 54.

28. Fulcher of Chartres, p. 223; Albert of Aachen, III.57; J. A. Brundage, 'Prostitution, miscegenation and sexual purity in the First Crusade', *Crusade and Settlement*, ed. P. W. Edbury (Cardiff, 1985), pp. 57–65. On St Augustine see: P. Brown, *Augustine of Hippo* (London, 1967).

29. Albert of Aachen, III.53.

30. *Gesta Francorum*, pp. 33–4.

31. Riley-Smith, *The First Crusade and the Idea of Crusading*, p. 51.

32. Raymond of Aguilers, pp. 54–6; *Gesta Francorum*, pp. 34–5; Albert of Aachen, III.38, IV.40. Anna Comnena, vol. 3, p. 20, has Taticius depart in May 1098 after being tricked by Bohemond. On the debate regarding Taticius' departure see: Lilie, *Byzantium and the Crusader States*, pp. 33–7; J. France, 'The departure of Tatikios from the army of the First Crusade', *Bulletin of the Institute of Historical Research*, vol. 44 (1971), pp. 131–47; France, *Victory in the East*, p. 243.

33. Raymond of Aguilers, pp. 53–5.

34. *Gesta Francorum*, p. 35.

35. Hagenmeyer, *Kreuzzugssbriefe*, pp. 146–9.

36. Albert of Aachen, III.55–6.

37. *Gesta Francorum*, p. 35; Raymond of Aguilers, pp. 51, 53, 55, 56; France, *Victory in the East*, pp. 281–2; J. Richard, 'La confrérie de la croisades:

à propos d'un episode de la première croisade', *Etudes de civilisation médiévale (IXe–XIIe siècles): Mélanges offerts à Edmond–René Labande* (Poitiers, 1974), pp. 617–22.

38. Raymond of Aguilers, p. 56.

39. *Gesta Francorum*, pp. 35–8; Raymond of Aguilers, pp. 56–8; Albert of Aachen, III.60–62; Ralph of Caen, p. 647; Hagenmeyer, *Kreuzzugssbriefe*, pp. 150–1, 158; Kemal ad-Din, p. 579. France, *Victory in the East*, pp. 245–51, attempts an extremely precise reconstruction of the battle, but may place too much faith in his exact identification of its site.

40. Raymond of Aguilers, pp. 57–8.

41. *Gesta Francorum*, pp. 37–8, 42; Raymond of Aguilers, p. 58; Hagenmeyer, *Kreuzzugssbriefe*, p. 151. Ibn al-Athir, *Kamel-Altevarykh, RHC Or.* I, p. 193, suggests that the crusaders had earlier sought to negotiate with Duqaq of Damascus. William of Tyre, pp. 267–8, writing in the later twelfth century, looked back on the negotiations with the Fatimids with relative equanimity, but made it clear that this contact ultimately concluded with the military defeat of these Egyptian Muslims.

42. Fulcher of Chartres, pp. 226–7; Hagenmeyer, *Kreuzzugssbriefe*, pp. 158. For views on the death rate see: France, *Victory in the East*, pp. 122–42; Riley-Smith, 'Casualties and the Number of Knights on the First Crusade', *Crusades*, vol. 1 (2002), pp. 13–28.

CHAPTER 6: TIGHTENING THE SCREW

1. Hagenmeyer, *Kreuzzugssbriefe*, pp. 165–6; Raymond of Aguilers, p. 59. On the question of whether Edgar the Aetheling accompanied this fleet see: France, *Victory in the East*, pp. 215–16.

2. Hagenmeyer, *Kreuzzugssbriefe*, pp. 151, 158, 166; *Gesta Francorum*, p. 39; Raymond of Aguilers, p. 59; Albert of Aachen, III.63.

3. *Gesta Francorum*, p. 40.

4. Ibid., p. 41.

5. Hagenmeyer, *Kreuzzugssbriefe*, pp. 151, 158, 166; *Gesta Francorum*, pp. 40–1; Raymond of Aguilers, pp. 59–62; Albert of Aachen, III.63–6. Runciman, *The First Crusade*, p. 227, dedicated only one paragraph to these events. France, *Victory in the East*, pp. 253–4, similarly offers only a brief comment.

6. *Gesta Francorum*, p. 42.

7. Raymond of Aguilers, p. 61; *Gesta Francorum*, p. 42.

8. Raymond of Aguilers, p. 62; *Gesta Francorum*, p. 42; Hagenmeyer, *Kreuzzugssbriefe*, pp. 151–2, 158–9, 166; Albert of Aachen, III.66.

9. This view of Raymond of Toulouse's motivation contrasts with that offered by: Hill, *Raymond IV, Count of Toulouse*, pp. 44–82.

10. Raymond of Aguilers, pp. 62–3; Peter Tudebode, pp. 78–9.

11. Raymond of Aguilers, pp. 63–4; *Gesta Francorum*, pp. 43–4; Peter Tudebode, pp. 81–2; Ralph of Caen, pp. 644–5; France, *Victory in the East*, pp. 229–30.

12. Albert of Aachen, IV.9; Raymond of Aguilers, p. 64.

13. Raymond of Aguilers, p. 117.

14. Peter Tudebode, pp. 79–81.

15. Hagenmeyer, *Kreuzzugssbriefe*, p. 159.

16. Anna Comnena, vol. 3, pp. 20–21; *Gesta Francorum*, p. 44; Raymond of Aguilers, p. 64; Fulcher of Chartres, pp. 230–33; Albert of Aachen, IV.15; Ralph of Caen, pp. 651–3; Hagenmeyer, *Kreuzzugssbriefe*, pp. 159; William of Tyre, pp. 285–7; Matthew of Edessa, p. 170; Ibn al-Qalanisi, p. 45; Kemal ad-Din, p. 580; Ibn al-Athir, p. 192. For an analysis of contemporary source variation see: France, *Victory in the East*, pp. 257–8.

17. *Gesta Francorum*, pp. 44–5.

18. Ibid., p. 45.

19. Albert of Aachen, IV.3.

20. *Gesta Francorum*, pp. 49–56; Hagenmeyer, *Kreuzzugssbriefe*, p. 159.

21. Matthew of Edessa, p. 170; Michael the Syrien, III, p. 184; Ibn al-Qalanisi, pp. 45–6; Kemal ad-Din, pp. 580–3; Ibn al-Athir, p. 194; Hillenbrand, *The Crusades: Islamic Perspectives*, pp. 56–9.

22. Albert of Aachen, IV.13.

23. Ibid., IV.14–15; *Gesta Francorum*, p. 45; Ralph of Caen, p. 654; William of Tyre, pp. 288–9; Anna Comnena, vol. 3, pp. 21–2.

24. Albert of Aachen, IV.10–12; Fulcher of Chartres, pp. 242–3; Matthew of Edessa, p. 170; Runciman, *The First Crusade*, p. 231; Mayer, *The Crusades*, p. 51; J. Richard, *The Crusades, c. 1071– c. 1291*, trans. J. Birrell (Cambridge, 1999), pp. 52–3.

25. *Gesta Francorum*, pp. 45–6; Raymond of Aguilers, pp. 64–5; Hagenmeyer, *Kreuzzugssbriefe*, p. 166.

26. Fulcher of Chartres, p. 228; Raymond of Aguilers, p. 77; *Gesta Francorum*, p. 63; Albert of Aachen, IV.13; Guibert of Nogent, pp. 227–9; Riley-Smith, *The First Crusade and the Idea of Crusading*, p. 74; Brundage, 'An errant crusader: Stephen of Blois', pp. 380–95.

27. *Gesta Francorum*, p. 46; Albert of Aachen, IV.20.

28. *Gesta Francorum*, pp. 46–7; Raymond of Aguilers, pp. 64–5; Ralph of Caen, p. 654; Fulcher of Chartres, pp. 232–3; Albert of Aachen, IV.21.

29. *Gesta Francorum*, pp. 46–7; Raymond of Aguilers, p. 65.

30. Raymond of Aguilers, p. 65; *Gesta Francorum*, p. 47.

31. Albert of Aachen, IV.22–3; *Gesta Francorum*, pp. 47–8; Raymond of Aguilers, p. 65; Fulcher of Chartres, pp. 233–5. Ibn al-Qalanisi, p. 44, remarked that the number of Antiochene's 'killed, taken prisoner and enslaved . . . is beyond computation'.

32. *Gesta Francorum*, pp. 47–8; Raymond of Aguilers, pp. 65–6; Hagenmeyer, *Kreuzzugssbriefe*, pp. 159, 166; Fulcher of Chartres, pp. 232–5; Albert of Aachen, IV.24–6; Ibn al-Qalanisi, p. 44.

33. Fulcher of Chartres, pp. 234–5; Raymond of Aguilers, p. 65; Albert of Aachen, IV.25.

34. Ralph of Caen, pp. 655–60.

35. H. Hagenmeyer, *Chronologie de le Première Croisade*, 1094–1100 (Paris, 1902), pp. 153–4.

CHAPTER 7: TO THE EDGE OF ANNIHILATION

1. Albert of Aachen, IV.27–8; Raymond of Aguilers, pp. 66–7; Hagenmeyer, *Kreuzzugssbriefe*, p. 159.

2. Albert of Aachen, IV.27; Matthew of Edessa, p. 171; France, *Victory in the East*, pp. 260–1, 269.

3. *Gesta Francorum*, pp. 50–1; Raymond of Aguilers, pp. 66–7; Albert of Aachen, IV.29.

4. Raymond of Aguilers, p. 67; Albert of Aachen, IV.33.

5. *Gesta Francorum*, pp. 50–1; Raymond of Aguilers, pp. 66–7; Albert of Aachen, IV.29–32; Kemal ad-Din, pp. 582–3.

6. *Gesta Francorum*, p. 56; Raymond of Aguilers, pp. 67–8; Peter Tudebode, pp. 96–7.

7. *Gesta Francorum*, pp. 56–7, 58–9, 61–2; Raymond of Aguilers, pp. 67–8, 74; Peter Tudebode, p. 97; Fulcher of Chartres, pp. 244–7, 262–3.

8. Albert of Aachen, IV.30–31; Peter Tudebode, p. 97; *Gesta Francorum*, pp. 61–2. According to Ralph of Caen, pp. 660–1, it was Robert of Flanders who set this fire. For an alternative view of this strange episode

of arson within Antioch see: Asbridge, *Creation of the Principality of Antioch*, p. 36.

9. Raymond of Aguilers, pp. 72–5; *Gesta Francorum*, pp. 57–8, 62; Fulcher of Chartres, pp. 242–6.

10. *Gesta Francorum*, p. 62; Fulcher of Chartres, pp. 262–3.

11. Albert of Aachen, IV. 27, 30, 32, 35; *Gesta Francorum*, pp. 61–2. The defence of this fortification seems to have been organised by Bohemond, with Rainbold Creton, Ivo of Chartres, Ralph Fontenais, Everard of Le Puiset and Peter son of Gisle among those manning the ramparts.

12. *Gesta Francorum*, pp. 62–3.

13. Albert of Aachen, IV.34; Fulcher of Chartres, pp. 247, 262–3; Raymond of Aguilers, pp. 76–7.

14. *Gesta Francorum*, pp. 62–3; Fulcher of Chartres, pp. 262–3; Raymond of Aguilers, pp. 76–7.

15. Raymond of Aguilers, pp. 68–72; *Gesta Francorum*, pp. 59–60; R. Rogers, 'Peter Bartholomew and the role of "the poor" in the First Crusade', *Warriors and Churchmen in the High Middle Ages: Essays Presented to Karl Leyser*, ed. T. Reuter (London, 1992), pp. 109–22.

16. Riley-Smith, *The First Crusade and the Idea of Crusading*, pp. 93–5. For further discussion of the role of relics in medieval society see: P. Geary, *Furta Sacra: Thefts of Relics in the Central Middle Ages* (Princeton, 1990).

17. Raymond of Aguilers, pp. 72, 74–5.

18. *Gesta Francorum*, p. 60; Riley-Smith, *The First Crusade and the Idea of Crusading*, pp. 95–6.

19. Raymond of Aguilers, p. 75; *Gesta Francorum*, p. 65; Peter Tudebode, pp. 107–8; Hagenmeyer, *Kreuzzugssbriefe*, pp. 159–60, 166–7; Fulcher of Chartres, pp. 235–8, 263; Albert of Aachen, IV.43; Matthew of Edessa, p. 171. Ralph of Caen, p. 678, suggests that a number of princes were immediately dubious about the lance, but his testimony is likely to have been coloured by hindsight and his anti-Provençal tendencies. Anna Comnena, vol. 3, p. 30, records the discovery of the relic, which she describes as a 'nail' but mistakes Peter Bartholomew for Peter the Hermit. Ibn al-Athir, p. 195, maintains that Peter Bartholomew buried the lance himself before duping the crusaders.

20. Mayer, *The Crusades*, p. 52. A similar line is taken by the following: R. Grousset, *Histoire des Croisades*, vol. 1 (Paris, 1934), p. 103; Riley-Smith, *The First Crusade and the Idea of Crusading*, p. 95; France, *Victory in*

the East, p. 279. See also: C. Morris, 'Policy and vision: The case of the Holy Lance found at Antioch', *War and Government in the Middle Ages: Essays in Honour of J. O. Prestwich*, ed. J. Gillingham and J. C. Holt (Woodbridge, 1984), pp. 33–45; S. Runciman, 'The Holy Lance found at Antioch', *Annalecta Bollandiana*, vol. 68 (1950), pp. 197–205.

21. Fulcher of Chartres, p. 263.
22. *Gesta Francorum*, pp. 65–6.
23. Raymond of Aguilers, pp. 75–8; Riley-Smith, *The First Crusade and the Idea of Crusading*, pp. 95–6.
24. Anna Comnena, vol. 3, pp. 27–9; *Gesta Francorum*, pp. 63–5; Ralph of Caen, pp. 658–9; Albert of Aachen, IV.37, IV.40–1; Lilie, *Byzantium and the Crusader States*, pp. 37–9.
25. Albert of Aachen, IV.41.
26. *Gesta Francorum*, pp. 66–7; Peter Tudebode, pp. 108–9; Raymond of Aguilers, p. 79; Hagenmeyer, *Kreuzzugssbriefe*, pp. 159–60.
27. Fulcher of Chartres, pp. 247–9; Albert of Aachen, IV.44–6; Ralph of Caen, pp. 663–5.
28. Matthew of Edessa, p. 171; Ibn al-Athir, p. 194.
29. Safe passage to Edessa, St Simeon or Cilicia might have been options for the crusaders, assuming they were prepared to give up Antioch, the city they believed to be the patrimony of St Peter. See: France, *Victory in the East*, p. 280, for an example of the refutation of the evidence presented by Matthew of Edessa.
30. Albert of Aachen, IV.46.
31. Raymond of Aguilers, p. 77; *Gesta Francorum*, pp. 67–8; France, *Victory in the East*, p. 279.
32. France, *Victory in the East*, pp. 280–96, provides a detailed and largely convincing analysis of the battle.
33. Albert of Aachen, IV.54.
34. Albert of Aachen, IV.55; Fulcher of Chartres, pp. 247–9, 252.
35. Ibn al-Athir, pp. 194–5.
36. *Gesta Francorum*, pp. 68; Peter Tudebode, pp. 110–11; Raymond of Aguilers, pp. 78–9; Fulcher of Chartres, pp. 252–5, 263; Albert of Aachen, IV.47–8; Ralph of Caen, pp. 665–6.
37. Raymond of Aguilers, pp. 80–1; Fulcher of Chartres, p. 263; *Gesta Francorum*, pp. 68–9.
38. Ibn al-Athir, p. 195.
39. Fulcher of Chartres, p. 263.
40. Ibn al-Qalanisi, p. 46; *Gesta Francorum*, pp. 69–70; Raymond of

Aguilers, pp. 80–3; Hagenmeyer, *Kreuzzugssbriefe*, pp. 160, 167; Fulcher of Chartres, pp. 255–7, 263; Albert of Aachen, IV.49–53; Ralph of Caen, pp. 666–71; Matthew of Edessa, pp. 171–2; Ibn al-Athir, pp. 195–6; Kemal ad-Din, pp. 582–3.

41. *Gesta Francorum*, p. 70; Fulcher of Chartres, pp. 256–7.
42. Raymond of Aguilers, p. 82; *Gesta Francorum*, p. 69.
43. Raymond of Aguilers, pp. 81–2; Albert of Aachen, IV.53.

CHAPTER 8: DESCENT INTO DISCORD

1. *Gesta Francorum*, p. 72; Raymond of Aguilers, p. 84. Fulcher of Chartres, pp. 265–6, seems to suggest that the delay was deliberately planned to allow the crusaders to rest and recuperate.
2. Asbridge, *Creation of the Principality of Antioch*, pp. 34–5.
3. *Gesta Francorum*, pp. 70–1; Fulcher of Chartres, p. 263; Raymond of Aguilers, p. 83. Ralph of Caen, pp. 675, 678, seems to be in error here when he suggests that the citadel fell to Raymond of Toulouse.
4. Asbridge, *Creation of the Principality of Antioch*, pp. 35–7.
5. Lilie, *Byzantium and the Crusader States*, pp. 39–41. For alternative readings of these events see: Hill, *Raymond IV, Count of Toulouse*, pp. 85–109; J. France, 'The crisis of the First Crusade from the defeat of Kerbogha to the departure from Arqa', *Byzantion*, vol. 40 (1970), pp. 276–308.
6. *Gesta Francorum*, p. 72; Raymond of Aguilers, pp. 83–4; Albert of Aachen, V.2–3.
7. Albert of Aachen, V.1; Riley-Smith, *The First Crusade and the Idea of Crusading*, pp. 93–4.
8. Albert of Aachen, V.1; William of Tyre, pp. 339–40; Asbridge, *Creation of the Principality of Antioch*, p. 195; B. Hamilton, *The Latin Church in the Crusader States: The Secular Church* (London, 1980), pp. 7–9.
9. *Gesta Francorum*, pp. 72–3; Albert of Aachen, V.15; Riley-Smith, *The First Crusade and the Idea of Crusading*, pp. 77–9.
10. *Gesta Francorum*, pp. 73–4; Kemal ad-Din, p. 584; Riley-Smith, *The First Crusade and the Idea of Crusading*, pp. 108–11.
11. *Gesta Francorum*, pp. 73–4.
12. Albert of Aachen, V.4.
13. Ibid.; *Gesta Francorum*, p. 74; Raymond of Aguilers, p. 84; Fulcher of Chartres, pp. 258, 263–4.

14. For differing views on Adhémar's significance see: Brundage, 'Adhémar of Le Puy: The bishop and his critics', pp. 201–12; Hill, 'Contemporary accounts and the later reputation of Adhémar, bishop of Le Puy', pp. 30–8.

15. Asbridge, *Creation of the Principality of Antioch*, pp. 129–30.

16. Raymond of Aguilers, p. 84; Asbridge, *Creation of the Principality of Antioch*, p. 28.

17. Albert of Aachen, IV.9; V.13.

18. Albert of Aachen, V.7–12; Raymond of Aguilers, pp. 88–9; Kemal ad-Din, p. 586; Asbridge, *Creation of the Principality of Antioch*, pp. 30–1.

19. Riley-Smith, *The First Crusade and the Idea of Crusading*, p. 61; K. B. Wolf, 'Crusade and narrative: Bohemond and the *Gesta Francorum*', *Journal of Medieval History*, vol. 17 (1991), pp. 207–16.

20. Raymond of Aguilers, pp. 75, 85–7; Riley-Smith, *The First Crusade and the Idea of Crusading*, p. 97.

21. Riley-Smith, *The First Crusaders*, p. 154.

22. Raymond of Aguilers, pp. 84–6.

23. Ralph of Caen, p. 679.

24. Albert of Aachen, V.3.

25. Fulcher of Chartres, pp. 258–64; Hagenmeyer, *Kreuzzugssbriefe*, pp. 161–5.

26. Fulcher of Chartres, p. 264.

27. Raymond of Aguilers, pp. 92–4; *Gesta Francorum*, pp. 75–6. Peter Tudebode, p. 118, actually suggests that Bohemond was unable to attend the meeting at Antioch on 1 November because ill-health detained him in Cilicia.

28. Raymond of Aguilers, pp. 93–4.

29. T. S. Asbridge, 'The principality of Antioch and the Jabal as-Summaq', *The First Crusade: Origins and Impact*, ed. J. P. Phillips (Manchester, 1997), pp. 142–52; Asbridge, *Creation of the Principality of Antioch*, pp. 37–42.

30. Raymond of Aguilers, pp. 91–2, 104–5; *Gesta Francorum*, pp. 74–5; Albert of Aachen, V.26; Fulcher of Chartres, p. 266.

31. Raymond of Aguilers, pp. 94–102; *Gesta Francorum*, pp. 77–80; Albert of Aachen, V.26, V.29–30; Ralph of Caen, pp. 674–5; Fulcher of Chartres, pp. 266–7; Ibn al-Qalanisi, pp. 46–7; Kemal ad-Din, p. 587; Ibn al-Athir, pp. 196. For outlines of the siege of Marrat an-Numan see: Asbridge, *Creation of the Principality of Antioch*, pp. 39–41; France, *Victory in the East*, pp. 311–15; Rogers, *Latin Siege Warfare in the Twelfth Century*, pp. 39–44.

32. Raymond of Aguilers, p. 94.

33. *Gesta Francorum*, p. 78; Raymond of Aguilers, pp. 94–8. Greek Fire was an incendiary weapon based around naptha developed, not surprisingly, by the Greeks. Its key properties were sticky adhesiveness and a resistance to being extinguished by water.

34. *Gesta Francorum*, pp. 78–9; Raymond of Aguilers, pp. 97–8.

35. *Gesta Francorum*, p. 79; Raymond of Aguilers, p. 98.

36. *Gesta Francorum*, pp. 79–80.

37. Ibid.

38. Ibn al-Athir, p. 196; Raymond of Aguilers, p. 98.

39. Raymond of Aguilers, pp. 98–9.

CHAPTER 9: THE FALTERING PATH

1. Raymond of Aguilers, p. 99; *Gesta Francorum*, pp. 80–1.

2. Raymond of Aguilers, pp. 99–100; *Gesta Francorum*, pp. 80–1; Ibn al-Qalanisi, p. 47.

3. Raymond of Aguilers, p. 101; Fulcher of Chartres, pp. 266–7; *Gesta Francorum*, p. 80. Peter Tudebode, pp. 124–5, suggests that the princes were worried that this type of atrocity might take place after the sack of Marrat and thus ordered the bodies of the dead Muslims to be dragged out of the city. For the suggestion that the incidence of cannibalism was linked to an organised group of 'poor' crusaders known as the *Tafurs* see: A. M. Sumberg, 'The "Tafurs" and the First Crusade', *Mediaeval Studies*, vol. 21 (1959), pp. 224–46. See also: M. Rouche, 'Cannibalisme sacré chez les croisés populaires', *La Religion populaire: Aspects du Christianisme populaire à travers l'histoire*, ed. Y.-M. Hillaire (Lille, 1981), pp. 29–41. It is worth noting that one crusader 'crime' at Marrat – the dismemberment of corpses in search of coins – mirrored closely the atrocities that Urban supposedly accused Muslims of committing against Christian pilgrims in Robert the Monk's version of the pope's speech at Clermont.

4. Raymond of Aguilers, pp. 100–1.

5. Ibid., pp. 101–2; *Gesta Francorum*, p. 81; Fulcher of Chartres, p. 268.

6. Raymond of Aguilers, p. 102; *Gesta Francorum*, p. 81. Hagenmeyer, *Kreuzzugssbriefe*, p. 150, indicates, for example, that Stephen of Blois seems to have been capable of distinguishing between different Islamic groups. In September 1099, however, Godfrey of Bouillon and

Raymond of Toulouse did, in the letter they authored with Daimbert of Pisa to Pope Paschal II (Hagenmeyer, *Kreuzzugssbriefe*, p. 170), seek to justify these dealings with Muslims, stating that they had been necessary 'because our army was not large, and it was the unanimous wish to hasten to Jerusalem, we accepted their pledges and made them tributaries'. For further discussion of the crusaders' relations with the Islamic powers of the Levant see: M. A. Köhler, *Allianzen und Verträge zwischen frankischen und islamischen Herrschern in Vorderren Orient* (Berlin, 1991), pp. 1–72.

7. Raymond of Aguilers, pp. 102–4; *Gesta Francorum*, pp. 81–2.

8. Raymond of Aguilers, p. 105.

9. Ibid., pp. 105–6; *Gesta Francorum*, pp. 82–3; Ibn al-Athir, p. 197. The classic study of Krak des Chevaliers was made by P. Deschamps, 'Le Crac des Chevaliers', *Les Château des Croisés en Terre Sainte*, vol. 1 (Paris, 1934).

10. Raymond of Aguilers, p. 107.

11. *Gesta Francorum*, p. 83.

12. Ibid., pp. 83–5; Raymond of Aguilers, p. 108; Albert of Aachen, V.31.

13. Raymond of Aguilers, pp. 107–9; *Gesta Francorum*, p. 85; Peter Tudebode, pp. 131–2; Fulcher of Chartres, p. 270; Albert of Aachen, V.31; Ibn al-Athir, pp. 196–7.

14. Raymond of Aguilers, pp. 109–10; *Historia Belli Sacri, RHC Occ.* III , pp. 181, 189–90, 212–15.

15. Asbridge, *Creation of the Principality of Antioch*, p. 42; *Gesta Francorum*, p. 84; Albert of Aachen, V.33.

16. *Gesta Francorum*, p. 84; Raymond of Aguilers, pp. 110–11; Peter Tudebode, pp. 129–31.

17. Albert of Aachen, V.33–4.

18. Raymond of Aguilers, pp. 111–12. Raymond's text has here been abridged.

19. Raymond of Aguilers, pp. 112, 124–5. For further comparison between the use of tribute systems in Iberia and the Levant see: T. S. Asbridge, 'The "crusader" community at Antioch: The impact of interaction with Byzantium and Islam', *Transactions of the Royal Historical Society*, 6th series, vol. 9 (1999), pp. 305–25.

20. Raymond of Aguilers, pp. 112–20.

21. On the medieval ordeal see: R. Bartlett, *Trial by Fire and Water: The Medieval Judicial Ordeal* (Oxford, 1986).

22. Raymond of Aguilers, pp. 120–4, 128–9.

23. Fulcher of Chartres, pp. 238–41; Albert of Aachen, V.13; Ralph of Caen, p. 682.

24. Raymond of Aguilers, pp. 125–7.

25. Albert of Aachen, V.34–5; Raymond of Aguilers, pp. 112, 127–30.

26. *Gesta Francorum*, pp. 85–6; Albert of Aachen, V.36–8. Raymond of Aguilers, p. 130, suggests that Raymond of Toulouse even tried to promote the investment of Tripoli itself.

CHAPTER 10: THE HOLY CITY

1. *Gesta Francorum*, p. 86; Albert of Aachen, V.38–9; Fulcher of Chartres, pp. 270–4.

2. Albert of Aachen, V.40–2; *Gesta Francorum*, pp. 86–7. On the question of the Fatimid reaction and military organistion see: France, *Victory in the East*, pp. 357–60; Y. Lev, 'Regime, army and society in medieval Egypt, 9th–12th centuries', *War and Society in the Eastern Mediterranean, 7th–15th Centuries*, pp. 115–52.

3. *Gesta Francorum*, p. 87; Raymond of Aguilers, p. 136; Fulcher of Chartres, pp. 274–8; Albert of Aachen, V.43; Hamilton, *The Latin Church in the Crusader States*, pp. 11–12; J. S. C. Riley-Smith, 'The Latin clergy and the settlement of Palestine and Syria, 1098–1100', *Catholic Historical Review*, vol. 74 (1988), pp. 539–57.

4. Fulcher of Chartres, pp. 278–80; Albert of Aachen, V.44.

5. *Gesta Francorum*, p. 87; Fulcher of Chartres, pp. 280–1; Raymond of Aguilers, p. 137; Albert of Aachen, V.45; Riley-Smith, *The First Crusade and the Idea of Crusading*, pp. 118–19; C. Auffarth, 'Himmlisches und irdisches Jerusalem. Ein religionswissenschaftlicher Versuch zur Kreuzzugeschatologie', *Zeitschrift für Religionswissenschaft*, vol. 1.1 (1993), pp. 25–49, vol. 1.2 (1993), pp. 91–118.

6. Raymond of Aguilers, pp. 136–7 suggests that the crusaders did debate the best strategy during their advance on Jerusalem. On Jerusalem see: Fulcher of Chartres, pp. 281–92; A. J. Boas, *Jerusalem in the Time of the Crusades* (London, 2001); J. Prawer, 'The Jerusalem the crusaders captured: A contribution to the medieval topography of the city', *Crusade and Settlement*, ed. P. W. Edbury (Cardiff, 1985), pp. 1–16; J. Osborne, 'A tale of two cities: Sacred geography in Christian Jerusalem', *Queen's Quarterly*, vol. 103 (1996), pp. 741–50; France, *Victory in the East*, pp. 333–5, 337–43.

7. France, *Victory in the East*, pp. 334–5.

8. Ralph of Caen, pp. 684–5.

9. *Gesta Francorum*, p. 87; Raymond of Aguilers, pp. 137–8; Albert of Aachen, V.46; Ralph of Caen, p. 687. France, *Victory in the East*, pp. 330–56, outlines the course of the siege.

10. *Gesta Francorum*, p. 88; Raymond of Aguilers, p. 139; Fulcher of Chartres, pp. 293–4; Albert of Aachen, VI.1; Ralph of Caen, pp. 688–90.

11. Albert of Aachen, VI.2; Fulcher of Chartres, p. 294.

12. Raymond of Aguilers, pp. 139–41; *Gesta Francorum*, pp. 88–9; Albert of Aachen, VI.6; Fulcher of Chartres, pp. 294–5.

13. *Gesta Francorum*, pp. 88–9; Raymond of Aguilers, pp. 141–2; Albert of Aachen, VI.4.

14. Albert of Aachen, VI.2; Raymond of Aguilers, pp. 145–6.

15. Raymond of Aguilers, p. 143.

16. Albert of Aachen, VI.8.

17. Raymond of Aguilers, pp. 145–7.

18. Albert of Aachen, VI.3, VI.10; *Gesta Francorum*, p. 91.

19. Albert of Aachen, VI.9, VI.15.

20. Ibid., VI.5, VI.8, VI.14.

21. Raymond of Aguilers, pp. 144–5.

22. *Gesta Francorum*, p. 90; Hagenmeyer, *Kreuzzugssbriefe*, pp. 170–71; Albert of Aachen, VI.8.

23. Raymond of Aguilers, pp. 146–7; *Gesta Francorum*, p. 90; Fulcher of Chartres, pp. 295–6.

24. Albert of Aachen, VI.9–10; Raymond of Aguilers, pp. 147–8; Fulcher of Chartres, p. 296.

25. Albert of Aachen, VI.10–11.

26. Raymond of Aguilers, p. 148.

27. Ibid., pp. 148–9; Fulcher of Chartres, pp. 296–7.

28. Raymond of Aguilers, pp. 148–9; *Gesta Francorum*, p. 91; Albert of Aachen, VI.12, VI.15; Ibn al-Athir, p. 198.

29. Albert of Aachen, VI.12, VI.15–16; Fulcher of Chartres, p. 296.

30. Albert of Aachen, VI.16–17.

31. Ibid., VI.17–18.

32. *Gesta Francorum*, pp. 90–1; Raymond of Aguilers, pp. 149–50; Fulcher of Chartres, pp. 297–9; Albert of Aachen, VI.19.

33. Raymond of Aguilers, p. 150; Fulcher of Chartres, pp. 299–300; Albert of Aachen, VI.20.

34. Raymond of Aguilers, p. 150.

35. *Gesta Francorum*, p. 91; Albert of Aachen, VI. 21–3; Hagenmeyer, *Kreuzzugssbriefe*, p. 171. Ibn al-Athir, p. 197, numbered the dead of Jerusalem at 70,000. Ibn al-Qalanisi, p. 48, indicates that a large proportion of Jerusalem's Jewish population were also slaughtered during the sack. France, *Victory in the East*, pp. 355–6, suggests that most of Jerusalem's population was massacred in cold blood three days after the city fell. I am most grateful to Professor B. Z. Kedar for allowing me to see a copy of his forthcoming article 'The Jerusalem massacre of July 1099 in the western historiography of the crusades' in advance of its publication in *Crusades*, vol. 3 (2004). His work provides an excellent overview of all the evidence for this episode and offers a useful summary of the material contained in the Geniza texts. These contemporary letters written by Jews living in the eastern Mediterranean make it clear that some Muslims and Jews did survive the sack of Jerusalem. Kedar also notes that the contemporary Arabic writer Ibn al'Arabi estimated the number of Muslim dead at Jerusalem at only 3,000, still a significant figure but far less than that offered by other Islamic sources.

36. Albert of Aachen, VI.20; *Gesta Francorum*, p. 91; Raymond of Aguilers, p. 151; Fulcher of Chartres, pp. 300–1; Ibn al-Athir, p. 198.

37. Fulcher of Chartres, pp. 300–4; *Gesta Francorum*, pp. 91–2; Albert of Aachen, VI.23; Ibn al-Athir, p. 199.

38. Fulcher of Chartres, pp. 301–2.

39. *Gesta Francorum*, p. 92; Peter Tudebode, p. 141; Raymond of Aguilers, p. 151; Fulcher of Chartres, pp. 304–5.

CHAPTER 11: AFTERMATH

1. *Gesta Francorum*, p. 92; Albert of Aachen, VI.20; Fulcher of Chartres, p. 304; Ibn al-Athir, p. 198.

2. *Gesta Francorum*, pp. 92–3; Raymond of Aguilers, pp. 152–3; Fulcher of Chartres, pp. 306–8; Albert of Aachen, VI.33. For the debate regarding the title and powers with which Godfrey was invested see: J. S. C. Riley-Smith, 'The title of Godfrey of Bouillon', *Bulletin of the Institute of Historical Research*, vol. 52 (1979), pp. 83–6; J. France, 'The election and title of Godfrey de Bouillon', *Canadian Journal of History*, vol. 18 (1983), pp. 321–9; A. V. Murray, 'The title of Godfrey of Bouillon as ruler of Jerusalem', *Collegium Medievale: Interdisciplinary Journal of Medieval Research*, vol. 3 (1990), pp. 163–78.

3. Raymond of Aguilers, p. 153.

4. Ibid., pp. 153–4; *Gesta Francorum*, p. 93; Hagenmeyer, *Kreuzzugssbriefe*, pp. 175–6; Albert of Aachen, VI.39–40.

5. Hagenmeyer, *Kreuzzugssbriefe*, p. 178; Raymond of Aguilers, p. 154; Peter Tudebode, pp. 145–6; Fulcher of Chartres, pp. 309–10; Albert of Aachen, VI.38; Riley-Smith, *The First Crusade and the Idea of Crusading*, p. 98; A. Frolow, *La Relique de la vraie croix* (Paris, 1961). On the later significance of the relic see: A. V. Murray, '"Mighty against the enemies of Christ": The relic of the True Cross in the armies of the kingdom of Jerusalem', *The Crusades and their Sources: Essays Presented to Bernard Hamilton*, pp. 217–37.

6. *Gesta Francorum*, p. 93; Raymond of Aguilers, pp. 155–6; Fulcher of Chartres, pp. 311–12; Hagenmeyer, *Kreuzzugssbriefe*, pp. 171–2; Albert of Aachen, VI.41.

7. *Gesta Francorum*, pp. 93–4; Raymond of Aguilers, p. 156; Fulcher of Chartres, pp. 311–12; Albert of Aachen, VI.41–2.

8. Raymond of Aguilers, p. 156; Hagenmeyer, *Kreuzzugssbriefe*, pp. 171–2; Fulcher of Chartres, pp. 312–13; Albert of Aachen, VI.43–4, VI.46; Ibn al-Qalanisi, pp. 48–9; Ibn al-Athir, p. 198; France, *Victory in the East*, pp. 360–5.

9. Peter Tudebode, pp. 146–7.

10. *Gesta Francorum*, pp. 95–7; Raymond of Aguilers, pp. 156–8; Fulcher of Chartres, pp. 314–18; Hagenmeyer, *Kreuzzugssbriefe*, pp. 171–3; Albert of Aachen, VI.45–50; Ibn al-Qalanisi, pp. 48–9; Ibn al-Athir, p. 198; France, *Victory in the East*, pp. 360–5.

11. Albert of Aachen, VI.51–3; Ralph of Caen, p. 703; Raymond of Aguilers, pp. 158–9.

12. Fulcher of Chartres, pp. 318–22; Albert of Aachen, VI.54–60; William of Tyre, pp. 436–8.

13. 'Vita Urbani II', *Le Liber Pontificalis*, ed. L. Duchesne, vol. 2 (Paris, 1892), p. 293.

14. Riley-Smith, *The First Crusade and the Idea of Crusading*, pp. 121–2; Riley-Smith, *The First Crusaders*, pp. 145–6, 151–2.

15. Riley-Smith, *The First Crusade and the Idea of Crusading*, p. 121; David, *Robert Curthose*, pp. 120–202.

16. Riley-Smith, *The First Crusaders*, pp. 144–5, 153–5, 166.

17. Ibid., pp. 156–7.

18. Ibid., pp. 155–6.

19. Ibid., pp. 144, 150–1, 155.

20. Riley-Smith, *The First Crusade and the Idea of Crusading*, pp. 120–34; J. L. Cate, 'The crusade of 1101', *A History of the Crusades*, ed. K. M. Setton, vol. 1, 2nd edition (Madison, 1969), pp. 343–67; A. Mullinder, *The Crusading expeditions of 1101–02* (unpublished Ph.D. thesis, University of Wales, Swansea, 1996).

21. Asbridge, *Creation of the Principality of Antioch*, pp. 42, 198–9; Hill, *Raymond IV, Count of Toulouse*, pp. 142–58; J. Richard, *Le Comté de Tripoli sous la dynastie toulousaine (1102–1187)* (Paris, 1945).

22. Asbridge, *Creation of the Principality of Antioch*, pp. 42–59.

23. Yewdale, *Bohemond I, Prince of Antioch*, pp. 85–134; J. G. Rowe, 'Paschal II, Bohemund of Antioch and the Byzantine empire', *Bulletin of the John Rylands Library*, vol. 49 (1966), pp. 165–202; Lilie, *Byzantium and the Crusader States*, pp. 72–82; Asbridge, *Creation of the Principality of Antioch*, pp. 94–8.

24. Asbridge, *Creation of the Principality of Antioch*, pp. 59–81; T. S. Asbridge, 'The significance and causes of the battle of the Field of Blood', *Journal of Medieval History*, vol. 23.4 (1997), pp. 301–16.

25. Mayer, *The Crusades*, pp. 61–3; A. V. Murray, 'Daimbert of Pisa, the *Domus Godefridi* and the accession of Baldwin I of Jerusalem', *From Clermont to Jerusalem: The Crusades and Crusader Societies, 1095–1500*, ed. A. V. Murray (Turnhout, 1998), pp. 81–102.

26. Mayer, *The Crusades*, pp. 68–72.

CONCLUSION

1. Hillenbrand, *The Crusades: Islamic Perspectives*, pp. 47–8; Hillenbrand, 'The First Crusade: The Muslim perspective', pp. 131–4.

2. Riley-Smith, *The First Crusade and the Idea of Crusading*, pp. 135–52.

3. Riley-Smith, *The First Crusaders*, pp. 74–5.

4. C. J. Tyerman has made a strong case for caution in the use of the term crusading 'movement' given that the form, ideology and practice of crusading evolved gradually over the course of the twelfth century and did not spring fully formed from the mind of Pope Urban II, nor exist as a clear entity in the years immediately following the First Crusade. See his works: 'Were there any crusades in the twelfth century?', *English Historical Review*, vol. 110 (1995), pp. 553–77; *The Invention of the Crusades* (London, 1998).

5. France, *Victory in the East*, pp. 26–51, 355–6.
6. Raymond of Aguilers, p. 117; Hillenbrand, *The Crusades: Islamic Perspectives*, pp. 78–81.
7. Asbridge, 'The "crusader" community at Antioch', pp. 319–21.

BIBLIOGRAPHY

ABBREVIATIONS

RHC Occ.   *Recueil des historiens des croisades, Historiens occidentaux*, 5
            vols, ed. Academie des Inscriptions et Belles-Lettres (Paris,
            1844–95)
RHC Or.   *Recueil des historiens des croisades, Historiens orientaux*, 5
            vols, ed. Academie des Inscriptions et Belles-Lettres (Paris,
            1872–1906)

PRIMARY SOURCES

Albert of Aachen, *Historia Hierosolymitana, RHC Occ.* IV, pp. 265–713.
Albert of Aachen, 'The *Historia Iherosolimitana* of Albert of Aachen: A
    critical edition', ed. S. B. Edgington (unpublished Ph.D. thesis,
    University of London, 1991).
Anna Comnena, *Alexiade*, ed. and trans. B. Leib, 3 vols (Paris, 1937–76).
    Translated into English: *The Alexiad of Anna Comnena*, trans. E. R. A.
    Sewter (Harmondsworth, 1969).
Anonymous Syriac Chronicle, 'The First and Second Crusades from an
    Anonymous Syriac Chronicle', ed. and trans. A. S. Tritton and H. A. R.
    Gibb, *Journal of the Royal Asiatic Society* vol. 92 (1933), pp. 69–102, pp.
    273–306.
Baldric of Bourgueil, bishop of Dol, *Historia Jerosolimitana, RHC Occ.* IV,
    pp. 1–111.

Caffaro di Caschilfellione, *De liberatione civitatum Orientis liber, RHC Occ.* V, pp. 41–73.

Frutolfs und Ekkehards Chroniken und die Anonyme Kaiserchronik, ed. and trans. F. J. Schmale and I. Schmale-Ott (Darmstadt, 1972).

Fulcher of Chartres, *Historia Hierosolymitana (1095–1127)*, ed. H. Hagenmeyer (Heidelberg, 1913). Translated into English: *A History of the Expedition to Jerusalem, 1095–1127*, trans. F. S. Ryan, ed. H. S. Fink (Knoxville, 1960).

Gabrieli, F., *Arab Historians of the Crusades* (London, 1969).

Gesta Francorum et aliorum Hierosolimitanorum, ed. and trans. R. Hill (London, 1962).

Gilo of Paris, *The Historia Vie Hierosolimitanorum*, ed. and trans. C. W. Grocock and E. Siberry (Oxford, 1997).

Guibert of Nogent, *Dei gesta per Francos*, ed. R. B. C. Huygens, Corpus Christianorum, Continuatio Mediavalis, 127A (Turnhout, 1996). Translated into English: *The Deeds of God through the Franks: A Translation of Guibert de Nogent's Gesta Dei per Francos*, trans. R. Levine (Woodbridge, 1996).

Hagenmeyer, H., *Die Kreuzzugssbriefe aus den Jahren 1088–1100* (Innsbruck, 1901).

Historia Belli Sacri, RHC Occ. III, pp. 169–229.

Ibn al-Athir, *Kamel-Altevarykh, RHC Or.* I, pp. 187–800.

Ibn al-Qalanisi, *The Damascus Chronicle of the Crusades, Extracted and Translated from the Chronicle of Ibn al-Qalanisi*, trans. H. A. R. Gibb (London, 1932).

Kemal ad-Din, *La Chronique d'Alep, RHC Or.* III, pp. 577–732.

La Chanson d'Antioche, ed. S. Duparc-Quioc, 2 vols (Paris, 1982).

Matthew of Edessa, *Armenia and the Crusades, Tenth to Twelfth Centuries: The Chronicle of Matthew of Edessa*, trans. A. E. Dostourian (Lanham, 1993).

Michael the Syrien, *Chronique de Michel le Syrien, patriarche jacobite d'Antioche (1166–1199)*, ed. and trans. J. B. Chabot, 4 vols (Paris, 1899–1910).

Odo of Deuil, *De profectione ludovici VII in Orientam*, ed. and trans. V. G. Berry (New York, 1948).

Orderic Vitalis, *The Ecclesiastical History of Orderic Vitalis*, ed. and trans. M. Chibnall, vol. 5 (Oxford, 1975).

'Papsturkunden in Florenz', ed. W. Wiederhold, *Nachrichten von der Gesellschaft der Wissenschaften zu Göttingen*, Phil.-hist. Kl. (Göttingen, 1901), pp. 306–25.

Papsturkunden in Spanien. I Katalonien, ed. P. F. Kehr (Berlin, 1926).

Peter Tudebode, *Historia de Hierosolymitano itinere*, ed. J. H. Hill and L. L. Hill (Paris, 1977). Translated into English: *Historia de Hierosolymitano itinere*, trans. J. H. Hill and L. L. Hill (Philadelphia, 1974).

Peters, E. (ed.), *The First Crusade: The Chronicle of Fulcher of Chartres and Other Source Materials*, 2nd edition (Philadelphia, 1998).

Ralph of Caen, *Gesta Tancredi in expeditione Hierosolymitana*, RHC Occ. III, pp. 587–716.

Raymond of Aguilers, *Le 'Liber' de Raymond d'Aguilers*, ed. J. H. Hill and L. L. Hill (Paris, 1969). Translated into English: *Historia Francorum qui ceperunt Iherusalem*, trans. J. H. Hill and L. L. Hill (Philadelphia, 1968).

Riley-Smith, L. and J. S. C., *The Crusades: Idea and Reality, 1095–1274* (London, 1981).

Robert the Monk, *Historia Iherosolimitana*, RHC Occ. III, pp. 717–882.

'Vita Urbani II', *Le Liber Pontificalis*, ed. L. Duchesne, vol. 2 (Paris, 1892).

William of Malmesbury, *Gesta Regum Anglorum*, ed. and trans. R. A. B. Mynors, R. M. Thomson and M. Winterbottom, 2 vols (Oxford, 1998).

William of Tyre, *Chronique*, ed. R. B. C. Huygens, Corpus Christianorum, Continuatio Mediaevalis, 63–63A, 2 vols (Turnhout, 1986). Translated into English: *A History of Deeds Done Beyond the Sea by William Archbishop of Tyre*, trans. E. A. Babcock and A. C. Krey, 2 vols (New York, 1943).

SECONDARY SOURCES

Abulafia, A. S., 'The interrelationship between the Hebrew chronicles on the First Crusade', *Journal of Semitic Studies*, vol. 27 (1982), pp. 221–39.

——, 'Invectives against Christianity in the Hebrew Chronicles of the First Crusade', *Crusade and Settlement*, ed. P. W. Edbury (Cardiff, 1985), pp. 66–72.

Adhémar-Labaume, G. J. de, *Adhémar de Monteil, évêque du Puy, légat d'Urbain II, 1079–1098* (Le Puy, 1910).

Amouroux-Mourad, M., *Le comté d'Edesse, 1098–1150* (Paris, 1988).

Andressohn, J. C., *The Ancestry and Life of Godfrey of Bouillon* (Bloomington, 1947).

Angold, M., 'The Byzantine state on the eve of the battle of Manzikert', *Byzantinische Forschungen*, vol. 16 (1991), pp. 9–34.

——, *Church and Society in Byzantium Under the Comneni, 1081–1261* (Cambridge, 1995).

——, *The Byzantine Empire, 1025–1204: A Political History*, 2nd edition (London, 1997).

Asbridge, T. S., 'The principality of Antioch and the Jabal as-Summaq', *The First Crusade: Origins and Impact*, ed. J. P. Phillips (Manchester, 1997), pp. 142–52.

——, 'The significance and causes of the battle of the Field of Blood', *Journal of Medieval History*, vol. 23.4 (1997), pp. 301–16.

——, 'The "crusader" community at Antioch: The impact of interaction with Byzantium and Islam', *Transactions of the Royal Historical Society*, 6th series, vol. 9 (1999), pp. 305–25.

——, *The Creation of the Principality of Antioch, 1098–1130* (Woodbridge, 2000).

Aubé, P., *Godefroy de Bouillon* (Paris, 1985).

Auffarth, C., 'Himmlisches und irdisches Jerusalem. Ein religionswissenschaftlicher Versuch zur Kreuzzugeschatologie', *Zeitschrift für Religionswissenschaft*, vol. 1.1 (1993), pp. 25–49, vol. 1.2 (1993), pp. 91–118.

Bachrach, B., 'The siege of Antioch: A study in military demography', *War in History*, vol. 6 (1999), pp. 127–46.

Bartlett, R., *Trial by Fire and Water: The Medieval Judicial Ordeal* (Oxford, 1986).

Beaumont, A. A., 'Albert of Aachen and the county of Edessa', *The Crusades and Other Historical Essays Presented to Dana C. Munro by His Former Students*, ed. L. J. Paetow (New York, 1928), pp. 101–38.

Becker, A., *Papst Urban II. (1088–1099)*, Schriften der Monumenta Germaniae Historica 19, 2 vols. (Stuttgart, 1964–88).

——, 'Urbain II, pape de la croisade', *Les Champenois et la Croisade. Actes des Ive Journées rémoises, 27–28 novembre 1987*, ed. Y. Bellenger and D. Quéruel (Paris, 1989), pp. 9–17.

Beech, G. T., 'A Norman-Italian adventurer in the East: Richard of Salerno 1097–1112', *Anglo-Norman Studies, XV: Proceedings of the XV Battle Conference and of the XI Colloquio Medievale of the Officina di Studi Medievali, 1992*, ed. M. Chibnall (Woodbridge, 1993), pp. 25–40.

——, 'Urban II, the abbey of Saint-Florent of Saumur, and the First Crusade', *Autour de la Première Croisade*, ed. M. Balard (Paris, 1996), pp. 57–70.

Bennett, M., 'First Crusaders' images of Muslims: The influence of vernacular poetry?', *Forum for Modern Language Studies*, vol. 22 (1986), pp. 101–22.

——, 'Travel and transport of the crusades', *Medieval History*, vol. 4 (1994), pp. 91–101.

Beshir, B. J., 'Fatimid military organization', *Der Islam*, vol. 55 (1978), pp. 37–56.

Blake, E. O., 'The formation of the "crusade idea"', *Journal of Ecclesiastical History*, vol. 21 (1970), pp. 11–31.

Blake, E. O. and Morris, C., 'A hermit goes to war: Peter and the origins of the First Crusade', *Studies in Church History*, vol. 22 (1985), pp. 79–107.

Blumenthal, U.-R., *The Investiture Controversy: Church and Monarchy from the Ninth to the Twelfth Century* (Philadelphia, 1988).

Boas, A. J., *Jerusalem in the Time of the Crusades* (London, 2001).

Boase, T. S. R., 'The history of the kingdom', *The Cilician Kingdom of Armenia*, ed. T. S. R. Boase (Edinburgh and London, 1978), pp. 1–33.

Brown, P., *Augustine of Hippo* (London, 1967).

——, *The Cult of the Saints* (Chicago, 1987).

——, *The Rise of Western Christendom* (Oxford, 1996).

Brundage, J. A., 'Adhémar of Le Puy: The bishop and his critics', *Speculum*, vol. 34 (1959), pp. 201–12.

——, 'An errant crusader: Stephen of Blois', *Traditio*, vol. 16 (1960), pp. 380–95.

——, *Medieval Canon Law and the Crusader* (Madison, 1969).

——, 'The army of the First Crusade and the crusade vow: Some reflections on a recent book', *Medieval Studies*, vol. 33 (1971), pp. 334–43.

——, 'Prostitution, miscegenation and sexual purity in the First Crusade', *Crusade and Settlement*, ed. P. W. Edbury (Cardiff, 1985), pp. 57–65.

Bull, M. G., *Knightly Piety and the Lay Response to the First Crusade: The Limousin and Gascony, c. 970–c. 1130* (Oxford, 1993).

——, 'The roots of lay enthusiasm for the First Crusade', *History*, vol. 78 (1993), pp. 353–72.

——, 'Origins', *The Oxford Illustrated History of the Crusades*, ed. J. S. C. Riley-Smith (Oxford, 1995), pp. 13–33.

——, 'The diplomatic of the First Crusade', *The First Crusade: Origins and Impact*, ed. J. P. Phillips (Manchester, 1997), pp. 35–54.

Cahen, C., 'La campagne de Mantizikert d'après les sources musulmans', *Byzantion*, vol. 9 (1934), pp. 628–42.

——, *La Syrie du Nord à l'epoque des croisades et la principauté franque d'Antioche* (Paris, 1940).

——, 'An Introduction to the First Crusade', *Past and Present*, vol. 6 (1954), pp. 6–29.

——, 'The historiography of the Seljuqid period', *Historians of the Middle East*, ed. B. Lewis and P. M. Holt (London, 1962), pp. 59–78.

——, 'The Turkish invasion: The Selchükids', *A History of the Crusades*, ed. K. M. Setton, vol. 1, 2nd edition (Madison, 1969), pp. 135–76.

——, *Introduction à l'histoire du monde musulman médiévale*, Initiation à l'Islam, vol. 1 (Paris, 1982).

——, *Orient et Occident aux temps des croisades* (Paris, 1983).

Cate, J. L., 'The crusade of 1101', *A History of the Crusades*, ed. K. M. Setton, vol. 1, 2nd edition (Madison, 1969), pp. 343–67.

Chalandon, F., *Histoire de la première croisades jusqu'á l'élection de Godefroi de Bouillon* (Paris, 1925).

Charanis, P., 'Byzantium, the West and the origin of the First Crusade', *Byzantion*, vol. 19 (1949), pp. 17–36.

——, *The Armenians in the Byzantine Empire* (Lisbon, 1963).

——, 'The Byzantine empire in the eleventh century', *A History of the Crusades*, ed. K. M. Setton, vol. 1, 2nd edition (Madison, 1969), pp. 177–219.

Chazan, R., 'The Hebrew First Crusade chronicles', *Revue des études juives*, vol. 133 (1974), pp. 235–54.

——, *European Jewry and the First Crusade* (Berkeley, 1987).

——, *God, Humanity and History: The Hebrew First Crusade Narratives* (Berkeley, 2000).

Chrysostomides, J., 'A Byzantine historian: Anna Comnena', *Medieval Historical Writing in the Christian and Islamic Worlds*, ed. D. O. Morgan (London, 1982), pp. 30–46.

Cole, P., *The Preaching of the Crusades to the Holy Land, 1095–1270* (Cambridge, MA, 1991).

——, 'O God, the heathen have come into your inheritance (Ps. 78.1): The theme of religious pollution in crusade documents, 1095–1188', *Crusaders and Muslims in Twelfth-century Syria*, ed. M. Shatzmiller (Leiden, 1993), pp. 84–111.

Constable, G., 'Medieval charters as a source for the history of the crusades', *Crusade and Settlement*, ed. P. W. Edbury (Cardiff, 1985), pp. 73–89.

Coupe, M. D., 'Peter the Hermit – a re-assessment', *Nottingham Medieval Studies*, vol. 31 (1987), pp. 37–45.

Cowdrey, H. E. J., *The Cluniacs and the Gregorian Reform* (Oxford, 1970).

——, 'The Peace and Truce of God in the eleventh century', *Past and Present*, vol. 46 (1970), pp. 42–67.

——, 'Pope Urban II's preaching of the First Crusade', *History*, vol. 55 (1970), pp. 177–88.

——, 'Cluny and the First Crusade', *Revue bénédictine*, vol. 73 (1973), pp. 285–311.

——, 'The genesis of the crusades: The springs of western ideas of holy war', *The Holy War*, ed. T. P. Murphy (Columbus, 1976), pp. 9–32.

——, 'Pope Gregory's "Crusading" plans of 1074, *Outremer*, ed. B. Z. Kedar, H. E. Mayer and R. C. Smail (Jerusalem, 1982), pp. 27–40.

——, 'Martyrdom and the First Crusade', *Crusade and Settlement*, ed. P. W. Edbury (Cardiff, 1985), pp. 46–56.

——, 'The Gregorian papacy, Byzantium and the First Crusade', *Byzantium and the West c. 850–1200: Proceedings of the XVIII Spring Symposium of Byzantine Studies*, ed. J. D. Howard-Johnston (Amsterdam, 1988), pp. 145–69.

——, 'The papacy and the origins of crusading', *Medieval History*, vol. 1 (1991), pp. 48–60.

——, 'Canon law and the First Crusade', *The Horns of Hattin*, ed. B. Z. Kedar (Jerusalem, 1992) pp. 41–8.

——, 'Pope Urban II and the idea of crusade', *Studi medievali*, ser. 3, vol. 36 (1995), pp. 721–42.

——, 'Pope Gregory and the bearing of arms', *Montjoie: Studies in Crusade History in Honour of Hans Eberhard Mayer*, ed. B. Z. Kedar, J. S. C. Riley-Smith and R. Hiestand (Aldershot, 1997), pp. 21–35.

——, *Pope Gregory VII, 1073–1085* (Oxford, 1998).

Crozet, R., 'Le voyage d'Urbain II et ses négotiations avec le clergé de France (1095–1096)', *Revue historique*, vol. 179 (1937), pp. 271–310.

Dajani-Shakeel, H., 'Diplomatic relations between Muslim and Frankish rulers, AD 1097–1153', *Crusaders and Muslims in Twelfth-century Syria*, ed. M. Shatzmiller (Leiden, 1993), pp. 190–215.

Daniel, N., *Islam and the West: The Making of an Image* (Edinburgh, 1960).

——, 'The legal and political theory of the crusade', *A History of the Crusades*, ed. K. M. Setton, vol. 6, 2nd edition (Madison, 1989), pp. 3–38.

——, 'Crusade propaganda', *A History of the Crusades*, ed. K. M. Setton, vol. 6, 2nd edition (Madison, 1989), pp. 39–97.

David, C. W., *Robert Curthose, Duke of Normandy* (Cambridge, MA, 1920).

Dédéyan, G., 'Les princes arméniennes de l'Euphratese et l'empire byzantin (fin Xie – milieu XIIe s.)', *L'Arménie et Byzance: Histoire et culture* (Paris, 1996), pp. 79–88.

Deschamps, P., 'Le Crac des Chevaliers', *Les Château des Croisés en Terre Sainte*, vol. 1 (Paris, 1934).

Despy, G., 'Godefroid de Bouillon, myths et réalités', *Academie Royale de Belgique, Bulletin de la Classe des Lettres et des Sciences Morales et Pollitiques*, ser. 5, vol. 71 (1985), pp. 249–75.

Downey, G., A *History of Antioch in Syria* (Princeton, 1960).

Duncalf, F., 'The Peasants' Crusade', *American Historical Review*, vol. 26 (1921), pp. 440–53.

——, 'The pope's plan for the First Crusade', *The Crusades and Other Historical Essays Presented to Dana C. Munro by His Former Students*, ed. L. J. Paetow (New York, 1928), pp. 44–56.

——, 'The councils of Piacenza and Clermont', *A History of the Crusades*, ed. K. M. Setton, vol. 1, 2nd edition (Madison, 1969), pp. 220–52.

Dupont, A., 'Raymond IV de Saint-Gilles et son role en Orient pendant la Première Croisade (1096–1099)', *Bulletin des séances de l'Académie de Nîmes*, vol. 47 (1970), pp. 19–21, 24–6.

Edbury, P. W. and Rowe, J. G., *William of Tyre: Historian of the Latin East* (Cambridge, 1988).

Eddé, A.-M., 'Ridwan, prince d'Alep de 1095 à 1113', *Revue des études islamiques*, vol. 54 for 1986 (1988), pp. 101–25.

Edgington, S. B., 'The doves of war: the part played by carrier pigeons in the crusades', *Autour de la Première Croisade*, ed. M. Balard (Paris, 1996), pp. 167–76.

——, 'The First Crusade: Reviewing the Evidence', *The First Crusade: Origins and Impact*, ed. J. P. Phillips (Manchester, 1997), pp. 55–77.

——, 'Albert of Aachen reappraised', *From Clermont to Jerusalem: The Crusades and Crusader Societies, 1095–1500*, ed. A. V. Murray (Turnhout, 1998), pp. 55–67.

——, 'Albert of Aachen and the *chanson de geste*', *The Crusades and their Sources: Essays Presented to Bernard Hamilton*, ed. J. France and W. G. Zajac (Aldershot, 1998), pp. 23–37.

Epp, V., *Fulcher von Chartres: Studien zur Geschichtsschreibung des ersten Kreuzzuges* (Düsseldorf, 1990).

Erdmann, C., *The Origin of the Idea of Crusade* (Princeton, 1977).

Favreau-Lilie, M.-L., *Die Italiener im Heiligen Lande vom ersten Kreuzzug bis zum Tode Heinrichs von Champagne (1098–1197)* (Amsterdam, 1989).

Fletcher, R., *The Conversion of Europe* (New York, 1988).

Fliche, A., 'Urbain II et la croisade', *Revue d'histoire de l'église de France*, vol. 13 (1927), pp. 289–306.

Flori, J., 'Mort et martyre des guerriers vers 1100. L'exemple de la Première Croisade', *Cahiers de civilisation médiévale*, vol. 34 (1991), pp. 121–39.

——, 'La caricature de l'Islam dans l'Occident médiéval. Origine et signification de quelques stéréotypes concernant l'Islam', *Aevum*, vol. 66 (1992), pp. 245–56.

——, *La Première Croisade: L'Occident chrétien contre l'Islam* (Paris, 1992).

——, 'L'église et la guerre sainte de la "Paix de Dieu" à la "croisade"', *Annales ESC*, vol. 47 (1992), pp. 453–66.

——, 'Un problème de méthodologie: La valeur des nombres chez les chroniqueurs du Moyen Age. A propos des effectifs de la Première Croisade', *Le Moyen Age*, vol. 99 (1993), pp. 399–422.

——, 'Faut-il réhabiliter Pierre l'Ermite? (une réevaluation des sources de la Première Croisade)', *Cahiers de civilisation médiévale*, vol. 38 (1995), pp. 35–54.

——, 'Pierre l'Ermite et sa croisades – légende et vérité', *Cahiers de Clio*, vols. 125–26 (1996), pp. 29–39.

——, *La formation de l'idée de croisades dans l'Occident Chrétien* (Paris, 2001).

Forse, J. H., 'Armenians and the First Crusade', *Journal of Medieval History*, vol. 17 (1991), pp. 13–22.

France, J., 'The crisis of the First Crusade from the defeat of Kerbogha to the departure from Arqa', *Byzantion*, vol. 40 (1970), pp. 276–308.

——, 'The departure of Tatikios from the army of the First Crusade', *Bulletin of the Institute of Historical Research*, vol. 44 (1971), pp. 131–47.

——, 'The election and title of Godfrey de Bouillon', *Canadian Journal of History*, vol. 18 (1983), pp. 321–9.

——, 'Anna Comnena, the Alexiad and the First Crusade', *Reading Medieval Studies*, vol. 10 (1984), pp. 20–38.

——, *Victory in the East: A Military History of the First Crusade* (Cambridge, 1994).

——, 'The destruction of Jerusalem and the First Crusade', *Journal of Ecclesiastical History*, vol. 47 (1996), pp. 1–17.

——, 'Patronage and the appeal of the First Crusade', *The First Crusade: Origins and Impact*, ed. J. P. Phillips (Manchester, 1997), pp. 5–20.

——, 'Technology and the success of the First Crusade', *War and Society in the Eastern Mediterranean, 7th–15th Centuries*, ed. Y. Lev, The Medieval Mediterranean, vol. 9 (Leiden, 1997), pp. 163–76.

——, 'The Anonymous *Gesta Francorum* and the *Historia Francorum qui ceperunt Iherusalem* of Raymond of Aguilers and the *Historia de Hierosolymitano Itinere* of Peter Tudebode', *The Crusades and their Sources: Essays presented to Bernard Hamilton*, ed. J. France and W. G. Zajac (Aldershot, 1998), pp. 39–69.

——, 'The use of the anonymous *Gesta Francorum* in the early twelfth-century sources for the First Crusade', *From Clermont to Jerusalem: The*

Crusades and Crusader Societies, 1095–1500, ed. A. V. Murray (Turnhout, 1998), pp. 29–42.

Frolow, A., *La Relique de la vraie croix* (Paris, 1961).

Gabrieli, F., 'The Arabic historiography of the crusades', *Historians of the Middle East*, ed. B. Lewis and P. M. Holt (London, 1962), pp. 98–107.

Gauss, J., 'Toleranz und Intoleranz zwischen Christen und Mulsimen in der Zeit vor den Kreuzzügen', *Speculum*, vol. 19 (1968), pp. 362–89.

Geary, P., *Before France and Germany: The creation and transformation of the Merovingian world* (Oxford, 1988).

——, *Furta Sacra: Thefts of Relics in the Central Middle Ages* (Princeton, 1990).

Gilchrist, J. T., 'The Erdmann thesis and canon law, 1083–1141', *Crusade and Settlement*, ed. P. W. Edbury (Cardiff, 1985), pp. 37–45.

——, 'The Papacy and the war against the "Saracens", 795–1216', *International History Review*, vol. 10 (1988), pp. 174–97.

——, 'The perception of Jews in the canon law in the period of the first two crusades', *Jewish History*, vol. 3 (1988), pp. 9–24.

Gindler, P., *Graf Balduin I. von Edessa* (Halle, 1901).

Golb, N., 'New light on the persecution of French Jews at the time of the First Crusade', *Medieval Jewish Life: Studies from the Proceedings of the American Academy for Jewish Research*, ed. R. Chazan (New York, 1976), pp. 334–52.

Grousset, R., *Histoire des Croisades*, vol. 1 (Paris, 1934).

Hagenmeyer, H., *Chronologie de la Première Croisade (1094–1100)* (Paris, 1902).

Hamilton, B., *The Latin Church in the Crusader States: The Secular Church* (London, 1980).

——, *Religion in the Medieval West* (London, 1986).

Head, C., 'Alexios Komnenos and the English', *Byzantion*, vol. 47 (1977), pp. 186–98.

Hiestand, R., 'Les canons de Clermont et d'Antioche sur l'organisation ecclésiastique des Etats croisés: Authentiques ou faux?,' *Autour de la Première Croisade*, ed. M. Balard (Paris, 1996), pp. 29–37.

Hill, J. H., 'Raymond of St. Gilles in Urban's plan of Greek and Latin friendship', *Speculum*, vol. 26 (1951), pp. 265–76.

Hill, J. H. and L. L., 'The convention of Alexius Comnenus and Raymond of St. Gilles', *American Historical Review*, vol. 58 (1952–53), pp. 322–7.

——, 'Contemporary accounts and the later reputation of Adhémar, bishop of Le Puy', *Mediaevalia et humanistica*, vol. 9 (1955), pp. 30–8.

——, *Raymond IV, Count of Toulouse* (Syracuse, 1962).

Hill, R., 'The Christian view of the Muslims at the time of the First Crusade,' *The Eastern Mediterranean Lands in the Period of the Crusades*, ed. P. M. Holt (Warminster, 1977), pp. 1–8.

Hillenbrand, C., 'The First Crusade: The Muslim perspective', *The First Crusade: Origins and Impact*, ed. J. P. Phillips (Manchester, 1997), pp. 130–41.

——, *The Crusades: Islamic Perspectives* (Edinburgh, 1999).

Holt, P. M., *The Age of the Crusades: The Near East from the 11th Century to 1517* (London, 1986).

Hunt, N., *Cluny under St Hugh, 1049–1109* (London, 1967).

James, E., *The Franks* (Oxford, 1988).

Jamison, E. M., 'Some notes on the *Anonymi Gesta Francorum*, with special reference to the Norman contingent from South Italy and Sicily in the First Crusade', *Studies in French Language and Medieval Literature presented to Professor Mildred K. Pope* (Manchester, 1939), pp. 195–204.

Katzir, Y., 'The conquests of Jerusalem, 1099 and 1187: Historical memory and religious typology', *The Meeting of Two Worlds: Cultural exchange between East and West in the period of the crusades*, ed. V. P. Goss (Kalamazoo, 1986) pp. 103–13.

Kedar, B. Z., *Crusade and Mission: European Approaches toward the Muslims* (Princeton, 1984).

——, 'Croisade et jihad vus par l'ennemi: une étude des perceptions mutuelles des motivations', *Autour de la Première Croisade*, ed. M. Balard (Paris, 1996), pp. 345–58.

Knappen, M. M., 'Robert II of Flanders in the First Crusade', *The Crusades and Other Historical Essays presented to Dana C. Munro by His Former Students*, ed. L. J. Paetow (New York, 1928), pp. 79–100.

Köhler, M. A., *Allianzen und Verträge zwischen frankischen und islamischen Herrschern in Vorderren Orient* (Berlin, 1991).

Krey, A. C., 'A neglected passage in the *Gesta* and its bearing on the literature of the First Crusade', *The Crusades and Other Historical Essays Presented to Dana C. Munro by His Former Students*, ed. L. J. Paetow (New York, 1928), pp. 57–78.

——, 'Urban's crusade, success or failure?', *American Historical Review*, vol. 53 (1948), pp. 235–50.

Lambert, M. D., *Medieval Heresy: Popular movements from Bogomil to Huss*, 3rd edition (Oxford, 2002).

Lawrence, C. H., *Medieval Monasticism: Forms of Religious Life in Western Europe in the Middle Ages* (London, 1984).

Lev, Y., 'Regime, army and society in medieval Egypt, 9th–12th centuries', *War and Society in the Eastern Mediterranean, 7th–15th Centuries*, pp. 115–52.

Lewis, B., 'The Isma'ilites and the Assassins', *A History of the Crusades*, ed. K. M. Setton, vol. 1, 2nd edition (Madison, 1969), pp. 99–132.

Lilie, R.-J., 'Der erste Kreuzzug in der Darstellung Anna Komnenes', *Varia II: Beiträge von A. Berger et al.*, Poikila Byzantina, vol. 6 (Bonn, 1987), pp. 49–148.

——, *Byzantium and the Crusader States, 1096–1204*, trans. J. C. Morris and J. E. Ridings (Oxford, 1993).

Lomax, D., *The Reconquest of Spain* (London, 1978).

Loud, G. A., 'Anna Komnena and her sources for the Normans of southern Italy', *Church and Chronicle in the Middle Ages: Essays Presented to John Taylor*, ed. I. Wood and G. A. Loud (London, 1991), pp. 41–57.

Mayer, H. E., 'Zur Beurteilung Adhemars von Le Puy', *Deutsches Archiv für Erforschung des Mittelalters*, vol. 16 (1960), pp. 547–52.

——, *The Crusades*, trans. J. Gillingham, 2nd edition (Oxford, 1988).

McGinn, B., 'Iter Sancti Sepulchri: The piety of the first crusaders', *Essays on Medieval Civilization*, ed. B. K. Lackner and K. R. Philip (Austin, 1978), pp. 33–72.

——, 'Violence and spirituality: The enigma of the First Crusade', *Journal of Religion*, vol. 69 (1989), pp. 375–79.

McKitterick, R., *The Frankish Kingdoms Under the Carolingians, 751–987* (London, 1983).

McQueen, W. B., 'Relations between the Normans and Byzantium 1071–1112', *Byzantion*, vol. 56 (1986), pp. 427–76.

Morris, C., 'Policy and vision: The case of the Holy Lance found at Antioch', *War and Government in the Middle Ages: Essays in Honour of J. O. Prestwich*, ed. J. Gillingham and J. C. Holt (Woodbridge, 1984), pp. 33–45.

——, *The Papal Monarchy: The Western Church from 1050 to 1250* (Oxford, 1989).

——, 'The aims and spirituality of the crusade as seen through the eyes of Albert of Aix', *Reading Medieval Studies*, vol. 16 (1990), pp. 99–117.

——, 'Martyrs of the Field of Battle before and during the First Crusade', *Studies in Church History*, vol. 30 (1993), pp. 93–104.

——, 'The *Gesta Francorum* as narrative history', *Reading Medieval Studies*, vol. 19 (1993), pp. 55–71.

——, 'Peter the Hermit and the Chroniclers', *The First Crusade: Origins and Impact*, ed. J. P. Phillips (Manchester, 1997), pp. 21–34.

Mullett, M., 'Alexios I Komnenos and imperial renewal', *New Constantines: The Rhythm of Imperial Renewal in Byzantium, 4th–13th Centuries. Papers from the Twenty-Sixth Spring Symposium of Byzantine Studies, St Andrews, March 1992*, ed. P. Magdalino (Aldershot, 1994), pp. 259–67.

Mullinder, A., *The Crusading Expeditions of 1101–02* (unpublished Ph.D. thesis, University of Wales, Swansea, 1996).

——, 'Albert of Aachen and the crusade of 1101', *From Clermont to Jerusalem: The Crusades and Crusader Societies, 1095–1500*, ed. A. V. Murray (Turnhout, 1998), pp. 69–77.

Munro, D. C., 'The speech of Pope Urban II at Clermont, 1095', *American Historical Review*, vol. 11 (1905–6), pp. 231–42.

——, 'Did the Emperor Alexius ask for aid at the council of Piacenza?', *American Historical Review*, vol. 27 (1922), pp. 731–33.

Murray, A. V., 'The Title of Godfrey of Bouillon as ruler of Jerusalem', *Collegium Medievale: Interdisciplinary Journal of Medieval Research*, vol. 3 (1990), pp. 163–78.

——, 'Questions of nationality in the First Crusade', *Medieval History*, vol. 1 (1991), pp. 61–73.

——, 'The army of Godfrey of Bouillon, 1096–1099: structure and dynamics of a contingent on the First Crusade', *Revue belge de philology et d'histoire*, vol. 70 (1992), pp. 301–29.

——, 'The Chronicle of Zimmern as a source for the First Crusade: The evidence of Ms. Stuttgart, Württembergische Landesbibliothek, Cod. Don. 580', *The First Crusade: Origins and Impact*, ed. J. P. Phillips (Manchester, 1997), pp. 78–106.

——, 'Daimbert of Pisa, the *Domus Godefridi* and the accession of Baldwin I of Jerusalem', *From Clermont to Jerusalem: The Crusades and Crusader Societies, 1095–1500*, ed. A. V. Murray (Turnhout, 1998), pp. 81–102.

——, '"Mighty against the enemies of Christ": The relic of the True Cross in the armies of the kingdom of Jerusalem', *The Crusades and their Sources: Essays Presented to Bernard Hamilton*, ed. J. France and W. G. Zajac (Aldershot, 1998), pp. 217–37.

Nicholson, R. L., *Tancred: A Study of His Career and Work in Their Relation to the First Crusade and the Establishment of the Latin States in Syria and Palestine* (Chicago, 1940).

Osborne, J., 'A tale of two cities: Sacred geography in Christian Jerusalem', *Queen's Quarterly*, vol. 103 (1996), pp. 741–50.

Ostrogorsky, G., *History of the Byzantine State*, trans. J. M. Hussey, 2nd edition (Padstow, 1968).

Porges, W., 'The clergy, the poor and the non-combatants on the First Crusade', *Speculum*, vol. 21 (1946), pp. 1–23.

Porter, J. M. B., 'Preacher of the First Crusade? Robert of Arbrissel after the Council of Clermont', *From Clermont to Jerusalem: The Crusades and Crusader Societies, 1095–1500*, ed. A. V. Murray (Turnhout, 1998), pp. 43–53.

Powell, J. M., 'Myth, legend, propaganda, history: The First Crusade, 1140–c.1300', *Autour de la Première Croisade*, ed. M. Balard (Paris, 1996), pp. 127–41.

Prawer, J., 'The Jerusalem the crusaders captured: A contribution to the medieval topography of the city', *Crusade and Settlement*, ed. P. W. Edbury (Cardiff, 1985), pp. 1–16.

Pryor, J. H., *Geography, Technology and War: Studies in the Maritime History of the Mediterranean 649–1571* (Cambridge, 1987).

——, 'The oaths of the leaders of the First Crusade to emperor Alexius I Comnenus: fealty, homage, *pistis, douleia*', *Parergon*, vol. 2 (1984), pp. 111–41.

Richard, J., *Le Comté de Tripoli sous la dynastie toulousaine (1102–1187)* (Paris, 1945).

——, 'Raymond d'Aguilers, historien de la première croisade', *Journal des Savants*, vol. 3 (1971), pp. 206–12.

——, 'La confrérie de la croisades: à propos d'un episode de la première croisade', *Etudes de civilisation médiévale (IXe–XIIe siècles): Mélanges offerts à Edmond-René Labande* (Poitiers, 1974), pp. 617–22.

——, 'Urbain II, la prédication de la croisade et la définition de l'indulgence', *Deus qui mutat tempora: Menschen und Institutionen im Wandel des Mittelalters. Festschrift für Alfons Becker zu seinem fünfundsechzigsten Geburstag*, ed. E.-D. Hehl, H.Seibert and F. Staab (Sigmaringen, 1987), pp. 129–35.

——, *The Crusades, c. 1071–c. 1291*, trans. J. Birrell (Cambridge, 1999).

Riley-Smith, J. S. C., 'The title of Godfrey of Bouillon', *Bulletin of the Institute of Historical Research*, vol. 52 (1979), pp. 83–6.

——, 'The First Crusade and St Peter', *Outremer*, ed. B. Z. Kedar, H. E. Mayer and R. C. Smail (Jerusalem, 1982), pp. 41–63.

——, 'The motives of the earliest crusaders and the settlement of Latin Palestine, 1095–1100', *English Historical Review*, vol. 98 (1983), pp. 721–36.

——, 'Death on the First Crusade', *The End of Strife*, ed. D. Loades (Edinburgh, 1984), pp. 14–31.

——, 'The First Crusade and the persecution of the Jews', *Studies in Church History*, vol. 21 (1984), pp. 51–72.

——, *The First Crusade and the Idea of Crusading* (London, 1986).

——, 'The Latin clergy and the settlement of Palestine and Syria, 1098–1100', *Catholic Historical Review*, vol. 74 (1988), pp. 539–57.

——, 'Early crusaders to the East and the costs of crusading', *Cross-cultural Convergences in the Crusader Period: Essays Presented to Aryeh Grabois on Sixty-fifth Birthday*, ed. M. Goodich, S. Menache and S. Schein (New York, 1995), pp. 237–58.

——, *The First Crusaders, 1095–1131* (Cambridge, 1997).

——, 'Casualties and the number of knights on the First Crusade', *Crusades*, vol. 1 (2002), pp. 13–28.

——, *What Were the Crusades*, 3rd edition (Basingstoke, 2002).

Robinson, I. S., 'Gregory VII and the Soldiers of Christ', *History*, vol. 58 (1973), pp. 169–92.

Rogers, R., 'Peter Bartholomew and the role of "the poor" in the First Crusade', *Warriors and Churchmen in the High Middle Ages: Essays presented to Karl Leyser*, ed. T. Reuter (London, 1992), pp. 109–22.

——, *Latin Siege Warfare in the Twelfth Century* (Oxford, 1992).

Röhricht, R., *Geschichte des Ersten Kreuzzuges* (Innsbruck, 1901).

Rouche, M., 'Cannibalisme sacré chez les croisés populaires', *La Religion populaire: Aspects du Christianisme populaire à travers l'histoire*, ed. Y.-M. Hillaire (Lille, 1981), pp. 29–41.

Rousset, P., 'Etienne de Blois, croise fuyard et martyr', *Genava*, vol. 11 (1963), pp. 183–95.

——, *Les origins et les caractères de la Première Croisade* (Neuchâtel, 1945).

Rowe, J. G., 'Paschal II, Bohemund of Antioch and the Byzantine empire', *Bulletin of the John Rylands Library*, vol. 49 (1966), pp. 165–202.

Runciman, S., 'The first crusaders' journey across the Balkan Peninsula', *Byzantion*, vol. 19 (1949), pp. 207–21.

——, 'The Holy Lance found at Antioch', *Annalecta Bollandiana*, vol. 68 (1950), pp. 197–205.

——, 'The First Crusade and the foundation of the kingdom of Jerusalem', *A History of the Crusades*, vol. 1 (Cambridge, 1951).

Russell, F. H., *The Just War in the Middle Ages* (Cambridge, 1975).

Savvides, A. G. C., 'Varia Byzantinoturcica, II: Taticios the Turcopole', *Journal of Oriental and African Studies*, vols. 3–4 for 1991–92 (1993), pp. 235–38.

Schein, S., 'Jérusalem: objectif original de la Première Croisade?', *Autour de la Première Croisade*, ed. M. Balard (Paris, 1996), pp. 119–26.

Shepard, J., 'When Greek meets Greek: Alexius Comnenus and Bohemond in 1097–98', *Byzantine and Modern Greek Studies*, vol. 12 (1988), pp. 185–277.

——, 'The uses of the Franks in eleventh-century Byzantium', *Anglo-Norman Studies, XV: Proceedings of the XV Battle Conference and of the XI Colloquio Medievale of the Officina di Studi Medievali, 1992*, ed. M. Chibnall (Woodbridge, 1993), pp. 275–305.

——, 'Cross purposes: Alexius Comnenus and the First Crusade', *The First Crusade: Origins and Impact*, ed. J. P. Phillips (Manchester, 1997), pp. 107–29.

Siberry, E., *Criticism of Crusading, 1095–1274* (Oxford, 1985).

Smail, R. C., *Crusading Warfare, 1097–1193* (Cambridge, 1956).

Somerville, R., 'The French councils of Urban II: some basic considerations', *Annuarium Historiae Conciliorum*, vol. 2 (1970), pp. 56–65.

——, 'The council of Clermont and the First Crusade', *Studia Gratiana*, vol. 20 (1976), pp. 323–37.

——, 'The council of Clermont (1095) and Latin Christian society', *Archivum Historiae Pontificiae*, vol. 12 (1974), pp. 55–90.

Southern, R. W., *Western Views of Islam in the Middle Ages* (Cambridge, 1962).

Sumberg, A. M., 'The "Tafurs" and the First Crusade', *Mediaeval Studies*, vol. 21 (1959), pp. 224–46.

Sumption, J., *Pilgrimage: An Image of Mediaeval Religion* (London, 1975).

Thomas, R. D., 'Anna Comnena's account of the First Crusade: History and politics I – The reigns of the emperors Alexius I and Manuel I Comnenus', *Byzantine and Modern Greek Studies*, vol. 15 (1991), pp. 269–312.

Tyerman, C. J., *England and the Crusades, 1095–1588* (Chicago, 1988).

——, 'Were there any crusades in the twelfth century?', *English Historical Review*, vol. 110 (1995), pp. 553–77.

——, *The Invention of the Crusades* (London, 1998).

Ullmann, W., *A Short History of the Papacy in the Middle Ages* (London, 1974).

Vryonis, S., Jr., 'The experience of Christians under Seljuk and Ottoman domination, eleventh to sixteenth century', *Conversion and Continuity: Indigenous Christian Communities in Islamic Lands, Eighth to Eighteenth Centuries*, ed. M. Gervers and R. J. Bikhazi (Toronto, 1990), pp. 185–216.

Ward, B., *Miracles and the Medieval Mind: Theory, Record and Event, 1000–1215* (London, 1982).

Wilkinson, J., *Jerusalem Pilgrims Before the Crusades* (Warminster, 1977).

Wolf, K. B., 'Crusade and narrative: Bohemond and the *Gesta Francorum*', *Journal of Medieval History*, vol. 17 (1991), pp. 207–16.

Yewdale, R. B., *Bohemond I, Prince of Antioch* (Princeton, 1917).

Zajac, W. G., 'Captured property on the First Crusade', *The First Crusade: Origins and Impact*, ed. J. P. Phillips (Manchester, 1997), pp. 153–86.

INDEX